Introducing Organizational Behaviour and Management

This textbook has been compiled for the following modules:

UMOCA8-20-1
UMOCX6-20-1
UMOCX7-20-1
UMOC9R-20-1

Introducing Organizational Behaviour and Management

David Knights and Hugh Willmott

Compiled by Harriet Shortt, Jenna Ward and Graham Baker

Australia • Brazil • Japan • Korea • Mexico • Singapore • Spain • United Kingdom • United States

Introducing Organizational Behaviour and Management, Custom Edition

David Knights and Hugh Willmott

University of the West of England

Compiled by Harriet Shortt, Jenna Ward and Graham Baker

Publishing Director: Linden Harris

Custom Solutions Manager: Jeni Evans

Production Controller: Paul Herbert

© 2010, Cengage Learning EMEA

ALL RIGHTS RESERVED. No part of this work covered by the copyright herein may be reproduced, transmitted, stored or used in any form or by any means graphic, electronic, or mechanical, including but not limited to photocopying, recording, scanning, digitizing, taping, Web distribution, information networks, or information storage and retrieval systems, except as permitted under Section 107 or 108 of the 1976 United States Copyright Act, or applicable copyright law of another jurisdiction, without the prior written permission of the publisher.

While the publisher has taken all reasonable care in the preparation of this book, the publisher makes no representation, express or implied, with regard to the accuracy of the information contained in this book and cannot accept any legal responsibility or liability for any errors or omissions from the book or the consequences thereof.

Products and services that are referred to in this book may be either trademarks and/or registered trademarks of their respective owners. The publishers and author/s make no claim to these trademarks.

For product information and technology assistance, contact **emea.info@cengage.com**.

For permission to use material from this text or product, and for permission queries, email **clsuk.permissions@cengage.com.**

British Library Cataloguing-in-Publication Data
A catalogue record for this book is available from the British Library.

ISBN: 978-1-4080-3256-5

Cengage Learning EMEA
Cheriton House, North Way, Andover, Hampshire, SP10 5BE
United Kingdom

Cengage Learning products are represented in Canada by Nelson Education Ltd.

For your lifelong learning solutions, visit **www.cengage.co.uk**

Purchase your next print book, e-book or e-chapter at **www.cengagebrain.com**

Printed by Cambrian Printers, Wales
1 2 3 4 5 6 7 8 9 10 – 13 12 11

Acknowledgements

The content of this text has been adapted from the following product(s):

Introducing Organisational Behaviour and Management, 1st Edition
Knights, David; Willmott, Hugh (978–1–84480–0353)

Full copyright details and acknowledgements will appear in the aforementioned publications.

Brief contents

Contents

Notes

Note to the reader

This customised text is an abbreviated volume comprised of only the chapters from *Introducing Organisational Behaviour and Management* (1st Edition), most relevant to the MOB modules at UWE. We have included Chapters 1, 2, 4, 7, 9, 13 and 14 and the Glossary. Copies of the full textbook are available at **www.cengagebrain.com**.

Timeline

The theories, organisations and social events that appear in the timeline have been chosen by the module leaders to provide students with an overview of theoretical developments and related subjects. However, this timeline is by no means definitive but instead highlights the concepts relevant for the MOB modules at UWE.

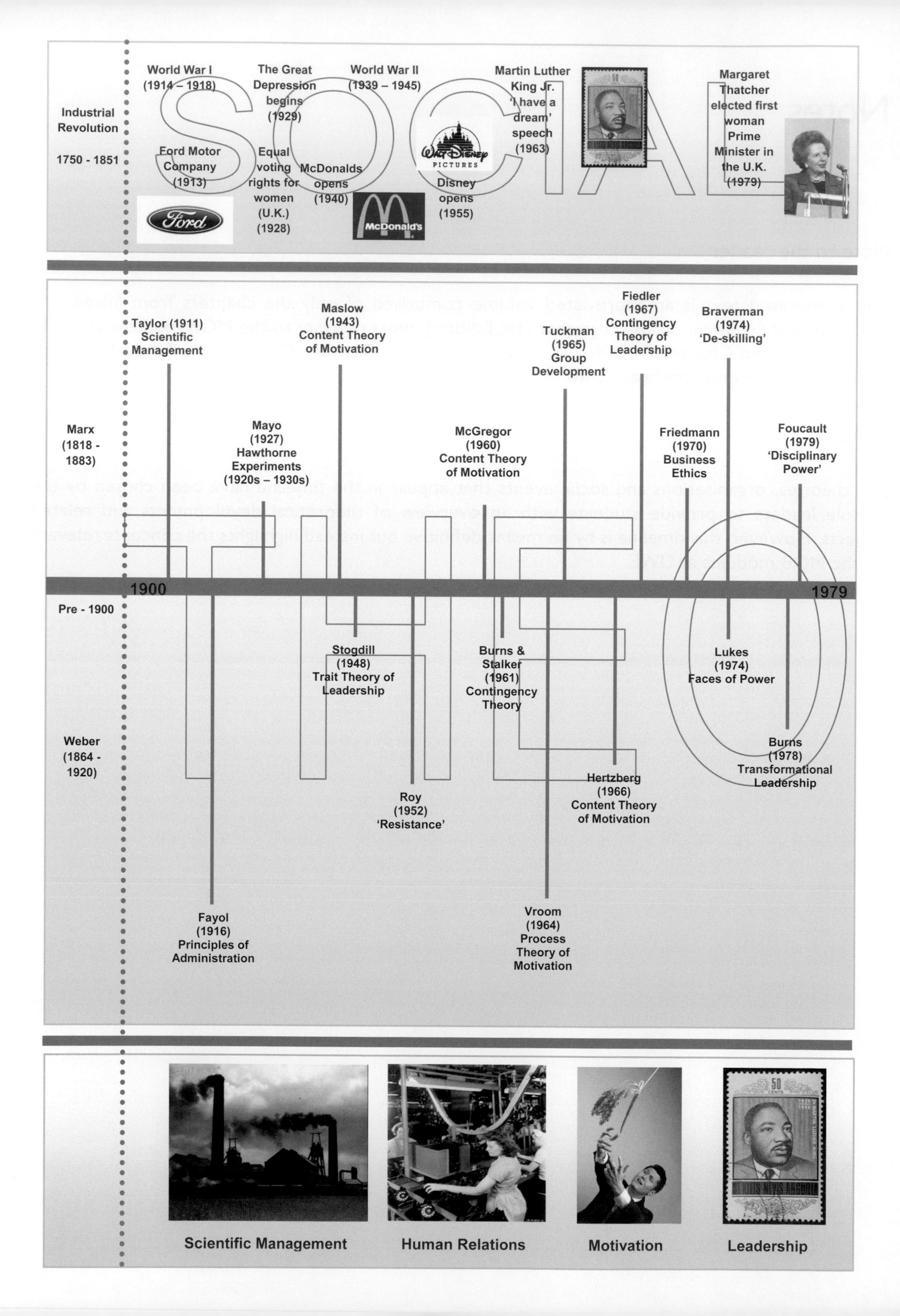
SOCIAL
Industrial Revolution
1750 - 1851
World War I (1914 – 1918)
Ford Motor Company (1913)
Ford
The Great Depression begins (1929)
Equal voting rights for women (U.K.) (1928)
McDonalds opens (1940)
McDonald's
World War II (1939 – 1945)
Walt Disney Pictures
Disney opens (1955)
Martin Luther King Jr. 'I have a dream' speech (1963)
Margaret Thatcher elected first woman Prime Minister in the U.K. (1979)
THEORY
Marx (1818 - 1883)
Pre - 1900
Weber (1864 - 1920)
1900
1979
Taylor (1911) Scientific Management
Fayol (1916) Principles of Administration
Mayo (1927) Hawthorne Experiments (1920s – 1930s)
Maslow (1943) Content Theory of Motivation
Stogdill (1948) Trait Theory of Leadership
Roy (1952) 'Resistance'
McGregor (1960) Content Theory of Motivation
Burns & Stalker (1961) Contingency Theory
Vroom (1964) Process Theory of Motivation
Tuckman (1965) Group Development
Hertzberg (1966) Content Theory of Motivation
Fiedler (1967) Contingency Theory of Leadership
Friedmann (1970) Business Ethics
Braverman (1974) 'De-skilling'
Lukes (1974) Faces of Power
Burns (1978) Transformational Leadership
Foucault (1979) 'Disciplinary Power'
Scientific Management
Human Relations
Motivation
Leadership

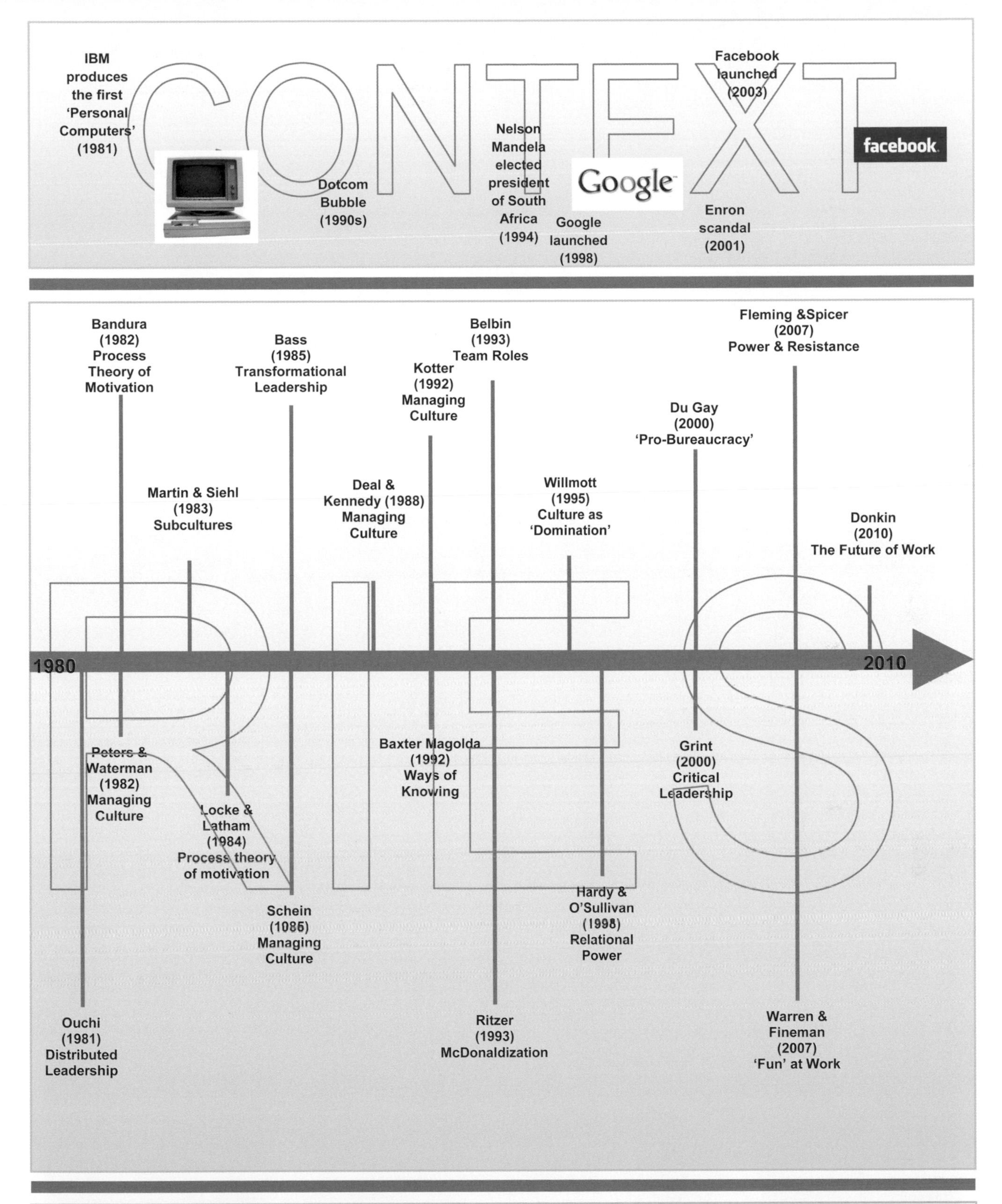
CONTEXT
IBM produces the first 'Personal Computers' (1981)
Dotcom Bubble (1990s)
Nelson Mandela elected president of South Africa (1994)
Google
Google launched (1998)
Facebook launched (2003)
facebook
Enron scandal (2001)
Bandura (1982) Process Theory of Motivation
Bass (1985) Transformational Leadership
Kotter (1992) Managing Culture
Belbin (1993) Team Roles
Fleming &Spicer (2007) Power & Resistance
Du Gay (2000) 'Pro-Bureaucracy'
Martin & Siehl (1983) Subcultures
Deal & Kennedy (1988) Managing Culture
Willmott (1995) Culture as 'Domination'
Donkin (2010) The Future of Work
1980
2010
RIES
Peters & Waterman (1982) Managing Culture
Locke & Latham (1984) Process theory of motivation
Baxter Magolda (1992) Ways of Knowing
Grint (2000) Critical Leadership
Schein (1985) Managing Culture
Hardy & O'Sullivan (1998) Relational Power
Ouchi (1981) Distributed Leadership
Ritzer (1993) McDonaldization
Warren & Fineman (2007) 'Fun' at Work

Culture
Teams
Power
Bureaucracy
Ethics

1 Introduction

David Knights and Hugh Willmott

Key concepts and learning objectives

Our intention for this book is to introduce management and organizational behaviour (OB) in a way that:

- Values your *own knowledge* and its contribution to understanding management and organizing.
- Encourages you to scrutinize and develop what you know about management and organization.
- Appreciates how the study of management and organization draws from a number of academic disciplines (e.g. sociology, politics, psychology and economics). It is, in this sense, multidisciplinary.
- Develops an awareness of how knowledge of management and organizations reflects and reproduces the particular framework or *perspective(s)* of the author (e.g. 'mainstream' or 'critical').
- Recognizes how different perspectives conjure up and provide contrasting and competing ways of making sense of management and organizations.
- Understands how knowledge of organization(s) is significantly dependent upon people's preoccupations and priorities and, in this sense, is *politically charged*.
- Challenges the way organizations are conventionally understood in mainstream texts as 'things' consisting of parts (e.g. people, functions, goals). This approach, we believe, is mechanical and removed from human experience.
- Appreciates how, fundamentally, 'management' and 'organization' are concepts. This encourages awareness of the diverse and multiple ways in which they are conceived. Each meaning associated with 'management' or 'organization' does not simply describe something 'out there' because it contributes to the very construction of what it claims to describe.
- Considers how the interrelated concepts of power, identity, knowledge, freedom, inequality and insecurity provide a framework for analysing aspects of organizational behaviour.
- Shows how key concepts in the study of management and organization are as relevant for making sense of everyday life as they are for studying behaviour in organizations.

Aims of this book

- This book seeks to connect the study of management and organization to readers' everyday experience.
- As this connection is made, the study of managing and organizing becomes more engaging and less remote.
- Ideas and insights explored in the following chapters should become more personally meaningful and therefore easier to recall.

Overview and key points

Much of our waking lives is spent in organizations: as students, for example, in schools or universities; as consumers in leisure organizations, such as shops and clubs; or as producers in work organizations, such as factories or offices (which, of course, include shops, schools and clubs). By relating our everyday *experience* to the study of management and organizations, we are likely to become more aware of how much we already know about them. Recognizing that we are already very familiar with organizations can increase our confidence when studying them. It can also encourage us to develop our understanding, question what we already know, and it may even result in us changing our habitual ways of thinking and acting. We illustrate this process in Figure 1.1.

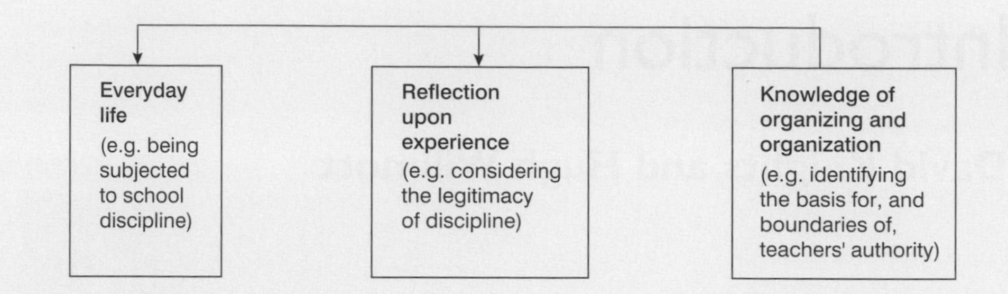

Figure 1.1 Experience, reflection and knowledge of management and organization

It would of course be possible to make further connections in this diagram – for example, by adding more boxes, by using double-headed arrows or by representing the elements as overlapping circles. How might additional elements and linkages offer other interesting ways of connecting our experiences, our reflections and our knowledge of organizations?

Before moving to the main part of the introduction, please have a look at the two boxes below.

Box 1.1: Learning as a challenging process

Learning best takes place when we relate meaningfully to what is being learned. If we take this view to heart, then it can make little sense for us to tell you *exactly* what you will have learned from each chapter of this book as each of the circumstances of each reader will differ. Instead, we encourage you to appreciate and explore your own understandings of the relevance of the various ideas and issues that we examine.

A very good and often enjoyable way to do this is by engaging in discussions with other students on your course. Consider how others are interpreting this text, and how these interpretations can challenge or advance your own understanding. For example, what assessments do you and they make of the arguments about learning and organizations presented in this chapter? What kinds of concepts and language are being used to articulate these views? What differences are emerging and how would you characterize these differences? Do others share your interpretation of these differences? Do these mixed reactions illustrate our point about the creativity, wilfulness and unpredictability of people?

Box 1.2: What you will find in this book

Each chapter of this book comprises an overview of key contributions to the mainstream study of its topic, followed by a reappraisal based upon a more critical approach to its analysis. What we mean by this is elaborated later in this chapter where we summarize our analytical framework based upon the concepts of insecurity, identity, inequality, power, freedom and knowledge. In each chapter we invite readers to go beyond the retrieval and storage of information from this book to reflect upon how the study of OB has relevance for everyday experience, and how this experience has relevance for OB.

Introduction

This book explores how people are organized and managed at work. Managing people is repeatedly identified by managers as the most demanding as well as the most important aspect of their jobs. Managing people is often troublesome. Why might this be?

Unlike other factors of production (e.g. raw materials and technology), human beings are wilful and comparatively unpredictable. Their creative power is crucial to production but it can also be deployed to frustrate, and not just facilitate, what they are paid to do. Organizational behaviour (OB) has emerged as a body of knowledge that identifies, explores and frequently suggests methods of controlling or 'empowering' the tricky 'people dimension' of managing and organizing.

As a field of study, 'organizational behaviour' comprises a wide variety of topics – such as motivation, leadership and organizational design – that relate to different aspects of behaviour in organizations. Examining these topics has involved incorporating perspectives and insights from a number of disciplines including psychology, economics, sociology and politics. (We elaborate this understanding later in this chapter in the 'What is Organizational behaviour?' section.)

Numerous disciplines that explore the complexity and diversity of collective human activity have contributed to the formation and development of OB. Something of this complexity is apparent in the sometimes conflicting purposes and objectives embraced by, or attributed to, 'management' and 'organizations'. These include: producing profits for shareholders, generating income for oneself and one's family, acquiring or building knowledge and skills, caring for others and so on. People rarely have just one purpose, and the various purposes do not always fit together neatly or achieve consistency one with another (see Box 1.3). To further complicate and confuse matters, people in organizations are affected by the changing circumstances in which they participate.

Providing a single definition of 'organization' is difficult and potentially unhelpful. At the same time we recognize that as we approach a new area of study, it can be helpful to have a working sense, or concept, of what we are studying. Provisionally, then, we will say that 'organization' is a concept used by both practitioners (e.g. managers) and analysts (e.g. academics) to make meaningful, and also to organize, the activities and interactions of people who are conceived to be doing organizational work, such as being engaged in creating, developing, and distributing products or services.

More specifically, in the current context, the concepts of 'organization(s)' and 'management' are deployed to indicate that people are able to accomplish together what they would find difficult or impossible to achieve when acting on their own or in smaller groups. They provide us with the possibility of thinking (or 'theorizing') about our experience, and especially, the practical, *collective* activity, such as the effort involved in making products or delivering services. (We explore the competing logics of organizing later in this chapter, in the 'Organizational behaviour as a contested terrain' section.)

Why study organizational behaviour?

Given the demanding nature of organizing and managing people, it is not surprising that OB is widely regarded as the foundation of management studies. Within the notion of 'behaviour', we include thinking and feeling as well as acting. OB aspires to have relevance for understanding the behaviour of people working at all **hierarchical levels** – from the workers employed part-time or on a casual basis on the **shop floor** or in the office to the most senior executive. Each is involved in processes of

Box 1.3: What about 'purpose'?

In order to explain their behaviour to others, individuals or groups often claim a purpose. But these claims may be rationalizations or simply socially acceptable accounts. Purposes, therefore, are not to be taken at face value or as the causes of behaviour. They are often invoked to make behaviour seem rational and coherent. Purposes are not self-evident. Sometimes we are only dimly aware of purposes after the event of their achievement. Only then are they identified 'on the hoof' (ad hoc) or after the next event (post hoc). (See Chapter 2.)

organizing and being organized, and managing and being managed. Whereas the management of lower hierarchy employees is transparent, it is also the case that boards of directors (or their equivalent), as well as less obviously personal assistants (PAs) or secretaries, often manage their senior executives.

We have emphasized how managing and organizing people to produce goods and provide services can be a demanding and perverse undertaking. As a student, you may well have experienced casual work, often undertaking jobs that are classified as 'unskilled' (and therefore poorly paid because there is no market shortage of people able to undertake them) but which require considerable concentration and effort, and can have damaging consequences if done badly. Equally, you may have found yourself in jobs where you have time on your hands and where your initiative and skills are underutilized or not used at all, except perhaps unofficially in looking for ways of minimizing your involvement in unpleasant tasks.

In principle, studying OB should enable you to better understand how and why people are organized; to identify and assess the likely consequences of making changes; and to introduce changes in ways that anticipate and minimize counter productive effects (see Box 1.4). As we have emphasized and illustrated, we believe that this understanding is facilitated by considering organization as a concept rather than a description or an entity, and by applying the insights derived from our conceptual framework that link identity, insecurity, power, inequality, freedom and knowledge (see Appendix: The conceptual framework).

Connecting ideas and experience

Consider your experience as a participant in a higher educational organization. With due consideration to what we have already said about how purposes are **invoked** and **ascribed**, one or more of your purposes in studying this course, which may change over time, might be identified from the following list:

1. Intellectual curiosity.
2. To understand the basics of business.
3. To enhance your management capabilities.
4. To avoid an alternative choice of degree that you view as impractical/boring/intellectually demanding.
5. To obtain a degree with the minimum of effort.

You can readily add to this list.

What about the purposes of your teachers, the university authorities (whoever you deem them to be) or the government?

You might also reflect upon how our 'attributes' towards studying (and work more generally) are influenced by our interactions with others – parents and teachers as well as fellow students. Such considerations are often described in OB in terms of motivation, involvement or group dynamics. They are significant for OB in so far as they affect the quality and direction of collective action. In the context of

Box 1.4: The relevance of organizational behaviour

OB may be of most direct relevance for understanding general management but its importance extends to specialist areas, such as accounting, production and marketing where, inevitably, organizing and managing people remain central activities. Indeed, OB is a 'subject' taken by a growing number of students, either as a single degree or as a core element of degree programmes in engineering, modern languages and sports studies among others. Specialists within different areas of management and business are inevitably working with others on whose cooperation and 'good behaviour' they depend. Likewise, generalist managers are involved in coordinating their activities with specialist functions of accounting (e.g. through constructing and monitoring budgets) and production (e.g. through liaison with suppliers and customers regarding production requirements and schedules). Crucially, these are not simply impersonal activities requiring technical skills but, rather, involve organizing capabilities that are identified as leadership, communication and motivation. Equally, everyday experiences, including work experience, have relevance for appreciating, assessing and challenging the body of knowledge that comprises OB.

higher education, this would include the extent to which students actively seek and encourage participation in class discussions, how much willingness there is to question the 'received wisdom' found in textbooks, and generally whether education is experienced as a process of passive or active learning.

Thinkpoint 1.1

Learning and relevance Think of some information that you find easy to remember – for example, popular singers, CD tracks, sports stars, soap opera characters and story lines, etc.

- What makes it easy for you to recall this information?
- Why is it often difficult to retain other kinds of information, such as the contents of some of the courses that you are studying?

Discuss with fellow students your conclusions. How might learning be organized differently to make easier what you find difficult?

The mixed and shifting motivations of students (as listed above, p. 4) presents teachers and textbook writers with a dilemma. Do we seek to 'manage' your learning by providing you with easily digestible 'nuggets of knowledge' that you can memorize and regurgitate with the minimum of effort or thought? This could be seen as the most 'efficient' (i.e. low-effort) way to satisfy (4) and (5) in the list, but is it 'effective' in enabling you to understand something of the basics of management and business (2) as a lived, practical activity, let alone in enhancing your management and organizing capabilities (1)? Think about the design of modules and courses that you have taken in the past, or are currently attending. In their contents and delivery, do some approximate to the 'efficiency' model while others incorporate some concern with 'effectiveness'.

As with all forms of management, this text might encourage and enable you to 'play the game' of appearing to be interested in (1) or (2) while secretly you remain closer to (5) or (4) or vice versa. If you can relate OB to your experience of everyday life, you may find it 'less boring' (4) than some courses and/or at least a comparatively 'easy option' (5). We, of course, believe that our approach is more capable of feeding and nurturing your intellectual curiosity (1), your understanding of business (2) and ultimately your management capability (3). We may, on the other hand, be wide of the mark. You might prefer something more conventional that is perhaps 'boring' but also less demanding because it does not expect your engagement. Instead it requires only that you memorize and regurgitate its contents.

It is worth pausing briefly to note the similarities and continuities, as well as some significant differences, between organizing people at work and processes of teaching and learning. Challenges and frustrations in the lives of teachers and students are often paralleled in the experiences of managers and workers. For this reason, when studying OB it is frequently helpful to reflect upon our own educational experiences in order to bring to life, and grasp the relevance of, key topics and concepts. We now move on to identify some of the distinguishing features of OB.

What is organizational behaviour?

OB draws upon elements from a wide range of social scientific disciplines. For example:

- *Sociology* examines human behaviour in relation to various social, political, psychological and economic conditions that affect it, but in turn are produced or reproduced by it.
- *Psychology* concentrates on how individuals think and behave.
- *Politics* focuses on competitive struggles for political power and influence in society (see Chapter 8).
- *Economics* examines how wealth is produced and distributed.

Each discipline generates a distinctive way of conceiving of 'organization(s)' and interpreting behaviour in them. There is also a tendency for each discipline to be antagonistic, or even closed to its rivals. Despite this limitation, the different approaches provide a check and challenge to our particular prejudices about organizations. They serve to focus and organize our thinking, and that is why we call them 'disciplines' (see Box 1.5).

Box 1.5: Single discipline domination

Despite incorporating some elements of 'rival' disciplines, most OB studies and textbooks are often dominated by a single discipline. A large number of introductory OB texts are influenced most strongly by the discipline of psychology. This influence has meant that the key OB topics are often focused upon the individual and group processes. An example is Ian Brooks (1999), who defines OB as 'the study of human behaviour in organizations with a focus on individual and group processes and actions'.

This text includes a consideration of the psychology of individuals and group processes (see 'The distinctiveness of this text' section later in this chapter), as is evident in our emphasis upon freedom, insecurity and identity as three of six key analytical concepts (see Appendix: The conceptual framework). At the same time, we understand the attitudes, motivations and dynamics of individuals and groups in terms of their social, not just their psychological, formation and development. We extend our vision to include an appreciation of how seemingly 'psychological' factors and forces are shaped by and deeply embedded in social relations that stretch beyond both organizational members and the boundaries attributed to organizations. People at work are simultaneously family members with diverse social affiliations (of gender, class, ethnicity, etc.) that directly or indirectly colour their behaviour as individuals and their participation in groups.

When considering the work undertaken by managers or other organizational members, for example, we recognize the importance of their perceptions and motivations for understanding their behaviour. We also appreciate how perceptions and motivations are formed and coloured by wider, historical and cultural (i.e. sociological) experiences and relations both at work and beyond the workplace. Behaviour in organizations is not just about perceptions and motivations. It is also, and perhaps more importantly, about the economic and political conditions and consequences of work. It is therefore highly relevant to pay attention to the historical and cultural formation of managers' and employees' material and symbolic aspirations (e.g. pay, pensions and position, as well as other possibilities or opportunities for improving their situation such as promotion, share options and moving jobs). In this context, we need to appreciate how, for example, managers of private sector companies (PLCs) are *legally* accountable to shareholders as especially privileged stakeholders.

Image 1.1 College as a global village

When placed in this wider context, awareness increases of how the disciplines of economics and politics are directly relevant for understanding work organizations. People who work in organizations come from diverse social backgrounds and have varied social responsibilities and affiliations outside, as well as within their workplaces. Quite widely divergent motivations and interests are forged and pursued in the process of developing and defending an individual and collective sense of security and identity. As a consequence, it cannot be presumed that, for example, employees or other stakeholders (e.g. customers, suppliers) fully support decisions (e.g. lay-offs, pay constraints, price rises, product range reductions) that are intended to advance the interests of shareholders.

Beyond mechanical prescription

We can illustrate the distinctiveness and value of our approach by considering the 'skill profile' attributed to effective managers (see Box 1.6), such as head teachers or departmental heads in schools. What is your reaction to the contents of this skill profile? Do you consider that knowledge of this profile would make managers that you have known more effective? If not, what else might be relevant? Give these questions a few moments of thought before continuing.

The 'skill profile' identified in Box 1.6 is based upon extensive research, with much of the data drawn from responses by managers' subordinates. Yet it contains few surprises or insights. In our experience, small groups of school students or undergraduates are able to produce very similar lists within a matter of minutes. If this is the case, it places in doubt the value of such lists, because they do little more than recycle and reinforce **common-sense** thinking (see Box 1.7).

Box 1.6: The effective manager's skill profile

- Clarifies goals and objectives for everyone involved.
- Encourages participation, upward communication and suggestions.
- Plans and organizes for an orderly work flow.
- Has technical and administrative expertise to answer organization-related questions.
- Facilitates work through teambuilding, training, coaching and support.
- Provides feedback honestly and constructively.

Source: From Kinicki and Kreitner, 2003, p. 8; emphases omitted.

Box 1.7: Isn't it all just commonsense?

When knowledge about something is considered to be 'commonsense', we tend to treat it as a self-evident or unquestionable 'truth'. How often have you been told, especially by parents or supervisors, to use your commonsense, or to be sensible? The term is used to convey the view that there is no room for debate or discussion about what is meant. Indeed, to challenge commonsense is to appear stupid or unreasonable. We use the term 'commonsense' to indicate what is believed to be obvious to any competent human being. 'Commonsense' is assumed to be clear-cut and straightforward, and so it is, but only as long as we do not challenge it. Terms that are not immediately recognizable as, or reducible to, commonsense – such as 'organization' or 'social structure', as contrasted to 'pecking order', for example – demand a little more thinking than commonsense expects.

An everyday example of commonsense is the notion that the sun rises and sets. Rising and setting is what the sun appears to do, yet if we accept contemporary scientific authority, then we should talk about the earth rotating: what commonsense tells us is misleading. Another, more directly relevant example of commonsense is the way that people describe economic self-interest as human nature. If we consider this claim more carefully, we find that it is problematic. This is because economic self-interest is also often denigrated as greediness – as in the 2002 scandals at Enron and WorldCom where false accounts were perpetrated to ensure high stock market ratings and big bonuses for the managers of those companies. In these examples, greed was condemned and executives have been urged to moderate their self interest, suggesting that it can be controlled and therefore it is not essential to human nature. If something is human nature, it is the equivalent of the dog barking when it senses that its territory is being invaded; and, as any dog owner knows, this is nigh impossible to prevent. In the example of economic self-interest, therefore, we can see that despite its claims to truth, commonsense is self-contradictory and rather impervious to reflection. It allows two mutually inconsistent or diametrically opposed views to be held at one and the same time.

We rarely think about organizations in a systematic way or seek to understand precisely why or how they failed to meet our expectations. There is a tendency to account for such failures by relying upon commonsense – for example, by diagnosing the failure as a 'lack of communication' or 'poor organization' as if, by labelling the problem in this way, we need pay it no further attention. Alternatively, we find a scapegoat like the incompetent boss. In principle, the study of OB can provide us with the conceptual and analytical resources for thinking beyond these sweeping and dismissive, commonsense 'explanations'. We might then better understand what renders communication 'lacking' or organization 'poor'. Or, to put this another way, we might begin to open the 'black box' of behaviour in organizations to discover what lurks inside.

Commonsense frequently relies upon assumptions that, on reflection, are shown to be simplistic. When the earth is conceived to be at the centre of the universe, it is 'obvious' that the sun rises and sets; when materialistic societies are conceived to be the most 'civilized', the greed that they inspire is readily identified as an essential feature of human nature. On reflection, economic self-interest is found not to be an essential quality of human nature. It is, rather, an effect of how in contemporary, materialistic societies, the individual and wealth are elevated as key values. In short, greed has become a widespread, normal pattern of behaviour – so widespread that economic self-interest is commonsensically regarded as inherent to human nature. But, saying this, there is no suggestion (either) that altruism (as the opposite of self-interest) is essential. Instead, we are drawn to the view that human nature is open and ambivalent. For this reason, to cite human nature as an explanation of a person's actions may be commonsensically plausible but, on reflection, it begs more questions than it answers. It invites us, for example, to ask why human nature is identified in particular ways that appeal to commonsense?

Having signalled its dangers and limitations, from time to time most of us, including scientists, rely upon commonsense thinking, or at least are prepared to suspend disbelief in it. We will, for example, rely frequently on a commonsense understanding of organization as an entity, even though we repeatedly question this commonsense 'truth'. Everyday conversations and communications would simply collapse if every word or statement that relied on commonsense were incessantly challenged or questioned.

What, then, is the alternative? In a nutshell, one possible alternative aims to provide insights into why, in practice, it is so difficult to develop and apply skills identified as effective. Take the example of goals and objectives. The list of effective skills implies that goals are already established and merely require elucidation. In practice, however, they are frequently ambiguous and conflicting as we noted earlier. Those involved may well perceive that the goals identified by the 'effective manager' are incompatible with their own preferences and priorities. In which case, 'participation' may well be more troublesome and even counter-productive in securing employee compliance. Even in situations where others can be persuaded to share goals or communicate and respond positively to honest feedback, competing priorities and limited resources frequently compromise or undermine effective managers' efforts to 'organize an orderly work flow' or 'facilitate work through teambuilding'. It is dangerous to assume that becoming an effective manager simply involves the acquisition of the desired skill profile. If this were so, a manager might be led to believe in the effectiveness of mindlessly applying those 'skills' to particular situations in the absence of interpreting appropriate usage on each and every occasion.

Box 1.8: Why are organizational behaviour texts so wide of the mark?

When considering the skill profile attributed to effective managers (see Box 1.6) we claimed that texts based upon such thinking are of limited value and relevance. This view immediately begs the question why, then, are they so popular and widely adopted? Our response is that their appeal resides in the highly positive image or 'spin' that they give to organizations and managers. This reassuring and even slightly glamorous image is attractive to future employers as well as to students as it portrays management as a respectable and responsible profession where the manager's role is 'simply' to enable others to achieve established, shared goals and objectives. Largely absent from the benign image of organizations and management presented in most OB texts is any recognition of how the practicalities of management are shaped – impeded as well as enabled – by insecurities and inequalities that are endemic to modern organizational life.

If this analysis is accepted, then what *is* of value to prospective managers? It is not, we believe, lists of effective skills or techniques. Rather, effective management involves drawing upon embodied insights into work relations as a means of developing a better understanding of how to manage without following simple prescriptions.

Our skill profile example is typical of an approach that introduces OB through the provision of abstract lists or idealistic prescriptions of management behaviour that students tend to find self-evident and/or remote from everyday experience. Because they are removed from an understanding of the ever-shifting complexities of human behaviour at work, they are likely to be of little assistance in practical situations of managing. Forms of management education and training based upon such prescriptive thinking tends to reinforce a passive learning experience in which students absorb and regurgitate information without ever reflecting upon its value to them, except as instrumental rational means of attaining a certification.

Without an awareness of the messy, politically charged practicalities of organizing and managing, any amount of worthy (and, we would add, often patronizing) prescription will be of little value and may even be damaging. It is foolhardy, and potentially disastrous, to apply a set of principles or 'best practices' without first making an assessment of the particular situation and developing an evaluation of their relevance.

We acknowledge that there can be value in identifying a set of skills that are seen to render managers effective. However, such profiles and checklists do not enable us to discern and diagnose why and in what circumstances these skills may be effective. In our view the point of studying OB is to scrutinize and move beyond apparently self-evident but ultimately simplistic and misleading ideas about working and managing in organizations. We elaborate our views in a later section of this chapter where we directly address the question 'Why study organizational behaviour?' For the moment, we focus upon organizations as the context for the study of human behaviour.

Thinking about organizations

So far, we have concentrated upon behaviour in organizations, but what about organizations themselves? When beginning to think about organizations, specific examples may spring to mind. We might think of a major retailer (e.g. Ikea), a manufacturer (e.g. Hewlett-Packard), a public sector organization, like the Health Service or a government department, a school, an office or a pub (see Box 1.9).

It is not difficult to reel off an extensive list of organizations, but what, if anything, do they have in common? Again, it is easy to identify some common features. Most organizations involve employment relations, a division of labour, hierarchy, and a degree of permanence or continuity. What other common features would you add to this list?

D) © STOCKPHOTO.COM/TOMAZ LEVSTEK

Image 1.2 Diverse work organizations: factory, school, office, public house

With the construction of this list, we appear to have identified a number of the distinctive characteristics of organizations. The difficulty is to find a single item on this list that is *exclusive* to organizations. Consider employment. We can think of examples of forms of employment that are not directly associated with organizations. Within the 'black economy' (e.g. where people work unofficially for cash in hand), many people are employed without being a member of an organization or indeed being recognized as employed for the purposes of tax and national insurance. Within organizations, a division of labour is present wherever members do not undertake identical tasks. But this is true of many other institutions, such as the family where certain jobs are frequently reserved by, or left to, particular members. For example, household tasks are often subjected to a gendered division of labour where women carry out most of the childcare responsibilities, cooking and cleaning, while men tend the garden or engage in DIY.

To take another example, a degree of permanence exists in families but we would not today readily identify families as organizations, even though, in small local enterprises, family members may run a business. In the pre-industrial era, work and family were not as separate as today, since domestic production was pre-eminent. The development of the internet and tele-computing communications has once again brought home and work closer together. Many people, like ourselves, do some or much of our work back in the family home partly because this allows us to concentrate, say, on writing this text without continuous interruptions from colleagues and students. However, through mobile communications, we usually make ourselves available to those who need to be in contact with us. Nonetheless, families are not readily conceived as organizations, perhaps largely because relations between their members are comparatively permanent, personal and intimate.

Thinkpoint 1.2

Working from home How many people do you know who work from home, at least part of the time, and what kinds of jobs do they do? What, if anything, differentiates the experience of doing these jobs from those carried out in offices, factories or other employer premises? Drawing upon your knowledge of people who work from home, what are some of the pros and cons of such work experience? How would you view 'housework' in the context of working from home?

There is further discussion of 'organization' in a later section in this chapter (see 'The distinctiveness of work organization: Instrumental rationality'). For the moment, it is worth repeating our earlier emphasis on organization as a concept that directs our attention and energies in particular ways, rather than assuming it to be a distinctive kind of social institution. It is also worth re-emphasizing that our purpose throughout this text is to connect its content with your experience of studying and working in a variety of settings or of consuming various products or services. In doing so, the intent is to make the contents of OB less remote and more personally relevant. In line with this approach, we now introduce an example from everyday life.

Box 1.9: What is a pub? A sociologist's answer

According to Clark (1983): . . .

the 'typically English pub' has its particular place in 'English' culture for its symbolic role as an 'icon of the everyday'. . . . Historically, in Britain, public houses have served as the social focus for geographical and occupational communities. The public house has taken different forms over time and has its origins in the 'inns', 'taverns' and 'alehouses' of the pre-industrial era. In that period, alehouses were more numerous than any other type of public meeting-place and were the focus for a huge range of social and economic activity. Ordinary people went there to buy and sell goods, to borrow money, to obtain lodging and work, to find sexual partners, to play folk games and gamble in addition to the usual eating, dancing, smoking and carousing.

However, it was not until the early 1800s that the purpose-built public house as we know it began to be built in large numbers and the 'alehouse' gave way to the 'public house'. By the beginning of the 19th century the term 'alehouse' had all but disappeared and by 1865, according to the *Oxford English Dictionary*, the word 'pub' had entered the language. (Watson, 2002, p. 18)

Organizational behaviour and everyday life: Going down the pub

We have already noted how difficult it is to draw a hard-and-fast distinction between organizations and other social institutions such as the family. The pub – or public house – provides a further example. For those who work in pubs, they are in many ways organizations that employ their specialist skills. In contrast, for regular customers, their 'local' is more like an extension of their family or community. In the following example of a pub – the Dog and Duck – we deliberately chose an example of an organization that is (a) familiar to most students and (b) ambivalent and shifting in its status as an organization.

In exploring the case of the Dog and Duck, we begin to introduce some of our key concepts (in italics) to demonstrate their relevance for analysing everyday life, including the pub as a work organization and a place of leisure where products (e.g. drinks and food) and services (such as live music and sports events) are consumed.

Our students tell us that the pubs that become student venues generally offer cheap deals on drinks and lower prices generally. In terms of material *inequality* (see the Appendix), many students are (albeit temporarily) low down on the social scale. The exceptions are students whose parents provide them with plenty of money, secure a large loan, or who get a well-remunerated job while at university. Even when not 'hard up', however, many students prefer drinking in student pubs rather than more expensive bars and clubs. Why is this? Take a moment to reflect upon what draws students to particular pubs. Do these work organizations have distinctive features?

Generally, student pubs are friendly toward young people and the management and staff are willing to put up with the boisterousness and noise where students gather in large numbers. They also provide attractions that students value, like pool tables and juke box music. But, beyond this, how does the student pub make you feel 'at home', relaxed and comfortable, and in what kinds of conditions

CASE STUDY 1.1 Jackie at the pub (1)

Jackie finished off her assessed work that was to be handed in the next day and felt she needed a drink. Her flatmates had gone out earlier that evening but she knew where they would be – at their local, the Dog and Duck. Her mates usually congregated in the pub around 7.00pm most weeknights because there were special deals on the drinks – two for the price of one. The landlady and landlord were happy for their pub to be full of students and did not hassle them when they got a bit rowdy. Also, in student jargon, the pub was good for 'pulling'. Jackie was now in her second semester of her first year and had already 'pulled' a couple of pretty fit lads she first met in the Dog and Duck. But the main reason for going to the D&D – or the 'B&Q' (the Bitch and Quackers) as it was known to her friends for reasons that Jackie would be embarrassed to explain – was that you could guarantee that your friends would be there.

However, on this occasion, Jackie arrived quite late because it had taken her longer than expected to finish her essay. Her mates had all disappeared. She had some idea that they would have gone off to one of the student discos in the town, but she was rather tired and so decided to have a quick drink on her own before heading back for a long-promised early night. At this time in the evening, most of the students had left and the bar was filling up with 'locals'. Like the students, the locals knew each other and therefore didn't ordinarily talk to the few remaining students unless they themselves were 'on the pull'. This was the first time that Jackie had found herself in the pub on her own and she felt a little embarrassed just standing at the bar with a drink. So she sat down in a corner of the pub, hoping she would be left alone. However, within a few minutes a group of young people, mainly lads, came towards her table. They seemed friendly enough and were talking in an animated way about the poor performance of the local football team. Jackie felt that she could fancy one of these lads. When he asked if anyone else was sitting at her table, the absence of other glasses made it difficult for her to refuse, and anyway her desire for a quiet drink had now been overtaken by her interest in the faceable lad.

Soon the conversation turned to the changing clientele in the pub and some of the group began running down the students, describing them as 'toffee-nosed' and 'cliquey'. It was clear to Jackie that they resented the 'takeover' of their local by the students, something that had happened earlier in the year when a new management at the pub made an effort to attract students. The pub had been quiet between about 6.30pm, when the early drinkers on their way home left and 8.30pm when the later regulars appeared after their evening meal. Jackie felt even more embarrassed that these locals were 'slagging off' students, as she thought, because she felt that they must know that she was a student, and were deliberately winding her up. She wasn't at all sure how, or even whether, to respond.

would you feel threatened? Does drinking with other students confirm or reinforce your *identity* (see the Appendix) as a student? Does that provide a key to understanding why we tend to gravitate to places where there are people like ourselves? When we find ourselves in a room largely full of strangers, we usually seek out a person we know. Why? Case Study 1.1 provides a story or scenario about going down the pub.

Like any other institution, the pub reflects a complex set of *power* relations (see the Appendix). As a customer, Jackie is dependent upon the staff of the pub to be served and, ultimately, for protection against verbal and physical abuse. But, as a customer, Jackie is important to the pub managers since they are determined to pursue the potentially highly profitable custom of students. Power relations operate to identify her not only as a student but also as a valued customer – and, quite possibly, as a customer who can encourage or dissuade her mates to use the pub. So even though Jackie and her friends occupy a comparatively low rung on the income scale, the existence of material *inequality* does not imply an absence of power as long as her custom, and that of her student friends, is valued. However, as our **vignette** or brief story shows, other customers, or even pub staff, may not share the positive value being ascribed by the pub managers to students as clientele.

Having read this account of Jackie's visit to the pub, what do you think you would have done in her position? Consider first what you perceive her position to be. What features of this position do you regard as significant? Once you have clarified your understanding of Jackie's situation, consider some possible responses Jackie could make:

- Pretend not to be listening to what they are saying?
- Confront the locals and attempt to defend the students?
- Pretend not to be a student and find a way of joining in on the stereotyping of them, if only as a way of attracting the attention of the Beckham-double? (After all, it is not too far-fetched to think that he may have targeted Jackie as a potential chat-up.)
- Ignore the attack but try to get into conversation with them?
- See the lads engaging in an alternative kind of 'chat-up' by trying to provoke some reaction instead of using a well-worn (institutionalized!) chat-up line – such as asking your name and what you did – so take the lads' (attention) in your stride?

Can you think of other ways that a student in Jackie's position might react?

We will return later to develop our analysis of this story. For the moment, we note only that what happened to Jackie indicates in a practical way how, even in places of leisure, experiences are

"Just for the minutes did anyone manage to catch the chairman's parting words?"

SOURCE: © CLIVE COLLINS/CARTOONSTOCK.COM

Image 1.3

unpredictable because others – in this example, other customers – act in ways that are experienced as intrusive and objectionable, and which can be characterized as friendly, wilful or mischievous. Traditionally, the pub has been associated not only with symbolic violence, as experienced by Jackie, who felt personally affronted by the lads' 'slagging off' of students, but also physical violence when, fuelled by alcohol, frayed tempers spill over into punch-ups.

Outright physical violence involving an exchange of blows is exceptional but not unknown in other work organizations. Symbolic violence, however, is much more widespread. It can be based on physical characteristics (e.g. sexual or racial harassment) or take the form of verbal bullying. Many critics of the workplace argue that simply the demand to perform repetitive, physical work tasks that hardly engage the brain is a form of symbolic violence, in which case a majority of employees experience it at some point. We hope to show in this text how employees suffer a sense of frustration less from the routine nature of their tasks than from the absence of any power to influence how tasks are decided and organized. In our case, Jackie's levels of stress and *insecurity* (see the Appendix) – in the form of anxiety, embarrassment, irritation and frustration – were raised by her sense of powerlessness and lack of control. While she desperately wanted to challenge the lads' stereotypical views about students, she felt inhibited and intimidated. Whether or not it was their intent, they had succeeded in winding her up and she was finding it difficult to calm down and collect her thoughts. The study of organizations encounters conflict and contested points of view in more ways than in the direct expression of verbal or physical violence.

Symbolic violence – in the form of mild or vehement expressions of disagreement – might include, for example, differences of opinion among bar staff (and customers) about the desirability of students as clientele, and the verbal and non-verbal communication directed at this group. In this process, there is an elevation of the symbolic value or identity (see the Appendix) of one group through a negation of the other. In its most extreme versions, there is a complete polarization so that the other(s) or 'out-group' are demonized as unworthy of proper human respect. At football matches, this has resulted in the necessity for institutional forms of crowd control, such as physical segregation and other restrictions on the away supporters.

Such violence extends to disagreements among researchers, consultants, and indeed employees about the usefulness and meaning of concepts that are deployed to analyse behaviour and pursue practices in organizations. These disagreements – such as our criticizing conventional texts – may not result in the trading of blows but they can, and do, involve passionate exchanges of views and uneasy 'stand-offs'. Even when people recognize discussion and debate to be healthy and a source of new ideas, they may still feel threatened when their own ideas are challenged. Take a moment to reflect on some of the ideas or beliefs that you are attached to and would defend against a challenge. Often these are so deeply ingrained or taken for granted (e.g. your gender, class, nationality, race or religion) that it takes considerable reflective effort to bring them to mind.

Organizational behaviour as a contested terrain

In leading textbooks, OB tends to be presented as largely cut-and-dried and settled, thus lacking any controversy, conflict or contest, yet such appearances are deceptive. There are fundamental differences of view – cultural, political and ethical – about how organizations are organized, how they should be organized and how they can be studied. To some extent, these mirror and amplify differences of opinion and preference among people working in organizations (between factions of senior managers, for example) about how to organize and manage their operation. As a general rule, theories that articulate and confirm our preconceptions and prejudices tend to be most appealing, as they are the easiest to grasp and make us feel secure in our views and identities. So, in general, women are more likely than men to appreciate how relations of gender implicitly or explicitly affect the workplace, especially in areas of recruitment, selection and promotion. We invite you to discuss and reflect upon why this may be the case.

Here we are highlighting the continuities between practitioners' and researchers' ways of making sense of behaviour in organizations. At the same time, it is relevant to note that these practitioners and researchers are positioned in different relations of power – relations of power that provide access to distinctive ways of thinking and that assign different weights and values to such thinking. Some researchers favour and elaborate forms of analysis that highlight and explore how organizing is largely consensual and routine; others contend that organizing is precarious and conflict-ridden. Such analyses can serve to illuminate practitioners' everyday experiences, but practitioners themselves, especially managers, may find more favour and comfort with ideas that assume organizing to be consensual and conflict-free; or, at least, which assume consensus to be the normal and natural state of affairs.

Differences within and between practitioners and researchers can be confusing and frustrating, not least for students of OB. But these differences are also what make the field dynamic and engaging. Glossing over these differences can make OB easier to present and absorb, but this does students and practitioners few favours when highly complex organizational processes are examined in technically simplistic and politically naive ways. Challenging thinking that skirts around or skates over this complexity is necessary for developing an awareness of it. It is through such conflict and debate – in practice as well as theory – that intellectual reflection and organizational innovation is stimulated. At least, it is difficult to imagine how reflection and innovation would occur without them.

Exercise 1.1

Encountering organization Consider an organization where you have worked or have been a customer. List some differences of view, or grievances, among employees and/or customers that you encountered. How do these concerns connect to how activities were being organized and managed. Are there other issues that *you* would raise as an employee or as a customer? Reflect upon how your values and preoccupations lead you to raise these issues.

Competing logics of organizing

We have repeatedly stressed that organizations are politically charged, complex, social institutions (see Chapter 8). Their complexity does not arise directly from their scale or even from the diversity of their operations, but rather from conflicting priorities and preferences of their members who, in turn, are caught up in webs of others' demands upon them (e.g. families, customers, shareholders, etc.). An expression of these conflicting priorities is found in the existence of competing logics of organizing material and human resources to provide diverse goods and services. We have seen, for example, how Jackie found herself in a situation complicated by the competing priorities and

Image 1.4

SOURCE: © ROBERT THOMSON/CARTOONSTOCK.COM

preferences of the pub managers and the local customers. Whereas the new managers wanted to maximize the use of the premises at all times, this priority risked losing their established customer base of local regulars who resented 'their pub' being taken over by students.

A much broader example of competing logics of organizing concerns the issue of how 'public goods', such as health and education, should be provided. In recent years, questions have been asked with increasing frequency and urgency about the adequacy, and even the viability, of provision of such goods by public sector organizations. Public sector organizations have been repeatedly criticized for being too bureaucratic, unresponsive and insufficiently alert to (changing) customer preferences and expectations. Their critics point to an ingrained inflexibility (i.e. of managers, professional staff and workers) as the greatest obstacle to delivering value-for-money public goods (e.g. education).

During the 1980s and 1990s many people were persuaded that the answer to problems identified in the public sector – such as waste, rigidity and inefficiency – was to run it as a private business (see Box 1.10).

For elements of the public sector that were not privatized, the 'modernization' plan was to populate the public sector with 'professional managers' and to introduce more entrepreneurial ideas from the private sector. This process has included provisional targets and financial incentives for staff. It has encouraged competition and discipline associated with performance measurement and comparisons between different services. In the United Kingdom, the reforms included the introduction of performance measures in the form of league tables to schools and hospitals, for example, so that their 'customers' (i.e. parents and doctors) would make an informed choice between alternative service providers. In making a choice of school or university course, you (or your parents) may have been influenced by such tables.

Thinkpoint 1.3

League tables Consider the pros and cons of introducing league tables to measure the performance of schools or university departments. Imagine that you are advising a government in a country that has no equivalent to these tables. Consider the probable effects of their use upon the organization – e.g. scope and delivery – of educational provision. What arguments would you make to recommend or resist the introduction of league tables? How would you illustrate your position by reference to your own experience and knowledge as a recipient of educational services?

Box 1.10: Privatization and the 'new enterprise culture'

The case for the privatization of public services, either through substitution or contracting out to the private sector, is based on the claim that employees and especially managers in most organizations, including many in the private sector, have to be shaken out of their complacency and become more willing to take risks and be innovative in pursuit of efficiency, productivity and improved performance. In many countries, a number of publicly owned utilities (e.g. electricity, gas, transport and telecommunications) were 'sold off' to the private sector through a process of 'privatization'.

The supporters of this move argued that it would serve to modernize these services by making their provision more cost-effective, in addition to releasing capital that could fund tax cuts, reduce debt or boost the financing of services retained within the public sector (e.g. armed forces). Its critics pointed to the loss of control of key services, the damaging consequences of making them objects of profit, the erosion of conditions for public services workers and the redistribution of wealth from the poor to the rich by expanding the private sector. For organizations that remain in the public sector, what is needed, it is claimed, is a set of targets linked to incentives that can substitute for the profit motive and competition, which are seen to drive private sector managers to deliver high levels of performance. Public sector management, its critics complain, lacks incentives to make radical reforms. Enabling managers to exercise greater prerogative, unhampered by established traditions of collective bargaining and custom and practice regarding such things as manning levels and job design, is the key to raising the quality as well as the cost-effectiveness of public service delivery.

While there is a continuing controversy about the wisdom of privatization, or selling off the family silver as Lord Macmillan once described it, the idea that the private sector has much to offer the public sector remains. In the United Kingdom, confidence in the capacity of private ownership and associated forms of organizing and managing reflects a wider embracing of values that have been characterized as part and parcel of a new 'enterprise culture'. Balanced against this, highly visible failures of privatization (e.g. UK railways) have somewhat tempered public opinion and policy making in this area.

In the United Kingdom, the substitution of private for public forms of financing and organizing has been welcomed, or at least tacitly supported, by a majority of people. This is unsurprising because a reluctance to fund public services through taxation increases has left them (us) on the receiving end of under-investment in a public sector run down and demoralized by this neglect.[1] Almost everyone has a tale to tell of poor or worsening standards of public housing, healthcare and education. People suffering a bad experience with the public sector are already receptive to the suggestion that government should be run like a business, with professional managers being given the prerogative and discretion to manage resources.

'New managerialism' in the public sector

What this new managerialism means or at least claims, in less abstract terms, is that only by running public services like a business can citizens (as customers) receive the value-for-money and quality services to which they are entitled (see Box 1.11). The reform of public services is advocated in order to ensure that they are run for the benefit of those who use them, and not for 'the bureaucrats' who provide them. Paradoxically though, the result of such 'reforms' is an increase of managerial and monitoring staff whose salaries are paid by slashing the numbers, and eroding the terms and conditions, of the front-line employees who are being 'modernized'. Various private sector managerial techniques of budgets, targets, financial incentives, project management, performance league tables and accounting procedures are applied to the public sector.

After the scandals at Enron and WorldCom, the ideology that commends the running of public services like a business may be less convincing. 'New managerialism' does not acknowledge how too much faith in a managerial view can readily lead to corruption and greed. This then might undermine the very conditions necessary for a successful economy (such as confidence, trust and security).

'So, do you still think the government should be run like a business?..'

Image 1.5

SOURCE: CLAY BENNETT/ © 2002 THE CHRISTIAN SCIENCE MONITOR (WWW.CSMONITOR.COM)

Box 1.11: The organization and managerialization of everything

Managerialism refers to a view that assigns to managers the exclusive power to define the goals of the organization and their means of achievement. In extreme form, it proposes that everything can be managed efficiently through the application of 'correct' techniques. Elements of this can be seen in the delivery of programmed education provided in modularized chunks, using standardized overhead transparencies and student workbooks. Likened to the provision of (fast) food, this has been described as the 'McDonaldization' of education. To cater for a mass education market, textbooks are being produced to a standard formula and, like burgers, are probably not to be recommended as part of a healthy diet.

Thinkpoint 1.4

Would you privatize? How do you feel about efforts to 'privatize' or 'modernize' the public sector? In considering this question, you might examine reports of the Fire Brigades Union dispute that occurred during the autumn of 2002 into 2003. You might also reflect upon your experience as a consumer of public services – education, health, transport, local public facilities, etc. Here you could assess the effects of privatization and modernization upon the availability, scope and quality of such services.

The recurrent complaint of those who favour enterprise or market-based solutions to all forms of resource allocation is that the public services have been organized primarily for the benefit of producers (e.g. public sector employees) rather than their customers. This echoes the discovery of an earlier generation of OB researchers who found that bureaucracies suffered considerably from what they described as **goal displacement** (Merton *et al.*, 1952). Conforming to the internal rules of the organization (perhaps for reasons of career advancement) was shown to be more important than fulfilling the objectives (service to clients) that the rules were designed to facilitate.

However, this complaint about self-serving public sector bureaucrats also deflects attention from the importance placed upon shareholders, rather than customers, in the organizing logic that distinguishes private sector service provision. Private sector companies are obliged not only to operate profitably, but also to compete to raise the return on capital deployed. Of course, they may fail to do this, in which case they are starved of capital, experience a cash flow crisis, and eventually go to the wall unless they are bailed out by government. Or they succeed in staying afloat by engaging in sharp (e.g. anti-competitive) practices, which restrict consumer choice and raise prices. Alternatively, they engage in 'creative accounting' to inflate their earnings or conceal the extent of their liabilities and expenses. Private sector companies frequently claim that it is their priority to serve customers as a way of retaining or increasing market share, but neither will be pursued unless they contribute to profits. The users of privately supplied public services in the United Kingdom (e.g. children taught by agency teachers or travellers using the privatized rail system) have routinely discovered this to their cost, sometimes with their lives.

It has become increasingly clear that the private sector does not have all the answers (see Box 1.12). In the worst case, customers experience increased prices, lower levels of service and safety and massive inconvenience – as in the case of the railways in the United Kingdom. Contractual services are also often far from perfect. For example, hospitals have been encouraged to contract out their cleaning to private companies. Through a bidding process, the costs may end up being lower, but the quality of the cleaning is often poor and perhaps dangerous to the health of patients.[2] Incentives can work in perverse ways. Basically, a low-cost supplier will tend to 'cut corners' in order to maintain profit margins rather than raise standards. (A comparison of the private and public sectors is set out in Table 1.1.)

In an effort to counteract this endemic problem of purely market-based relations, increasing interest is being shown in private–public partnerships. In principle, the entrepreneurial features of private business are conceived to shake up and inspire improvements in public sector organizations without entirely abandoning an ethos of public service delivery. The assumption underlying this move was that market competition between private contractors would reduce the cost while maintaining or even improving quality. However, this calculation does not take significant account of the capacity/expertise of inexperienced staff in the public sector to secure a good deal.

Box 1.12: Denting confidence in private sector rationality

During the 1990s, the failure of many dot-com companies and e-commerce ventures indicated that private sector methods and strategies are not guaranteed to be superior to other (e.g. democratic, bureaucratic) ways of running an organization. In historical terms, the bursting of the dot-com bubble is not new;[3] and indeed, on a smaller scale, a high proportion of new businesses go bust every year. This is the nature of private enterprise and indeed the stock market has been likened to a giant global gambling casino (Strange, 1997). When the market crashed, those that spread their risks across a wide range of investments fared much better than those who were sucked into the idea that the boom could go on forever. Perhaps we should be just as circumspect when it comes to delivering public services.

Table 1.1 Comparing private and public sectors

Sector	Private	Public
Focus	Produce what is profitable for investors	Provide what is demanded by voters
Governance	Accountability to shareholders	Accountability to electorate
Logic of organization	Innovation to produce better returns on capital invested	Standardization to provide continuity of service and security of employment
Shortcomings	Lack of concern with anything (e.g. the environment, ethics, other stakeholders) that does not contribute to profits	Under-investment, bureaucratic rigidity and ineffective use of resources

Instead of surrendering, as it were, much of the public sector to private sector operators and their market-driven logics, there is increasingly an attempt to forge longer-term partnerships between the two sectors to secure the best of both worlds. Supporters of this middle way suggest that entrepreneurial flair can be transferred without damaging the ethos of public service delivery. In place of the lowest bidder, 'best value' is taken as the baseline for evaluating competing private sector bids for public service contracts. Best value can incorporate a concern with the ethos of the contractor, including their track record on collaborating in long-term partnerships, to find mutually acceptable ways of securing cost-effective improvements in service delivery.

Whether or not faith in public–private partnerships is justified or sustained, there is no doubt that a defining feature of capitalist business is risk. Critics of the 'enterprise culture' have asked the question: 'If you are ill do you want to be treated by an entrepreneur or a doctor following professional and regulated standards of good practice?' This question became all the more poignant or significant when in 2002 senior executives at major international companies (e.g. Enron, WorldCom) were exposed for fraudulently massaging their balance sheets to secure better stock market share prices. As major shareholders, many of these executives were the direct beneficiaries of the increased valuations and in many cases offloaded their shares prior to the company's collapse (see Box 1.13).

Contexts of organizational behaviour

Apart from the tragedy for employees losing their jobs, the Enron and WorldCom scandals had the effect of scaring already jittery investors who had experienced the pain of the dot-com bubble into a mass exodus from the stock market that brought share prices tumbling down and reminded people of the Great Crash on Wall Street in 1929. Because the whole world experienced several

Box 1.13: 'Enronomics'

The collapse of Enron followed by WorldCom begged a number of questions: How many more companies might be fraudulent? It led investors to ask: 'Can we trust executives – even, and perhaps especially, those with MBAs – with our money?' Almost overnight, senior executives and their so-called independent audit firms suffered worldwide disrepute. From being popular American heroes, corporate executives were reduced to pariahs – viewed with increasing suspicion and scorn when previously they had been lavished with bonuses and praise.

years of deep recession and mass unemployment after the 1929 crash, any parallel is viewed with great fear.

Of course, not every company is an Enron or a WorldCom, and not every dot-com company was badly managed or went bankrupt. But their 'excesses' are a reminder that the values and priorities of private business are financial profit. Companies stay in business only so long as investors (e.g. shareholders and banks) have confidence in the executives to deliver an acceptable rate of growth on their capital. When confidence is dented, investment is withdrawn as capital is transferred towards less risky ventures. Depleted of capital, financially weak companies based upon optimistic or 'unrealistic' business models then struggle to survive when an economic downturn favours companies with sufficient reserves to slash prices and/or weather the storm.

Combined with misgivings about the performance of privatized public utilities and private contracting, the 1990s dot-com bubble burst and the subsequent loss of confidence in audited accounts can only help to moderate the enthusiasm of governments for exclusively private sector solutions to public sector reform. In the wake of major scandals and collapses, the idea that 'government should be run like a business' is destined to lose some of its common-sense appeal. Perhaps, after all, solutions for organizational problems are not so simple, and maybe despite the problems of rigidity characteristic of bureaucratic organizations, there is some merit in the checks and balances built into 'old' public sector management (Du Gay, 2000).

At the time of writing (early 2003) world markets were struggling to avoid or climb out of recession, which, despite governments' best endeavours, tend to occur in cycles. Part of this problem was a global crisis of over-production (i.e. too many goods/services chasing too few consumers) but depressed stock markets resulting from global uncertainty about an Iraqi war plus the accounting scandals discussed above exacerbated the sense of crisis. Despite relatively high rates of employment, exceptionally low income tax and interest rates that would normally fuel consumer spending, the talk of economic gloom was fuelling the crisis. Contexts such as this cannot be ignored when studying organizations because they provide good or legitimate reasons (or excuses) for decisions that, for example, lead to downsizing, mergers and acquisitions, or liquidating a company.

Instead of focusing narrowly upon the behaviour of individuals and groups in organizations, we have sought to locate 'organizing' within a wider context – such as the private or public sectors of goods and services production (see Box 1.14). It is important to remember that organizing takes place within wider historical, cultural and institutional contexts. Organizational behaviour is embedded in this context, which it reproduces or transforms. How would you characterize the contemporary context? Modern? Capitalist? Industrial? Post-industrial? These and other terms may spring to mind, but there is also a case for describing contemporary society as simply organized. Many contemporary activities and arrangements are characterized as the properties of organizations – bodies that cater for virtually every aspect of our lives.

Organizations have become central to, and now dominate, processes of producing and consuming goods and services of all kinds. To earn a wage or salary, a majority of people find employment within organizations – the self-employed being an exception (although many of them are contracted to work for organizations on a casual or temporary basis). While we usually work in one organization, we spend most of our earnings in other organizations, notably in the retail outlets where we buy food, clothing, cars, mortgages and so on. Organizations provide us with most of our material, and a considerable number of our less material (i.e. leisure and other service) wants. In their absence, many people would struggle to obtain an equivalent income, and there would be an acute shortage of goods and services. Organizations have become crucial to our material lives and perhaps survival.

Box 1.14: The 'unnaturalness' of organizations

The provision of goods and services through the creation of organizations is clearly not a 'natural' (i.e. a part of the human condition like food, water and oxygen) or necessary way of sustaining our lives. We need only think of how (even today, and more so in the past) a majority of people in the world produce and consume their everyday goods by depending much more on family and community than they do upon the activities and arrangements that we describe as organizations.

Back to the pub: The personal and the organizational

When thinking of organizations, there remains a tendency to think first of manufacturing industry or perhaps an established public sector organization, such as a school or hospital. We could easily have situated Jackie's experience of organization in a school, office or factory instead of a pub. The pub is however an interesting space as it combines processes of production, in the form of service delivery and sometimes brewing, with processes of consumption that are partly commodified (e.g. through purchasing and branding of goods) but largely self-organized (e.g. through socializing, conversing, etc.).

In contemporary, post-industrial societies, leisure has become a distinctive sphere of (recreational) life by virtue of other time that is sold to an employer or taken up with routine chores and 'maintenance' activities. Historically the 'public house' has been a recreational space and of central significance in 'disposing' of leisure time. Increasingly, however, advanced industrial societies are becoming de-industrialized as manufacturing is more profitably undertaken in industrializing economies where access to labour and raw materials is cheaper, more plentiful and less regulated. As the proportion of income available to be disposed on non-essentials (e.g. accommodation, food, clothing) has grown, the leisure sector has enjoyed sustained growth by commodifying the means of entertainment. That is to say, forms of leisure are increasingly 'packaged' for sale in the market-place rather than self-organized within families or communities.

Let us therefore go back to our narrative about Jackie in the Dog and Duck, a pub owned by the brewery, which has not (yet) sought to give it a 'theme' or 'facelift'. Remember she was sitting in a corner of the pub, having to listen to a gang of locals openly engaged in what she experienced as a character assassination of students.

We invite you to reflect further upon Jackie's visit to the pub (see Case study 1.2), concentrating this time upon the landlord and landlady's approach to managing this organization. To assist in this process, we encourage you to consider, preferably with other students on your course, the following questions:

1. Jackie is taking a course on organization studies. How do you think her experience of working in the pub might help with her studies and, how might her studies help her in the work?

CASE STUDY 1.2 Jackie at the pub (2)

Instead of choosing the various options suggested after presenting our vignette earlier, Jackie decided to leave the table and return to standing at the bar. After a short time she entered into conversation with the landlady and landlord who, for a few minutes, were sitting on the customer side of the bar. The conversation meandered through a number of topics, until Jackie felt sufficiently relaxed to bring up the experience of being criticized by the locals.

The landlady sympathized with Jackie, recognizing that there was a good deal of animosity between the locals and the students, especially since they had made considerable efforts to attract students into the pub. Ordinarily there was little trouble as the students were inclined to move on to other bars or discos nearer the centre of town before the locals came in. The landlord went on to explain his policy in seeking to attract the students when he became the tenant of the pub 12 months ago. He pointed out that they were hoping to make their tenancy a great success, as this was the way to obtain a much bigger pub from the brewery. Eventually they were hoping to buy their own pub in a nice coastal village in Cornwall where the tourist trade during the summer would provide financial security and allow them more time to pursue their hobbies – of astronomy and art work – during the quieter winter months. As they were talking, some customers were becoming impatient at not getting immediate service, and the landlord went back behind the bar for a while. The landlady then confided in Jackie that the growth in business in the pub had presented a staff problem for them.

As she left the pub Jackie felt a lot more at ease. The friendliness of the landlord and landlady had reassured her that students were really welcome and she knew that, in future, she could always talk to them when waiting for her friends to arrive. In fact she had found herself saying that if ever they were short of staff, she would be happy to help out. On her next visit to the pub, Jackie was asked by the landlord if she could do a few hours the following night when one of the staff had to visit her mother in hospital.

2. How does the case illustrate the concepts of identity, insecurity, power and inequality, and illuminate the practicalities of management and organization? (See the Appendix for further discussion of these concepts.)
3. Are there any other questions relating to this case study that you feel are important? If so, discuss these and feedback your results to our website.

It might be assumed that organizations have relevance, value or significance only as instruments for producing and providing goods and services. Yet organizations are also of central importance in producing and providing *a* sense of identity for both employees and customers. It is through our participation in organizations (e.g. as producers or consumers) that we develop, confirm or manage our sense of identity – for example, as employable (in work organizations), as prosperous (in retail outlets), as sick or cured (in hospitals), as well-educated or ignorant (in schools), and as enjoying ourselves (in pubs and clubs). But, as we have seen in our case study of the Dog and Duck, pubs can also be contexts where our identities are threatened in ways that fuel our insecurities. We saw how Jackie experienced this when the local lads voiced their assault on students – an assault that was provoked by insecurities aroused because of the pub's concern to attract students into their local.

Formation, development and change in our identities occur through social interactions – with ourselves as well as others – as we reflect upon our experiences and resolve, perhaps, to change our ways. This is, of course, not easy as is evidenced but the number of new year resolutions that are broken as our habitual patterns of action override our good intentions before the end of January.

Inescapably, what happens in organizations has personal as well as **instrumental** significance. Our experiences in organizations reinforce (or threaten) our sense of who we are and what is meaningful and valuable to us (and about us). In this process, relations of power operate to enable or obstruct how interactions and identities are accomplished. For example, Jackie's identity as a student is not just created by herself but also by the locals and the landlord and landlady. This identity degrades her value in the eyes of the locals but enhances it from the perspective of the landlady. She regards Jackie as a potential employee who can assist in developing a student clientele.

From Jackie's standpoint, her limited income as a student made the opportunity to do some part-time bar work more attractive than for someone in a healthier financial situation. But it was not simply material inequality that rendered Jackie more alert to this job opportunity. She also regarded it as a chance to enhance her status in the eyes of her parents who had been exerting pressures upon her to find part-time work. It is hardly surprising then, that Jackie felt much better after having had a more pleasant interaction with the landlord and landlady, being eventually offered a part-time job behind the bar. A few months later, after demonstrating a flair for interacting with customers, she was asked by the landlord if she would be able to manage the pub for a weekend. We take up the story on her first night in this enhanced role (see Case study 1.3).

CASE STUDY 1.3 Jackie at the pub (3)

Jackie was in some trepidation about managing the pub and, in particular, the reactions of the two other bar staff. They were both slightly older and also locals. John was pretty relaxed and she didn't expect much of a problem, not least because he displayed a 'soft spot' for her and this gave her a sense of control. Christine, however, was a different kettle of fish. When Christine had found herself working behind the bar with a student, she had felt threatened. As the elder and more experienced bartender of the three, Christine was upset that she had not been asked to manage the pub. This was particularly galling because she had ambitions to become a landlady.

Things were going all right on this Saturday evening until it got very busy. One of the customers was clearly expressing impatience at not getting served. Both Jackie and John were serving customers but Christine was engaged in a lengthy chat with a friend who was sitting at the bar. Jackie asked Christine if she could serve the waiting customer and she appeared to accept the request but then continued to chat with her friend. A bit of a row then occurred as Jackie tried to get Christine to come into the back where they could discuss the problem. Christine simply blew her top, condemning Jackie for embarrassing her in front of the customers. Christine walked out, saying she was not going to be bossed about by a trumped-up student who knew nothing about bar work.

The pub was very busy and it was going to be extremely difficult to manage with just two bar staff. At the first opportunity

Jackie tried to ring the landlord but couldn't get an answer. So she rang one of her flatmates – Carol – to see if she would come and help out. Fortunately Carol agreed to come at once and, despite needing a lot of help, the evening went reasonably smoothly. Eventually the landlord rang back and Jackie was able to explain the situation. He was sympathetic but was also a bit worried about how to replace Christine who, he feared, was gone for good. Maybe Carol, he suggested, would fill in for Christine, although Christine was working more hours than might be expected from a full-time student. Carol seemed quite keen. She had seen how Jackie had flourished since taking the job, plus the money was not to be sneezed at.

Jackie had experienced a big boost to her self-esteem by being asked to manage the pub. In contrast, not being chosen to manage the pub was a terrible blow to Christine. Not least, this was because she was more experienced in pub work, older, and of even more importance, she had ambitions to run a pub of her own. This helps us to understand Christine's reactions when Jackie sought to manage her defiance. Christine's defiance threatened Jackie's sense of identity, and especially her stand-in role as manager of the pub. She felt that her position as temporary manager had been undermined in the eyes of the clientele, and that her standing with the landlord and landlady would be damaged. Jackie was also concerned about how the landlord would react to the possible loss of Christine as a valued employee. While she had been embarrassed by Christine's walkout, Jackie's dignity and self-esteem remained intact by virtue of her not exploding in the same way as Christine. However, she felt some mild resentment towards the landlord who, she believed, must have had some inkling of how Christine might react. She felt that she had been placed in a difficult situation, and it crossed her mind that the landlord and landlady had perhaps seized, or even created, an opportunity to force Christine out so as to replace her with someone who they could trust to act as a reliable manager in their absence.

Once again, we encourage you to reflect upon staff relations at the Dog and Duck as illustrative of different aspects of behaviour in organizations. Here are some questions:

1. If Jackie is right that the landlord had contrived a situation that would provoke Christine into walking out, what implications does this have for 'the effective manager's skill profile' presented and discussed earlier.
2. How are the concepts of insecurity, identity, knowledge, power, freedom and inequality (see the Appendix) relevant for exploring and analysing the dynamics of the relationship and interactions between Jackie, Christine and the landlord?
3. Can you draw some parallels between the actions of the landlord, Jackie and Christine and your own experiences of work or leisure relationships?
4. Can you think of media reports of disputes at work, past or present, whose content might be illuminated through a similar analysis to the one we have sketched to interpret aspects of organization and management at the Dog and Duck?

Jackie's experience illustrates how organizations are not only important to our material existence, but they also have *symbolic* significance. For organizations involve not just our objectives and interests, but also our feelings, sentiments and identities. Organizations are among the core institutions – including the family and school – that foster and shape our aspirations and our attachment to particular social identities.

Organization and institutionalization

When we highlight the personal and social significance of organizations, we are also acknowledging their status and importance as institutions within which people – employees and customers – become institutionalized. You have probably heard the phrase 'the British pub is an institution' and never thought to reflect upon what it means. The phrase signals, we suggest, the distinctiveness of the social interactions as emblematic of British society. More sceptically, it could be argued that the pub is invoked to support a romantic ideal of how many people prefer to think of Britain.

Of course, there are many institutions that are not readily or plausibly identified as organizational. For example, a series of activities may become institutionalized around preparing for mealtimes, such as breakfast. The kind of breakfast that is prepared and the particular interactions, or grunts, exchanged with others during the process of preparing and consuming breakfast, assumes a pattern that becomes 'normal' and taken-for-granted. It is only when this pattern is disturbed, intentionally or otherwise (e.g. a valued ingredient runs out or a guest requests a very different kind of breakfast), that an awareness of the routine is aroused. The routine is an element of 'an institution' in the sense that it is the outcome of an orderly set of social relations that ensures, most of the time, that, in the case of the breakfast routine, the desired ingredients have been bought and that the usual grunts are exchanged (see Box 1.15).

Thinkpoint 1.5

It's just routine Consider some other routines (e.g. going to lectures) and how their presence and significance only comes to light when they are disrupted, or when we reflect critically upon them by imagining the possibilities of their disruption.

An example of 'breaking with routine' is the inability to 'make' the 9.00am lecture because of a hangover or lack of sleep the night before (assuming, of course, that such a routine was ever established). Student life can result in late nights and leisure becoming the routine, and this might only be disrupted when realizing that the lifestyle could result in failing the degree.

The significance of routines

Actions and relations are institutionalized in the sense that there is regularity and routine – for example, in how pupils relate to teachers, how doctors treat patients and how ticket inspectors check passengers. This process does not occur automatically. Rather, actions become institutionalized as people become attached to routines for material reasons (i.e. income flows from the routines of a job) or social acceptance (i.e. 'fitting in' with the routines of our mates). In both cases, our identity is confirmed, thereby making us feel secure – unless, of course, we are striving to establish a sense of identity in opposition to established conventions and lifestyles (in which case, we are involved in a process of institutionalizing alternative values and forms of behaviour).

As we noted earlier, over the past decade or more, pubs as work organizations have been expanding their services in an attempt to appeal to new customers. Providing play areas for children can attract young families, those seeking to eat out inexpensively can be catered for by pub food, and some pubs might (like the Dog and Duck) seek to specialize by encouraging a potentially profitable segment (e.g. students). In each case, the traditional clientele may feel (as we saw at the Dog and Duck) 'pushed out' or denied their institutionalized expectations when going down the pub.

More generally, employees as well as customers in many organizations have been obliged to make sense of, and deal with, disruptions to established practices and routines as companies have sought to use their (human and material) facilities in more productive, profitable and cost-effective ways. Think, for example, of the use of call-centres to replace face-to-face services, the shift to self-service

Box 1.15: Institutions and institutionalization

When sets of actions and relations are seen as fairly predictable, they are termed 'institutions'. Institutions involve common ways of doing things. Members of institutions (e.g. students within a university system) may not always agree with the rules (e.g. examination regulations) but usually comply (e.g. because of the concern to gain a degree). Processes of institutionalization are simply the outcome of our routinely behaving in accordance with what the institution (e.g. the family, school or work organization) deems appropriate. So, for example, in schools and work organizations, the process of institutionalization includes the acquisition of habits, aspirations and discipline (e.g. time-keeping and deference to authority) that enable classes to run on time, students to attend and a degree of order to be maintained.

Image 1.6 Everyday routines – having a meal, cleaning the fridge

(e.g. bank ATMs, supermarket consumption) or the exploitation of brands to generate customer loyalty and a high pricing strategy. Do these changes have implications for how people use products and services (e.g. how customers use pubs) and become 'institutionalized' through their interactions within them?

Thinkpoint 1.6

Branding and consumption When companies brand products (e.g. themed pubs), what assumptions are they making about the organization of consumption (and the production of such goods and services)?

Whenever we participate in an institution, we take with us implicit as well as explicit knowledge of the routines and conventions that we expect to find in such contexts. As a regular customer in a supermarket, for example, we learn how the store is arranged in terms of how the goods are grouped and where they can be found on the shelves. Again, this knowledge may be so taken-for-granted that it surfaces only when there is a 'reorganization'. Such changes are usually justified by a managerial calculation that they will produce more traffic down the aisles and thereby increase revenues. It disrupts our shopping pattern, and perhaps makes us more aware that we had such a pattern, but it is effective from the viewpoint of the supermarket's managers and shareholders if it has the effect of us purchasing other goods that had previously been invisible to us.

What such disruptions risk, of course, is a negative reaction from customers who, in the absence of any marked loyalty, may respond by changing their routines as they decide to shop elsewhere. A parallel analysis could be applied to the locals, as customers, at the Dog and Duck (see earlier) who were reacting negatively to what they were finding on the equivalent of 'the shelves' in the supermarket – that is, the influx of a student clientele. Can you think of other examples where a change in what is available to consumers upsets their routine?

The centrality of people

As we all know, our everyday relationships with parents, friends or lovers can be difficult. The more we try to organize them the more difficult they often become. Work organizations exhibit these same difficulties, except we do not usually or necessarily share the same intensity of commitment and loyalty to relationships at work. In general, it is easier to leave the organizations in which we work than to walk out of personal relationships, unless of course they coincide!

Exercise 1.2

Organizing in everyday life Think about a tension or conflict you have had personally with someone close and reflect on the degree to which it can illuminate an aspect of organizing, being organized or relating to some organized activity (e.g. a place of education, work, consumption or leisure). If convenient, this could be done in pairs whereby one of you probes the other and vice versa so as to try and avoid the tendency that we all have of rationalizing (i.e. reinterpreting unpleasant experiences in a more favourable light in terms of our own part in them). Consider, for example, how a sense of 'fairness' is negotiated or imposed, or reflect upon how trust is established or undermined.

When faced with pressures to increase productivity or improve levels of service, managers may attempt to coerce staff into working harder (e.g. by bullying or imposing penalties). Earlier, when considering the actions of the landlord at the Dog and Duck, we raised the possibility that he engineered the situation that resulted in a staff member (Christine) walking out. When detected or even suspected by staff, such methods reinforce the impersonality of the relationship, and make it more difficult to engineer more personal or involved forms of motivation and leadership. This tells us something significant about work organizations. Participation in them is usually based on an impersonal contract of employment in which a wage is paid for the application of skill and effort. In itself, this impersonal contract carries with it no moral obligation to work diligently or to be loyal to the employer.

People in organizations may be more or less willing to accept being organized. Ultimately, willing cooperation or grudging compliance depends upon their sense of the legitimacy (fairness) of the demands made upon them, and of course the capacity of managers to influence the conditions that make compliance the normal employee response. We saw earlier how compliance is not to be taken for granted when Christine was unwilling to be managed by a younger barmaid in the pub in which they both worked. People can be creative, responsible, dedicated and loyal, but, equally, they can act in ways that, from a managerial perspective, are destructive, subversive, irresponsible and disloyal.

Views of organization: Entity, process and concept

Identifying organization

On the face of it, what 'organization' means is obvious or self-evident. Ask anyone to name six organizations, and they would have few problems providing a list. What would you name? Let's make the question a little more testing by asking you to identify six *educational* organizations. Which six would you choose from the list in Table 1.2?

Table 1.2 Types of educational organization

❖ School	❖ Workplace	❖ University	❖ Community centre
❖ Family	❖ Hockey club	❖ Night class	❖ Beach party
❖ Friendship group	❖ Garden centre	❖ Chat room	❖ Toddler group
❖ Bookshop	❖ Library	❖ Cinema	❖ Media

Once you have chosen the six that, in your view, are 'educational organizations', think back to what led you to pick them. If you now had to justify your selection, what would you say? What is it about your six selections that differentiate them as 'educational *organizations*'?

Perhaps the most obvious candidates are 'school' and 'university'. These, commonsensically, are bodies that provide educational goods or services. When we think of 'education' we tend to privilege *formal* methods of teaching – as found in classrooms. That is what education commonsensically means, even if there are alternatives which challenge that understanding, like 'the school of hard knocks' which celebrates learning through the 'university of life' – doing and making mistakes.

Parents, for example, are also involved in educating their children – by teaching them how to speak and to interact with others. Parents may also try to compensate for perceived shortcomings in their children's formal education by supplementing it with their own instruction or employing tutors. Governments may even build this view of 'responsible parenting' into educational policy by, for example, prosecuting (even gaoling) parents of truanting children for not instilling the values of education in their offspring. So, do we count the family as an educational *organization*?

In the workplace, various kinds of education abound, both in training and through learning from others as mates and mentors. The same could be said for many other forms of human association. In the process of meeting up with friends, going to discos, clubs, pubs and parties, playing sports and even watching TV, visiting retail stores, chat rooms, etc., we become educated about various aspects of the world in which we live. Many of these activities are 'organized' and/or take place in organizational contexts. Indeed, they can and do provide alternative forms of education, even to the point of placing in question the authority and value of formal education. From a critical perspective, formal education can be seen as a narrow indoctrination into certain 'respectable' patterns of belief and behaviours that restrict rather than expand intellectual and moral horizons. Critics of formal education might well wish to place some scare quotes around much of the 'education' provided by schools and universities. Purposely, we also placed on the bottom row of our list a number of non-educational organizations/institutions that, nonetheless, may facilitate education. The last two – cinema and media – indicate that almost anything can be educational; it depends on how we relate to them.

When education is seen as a process, almost everything we do has educational significance and implications; it all depends on how we *relate* to what we do. Learning can be seen as synonymous with our everyday practices of talking, interacting and relating with one another and the world around us. Take the case of organizations. Why assume that we know little or nothing about organizations or organizing just because we have never attended an OB course or read a textbook and, therefore, jump to the conclusion that we are ignorant of the subject? In doing so, we effectively disempower ourselves as we cede authority to 'experts' who are deemed to possess a monopoly of knowledge in this field – a view that allows our experience of organizations and organizing to be ignored or marginalized. Instead, we might usefully recognize how frequently and continuously we have participated in organizations and organizing processes, and how much we have 'picked up' or learned in this process. Unfortunately, many textbooks fail to recognize and facilitate the exploration of this knowledge as part of studying OB.

Box 1.16: Education in business schools

Associated with the idea that organizations are distinguished by the presence of formal, impersonal relationships and procedures is a conception of business and management education that emphasizes and reinforces this understanding. The ultimate expression of this thinking is the treatment of people as mere factors of production or commodities.

Since the Enron and WorldCom scandals, there has been considerable soul-searching about the education of executives. The content of MBAs (Masters of Business Administration), in particular, has been criticized for the lack of attention to the ethics of managing. Finance-centred courses in particular have encouraged and legitimized the ruthless pursuit of shareholder value fuelled by the rising value of stock options used to compensate executives. Commonsensically, the term 'education' is reserved for what happens in schools, colleges and universities, and increasingly tends to focus upon abstracted forms of knowledge comprising sets of information and techniques. Even case studies, which offer a potential means of exploring issues of politics and ethics in decision making, tend to concentrate on the analysis of information and the identification and application of appropriate techniques. This commonsense notion of education revolves around treating education as a 'thing', which is confined to specific settings, rather than a process that occurs within all spheres of everyday life.

In the next three sub-sections, we consider some different ways in which 'organization' can be defined, identified and analysed.

An entity view

Box 1.17: Mainstream definitions of 'organization'

- 'Organization refers to social arrangements such as factories, bureaucracies, armies, research and development teams, and so on, created to achieve technical, productive ends'. (David Buchanan and Andrei Huczyinski, *Organizational Behaviour: An Introductory Text*, third edition, London: Prentice Hall, 1997, p. 552.)
- 'An organization is a consciously coordinated social unit, composed of two or more people, that functions on a relatively continuous basis to achieve a common goal or set of goals. It's characterized by formal roles that define and shape the behaviour of its members'. (Stephen P. Robbins, *Essentials of Organizational Behaviour*, seventh edition, Upper Saddle River, New Jersey: Prentice Hall, 2003, p. 2.)

When considering the definitions set out in Box 1.17, you may well respond by thinking: 'Yes, that makes sense. It is a bit technical but it is along the lines I was expecting'. We acknowledge the contribution of such thinking, at least to the extent that it highlights how, in work organizations, there is a great deal of emphasis on the means to achieve what are presumed to be shared objectives. In families or in friendship groups, in contrast, doing things more efficiently or effectively is generally of lesser importance than preserving the quality of our relationships, as an end in itself. In this respect, at least, there is logic when studying organizations in emphasizing the impersonal and objective criteria of appointment and promotion, as often based primarily upon qualifications and/or measurable length of service.[4] In the process, however, other ways of understanding organizations are screened out.

Mainstream definitions reflect and reinforce the common-sense understanding of 'organizations' as *entities* consisting of a distinguishing set of characteristics. Organizations are portrayed as unified entities comprising 'formal' rules and structures. Roles, or positions, are hierarchical – meaning that those who occupy senior positions always 'define and shape' the behaviour of subordinates (see Box 1.18).

Box 1.18: Roles, security and power

The notion of role is not unlike that used in the theatre but the script is unwritten and therefore, in principle, more open to interpretation, improvisation and inspiration than is the case for the actor. A role, however, consists of a set of expectations and obligations. To the extent that people identify with these roles as a source of security and/or sense of power, they operate to constrain the individual almost as much as scripts constrain actors on stage.

Definitions should not be dismissed as simply the ritualistic elements of a textbook. Definitions are significant insofar as they distil and frame a particular way of thinking that is exemplified through a text. How 'organization' is defined frequently provides an important clue to how the boundaries of the field are being drawn and how its contents are being examined.

Like the common-sense idea of education as something that occurs within specific organizations, the definitions provided in Box 1.17 are not so much wide of the mark as limiting and potentially misleading. They focus attention principally upon aspects of organizing that coincide with the concerns of those occupying the senior ranks of organizations. It is a view of organizations developed by their designers, and it is one that portrays organizations as malleable, instrumental tools for achieving their established objectives. Minimal attention is given to the conflicting priorities of other members of the organization or the dangers in managing organizations as if such conflicts were of little consequence.

Definitions found in mainstream textbooks may appear to be uncontroversial and politically neutral, but this is far from the case. Their adequacy and credibility can be challenged on account of the exclusion of issues of power, domination and exploitation. Silence on these issues casts doubt upon the practical relevance as well as the scholarly standing of their contents. It is important to recognize how their contents operate not only to describe but also to define and discipline how organization is thought about and how we act within them (including ourselves as lecturers and students).

The effect of these texts, when we accept them as common-sense truths, is to equate the meaning of organization with their contents. They invite us to accept their knowledge of organizations without presenting alternatives and without actively encouraging us to reflect critically upon their analyses and prescriptions. To assume that organizations are created and/or maintained simply 'to achieve technical, productive ends' is simplistic since it excludes consideration of many (mixed) 'motives' and 'preoccupations' that inspire and shape their design and development. Similarly, presuming that the goals of senior managers are identical to those of other members of the organization is politically unrealistic. To believe (commonsensically) in the entity view is the equivalent of thinking of the sun rising, rather than the earth rotating.

A process view

To say that organization is a process rather than an entity is not to deny that there are activities occurring that are identifiable as 'organized', and that are located, as it were, in organizations. By conceiving of organization as a process, however, the study of (organizing) processes is not confined to what are commonsensically identified as large, formal organizations or their structures, roles and so forth. The focus of analysis is not upon organizations as entities, but upon processes of organizing wherever organized activities occur – in families, beach parties, toddler groups, etc.

Box 1.19: A process view of 'organization'

'The concept of "the organization" is extremely difficult to define and, additionally, depends upon what use is to be made of the definition . . . For this reason, *our focus is not on organization as a thing but on organization as process*: the activity of organizing and being organized. All particular organizations are examples of this process . . . The process of organization in this context is the configuration of people and things in ways that are not given in nature . . . when we talk about organizations we mean any organization, whether big or small, multinational or local, formal and informal, for profit and not for profit, involuntary or voluntary'. (Norman Jackson and Pippa Carter, *Rethinking Organizational Behaviour*, London: Prentice Hall, 2000, p. 7, emphasis added.)

The process view draws our attention to the ways in which organizing, in diverse settings, is accomplished through social interactions in which we seek to manage ourselves as well as others. It understands behaviour in all human associations as a process of skilful negotiation in accomplishing whatever is done. This view invites us to scrutinize how various activities happen or are disrupted in the everyday life of an organization, whether this is in settings commonsensically identified as 'organization(s)' or outside of such settings. Importantly, it recognizes the continuity of organizing processes across institutions, and does not confine them to, or reserve them for, 'organizations'. Organizations – such as the multinational enterprise or the local voluntary group – are understood to be products or expressions of such 'organizing processes' that should not to be reduced simply to formal role-playing or goal-orientated behaviour.

A process view of organization might perhaps be seen as more theoretical. Yet it is arguably more focused on the practices that comprise organization than on the entity approach. For an entity definition tends towards a concern with prescriptions and models, such as the allocation of tasks, the grouping of activities, systems of measurement and reward, and so on, rather than the activities and interactions that comprise organizing as a dynamic process.

A concept view

As Jackson and Carter (2000) point out, the difficulty of single, universal definitions is that they cannot take account of how a definition will change in relation to how it is used in a particular context. We see no problem, in principle, in engaging alternative definitions of organization for different purposes. Yet it would be devious not to declare our own preference for a third, 'concept' view of organizing and organization. In doing so, we acknowledge that 'the concept of "the organization" is extremely difficult to define' (Jackson and Carter, 2000, p. 7). Its meaning is multiple and contested. Does this imply that differences over the meaning of organization can be settled? In our view, they cannot. Instead each definition, or way of conceiving of organization, is partial and political. It is partial not in the sense that it reveals just one aspect of organization, but, rather, because each definition necessarily excludes other ways of thinking about organization as it supports and champions a *particular* view. It is political because it invites and encourages people to 'see' *and organize* the world in particular ways. As a consequence, the world – including the world of organizing and organizations – takes a form associated with specific ways of thinking and associated actions. When a particular complex of thought and action assumes prominence and dominance, it becomes the 'common-sense' view (until it is disrupted and supplemented by an alternative).

What makes the 'concept view' distinctive? The concept view understands that 'organization' is first and foremost a word that assumes a variety of meanings and exerts a number of effects. The concept view recognizes that 'organization' can be conceived as an entity; and it can also be conceived as a process. But it is neither an entity nor a process. Organization is rather a concept to which a variety of meanings are attributed – including the view that it is a concept. We have already observed how, for those who favour a process view of organizations, it is the *activity of organizing*, wherever this takes place. Definitions of both entity and process make reference to organizations as identifiable social units or as examples of organizing activities. The concept view draws attention to how all definitions are politically charged as they construe activity in particular ways and anticipate or expect certain behaviours in the future. In this sense, ideas of organization do not just describe but also *prescribe* (i.e. outline what should happen) and act to *discipline* the behaviour of their members. That is what makes them partial and political.

Thinkpoint 1.7

It's kind of hard to define . . . Given our concern to make studying organizations more interesting and connected to everyday life, you might justifiably object that our attention to definitions is contradictory. Surely, you might say, definitions are abstract and boring and that is why, in everyday life, we prefer to point to the object that we are talking about rather than define it. Our response is that definitions remain important for communication and disciplining thought. Clarifying how terms are being defined can minimize the danger of talking at cross-purposes. Even so, we prefer to regard definitions as 'views'. The term 'definition' tends to imply that words can capture the basic features or essence of what they aspire to describe, whereas 'view' better conveys our understanding that words operate to make us see, make sense of and perform the world around us in particular ways.

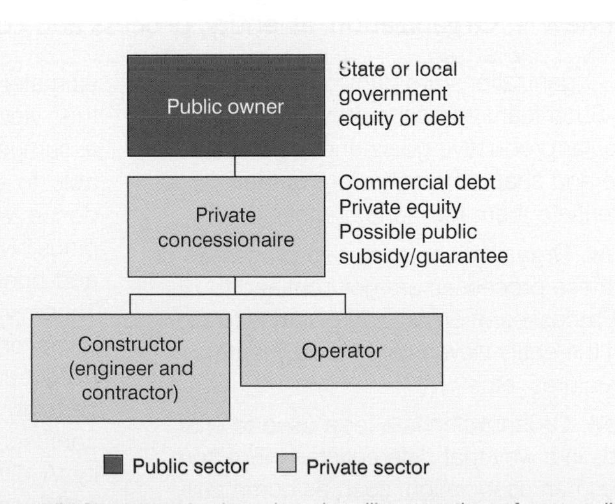

With the design-build-finance-operate (DBFO) approach, there is a bundling together of responsibilities for designing, building, financing and operating, which are transferred to private sector partners. A common feature of such schemes is their part or total financing by debt leveraging revenue streams. For example, direct user fees (tolls) on roads constructed by the DBFO approach can provide a revenue source. In such cases, future revenues are leveraged to issue bonds or other debt that provide funds for initial capital and project development costs (e.g. building roads, hospitals, etc.).

SOURCE: ADAPTED FROM WWW.FHWA.DOT.GOV/PPP/DBFO.HTM

Figure 1.2 Public–private partnership: design, build, finance, operate (DBFO)

The principal merit of identifying organization as a concept is that it disrupts the tendency to assume that language (e.g. organization) reflects or captures some element(s) of the world that are external to it – such as the features of the 'entities' and 'processes' the views discussed earlier claim to describe. To put this another way, the concept view reminds us of our involvement, as subjects or agents, in helping to produce, sustain and change the social world of organizations that otherwise appears to exist independently of us.

Box 1.20: The origin of the term 'organization'

The word can be traced to the Latin word organum, meaning a musical instrument and the disciplined playing of pre-arranged notes. Organization then continues to have this association with order and discipline (hence the ease with which the entity view prevails) but the discipline is implicit rather than explicit as in a musical score. Moreover, perhaps (to retain the musical analogy) an organization is more akin to music such as jazz, rock or heavy metal where there are greater degrees of interpretation and improvisation. Over time, it has come to assume a related but rather different meaning in which there remains continuity with order and discipline, and where the disciplined setting and playing of notes has parallels with activities that are identified as what is meant by organization. As we have seen, however, this emphasis on discipline and order is implicit rather than explicit in mainstream definitions of organization, and the political nature of the definition is thereby concealed. This does not mean that alternative definitions (e.g. the process view – see Box 1.19) are free of politics. Refusing to follow the convention of defining organizations as formal structures designed to achieve shared goals is a political statement, but one that disrupts rather than conserves commonsense ways of thinking and acting.

The concept view indicates that there is no one universal way to define or study organizations. When we accept or adopt a particular view, we are engaging in a political, reality-defining act. In that moment of decision, we act in a way that construes any object (e.g. organization) in the world as 'this' rather than 'that'. From this it follows that different definitions of 'organization' should not be evaluated according to their claimed correspondence to what they aspire to describe.

We conceive of organization as a potent concept, while commonsense tends to treat it as an entity. Organizations are identified and discussed as if they exist 'out there' in a way that implies that they are virtually identical with the buildings or that social space they occupy. Most textbooks on organizational behaviour perpetuate this common-sense understanding as they favour an entity definition of organizations. We have sought to question this approach.

Box 1.21: Overview – 'Organization' as entity, process and concept

- *The entity view*. Organizations are particular kinds of unified entities. Such features as their design for achieving particular productive goals and the formal roles that define and shape the behaviour of their members differentiate them from one another.
- *The process view*. Organizations comprise processes of organizing but these processes are not confined to organizations. Processes of organizing give rise to the activities, which the entity view aspires to delineate as tasks, roles, structures, etc.
- *The concept view*. Organization is a term used to characterize activities in a way that differentiates them from other forms of human association, such as community or family. It also indicates how we are active agents in organizing whatever it is that the entity or process view defines as organization.

When we examine different definitions of organizations or texts that amplify these definitions, it is tempting, yet ultimately mistaken, to ask the question: 'How realistic is this view?' The difficulty with this question is that it assumes that we have direct access to reality and are able to evaluate definitions in terms of their correspondence with it. On reflection, this seems unlikely. More plausibly, we rely upon a set of interpretations, prejudices and hunches to assess the credibility of different views. These views are relevant in enabling us to elaborate, refine or even abandon our interpretations and thereby (re)direct our actions. Learning from competing views is certainly possible, but it should not be conflated or confused with assessing their correspondence with reality. A diversity of views can open up alternative lines of action and/or provide ways of challenging dominant thinking, but their summation does not produce a more comprehensive grasp or map of the terrain. Attention is more appropriately directed to scrutinizing the values, preferences and *effects* embedded in different conceptions of organization and organizing.

Distinctiveness of work organization: instrumental rationality

'Bureaucratic work shapes people's consciousness in decisive ways. Among other things, it regularizes people's experience of time and indeed routinizes their lives by engaging them on a daily basis in rational, socially approved, purposive action' (*Jackall, 1998, p.p. 5–6*).

'Community and family are conserving institutions. In general, their members act to maintain stability and to prevent, or at least to slow down, change. But the modern organization is a destabilizer. It must be organized for innovation, and innovation, as the great Austro-American economist Joseph Schumpeter said, is "creative destruction" ' (*Drucker, 1992, p. 96*).

Earlier, when considering the entity view of organizations, we noted how organizations are conventionally and commonsensically associated with the use of an instrumentally rational means to achieve explicit purposes or goals. Such instrumental rationality is reflected in the definitions of organization provided by the entity view, where 'organization' is seen largely in terms of the technical or functional means to achieve 'a common set of goals'.

In discussing instrumental rationality, we have repeatedly drawn upon the entity view of organization – for example, when we talk about organizations (as entities) pursuing objectives or refer to managers in organizations engineering employee loyalty. This is not surprising because we understand the entity view to be closely associated with, or even a product of, instrumental rationality. Organization is conceived as an entity as it is identified as an instrument for attaining objectives as defined by senior managers. In other words, we regard the entity view as a product of the instrumental rationality that it also aspires to advance. Equally, both are seen to reflect commonsense because, as soon as we use the word organization, we tend to associate it with the concrete entity (i.e. the building) in which it is located and the very entity is assumed only to exist to serve some instrumental purpose.

Box 1.22: Instrumental rationality

An instrumentally rational organization or person is concerned primarily, if not exclusively, with the most effective means to achieve specific ends or objectives. The *value* of those objectives is taken for granted and therefore is not open to debate or challenge. One might suggest, for example, that private companies are preoccupied with the best means to increase profits; or that public corporations are concerned with the most efficient means of providing a public service such as health or education. Each is geared to increasing labour productivity and reducing the costs of production.

We have also suggested that organizing is fundamental to human existence but that this activity occurs within different kinds of institutions (e.g. the family or peer groups) and is not confined to organizations. We have differentiated (work) organizations from other institutions by the degree of dependence upon instrumental rationality. While instrumental rationality may be present to some degree in many institutions, it is most dominant and legitimate within (work) organizations. This is why we describe them as organizations, rather than families or communities. We can say, then, that the concept of organization, and the associated notion of organizational behaviour brings with it a particular, instrumentally rational view of *how to organize* – what is expected from us when becoming a member of an organization.

Box 1.23: Legitimacy

Legitimacy is a term used to convey an unquestionable or legal right to something. Once it is legitimate to exercise power over someone, it is difficult to challenge that right, although this does not rule out resistance. Indeed it is only by challenging or resisting the legitimacy of established power relations that social change occurs. People had to resist the legitimate power of slave-owners to abolish slavery, the absolute sovereignty of the monarchy and aristocrats to achieve democracy, and the imperial powers of Western nations to achieve independence for ex-colonies and protectorates.

Given the pervasiveness of organizations in modern societies and the centrality of instrumental rationality in schools and workplaces, it would be surprising if their influence did not extend to family life and friendship groups who may come to resemble organizations when planning, resourcing and implementing an event or set of tasks. Peer groups often try to organize an event, trip, or perhaps just a party; and then what they do can begin to look like the activities associated with organizations.

Consider the party. Someone proposes a party and usually individuals or groups agree to take on particular tasks such as arranging an appropriate venue, ordering or preparing the food and drink, getting the music sorted, etc. This way of 'making it happen' is routinely conceived or calculated to be the least time-consuming and individually onerous. So, a leisure group can, for limited periods, look not dissimilar to a work organization. You might raise the objection that the peer group does not get paid, or seek to make a profit. These are relevant distinctions but ones that define an *economic* work organization as opposed to an organization per se. What makes holding a party similar to a work organization is reliance upon instrumental rationality that supports the logic of a division and coordination of the labour involved in making it happen.

Box 1.24: Mixing rationalities

The predominance of a means–ends (instrumental) rationality is, we have suggested, what distinguishes the entity view of organization from other human associations such as families, friends or communities where we expect love, loyalty and commitment to prevail. In principle, organizations are those institutions to which a greater influence of calculative, means–ends rationality is attributed. There are, however, continuities and overlaps.

Instrumental reasoning enters other social institutions and arrangements when, for example, someone marries for money, uses friends to advance their career, or engages in community work to enhance their status and reputation. Conversely, managers often try to secure loyalty, cooperation and commitment from employees by emphasizing family and community values of solidarity. But, of course, their motivation is an instrumental one: they calculate, perhaps correctly, that developing a more attentive and friendly attitude towards their staff will improve morale and employee retention. In 2003, the UK government passed family friendly legislation that gave employees with children under six the right to flexible working hours. A popular device for securing both cooperation and commitment is teamworking drawn from team sports. Here an identification and solidarity with the 'in-group' in opposition to the 'out-group' is used as a competitive device for raising productivity. However, where cooperation and collaboration between different groups or teams is important, this competitive ethos may be counter-productive.

Conversely, a family can be seen as an economic work organization when, for instance, some of its members run a small business, such as the corner shop or a small farm. In such cases, there is generally a blending (or uneasy union) of instrumentally rational principles, such as a division of labour with respect to particular tasks (and associated responsibilities), and other, familial values that demand a degree of flexibility and commitment – qualities in a workforce that are more difficult to engender and mobilize in the absence of family and community ties. The significance and impact of instrumental rationality is well illustrated when, for example, a hobby or leisure activity, like playing football, is turned into a job that provides a source of income (see Box 1.25). What previously was pursued casually and in an ad hoc manner then becomes a target of more careful calculation, as time becomes money.

Manchester United is not just a work organization because, unlike many football clubs throughout the world, it has been highly profitable and has an international image and thus is a global brand – something that has been a major attraction to corporate predators wishing to take it over. It is also a work organization because it is identified as such by others (e.g. staff, investors, etc.) who emphasize its likeness (in terms of hierarchical and formalized organizing practices, for example) to other institutions that are characterized as work or business organizations. This identity is further reinforced by players insofar as they regard their activity as work (albeit comparatively pleasurable) in which they participate in the development and promotion of a business and expect a substantial income in exchange for their efforts, skill and time. It is difficult not to be aware of the superficiality of family-like solidarity and loyalty within football when key members of the team (e.g. David Beckham) are 'sold off' to help balance the books. Business values almost always take precedence when push comes to shove – something, that invariably disaffects hard-core fans who are more interested in retaining star players than in making profits for shareholders who have only a financial interest in 'their' club. A similar analysis could be made of the British royal family, which its members privately but revealingly describe as 'The Firm'.

Box 1.25: Family, community, organization and Manchester United

Concepts such as 'family' or 'community', rather than 'organization', may be emphasized when characterizing a football team. Managers often seek to engender a 'happy family' atmosphere among their teams, despite its obvious superficiality when key players can be 'sold off' to make room for the latest superstar or to 'balance the books'. A family friendly image has also become a major marketing tool of the big clubs, with family stands, etc.

Consider the appalling tragedy at Hillsborough football ground in Sheffield. Due to a combination of barriers, overcrowding on the terraces and police incompetence large numbers of spectators died or were seriously injured because of a sudden surge of fans crushing those in front of them. The outcome of this tragedy was government insistence on seating-only stadiums, an unintended consequence of which was to make football more of a family spectator pastime as the standing-only terraces were swept away.

Fans of Manchester United have appealed to family and community notions when seeking to question or resist multinationals taking over the club. In 2000 the community of fans demonstrated their power when Rupert Murdoch and his media empire tried to takeover the club partly to strengthen its TV rights monopoly over the most attractive football matches. The official fan club mobilized the community of Manchester United fans to persuade the directors not to pursue the offer, and this probably had some effect. Eventually the Competition Policy Committee outlawed the bid on monopolistic grounds, but it is likely that the community protest had some effect on the outcome. It had much less effect, though not for want of trying, when Malcolm Glazier bought the club through enormous borrowing in 2005 and saddled what was previously the most profitable soccer club in the world with huge debts. Amidst considerable anger from the fans and even the wider public, Manchester United became a private company owned solely by Malcolm Glazier, whose interest would seem to be the purely financial one of exploiting the brand to maximum effect. It is expected that he will sell the club on once this further exploitation of the brand is realized.

Game-playing and resistance

In practice, there can be considerable resistance to instrumental rationality in organizations. As we have repeatedly noted, other rationalities are present that are resistant to being supplanted or **colonized** by instrumental rationality. People enter organizations with their own values, their own objectives and their own sense of what is reasonable. In doing so, they may think, or be persuaded, that it is appropriate to forget or suspend their values and priorities once they set foot in the office or factory. But they may also resent and resist demands to be compliant. Or they may become more instrumentally rational – not by directly pursuing corporate objectives but by calculating how to set, protect and fulfil their own agendas, while managing an impression of dedication, loyalty and commitment. Career systems allow some coincidence of personal and corporate agendas as commitment can be demonstrated and rewarded with promotion and/or pay. But because of the complexities of organizations, where outcomes cannot easily be attributed directly to the efforts or skills of a single individual, there can be a lot of game-playing in which individuals claim responsibility for 'successful' outcomes and endeavour to shift the blame for 'unsuccessful' ones.

Box 1.26: Game-playing in higher education

Students and staff engage in various forms of game-playing. Lectures, tutorials/seminars, and self-study or library work are regarded as the instrumentally rational way of enabling large numbers of students to gain degree-level education. This education is meant to involve a creative component that takes students beyond the comparatively programmed and packaged experience of A levels. In practice, many management students (at least) discover that much degree level work is less demanding and less creative than some of their A level courses.

There is often ambivalence about this. On the one hand, it is frustrating and disappointing, with a sense of being cheated or 'conned'. On the other hand, it is a relief and leaves more time for leisure pursuits. What tends to emerge is a conspiracy of silence – a kind of grand game-playing – in which neither students nor staff are inclined to acknowledge this particular 'elephant in the room'. Staff say that some creative input into essays is required but then often penalize students when it appears. To do otherwise, would require considerable time in assessing the merit of eccentric approaches that deviate from the model answers often required to standardize the assessment process.

Cutbacks in resources and associated pressures to secure research grant income and generate publications make it unlikely that staff will sacrifice their careers or their leisure time by giving assignments that are demanding to assess. Students realize that regurgitating lectures and textbooks is a less risky way of achieving a good (but perhaps not outstanding) mark. Both students and staff act in an instrumentally rational way to reproduce a system that is ostensibly organized to provide degree level education but which routinely falters in its delivery. At the same time, performance systems for teaching as well as research are introduced, which staff become adept at 'gaming' in order to provide the required evidence of educational quality. In this, students are encouraged to collude by accepting the logic of the calculation that the value of their degree depends in some measure upon the reputation of the department that is being assessed.

Less-privileged (i.e. lower-ranking) staff in organizations generally have fewer opportunities to play games that substantially improve their material (income) or symbolic (social status) wealth. Nonetheless, they may pretend to be committed while remaining psychologically distant from what they are doing. This occurs frequently when they are engaged in mundane routine tasks such as performing data entry, routine office work, or working on the mass assembly line in car production and other manufacturing work. Staff may daydream or spend much of their time chatting except when the supervisor appears, at which time they put their heads down and give the impression of being engaged on the task. Occasionally resistance to the instrumentally rational pursuit of production goals will be more disruptive or subversive. Workers may purposely slow down the machine or **sabotage** the conveyor belt by causing it to break down. In this way, they demonstrate the dependence of managers and shareholders upon their productive efforts. This dependence is even more dramatically demonstrated when there is a strike or 'work to rule' in labour relations. For then there are no products and services from which profits can be extracted.

Theory and practice

An underlying assumption of educational provision, including the delivery of OB modules, is that exposure to academic or 'scientific' knowledge about behaviour in organizations will make workers, and especially managers, more efficient and effective. More specifically, it is anticipated that the expertise, or at least the qualifications (e.g. an MBA), will add legitimacy to the exercise of authority. Either way, there is an expectation that knowledge of human behaviour will result in improved practices.

This view is seductive but also problematic. Its limitations are manifest in the manager who is highly qualified – let us imagine someone who possesses a first degree in business studies followed by an MBA – yet is notoriously bad at organizing and managing people. Such a manager has sat through numerous courses, including OB modules, to gain such qualifications, and has also passed examinations that apparently demonstrate an expert knowledge of the field. So, why doesn't this expertise translate itself into effective ways of managing and organizing people?

We doubt that there is a simple or universal answer to this question. To assume that there is would be to fall into the trap of believing that a medical model is appropriate for 'treating' problems attributed to organizations: all that is required is to diagnose what is wrong, prescribe the medicine and await the recovery. The assumption that organizations can be likened to the human body has attracted many students, and particularly management consultants, who propose a whole range of prescriptions for diverse symptoms of 'organizational ill health'. We have yet to find the organizational equivalent of the aspirin, let alone antibiotics; and we argue that we never will because organizations are not the same as bodies. To put this another way, the theory – including its conception of the relationship between practice and theory – is poorly aligned with the practice.

Nor are organizations like machines. Yet the metaphor has been another influential way of thinking about organizations, with the assumption that knowledge of engineering will yield effective solutions to perceived problems. Indeed, some of the most influential classical, and a number of more recent theorists of organization (e.g. Fayol, Taylor, Crosby and Deming) were engineers by training. Students of organizations have sought to treat them as machines in order to bridge the gap between theory and practice in one 'quick fix'. Our own view is that thinking drawn from the social sciences rather than biology or engineering is more relevant. Ideas of **contextual embeddedness**, for example, can help us to explore possible reasons for the gap between theory and practice.

On the basis of what we have explored so far, we can sketch a number of reasons for the theory–practice gap, and we invite you to add others:

- Theory presented in textbooks, or underpinning influential practice provides an over-rosy ('idealized' to use a bit of social scientific jargon) view of complex behaviour, leading to simplistic interventions. Textbook knowledge fails to appreciate particular, contextually embedded aspects of the situation and thereby offers seemingly universal but locally inappropriate solutions to problems.
- Students view knowledge of organizations and management instrumentally as a means of gaining qualifications. There is little thought for, or grasp of, its potential relevance for the messy practice of managing and organizing. Knowledge is often viewed inappropriately as a reliable instrument of power and thereby applied mechanically or naively to practice.
- Politics and power operate to frustrate consultants and managers' efforts to reorganize activities by applying theories, even of the most sophisticated variety. Attempts to impose control provoke resistance that is unanticipated because it is assumed that those being managed will share managers' sense of priorities.
- The practice of managing and organizing involves, above all else, interaction with people – colleagues and superiors as well as subordinates. There is little in management textbooks or indeed in education and training that directly addresses this critical issue.

What other possible factors behind the theory–practice divide can you think of?

We have cautioned against using commonsense as a guide to the study of organization (see earlier examples). Yet we have also recognized how it is drawn upon in developing theory and in management practice. Jackie was hardly consulting a textbook when running the pub for the weekend. She just drew on her everyday experience of organizing, and as we have said, this is extensive for us all. If you think about it, every day of our lives consists of a great deal of organizing. Some, of course, we have learned consciously at school or elsewhere. Knowing this, the managers of the pub could assume that Jackie would be able to add up the takings at the end of the day and communicate with the other bar staff. Yet, as we saw, in the case of Christine, not all such tasks are simple. What Jackie did not appreciate or anticipate was how Christine would interpret and react to the landlord's decision, and how this would result in an embarrassing and threatening display of defiance. What Jackie lacked was a theory of organizational behaviour that would have sensitized her to this possibility and thereby enabled her to think through how she might deal with such an eventuality. Yet even had she studied OB, there is no guarantee that in the heat of the moment she would have been able coolly to apply its insights rather than just react spontaneously as she did.

Distinctiveness of this text

In general, the curriculum and teaching of OB has given priority to ideas that are conservative and broadly pro-managerial. OB has been superficially pro-managerial in the sense of presuming that managers *alone* have a monopoly of knowledge of, and an almost divine right to determine, how work should be organized. As a consequence, the orthodox treatment of OB has taken the form of a technology of control, with each of its topics (e.g. motivation, leadership) being presented as an element of a control toolkit. Ideas and perspectives that do not fit neatly into this toolkit are either ignored or accommodated as just one more dimension to consider. Efficiency, performance and/or profit are seen to inform everything that occurs in organizations, whereas social and moral responsibility are either seen as outside the sphere of OB or simply tagged on as an afterthought. Even where ethical issues are included, and this has become more relevant in recent time because of various corporate scandals, the focus is on compliance with regulations to avoid bad publicity or financial sanctions against the organization. In short, the concern with business ethics (see Chapter 14) is simply another instrumental means to the end of preserving the status quo.

Our text attempts to be different primarily by presenting and contrasting alternative conceptions – orthodox or mainstream and critical – of OB. In each of the following chapters, an account of the subject matter found in mainstream texts familiarizes the reader with what is conventionally studied in this field. The orthdox approach is not presented here as an end in itself, however. Instead – as we have shown in relation to the 'entity' concept of organization – orthodox thinking is treated as a foil for introducing critical or unorthodox thinking on OB. To do this, we rely upon an approach with which all the contributors have been closely associated for several years.

Box 1.27: Orthodox and critical wings of organizational behaviour

What do we mean by 'orthodoxy'? The term orthodox is used to describe what most people *currently* recognize as a legitimate way of doing or thinking about things – it is conventional and conservative, or a continuation of the way things have always or traditionally been done. The orthodox view regards managing as a technical activity and organization as a neutral instrument for achieving shared goals.

What do we mean by 'critical'? The term 'critical' is used to signal an interest in interrogating and challenging received wisdom – both theory and practice – by drawing upon social science perspectives that are routinely ignored or excluded from OB. Critical refers to approaches that challenge the orthodoxy in some way. The critical view regards organization as a political instrument for achieving contested goals.

Of course, if widely accepted, a critical approach may become the orthodoxy. Examples that spring to mind include the challenge to religion made by science, the challenge to monarchy posed by republicanism, the discrediting of imperialism generated by anti-colonialists, and the challenge to anti-apartheid in South Africa represented by the (after the fact) heroic figure of Nelson Mandela.

Each chapter of this book addresses a core topic of OB. In each chapter both mainstream and critical contributions to knowledge of this topic are presented and explored through one or more of the six central concepts – identity, (in)security, freedom, power, inequality and knowledge – around which the more critical content of this book is organized (see the Appendix for a definition of these concepts).

Throughout the book, we endeavour to make the subject matter more relevant and accessible by viewing organizational behaviour first and foremost as practices of organizing and meaning-making, involving thinking, feeling and acting, that are not so dissimilar to everyday life. An important implication of this approach is that it acknowledges, rather than denies, the politically and emotionally messy human detail of organizations. This approach, as we explained earlier, makes it easier to learn about organizations as work relations and management activities are understood to be less remote from everyday life.

More specifically, we seek to appreciate and emphasize the continuities between the experiences of students and employees. Both are engaged in, and shaped by, a world in which organizations are as central as they are familiar. We also endeavour to capitalize upon the closeness of this understanding with the view that we all learn best when we can identify and participate in the 'object' of our learning. This may sometimes demand a leap of imagination and a refusal to compartmentalize our everyday lives (e.g. going to clubs, pubs, bars or parties) from what we are studying. Of course we are not suggesting that the social world of the student is equivalent, let alone identical, to that of a manager or administrator. As we have emphasized earlier, we do not deny the distinctiveness of organizations in which the working lives of employees are routinely conditioned by the demands and trappings of instrumental rationality. But, at the same time, we reject the reduction of the messy complexities of organizing to the abstracted and idealized ways of representing this complexity in the mainstream, orthodox OB literature.

In turn, this approach leads us to recognize and stress that (i) instrumental rationality is neither politically and morally neutral nor free of specific values for it cultivates a particular, **impersonal and disembodied** way of living; and (ii) it is introduced and applied by economically and politically interested managers and employees who are also gendered, sexually charged, ethnically located, emotionally involved, and more or less passionate human beings. These interests, emotions and identities after all comprise some of the most fundamental of our experiences, whether at work or not (Knights and Willmott, 1999). Put at its simplest, we challenge the very idea that the organization is separate from life outside it and vice versa. To explore this connection, contributors to this text have been guided by a framework of six interrelated concepts.

Six key concepts

The central concepts that provide the framework for all the chapters are outlined here, together with the principal and secondary disciplines that are ordinarily associated with them (see Table 1.3).

Table 1.3 Key concepts and disciplines

Concepts	Principal discipline	Secondary discipline
Insecurity	Psychology	Economics
Identity	Social psychology	Sociology
Inequality	Economics	Sociology
Power	Sociology and politics	
Knowledge	All disciplines	
Freedom	Philosophy, politics and economics	

We deployed these six concepts earlier in this chapter but now seek to define them a little more closely in relation to Jackie's experiences in the pub. If you return to the vignette, you will recall that when first standing at the bar Jackie had felt uncomfortable and perhaps a little *insecure*, as all the students had already left the pub to go to the disco. Our assumption is that uncertainties and associated insecurities are a widespread feature of working in organizations. They may range from a general feeling of uneasiness to more fundamental questioning of its purpose, accompanied by unvoiced doubts such as 'is this all there is?'

Box 1.28: Insecurity

Insecurity arises when people are unable to interpret a situation in a way that confirms their own sense of themselves – for example, as a 'bright student' or as a 'caring person'. Social situations are especially difficult in this respect since we can never be fully sure of, let alone control, how others view us. Yet, it is through our sense of how others view us that we develop and evaluate self-identity. 'Knowing' someone reduces the stress or tension of this uncertainty in social encounters. However, this uncertainty cannot be entirely eliminated as people are continually changing as a result of new circumstances, experiences and relationships.

When the local lads who sat at her table started criticizing students, Jackie felt her *identity* was under attack. Perceiving her identity as a student, she did not like the lads undermining it. People routinely attribute an identity to us, in past as a way of dealing with their own uncertainties and insecurities. We also, often subconsciously, take on identities and only realize the extent of our identifications when they are challenged. Much of the time we are unconsciously striving to reproduce an habitual sense of identity (or identities – student, brother/sister, son/daughter, man/woman, etc.) that we have largely taken for granted.

As we all know, attacks on our identity can be almost as bad as being physically assaulted. As an example, in 2002 the Republic of Ireland and Manchester United soccer captain, Roy Keane, became a household name less for his footballing brilliance than for his violence (both physical and verbal) in what can only be seen as an attempt to assert and/or defend his identity against the Irish manager of the 2002 World Cup squad. Zidane's head butt in the 2006 World Cup final provides a further example.

Box 1.29: Identity

Identity refers to how people are identified or classified – as a man, brother, student, fighter, etc. Our sense of self-worth or significance is related to our social identity. But an identity is not only an image presented by oneself or attributed to us by others. It is also associated with expectations and obligations about how to behave. When how we behave is consistent with what others expect there will tend to be coherence between our sense of self-identity and the social identity ascribed to us.

Returning to Jackie, when she was on her own in the pub, she felt *power*-less to intervene to defend her own identity. She had a sense of being subjected to the *power* of the locals and thereby unable to do much about their ridiculing students. More generally, her very sense of identity as a student was an effect of the power that produced this identification. We frequently think of power as a possession – the lads had it, Jackie lacked it – but it is perhaps more illuminating to conceive of power as shaping who we are and what we do. Thinking of power in this way enables us to consider the extent to which both the lads and Jackie were objects and agents of power (e.g. the power that defined Jackie as a student) – the power that placed them in a particular way in relation to each other.

Box 1.30: Power

Power has traditionally been associated with the coercive and repressive means through which respectively a class of capitalists exploits proletarian labour (Marx), political elites control the masses (Pareto) or management cadres dominate subordinate employees (Burnham). Such concepts of power see it as a wholly negative control of one group or person over another. More recently, an alternative has rejected this negative or purely coercive conception of power. Instead, allowing that there are no social relations that are 'free' of power, it is seen not just as constraining in its effects but also productive and positive (Foucault, 1980, 1982). An individual or group can exercise power positively by transforming individuals into subjects who find meaning, purpose and identity in the practices that it demands or expects. The effect of power then can be to make those over whom it is exercised more creative, productive and powerful, which, of course, does not imply that they always and everywhere accept or defer to the ostensibly powerful. Sometimes subjects will exercise their own power to resist what is demanded or expected of them.

Why did Jackie feel powerless to resist the negative stereotypes or stigmas of students that the local lads were constructing? Largely it was because of being outnumbered and this *inequality* making her feel insecure in a way not dissimilar to when she had stood alone at the bar. This situation of inequality would have been reversed had she come to the pub earlier when the students outnumbered the locals. However, were we to examine the future prospects of the students compared to those locals who had not attended university, we would probably conclude that many of them suffered more from inequality – in terms of housing, employment opportunities, life expectancy, pension provision, etc. – than the students.

Box 1.31: Inequality

Inequality describes differences in wealth and status, such as the inequalities of income and privilege between managers and employees and between men and women, or those suffered by ethnic minorities. These inequalities may be seen as institutionalised insofar as they are embedded in, and reproduced by, working relations (e.g. hierarchy and job segregation by gender or ethnicity) and employment practices (e.g. recruitment and promotion). They are also reproduced by other social formations such as markets, where inequalities of wealth are reinforced because money, makes money, or the family, where inheritance guarantees intergenerational inequality.

Indeed, it is this *knowledge* of how inequality works that might explain the perhaps semi-conscious purge for the locals to verbally abuse the students. Arguably, the locals were feeling swamped by students who had begun to 'take over' a pub that they regarded as 'theirs'. This antagonism was, in all likelihood, prompted and fuelled by an implicit awareness and resentment of how students can trade on their knowledge to secure privileged jobs and a superior social status in life.

Box 1.32: Knowledge

Knowledge is sometimes referred to as power ('power is knowledge'), and this is probably because invariably, when exercising power, knowledge is drawn upon. Knowledge – both everyday knowledge and more specialist knowledge – leads us to interpret and produce the world in particular historically and culturally specific ways. Just think of how disempowered we feel when, as we move out of our sphere of knowledge, we do not *know* the language or *know* the culture. It is not coincidence that a majority of football managers are ex-footballers as they can draw upon their knowledge of playing as well as of more recently acquired management skills.

Knowledge and power are so intimately related that Foucault (1980) insisted on speaking about power/knowledge relations. However, it is not just that knowledge is a resource for the exercise of power. Knowledge is also often an effect of, or produced by, the exercise of power. So, for example, the very exercise of power over a football team will generate knowledge of how to exercise that power, and this is why nothing is seen to entirely substitute for experience. Acquiring knowledge through education is something that you are doing as students, and you may be doing it largely not for its own sake but as a means to getting a 'good' job.

Perhaps the reason why the local lads were antagonistic to the students was because they also resent the *freedom* that students appear to enjoy. Students do not have to get up at a certain time every day for work, enjoy long holidays, experience few controls, etc. The locals overhear them recounting exciting experiences overseas in the summer vacation and they always seem to be partying.

Box 1.33: Freedom

Freedom has often been defined as autonomy or an absence of constraints on the individual. However, while we all may seek fewer constraints on our choices and behaviour, a moment's reflection would suggest that an absence of all constraints would be chaotic or anarchic. We have to use our freedom (and power) responsibly so that it at least does not directly violate other people's freedom. We can see here that our very concept of freedom is based on a (humanistic) constraint of being respectful to the 'other'. With the development of the environmental movement, this respect is extended from the world of human beings to that of nature. Human freedom or autonomy then, as Foucault (1982) reminds us, is both liberating and disciplining.

We use this conceptual framework to interpret the key elements of, and present an alternative to the orthodox or mainstream treatment of OB topics. In addition to providing some insights into behaviour in organizations, these six concepts can also readily be related to your own experiences, thereby making the study of OB more meaningful and memorable.

Box 1.34: Mainstream, orthodox texts

Mainstream texts tend to present a (exhaustive) body of knowledge that aspiring managers are invited to absorb in a way that is abstracted from their everyday experience. In the absence of any overall and explicit sense-making framework, it is difficult to grasp the relevance of the knowledge and to incorporate it into what is done in organizations. In contrast, by exploring a web of concepts, students are able to draw and build upon their own experience of organizations. Then, the relevance and value of the orthodox body of knowledge can be scrutinized and selectively drawn upon.

We are not of course suggesting that the combination of these concepts is all that matters. Clearly you could think of lots of other concepts (e.g. emotion, rationality) that would help us to understand behaviour in organizations, including Jackie's experiences and actions. However, when speaking about Jackie's emotions or rationality, it would be difficult to ignore one or more of the six concepts. Her emotions revolve around insecurity and identity, and her rationality is dependent on (because it is exercised through) her freedom, knowledge and power. Jackie also deploys both rationality and emotion in securing knowledge and maintaining her position within a system of social inequality through succeeding in education, and through her social skills and capacity to present a favourable impression to the landlord and landlady, thereby gaining a job as a barmaid.

Each concept in our framework is intuitively relevant for understanding people in organizations. For example, we are all routinely ascribed an *identity* – as students, employees, customers, suppliers, etc. – that will have some influence upon how we present (and manage) ourselves. We may invest in more than one identity, and sometimes these may conflict. At this point, you may usefully return to the case study of the pub to list the different identities that relate to Jackie and consider whether there are conflicts between them. Take the issue of gender and sexual preference. These are important identity issues for most people. Misconceptions and misunderstandings in these areas can cause considerable offence, embarrassment and pain when they are not a source of amusement and pleasure. When others (e.g. customers) identified Jackie as a barmaid, she was seen differently. The sexist stereotype of this role might help to explain the numerous sexual advances that she experienced, some of which she found flattering or amusing, but most of which she experienced as awkward or demeaning. Again, you might wish to reflect upon the possible explanations of such mixed reactions.

As employees, we may comply with certain expectations but we may also seek to challenge and change them. In dealing with others, including those who hope to persuade or coerce us to perform organizational tasks, we mobilize everyday *knowledge* of others as well as of ourselves. In doing so, we exercise both *power* and *freedom*. In this process, we encounter relations of *inequality* as we discover that others have more money/income or status than ourselves. This, combined with the difficulties of fulfilling or wanting to challenge other people's expectations, can make us feel insecure – as was Jackie when, as a student, she felt personally subjected to a character assassination of students by the locals. This was so despite the oblique nature of their assault.

This way of thinking about behaviour in organizations rarely surfaces in mainstream, orthodox OB texts. Why not? It is because, on the whole, orthodox texts are preoccupied with conveying an exhaustive and comprehensive list of theories and topics so that their authors cannot be criticized as failing to cover all the literature.

They are less concerned with showing how behaviour in organizations can be illuminated and made meaningful to students by approaching its topics through a linked set of concepts or a conceptual framework. Such a framework provides a basic analytical *aide-mémoire* that has wide applicability for interpreting, and participating in the dynamics of OB. Of course, we hope that you find it helpful when studying OB. But we hope even more that you will continue to find it useful when you have completed your studies and are facing the challenges of working with people in organizations.

References

Brooks, I. (1999) *Organizational Behaviour: Individuals, Groups and the Organization*, London: FT Pitman.

Buchanan, D. and Huczyinski, A. (1997) *Organizational Behaviour: An Introductory Text*, third edition, London: Prentice Hall.

Clark, P. (1983) *The English Alehouse: A Social History 1200–1850*, London: Longman.

Drucker, P. (1992) 'The New Society of Organizations', *Harvard Business Review*, 70(5): 95–104.

Du Gay, P. (2000) *In Praise of Bureaucracy*, London: Sage.

Foucault, M. (1980) *Power/Knowledge*, edited by Colin Gordon London: Tavistock.

Foucault, M. (1982) 'The Subject and Power', in H. Dreyfus and P. Rabinow (eds) *Michel Foucault: Beyond Structuralism and Hermeneutics*, Brighton: Harvester Press.

Huczynski, A. and Buchanan, D. (2001) *Organizational Behaviour: An Introductory Text*, fourth edition, London: Financial Times/Prentice Hall.

Jackall, R. (1998) *Moral Mazes: The World Corporate Managers*, New York: Oxford University Press.

Jackson, N. and Carter, P. (2000) *Rethinking Organizational Behaviour*, London: Financial Times/Prentice Hall.

Kinicki, A. and Kreitner, R. (2003) *Organizational Behaviour: Key Concepts, Skills and Best Practices*, New York: McGraw-Hill.

Knights, D. and Willmott, H. C. (1999) *Management Lives: Power and Identity in Work Organisations*, London: Sage.

Merton, R. K., Gray, A. P., Hockey, B. and Selvin, H. C. (1952) *Reader In Bureaucracy*, New York: Free Press.

Robbins, S. (2003) *Essentials of Organizational Behaviour*, seventh edition, Upper Saddle River, New Jersey: Prentice Hall.

Strange, S. (1997) *Casino Capitalism*, Manchester: Manchester University Press.

Watson, D. (2002) 'Home From Home: The Pub and Everyday Life', in T. Bennett and D. Watson (eds) *Understanding Everyday Life*, Oxford: Blackwell.

Notes

1 In addition, those who bought shares in privatized industries at knock-down prices made substantial capital gains, provided that they sold their investments before the privatization bubble was burst by scandal and subsequent regulations.

2 We have direct experience of contract cleaners rarely doing more than emptying the waste bins in universities, but in hospitals cleanliness is more than a mere aesthetic.

3 When the high valuation given to internet and new technology stocks was dramatically cut.

4 These are the kinds of criteria used to justify the shortlisting of candidates. Thereafter, other less readily auditable and quantifiable criteria come into play, such as assessments of their character and ability to lead, or the knock-on effects of appointing particular or disappointing individuals.

PART I
The Human Dimension

Part I examines a number of topics and themes that are closely interrelated in the mainstream literature. These chapters draw primarily on a psychological approach to understanding organizational behaviour in which the individual in the group is centre stage. They complement this orientation by drawing extensively on a wider social science literature and, in particular, on a critical literature that pays attention to their wider significance in relation to society and politics. The chapters consider the standard approaches to managing people at work through motivation, attitude and personality analysis, teamworking and learning strategies, but challenge their assumptions so as to provide alternative insights.

2 Motivation and the Self

John Roberts

Key concepts and learning objectives

By the end of this chapter you should understand:

- The key mainstream approaches to motivation, as well as their limitations.
- Some of the shared and opposed interests that shape motivation at work.
- How our sense of self is socially constructed and maintained.
- How our so-called 'ego needs' mean that we are always vulnerable to the attitudes of others towards us, and how they serve as a key way in which our conduct can be controlled and influenced.
- How power comes to work largely through processes of self-discipline in which we appraise and judge ourselves against an internalized standard of how we should be.

Aims of the chapter

This chapter will:

- Explain why the study of motivation at work has received so much attention.
- Explore some of the key ideas that have marked the evolution of management's understanding of the different factors that shape motivation.
- Examine some of the key mainstream studies of motivation.
- Explore some of the important ideas that have marked the evolution of critical understandings of motivation theory.
- Examine some of the critical studies of motivation.
- Explore the linkages between insecurity, identity and the workings of power relationships in order to better understand motivation.

Overview and key points

When we get a job there is typically an employment contract with the organization, which specifies what we will do, for whom and for how long, and what we will get in return by way of pay, holidays, etc. But the contract does not determine what then happens. There can be a huge difference in both the quantity and quality of our work depending on our experiences and attitudes, and the response of others to us. It is this difference that is the focus of 'motivation theory' and both manager and employee have an intense interest in the subject. As employees, given that work occupies such a large part of our lives, we have a very strong interest in the satisfaction to be drawn from work. As a manager, a highly motivated employee is likely to be both happier and also more productive. He or she will therefore be both easier to manage, though possibly more demanding, and will help realize the objectives by which the manager is judged and appraised. These dual interests in motivation have ensured that the search for the key to effective motivation has served as the 'holy grail' of management theory; a search for the key that will unlock the virtuous circle of productivity *and* satisfaction.

This chapter will first review some of the key mainstream ideas that emerged during the 20th century as part of this quest for the secrets of what releases human energy and effort. We start with what are termed **content theories of motivation**; the ideas of Maslow on human needs and how these were developed by subsequent theorists of motivation such as McGregor, McClelland, Herzberg and Hackman. We then look at **process theories of motivation**; Vroom's expectancy theory and

SOURCE: © IMAGES.COM/CORBIS

Image 2.1 Beyond the carrot and the stick

contemporary theories of motivation and the emphasis they place on an employee's autonomy and self-motivation, supported by management empowerment.

In the second half of the chapter we will take a more critical look at what is involved in motivation. We look first at Marx's analysis of 'alienation' at work and his suggestion that in capitalism there is a fundamental conflict of interests between owners and their agents and employees. Secondly, we take a critical look at the current interest in promoting individual autonomy at work and suggest that motivation techniques now involve not just the use of economic insecurity but also the deliberate manipulation of a person's sense of self and self-worth.

Mainstream approaches to motivation and the self

Introduction

Late in the 19th century Frederick Taylor developed one of the earliest conceptions of management and the management role – his 'principles of scientific management'. Here we merely want to touch on some of these principles as they reflect a set of assumptions about motivation against which many of the writers on whom we will later focus can be seen to be reacting and responding.

Taylor was the first person to have attempted to provide a rationale for the emergent role of the manager in increasingly large American enterprises. The foreman or chargehand was no longer merely the stand-in for the absent owner, free to exercise power in a personalized and arbitrary fashion. Instead, Taylor drew upon the wider authority and methodology of science to offer a version of what the manager should do. The division of labour between worker and manager was seen in terms of a separation of the planning function from that of execution. It was the manager's job to make a 'scientific' study of tasks and on this basis to develop the most efficient form of work that could then be taught to new employees. The division of labour could then be greatly extended, allowing relatively unskilled labour to be trained in the most efficient means for carrying out a particular part of a task. It was also part of the management task to then control this labour through close monitoring and through the use of piece rates to ensure that the economic rewards of work were tied to actual productivity. It is this attempt to relate reward to the efficiency of effort and output that has led many to insist that Taylor placed a primary motivational value upon money.

For Taylor there was no necessary conflict between the interests of workers and those of management. Instead, if managers were to exercise their responsibilities in the ways in which he described, then what was possible was a rational division of labour that made optimal use of the purely manual skills of labour through the mental skills associated with the study and optimization of work, planning and monitoring by managers. The laziness or 'systematic soldiering' that Taylor observed in employees could in this way be resolved in the service of both the organization and the employee. Both would gain economically from the application of this new managerial rationality.

The separation of mental and manual capabilities, the focus on the efficiency gains of an intense division of labour, coupled with management training and monitoring, offer us an early image of the beliefs and practices that shaped human motivation. One of the targets and exemplars for Taylor for these new management techniques was a pig-iron shoveller called Schmidt – a man who was seemingly deficient in all respects bar brute physical strength. Once his labour had been scientifically studied and analysed his capacity for shovelling increased enormously and seemed to offer clear evidence of the potential gains for all, including Schmidt, of this new scientific version of the manager's role in relation to labour.

In the 1920s and 1930s a set of American studies at the Western Electric Company, often referred to as the Hawthorne Experiments, began to unravel the assumptions of Taylor's early work. The experiments began with a scientific study of the impact of different levels of illumination on worker output. Much to the surprise of all those involved, output increased whatever adjustments were made to the level of lighting; a result that gradually led to the recognition of the importance of individuals' social needs. The economic atom that Schmidt symbolized is seen now as a person who craves the attention of the manager, and who, as a social being, is found to be highly responsive to the pressures brought to bear by his or her work group. While the Hawthorne studies are typically held to have founded the human relations movement, it was left to later theorists to draw out and develop the more complex view of human motivation that the studies began to uncover. In what follows we will briefly review some of the seminal studies and theories that then shaped something of a revolution in how managers were supposed to understand, and ideally practise motivation.

Central problems and major issues in mainstream approaches

The major issues that mainstream motivation theory has sought to address are:

- What motivates a person? Should we look for the answer 'inside' the person in their 'needs' for money, status or power? Should we look outside at the work they do and how they are managed?
- Is there a universal truth to be discovered, or is motivation highly contingent and dependent on the specific character of a person and situation?
- How does motivation change over time? Is what motivates the same as what demotivates?
- Can my manager know more about what motivates me than I do, or does my motivation depend on the sense I make of my experiences?
- Can a manager motivate someone else or is motivation always something I do to myself?
- What allows or gets in the way of such self-motivation?

Key ideas and contributions

Motivation: It is about fulfilling human needs (Abraham Maslow) Although Maslow was writing over 60 years ago, his ideas about a '**hierarchy of needs**' have retained a peculiar currency. At the bottom of the hierarchy are what he called 'physiological' needs; the needs for food, sleep, drink, etc. Maslow suggests that while such needs are unsatisfied then we are completely preoccupied by them and all our capacities are put to the service of meeting them. Other needs or concerns are in this way marginalized and become unimportant. But Maslow, writing in a US context, suggests that the dominance of such physiological needs is very rare; appetite should not be confused with hunger in this sense – men live by bread alone only when there is no bread.

So what happens when such physiological needs are routinely met. It is here that Maslow introduces his notion of a hierarchy of needs. He suggests that as one level of need is met 'at once other (and "higher") needs emerge' and come to dominate. In this sense the meeting of a need is

CASE STUDY 2.1 A problem (of motivation) at PYT plc (1)

Peter Drake has just been appointed as the Sales Manager of the Manchester office of PYT plc. He has been with PYT since leaving school nine years ago. At school he had done all right, and his teachers had told him that if he worked hard at his A levels he could get to college. Peter, however, was keen to get out and start earning some money as soon as possible, but he was clear that, unlike his dad who was a school caretaker, manual work was not for him; he wanted a job in an office. The job at PYT seemed ideal. He started as a telephone sales representative, and four years later became a section leader.

PYT had a contract with the national telephone company to publish a telephone directory of business services. Every business in the country had a free entry in the directory but PYT made its money from selling additional advertising space to individual businesses. Looking back, Peter thought that part of his success was simply a matter of good luck and timing. When he first joined PYT it had only been going for a year and he quickly discovered that there were rich pickings to be had. The product was new to the UK and the potential market for additional advertising was huge. The company did not put him straight on the phones but instead took him away for a two-week training course at a hotel in the south of England. Here he was taught all the benefits of the product and introduced to the skills of selling.

His mum and dad had always told Peter that he would go far because he had the 'gift of the gab' and telephone sales offered him the chance to make good use of this. For every bit of additional space he sold he was paid a commission that meant that, in a good month, he could add something like 50 per cent to his basic salary. Within a year he had bought himself a car and had moved into a shared flat in town. Compared to his friends who had gone to college, he had loads of money and the chance of getting on if he did well.

Peter had just got back from his first sales managers' meeting – a meeting of all the Office, Regional and National Account managers, held in Birmingham with the Sales Director. The picture of the state of the company that Peter had gathered from this meeting was not very encouraging. Given the strength of PYT's sales training, new sales had always been good, but two problems had begun to emerge. The latest figures indicated that a growing number of their customers were not renewing their adverts from one year to the next. In the past this had not mattered much – there were plenty of new 'punters' to be caught – but the Sales Director had pointed out that, if current trends continued, in three years time they would be losing more business than they were selling. Their licence for publishing the directory was also due for renewal in two years time. Matters were possibly being made worse by the fact that staff turnover in the offices was approaching 100 per cent. Not only was this a big cost to PYT, given its initial training costs, but it also meant that there was no incentive for staff to be realistic in what they sold to customers. Staff would oversell one year and then leave rather than go back to the same customer a year later. At the meeting the Sales Director had announced a number of changes and initiatives that were to be introduced across the company to address the situation. There were to be immediate changes to the incentive system; in future staff would only be paid commission for any net gain in sales (new sales less drop-out from the previous year). Managers were also encouraged to change the profile of the people they recruited; it was thought that older, more mature people would probably stay longer. Finally there was the suggestion that part of the problem was poor management and Peter heard that he was to attend a one-week management development course next month.

Question

Drawing on the above and your own experiences, what factors do you think might affect the motivation of a group of sales staff?

important in allowing other, more social needs to emerge. At the same time, however, a need that is satisfied no longer motivates.

The second set of needs that Maslow identified in his hierarchy he termed 'safety' needs. Such a need for safety, Maslow suggests, is evidenced in our taste for routine and predictability. When safety is disturbed, panic or terror set in. Maslow suggests that, in developed societies, one must look to the neurotic or the 'economic or social' underdog to see where these needs dominate. According to Maslow (1989, p. 26) 'Their reaction is often to unknown, psychological dangers in a world that is perceived to be hostile, overwhelming, and threatening. Such a person behaves as if a great catastrophe were almost always impending'.

As with physiological needs, once met safety needs no longer dominate attention and leave room for yet higher needs to emerge. The next hierarchal set of needs to emerge is framed by Maslow in terms of needs for 'love, affection and belongingness'. While some of these needs may well be met through relationships outside work, in the context of work Maslow was thinking of a person's need to find their place within a group; a need to make contact and establish friendships with colleagues.

The fourth set of needs that emerge, once 'love' needs are met, Maslow termed 'esteem' needs. He describes these in the following terms: 'all people in our society (with a few pathological exceptions) have a need or desire for a stable, firmly based, (usually) high evaluation of themselves, for self-respect, for self-esteem, and for the esteem of others' (Maslow, 1989, p. 27). This, he suggests, should be based on real capacity, achievement and respect for others. He further divides these needs in terms of, first, 'the desire for strength, for achievement, for adequacy, for confidence in the face of the world, and for independence and freedom', and secondly, as the desire for 'reputation or prestige, recognition, attention, importance or appreciation'. If such needs are met, he suggests that they lead to feelings of 'self confidence, worth, strength, capability and adequacy, of being useful and necessary in the world'. If they are thwarted they lead to feelings of 'inferiority, of weakness and of helplessness'.

But even with the meeting of such 'esteem' needs, Maslow suggests that a 'new discontent and restlessness will soon develop', which arises from needs for what, at the top of the hierarchy, he terms the need for 'self-actualization'. He uses this term to refer to the desire for self-fulfilment; the desire to make actual all that is potential within the self.

Importantly, Maslow sees the thwarting of these basic needs as a source of sickness. For him a 'healthy man is primarily motivated by his needs to develop and actualize his fullest potentialities and capacities'. Such a notion of health is very demanding. In so far as the pursuit of such self-actualizing needs characterizes only a few people in organizations, then the sad conclusion is that there is much sickness in our organizations.

Exercise 2.1

Consider the following questions:

1 From your own experience and what you know of the experiences of your parents, siblings or friends, what merits are there to Maslow's idea of a hierarchy of needs?
2 Think of occasions when each of the different needs – physiological, safety, love, esteem and self-actualization – have been dominant in your mind. What feelings arise with the satisfaction of each need? What feelings dominate when these needs are frustrated?
3 Can you see in different others the dominance of different needs?
4 In terms of each set of needs, think about what might need to be done by colleagues, managers and those who design organizations to make the meeting of such needs possible.
5 Where in the hierarchy would you place money as a motivator?
6 What is your potential?
7 How 'sick' is our society in terms of the satisfactions it offers people in their work?

In what follows we will explore how Maslow's ideas have been taken up and developed in at least two different directions. The first looks at how behaviour at work, or the lack of motivation, may be the *unintended consequence* of how manager's think about employees – they simply do not understand their needs. The second takes these needs more seriously and then looks at the design of work to understand what motivates.

Motivation: It is managers' assumptions that matter (Douglas McGregor) We turn to Douglas McGregor's work immediately after looking at Maslow because there is a clear and explicit link between Maslow's view of 'sickness' as the failure to be able to meet one's basic needs and McGregor's attempts to think this through in terms of the effects that *manager's own assumptions* have on how they then go about seeking to motivate others. While Maslow focused on defining a hierarchy of largely unconscious needs that shape conduct, McGregor is more interested in how managers' *beliefs* about what drives others (and themselves perhaps) feed through into their practice of motivation.

The story McGregor tells contrasts a conventional conception of management's task – theory X – with a new, theoretically informed theory Y. **Theory X** propositions are as follows (McGregor, 1989, p. 315):

1. 'Management is responsible for organizing the elements of productive enterprise – money, materials, equipment, people – in the interest of economic ends.
2. With respect to people, this is a process of directing their efforts, motivating them, controlling their actions, modifying their behaviour to fit the needs of the organization.
3. Without this active intervention by management, people would be passive – even resistant – to organizational needs. They must therefore be persuaded, rewarded, punished, controlled – their activities must be directed.'

McGregor suggests that other, less conscious assumptions inform this conventional theory including the belief that the average person is lazy, lacks ambition, prefers to be led and dislikes responsibility. These assumptions, he suggests, shape organizations in the way that they come to be embedded in structures, policies and practices.

It is not that these assumptions are wrong, but rather that they are *assumptions*, and, once embedded in management structures, policies and practices, they begin to have effects on how people behave. McGregor's innovation was to suggest that while behaviour supporting the assumptions of theory X could easily be discovered in organizations, it was the result not of human's inherent nature, but rather an unintended consequence of management philosophy, policies and practice. The problem of motivation lies not in the worker but in the mind and assumptions and resulting conduct of the manager.

It is at this point that McGregor draws on Maslow's work to offer a critique of current management practice. He suggests that arbitrary management action, uncertainty over continued employment, favouritism or discrimination, all serve to keep safety needs strong in the employment relationship. Similarly, he suggests that management can fear group resistance to the pursuit of its objectives and therefore leave what he calls employees' 'social' needs unsatisfied. In relation to the needs for self-esteem, status and respect, McGregor suggests that, at least at lower levels in the hierarchy, these needs

SOURCE: © CLIVE GODDARD/CARTOONSTOCK.COM

Image 2.2

are completely ignored, and thereby thwarted. This is even more so for the needs for self-actualization: 'People, deprived of opportunities to satisfy at work the needs which are now important to them, behave exactly as we might predict – with indolence, passivity, resistance to change, lack of responsibility, unreasonable demands for economic benefits. It would seem that we are caught in a web of our own weaving' (McGregor, 1989, p. 320).

McGregor then offers an alternative '**theory Y**' based on what he argues is a more adequate set of assumptions about human nature and motivation (McGregor, 1989, p. 321).

1. Management is responsible for organizing the elements of productive enterprise – money, materials, equipment, people – in the interest of economic ends.
2. People are *not* by nature passive or resistant to organizational needs – they have become so as a result of their experience in organizations.
3. The motivation, the potential for development, the capacity for assuming responsibility, the readiness to direct behaviour towards organizational goals are all present in people. Management does not put them there. It is the responsibility of management to make it possible for people to recognize and develop these human characteristics for themselves.
4. The essential task of managers is to arrange organizational conditions and methods of operation so that people can achieve their own goals best by directing their effort toward organizational objectives.

Change, McGregor suggests, will inevitably be slow, but in job enrichment and new forms of decentralization, delegation, participation and consultation he sees hope of the gradual implementation of theory Y. Management by objectives is to replace management by control. External control will be replaced by '*self-control and self-direction*'.

Thinkpoint 2.1

Think about the good and bad teachers, lecturers or managers that you have encountered. How do you think your own behaviour was influenced by the assumptions they seemed to have about your ability and motives?

What motivates managers? (McClelland and Burnham) A striking feature of studies of motivation is that they are typically addressed to those who would motivate others. As an exception to this, in the 1970s David McClelland and David Burnham published an article in *Harvard Business Review* called 'Power is the great motivator' that focused directly on manager's motivation. Drawing on studies of managers in the United States they contrasted three possible sets of motives – the need for achievement, the need for power, and the need to be liked. They argued that the 'need for achievement' had typically been assumed to be the measure of business success, for example, with successful entrepreneurs. Their innovation was to question whether such a need for achievement was related to good management, particularly in large complex organizations. They argued that, in practice, a high need for achievement may encourage an individual to focus on personal improvement, and encourage them to do things themselves. The need to achieve might typically also be associated with a need for concrete short-term feedback. Against this they argued that, in large complex organizations, the key requirement is to manage others to perform, and this will often mean a lack of immediate and personal feedback for the manager. Here they suggested that the 'need for power' might be more important and appropriate than the 'need for achievement'.

They decided that perhaps the best index of a manager's effectiveness would be the climate he or she creates around themselves and that this would be reflected in the morale of subordinates. It was this that they then measured. Their version of a good manager was as follows (McClelland, 2003, p. 109):

> a good manager is one who, among other things, helps subordinates feel strong and responsible, rewards them properly for good performance, and sees that things are organized so that subordinates feel they know what they should be doing. Above all, managers should foster among subordinates a strong sense of team-spirit, of pride in working as part of a team.

Through their surveys they found that some 70 per cent of managers had a higher than average need for power, suggesting that the need for power is important in managers. They also found a strong correlation between the strength of a manager's need for power and good team morale. But the results also contained a surprise, for the main driver of high morale turned out to be not whether a manager's need for power was higher than their need to achieve, but whether it was higher than their need to be liked. This latter group they termed 'affiliative managers', whose strongest need was to be liked. This, they argued, would result in a kind of weakness that would make exceptions out of sentiment or the desire to be thought well of by a particular subordinate. The result would be a team-wide perception of unfairness that led to low morale. This thought about the impact of perceived fairness on motivation has been further developed in Adams '**equity theory**', and more recently by Greenberg's work on '**procedural justice**'.

Maslow's early ideas about a hierarchy of needs and the way in which these were then taken up by McGregor define at least two key axes along which motivation can be understood – the nature of human needs and, as importantly, a manager's assumptions about the needs of those they manage. McClelland and Burnham's studies were an interesting addition, for in Maslow's terms, they suggest that a manager's love and status needs may well get in the way of effectiveness. Manager's should need power but in a mature and non-egocentric way if they are to manage well.

Exercise 2.2

Consider the following question: In your experience of teachers, lecturers and managers can you think of instances where it seemed as if their own needs to be liked, or for power or for achievement, helped or hindered their work?

In the next section we will explore another, slightly different approach to motivation; one that gives primary importance to the work itself as a source of motivation. We will begin by looking at the very influential ideas of Frederick Herzberg.

Motivation: What satisfies is different from what causes dissatisfaction (Frederick Herzberg) Herzberg made the useful observation that it is often the manager rather than the employee who is motivated. Managers want to get people to do things – in this sense they are motivated – but the means they use, he suggests, often serve only to produce movement rather than motivation in employees. His own views on motivation emerged as result of his asking this question to a wide variety of people in different jobs: 'what job events had occurred in their work that had led to extreme satisfaction or extreme dissatisfaction on their part?' Answers typically suggested that the factors that cause dissatisfaction are almost entirely different from those that cause satisfaction. His conclusion was that job satisfaction and dissatisfaction involve different feelings and are not polar opposites. As he puts it (Herzberg, 2003, p.p. 55–56): 'The opposite of job satisfaction is not job dissatisfaction but, rather, *no* job satisfaction: and similarly, the opposite of job dissatisfaction is not job satisfaction, but *no* job dissatisfaction.'

Herzberg argued that two different needs of human beings are involved here. One set of needs can be thought about as stemming from human's animal nature – the built-in drive to avoid pain from the environment, plus all the learned drives that become conditioned to the basic biological needs. The other set of needs relates to what he argued was a unique human characteristic – 'the ability to achieve and, through achievement, to experience psychological growth'.

SOURCE: © (2006) UNITED FEATURE SYNDICATE, INC. REPRODUCED BY PERMISSION.

Image 2.3

The growth or 'motivator factors', he argued, were intrinsic to the job. They are achievement, recognition, the work itself, responsibility and growth or advancement. The dissatisfaction–avoidance or what he termed 'hygiene factors' are extrinsic to the job and include company policy and administration, supervision, interpersonal relationships, working conditions, salary, status and security. 'Motivators are the primary cause of satisfaction, and hygiene factors the primary cause of unhappiness on the job' (Herzberg, 2003, p. 57).

On the basis of his studies Herzberg was scornful of many of the personnel practices that were the outgrowth of the Hawthorne experiments and the human relations movement. Things like sensitivity training, employee participation and counselling. The primary implication of his work was that the focus of motivational effort should be on work itself and the way it could be 'enriched' to bring about the more effective utilization of personnel.

Rather than pursue Herzberg's ideas on job enrichment we will look at some slightly later work of Hackman, who, in collaboration with Oldham, tried to discover what creates what they called 'intrinsic' motivation, and what job characteristics are associated with such motivation.

Motivation: It is the design of jobs that can make a difference (Hackman) A lot of the problems of motivation fall away when someone is well matched to the job they are doing. In such circumstances working hard and performing well happens simply because it is rewarding and satisfying. Hackman and Oldham (1980) talk about this happy congruence of person and job as 'internal motivation', and suggest that this depends upon three key conditions:

1. The work should be experienced as 'meaningful' – as something that matters to the person.
2. Work must involve the experience of 'responsibility' for the results.
3. A person must have 'knowledge of the results' of their work. Without this kind of feedback a person will have no basis upon which to feel good or bad about what they are doing.

Problems of motivation arise when one or more of these 'critical psychological states' is missing. While the three psychological states are internal to the person, Hackman and Oldham suggest that they are related to five key job characteristics.

In order to experience work as *meaningful*, three job characteristics are necessary:

1. '*Skill variety*'. A job needs to involve a variety of different activities drawing upon a variety of skills.
2. '*Task identity*'. A job needs to involve completion of a whole or complete piece of work with a visible outcome.
3. '*Task significance*'. A job and its output needs to make a difference to others either inside or beyond the organization.

In order to encourage feelings of *responsibility* for what one does, a job needs to involve substantial freedom, autonomy and discretion in how it is carried out. Only with this will there be a sense that outcomes are the result of one's own efforts and therefore something for which one has personal responsibility.

Box 2.1: Comment

The ideas of Maslow, McGregor, McClelland, Herzberg and Hackman that we have looked at so far, when taken together sketch the three main dimensions around which motivation has and continues to be thought about; (a) the person and their needs, (b) the manager's needs and beliefs and (c) the characteristics of the job itself. Together they bring us a long way from Taylor's view of scientific management. The employee is not merely a body but a human with 'social' needs. Taylor's scientific view turns out to a set of assumptions he was making about others and these assumptions were part of the motivational problem. They assumed the need for close control and monitoring without seeing how this thwarted human needs. The fragmentation of jobs that he then promoted in the name of efficiency in effect robbed work of any 'intrinsic' motivation.

Finally, in order to have *knowledge of the results* of what one does a person needs feedback. Such feedback they suggest needs to come directly from the work, rather than indirectly through one's boss.

In contrast to Maslow's focus on needs, Hackman and Oldham conclude that: 'motivation at work may actually have more to do with how tasks are designed and managed than with the personal dispositions of the people who do them'.

The theories that we have looked at so far are often referred to as 'content' theories; they offer a concrete view of what motivates – needs, behaviour, and different aspects of work and the organization of work. Such theories are then contrasted with what are called 'process' theories that explore motivation as the outcome of experience and the sense made of experience. We will begin with the ideas of Vroom, who in the 1970s developed what he called an expectancy theory of motivation.

Motivation: It is a person's expectations that count (Victor Vroom) One of the problems of Maslow's theory of needs is that motivation seems to be the product of needs that are largely given as part of 'human nature' and that for the most part are largely unconscious. This is a convenient myth for managers for it denies that what people do – the level of effort that they put into their work – is in part the *product of their experiences at work* and the sense that they have made of these. The employee is not just a need-driven entity but rather a self-conscious person making sense of their experiences and adjusting their effort in the light of earlier experience. It is here that Victor Vroom, writing in the early 1970s, made an important contribution to conventional theories of motivation with what became known as 'expectancy theory'.

In line with earlier behaviourist theories, Vroom assumes that humans are motivated to maximize pleasure and minimize pain, but humans are capable of choice, and such choices will depend upon their perceptions and the beliefs and attitudes that are formed from these. 'Valence', 'instrumentality' and 'expectancy' were the terms that Vroom selected to identify three sets of belief involved in deciding to commit effort to a course of action.

Valence refers to largely emotional orientations people have in relation to particular outcomes. These can be both positive (I want these) and negative (I'm keen to avoid these.) It is also possible to be indifferent to some outcomes. What was significant about Vroom's formulation was to suggest that in relation to work it is people's *expectations* rather than actual outcomes that matter. For example, the effort you make at any moment will be driven by what you expect to get out of your course, rather than its actual outcomes. So valence is about the expected levels of satisfaction and/or dissatisfaction that employees expect to flow from their efforts.

The second term – instrumentality – explores the factors that shape the expectations or valence for an employee. Something is instrumental if it is believed to lead to something else. So you may expect that reading this text will allow you to write a good essay and get a good degree, which in turn may mean that you can get the job you really want. However, the relation between effort and outcome is not certain, or rather we will have different expectations, born of experience, of the certainty or otherwise with which outcomes will follow from effort. For example, your past experience may lead you to believe that there is a strong positive relationship between your essay writing efforts and the feedback and results that you get. This will create a positive valence. On the other hand, your experience may have been negative or frustrating and leave you feeling that it was not worth the effort, or that those who make no effort are also rewarded by high marks. How have your own efforts on your course been changed by the sense you have made of your experiences so far?

The third belief involved in Vroom's model he termed expectancy, and he writes of this as the 'action–outcome' association in a person's mind. Several things might shape your expectations about the outcome of your essay writing. Do you think that you have the ability to do the course? Will your lecturers give you the help you need? Will the library have the right books?

It is the combination of beliefs about valence, instrumentalities and expectancies that results in a certain level and pattern of motivation. Motivation and the performance that flows from this is the product of *choice*; choice shaped by expectations born of past experiences.

One implication of Vroom's ideas is that, like it or not, managers and the jobs they design, and the decisions and systems that they put in place, are shaping employees' expectations and choices as to whether it is worth the effort, or at least how much effort to make for what. The second implication is that the employee is not a 'need' driven entity but rather a self-conscious person capable of autonomous choice. Behaviour is shaped not just by needs but by 'cognitions'; by an active process of sense making.

Motivation: A new competitive imperative In the late 1970s and early 1980s a new urgency was given to the topic of employee motivation by the emergence of Japan as a major competitor in the world economy. Many of the subsequent studies of the Japanese employment system, often by Western academics or consultants, were used to hold up a less than flattering mirror to the West's own

CASE STUDY 2.2 A problem (of motivation) at PYT plc (2)

Peter's management training course was a real eye-opener to him. He had never thought much about human needs or management styles. What he knew about managing came from what he'd learnt working for his old boss, Mr Thomas. But the course had made him think about this experience a bit differently. For some reason Peter had always got on well with Mr Thomas; he encouraged Peter even when things were not going so well and it was Mr Thomas who had encouraged Peter to put in for his first promotion. But with the rest of the staff Mr Thomas was often very strict; and some of his colleagues used to call Peter the 'teacher's pet' as a result. Mr Thomas regularly listened in to sales calls and told people where they were going wrong. You had to ask permission if you wanted to leave your desk, and apart from at breaks, talking to colleagues was discouraged. At the end of each day he would check on who had sold what to whom and, if people had failed to meet their targets, it was not unusual for him to shout at them in front of the whole office.

Thinking about this on the course, Peter began to wonder whether this was good management. He had been particularly impressed by the ideas about 'theory X' and 'theory Y', and that being a manager should really be about creating opportunities for people to grow. His own time at PYT had allowed him to grow a lot and become a supervisor and now office manager. It was clear enough that profits were important but he liked the idea that he was also able to help people develop and grow. That way there was no 'us' and 'them'.

Question

Drawing on all the ideas presented above, what suggestions could you give Peter for improving staff motivation at PYT? What might he need to do to implement theory Y in relation to both staff and managers? What other factors would he need to consider to improve motivation?

Box 2.2: 'From Control to Commitment in the Workplace'

Richard Walton's 1985 *Harvard Business Review* article announced a 'significant change' that was under way throughout US industry in approaches to organization and the management of work. Comparing two plants, Walton argued that the differences could be traced to two 'radically different strategies' for managing the workforce; a strategy based on 'imposing control' and a strategy based on 'eliciting commitment'. The traditional 'control' strategy involved a rigid division of labour and individual accountability that assumed low levels of staff skill and motivation. Managers in control mode were organized in a hierarchy of specialist roles with clear status demarcation. Labour was treated as no more than a variable cost, and assumed to have an inevitably adversarial relationship to controlling managers. Walton argued that at the heart of this traditional model was the 'wish to establish order, exercise control and achieve efficiency in the application of the workforce'(Walton, 1985, p. 78). However this wish, Walton argued, was now threatened both by changing worker expectations and the inability of this strategy to meet the 'standards of excellence' set by world-class competitors. Market success, he suggested, required a superior level of performance that needed 'the deep commitment, not merely the obedience – if you could obtain it – of workers', and it is in the context of this need that the new strategies of eliciting commitment began to emerge. Unions and managers began talking of common interests and the need for mutual trust, layers of hierarchy were stripped out and overt status differentials reduced. Responsibility for integration and quality were being pushed back down to the shop floor. Jobs were being redesigned to be broader and more flexible and included responsibility for continuous improvement. Accountability was shifted from the 'individual' to the 'team' with an acknowledgement of the 'heightened importance of group achievement, the expanded scope of individual contribution, and the growing concern for such questions of "equity" as gain sharing, stock ownership and profit sharing'. To help elicit commitment from the workforce companies were giving employees some assurance of security with retraining, and consultation. Unlike the old control strategy with its exclusive focus on the rights of shareholders, management now acknowledged the 'legitimate claims' of a company's multiple stakeholders – owners, employees, customers and the public.

management and motivational practices. The contrast was perhaps sharpest at the level of production workers in Japan. Here a system of company unions and associated security for core employees apparently allowed for much greater flexibility and responsibility among employees and was enabling the Japanese to achieve both high-quality and low-cost production. That other systems could be both more profitable and encourage greater employee motivation was alarming.

The result in the West has been two decades in which human resource strategies have come to be seen as central to business recovery, and old motivational certainties have been augmented by a growing emphasis upon the team, on creating commitment and on encouraging high performance. The high-performance team it is argued is now a competitive necessity. While Walton announces an American corporate revolution, in practice there is a great deal of continuity between current human resource management and the earlier theories of motivation that we have already looked at. In this way current motivation theory both builds upon the past as well as adding new points of emphasis and focus. Some aspects of these – the focus on groups and teams, and on organizational culture – will be covered in other chapters. Here we will look at the emphasis that is now placed on autonomy and self-management and the ways that the manager can support these.

In one sense, Walton's recognition of the counter-productive consequences of control marks the triumph of motivation theory over management. What starts with a concern to find ways that managers can control employees' motivation ends with the grudging recognition that people manage themselves, and that, at best, managers can seek to create the conditions under which employees will commit their energies to the organization. But in another way, recognizing and coming to understand the reality of 'self-management' has also opened up new avenues for management influence.

Self-motivation: It is the ideals we have for the self that motivate (Harry Levinson) One clear statement of the reality of self-motivation came from a psychoanalyst and management writer, Harry Levinson, who in a *Harvard Business Review* article in the 1970s – 'Management by Whose Objectives' – suggests that we need to begin with an understanding of a person's own objectives since managers' objectives will have no incentive effect if they are unrelated to a person's own dreams and wishes. These he talks about as an 'ego-ideal' (Levinson, 2003, p. 111):

> If a person's most powerful driving force is comprised of needs, wishes, and personal aspirations, combined with the compelling wish to look good in her own eyes for meeting those deeply held personal goals, then management by objectives should begin with her objectives. . . . Each of us has a built-in road map, a picture of his or her future best self. Psychologists speak of this as an ego-ideal, which is comprised of a person's values, the expectations parents and others have held out for competences and skills, and favourite ways of behaving. An ego-ideal is essentially the way an individual thinks he or she ought to be.

Some of the focus on leadership, on corporate vision and values, and on culture management (see Chapters 7 and 9) can be understood as attempts to shape such ideals.

Self-motivation is shaped by a person's sense of 'self-efficacy' (Albert Bandura) Another aspect of the self that has become the object of attention is a person's belief about how effective they are. As part of his 'social cognitive theory', Albert Bandura suggests that a person's sense of their own efficacy is one of the most important and pervasive influences on how they act. Some people, he suggests, do not even try to do something because they simply doubt that they have what it takes to succeed. Conversely, others have a strong belief in their capacity to succeed even in the face of setbacks and obstacles.

Such beliefs about self-efficacy will have a pervasive effect on what a person aspires to do and how to approach almost any aspect of work in an organization, including a person's resilience to stress. Bandura suggests that we cannot influence our own motivation and actions very well if we do not keep track of our thought patterns and performance, what is happening around us and the effects we are having. Self-observation of behaviour is part of the solution, as are various forms of goal-setting and emotional 'self-regulation'. Although such beliefs will most probably have been shaped early in life, Bandura suggests a number of strategies that can be pursued to develop and strengthen a 'resilient' sense of self-efficacy. As regards perceptions of self-efficacy, he says (Bandura, 2000, p. 121):

> People of high efficacy focus on the opportunities worth pursuing, and view obstacles as surmountable. Through ingenuity and perseverance they figure out ways of exercising some control even in environments of limited opportunities and many constraints. Those beset with self-doubts dwell on impediments which they view as obstacles over which they can exert little control, and easily convince themselves of the futility of effort. They achieve limited success even in environments that provide many opportunities.

Exercise 2.3

Think about your own sense of 'self-efficacy'. Is it 'high' or 'low'? How might this be shaping what you do, along with what you try to do? With these ideas, how might you try to strengthen your sense of how effective you can be? How might others help in this?

As a resource for thinking about motivation, Bandura's ideas focus not on an assumed set of needs that we possess by virtue of being human, but rather on the very ways in which we have come to think about ourselves. In terms of the development of motivation theory, this involves a step change – a new focus of knowledge on thought processes within the person.

Self-motivation: It is the goals set for the self (Locke and Latham) This theory, which the authors claim has been tested on over 40 000 people in many countries, suggests that the most simple and direct explanation of why some individuals perform much better than others lies in the fact that they have different performance goals. The theory builds on four broad propositions:

1. Difficult goals lead to higher performance than easy goals, or no goals, or abstract injunctions like 'do your best'.
2. The higher the goal the higher the performance.
3. Praise, feedback or participation in decision making makes a difference to what people do only in so far as it increases commitment to a difficult goal.
4. In addition to affecting choice, effort and the persistence of effort, goal-setting can also increase the effort people make to discover ways of meeting a goal.

Latham and Locke argue that, in addition, a goal must be challenging and specific. Their idea is that as well as serving as *targets* to attain, goals are 'the standards by which one judges one's adequacy or success'. There is a competitive element here so that part of the pleasure of setting high goals is that they are higher than other people's goals. Moreover, high goals are accompanied by expectations that achievement will bring feelings of self-efficacy, as well as recognition by one's peers, along with the more tangible benefits of salary increases and promotion.

Latham argues that 'the management of oneself lies at the core of goal setting theory' and that 'without commitment goal-setting is meaningless'. In other words goal-setting is something that we should do in order to motivate ourselves. But managers can support this self-management. Feedback is important because measurement signals what is actually valued in an organization rather than what is claimed to be valued. Relatedly coaching aimed at improving performance through increasing a person's sense of self-efficacy can be most effective. Managers should set *'SMART' goals* – that is, goals should be specific, measurable, attainable, relevant and have a clear time frame. The manager's own expectations of employees can also be important in shaping the goals they set themselves.

Self-motivation involves empowerment (Thomas and Velthouse) While empowerment is often presented as a management initiative, Thomas and Velthouse (1990) argue that empowerment should be understood in terms of four different cognitions related to a person's sense of meaning, competence, choice and impact. Meaning is about my assessment of the value of a task in relation to my own ideals and standards. Competence relates to my beliefs about my own capability (self-efficacy). Choice refers to my beliefs as to whether I can direct my own actions, and Impact to my sense of being able to 'make a difference'. Conger (2000) later suggests that understanding empowerment requires understanding the psychology of power and control. Power must be understood as 'an intrinsic need for self-determination along with a belief in self-efficacy'. But if employees have such a need for self-determination, management can effect this in a variety of ways.

- *Factors that undermine empowerment cognitions.* A rigid and impersonal hierarchy may limit a person's sense of being able to exercise initiative, or exercise real responsibility. Authoritarian styles of management can deny any sense of self-determination. Rewards may be allocated in a way that is perceived as unfair or unresponsive to competence or creativity. Similarly, as we have seen, jobs that have little meaning or challenge, or where there is overload or conflict, readily produce a sense of powerlessness.
- *Factors that encourage empowerment cognitions.* Organizational policies and cultures that emphasize self-determination, collaboration over competition, and high performance standards and open communication systems help create the conditions for empowerment. Leadership or supervision that sets high expectations while expressing confidence, allows autonomy, and sets inspirational or at least meaningful goals, also contributes to empowerment. Jobs with high variety, relevance, autonomy and control as well as good advancement prospects empower, as does rewarding innovative and creative performance.

Self-motivation: Selective recognition by managers helps (Luthans) Along with a focus on how management can create the conditions for empowerment cognitions, the other focus in the 1990s has been on the effect of recognition on performance. Some of this takes us back to our initial focus on the impact of pay on performance. The 1980s and 1990s saw a renewed interest in pay as a way to influence performance, and both attract and retain employees. Along with traditional practices, many advocated new forms of profit sharing and share ownership schemes for employees at all levels as an inducement for better performance. Interest in such traditional forms of recognition were accompanied by a new awareness of the power of 'social recognition'. Luthans and Stajkovic (2000), for example, argue (at p. 167) that: 'If social recognition is provided on a contingent basis in managing employee behaviour it can be a powerful motivator of employee behaviour'. Such a use of 'contingent recognition' by management, they suggest, both shapes expectations of future reward as well as offering a signal of belonging. It also has a direct regulatory effect.

> Based on the recognition received and, thus, the perceived prediction of desired consequences to come, people will self-regulate their future behaviours by forethought. By using forethought, employees may plan courses of action for the near future, anticipate the likely consequences of their future actions, and set performance goals for themselves. Thus people first anticipate certain outcomes based on recognition received, and then through forethought, they initiate and guide their actions in an anticipatory fashion. *(Luthans and Stajkovic, 2000, p. 170)*

By using recognition selectively managers can influence how staff will manage themselves. Self-management it seems does not mark the end of managers' attempts to control staff after all. Rather, a clearer understanding of the self – the ideals, and standards by which we judge ourselves, our beliefs about our own competence, and the value, meaning and effects of what we do – offers both a new object for our own self-observation and self-management, and new opportunities for managers to influence the very ways in which we exercise our autonomy.

SOURCE: © (2006) UNITED FEATURE SYNDICATE, INC. REPRODUCED BY PERMISSION.

Image 2.4

Contribution and limitations of the mainstream theories of motivation

We began this review of mainstream theories of motivation with the work of Frederick Taylor, his development of a 'scientific' view of management, and, within this, his assumption that money in the form of piece rates would be enough to motivate Schmidt, the pig-iron shoveller. In the subsequent century of work on motivation our understanding has come a long way.

We saw how the humanist views of Maslow challenged the patronizing views of Taylor, insisting that managers recognize a much broader range of needs, beyond money, in their employees. McGregor took this a step further by suggesting, with his distinction between theory X and Y managers, that the laziness Taylor imagined to be a part of Schmidt, may have been no more than a reflection of Taylor's own negative assumptions and the way that these informed his treatment of Schmidt. Herzberg's and Hackman's work then challenged Taylor's views on the separation of mental from manual labour, and the efficiency of an intense division of labour, by insisting that it was the nature of jobs, rather than human needs that was the key to motivation. Schmidt was not stupid or lazy, but bored out of his head by the mindless, fragmented work that he was asked to do. To be meaningful and motivating jobs need to allow one to use a variety of skills, to deal with complete tasks rather than fragments, and allow one to feel that what one does is important to others and the success of the organization.

But these early attempts to uncover the universal truths, or 'content', of what motivates – individual needs, the task, the managers' assumptions and conduct – were themselves challenged by ideas that insisted that motivation is a dynamic 'process'. Schmidt had perhaps learnt through long experience to expect little beyond money from his work. He was not, as Taylor imagined, just a body to be trained, or even a bundle of needs, but a self-conscious person who acted on the basis of the sense he made of his experiences.

Now if the employee is a self-conscious, thinking being, just like the manager, then suddenly motivation theorists realized that motivation could never be what a manager *does* to an employee. People motivate themselves, and the most that managers can do is to create an enabling

CASE STUDY 2.3 A problem (of motivation) at PYT plc (3)

Val had worked as a sales representative at PYT for a couple of years when she was promoted to a vacant post on John's team of sales executives. She was a bit worried about this move; she wasn't sure she could handle the larger clients, and John had the reputation of being fiercely ambitious and felt much less approachable than her present boss Mel. Her fears were quickly confirmed. She was having some problems with her partner outside work and she began to slip behind on her sales targets for her first campaign. John said he would give her some training and spent one Friday morning listening in to her calls. But the training in practice involved John telling her all the things she was doing wrong. She tried to explain to him that it was just a bad patch she was going through. She even hinted at the troubles she was having outside work but John ignored this. By the end of the morning she was feeling awful about herself and finally burst into tears and rushed out of the office. She went to the doctor and was off sick for the next week. When Mel, her old team leader, heard about what had happened she was furious with John for what she saw as the way he had undermined Val. He, however, insisted that she was simply 'no good' and 'not up to it' and would have to leave or take a demotion. When Val returned fearfully the next week, John took her into an office and told her that she had the choice either to leave the company or go back to her old job on Mel's team. Val was shattered. It was Mel who later came and found her in the toilets, took her out to lunch, and tried to persuade her to give it a go with her old job. 'Never mind what John said, I know that you're a great sales person and I want you on my team.' Val went back to work for Mel, but it was weeks before she began to regain her confidence.

Question

How do theories of self-motivation in relation to ideals, self-efficacy, targets, empowerment and selective recognition help understand Val's contrasting experiences of being managed at PYT? What does her experience suggest about the problems of these new forms of self-motivation?

environment for this. Under the pressure of growing international competition since the 1970s this has led to an explosion of interest, and study, of all the different dimensions of self-motivation. In part this depends on the ideals we have of what we should seek to become, the beliefs we have acquired about how effective we can be, and the goals we set for ourselves. The role of managers in relation to self-motivation involves them thinking about whether the environment they create is empowering for staff, and whether they create opportunities for achievement, as well as offer staff recognition.

So after this century-long journey of 'discovery' about motivation have we reached the promised land of healthy, productive and satisfied employees? What does your own experience tell you? Is this the sense you have of your own experiences of working, or those of your friends or parents?

Many of the studies we have described were sincerely motivated by a concern to address what the writers felt was the waste of human potential at work, but the interest their work aroused was perhaps less noble in its intentions. Who was investing in developing our understanding of motivation, and why? On the one hand, managers like to think well of themselves and how they treat their staff. But, on the other hand, they know that their own success will depend on their ability to get as much as they can from staff. So although thinking about motivation seems to have moved way beyond Taylor, in another way it still shares his *instrumental* interest in efficiency. Other people are still seen as a means to an end. Managers' interests lie in about making full use – exploiting – other people; their job and future career as a manager depends on this. We might also ask why it has taken a century for theory to discover that employees are people like us. Do we really need social scientific studies to discover what should be obvious from our own experience of families and friendship. And why is it still so easy in the course of our work to find discontent and unacceptable conduct?

The unspoken story in all these studies of motivation is about power. The desire to fully use others' power in the service of our careers and the organization, and all the resources – research and training – that are put into this. The power that allowed Taylor to treat Schmidt like a mindless machine, and kept Schmidt working despite this. The power that makes the use of motivation theory a sort of optional extra for managers; something that they can embrace but also ignore if they choose to do so.

Superficially, the recognition of the damaging impact of imposed control, and the apparent recognition of employee autonomy suggests that, in theory at least, motivating managers have given up using their power in this way – they merely empower and enable. But as we shall explore in what follows, the more recent attention to the autonomous self – its ideals, self-beliefs and aspirations – can be seen as an even more intense, intrusive and effective form of power in the service, not of the employee, but of corporate profit.

Box 2.3: James Wolfensohn – President of the World Bank

'I personally feel that the world is out of balance. The way the world is dealing with problems of poverty and peace seem to be disconnected. Military spending is now probably US$1000 billion and spending on subsidies or tariffs to protect the developed world farmers is about US$300 billion. Meanwhile the rich countries offer no more than US$50–60 billion in aid to developing countries while blocking most of their agricultural exports – one of the few ways these countries could pull themselves out of poverty.'

'The three things are linked. There are 5 billion people in the developing world, 3 billion earning under US$2 a day, and 1.2 billion earning under US$1 a day. If you can't give them hope, which comes from getting a job or doing something productive, giving them their self respect, these people become the basis upon which terrorists or renegades or advocacy groups can flourish. Its an essentially unstable situation.'

'If you cannot deal with the question of hope or economic security there is no way that with military expenditure you can have peace . . . if you do nothing about poverty and development you're not going to have stability.'

Source: The *Australian*, 4 February 2004.

Critical perspectives on motivation and the self

Overview

While many of the studies that we have looked at in the first part of this chapter were very critical of current management practice, what they all share is a hope or a belief that the 'problem' of motivation can be solved through the development and application of knowledge; i.e. a better understanding of human needs, the redesign of work and more appropriate management behaviour. Critical views of motivation theory challenge the adequacy of these mainstream approaches on two very different but related bases. In the first – views shaped by Marx's analysis of the structures of capitalism – we return to the role that economic interests have in shaping conduct at work. While mainstream theory emphasizes the unitary nature of interests in organizations, for Marx, capitalism involves an essential *conflict of interests* between ownership (and its agents) and those who must sell their labour in order to live. Acknowledging this fundamental conflict of interests arguably offers a more historically accurate account of how management have been able either simply to ignore employee interests, or alternatively have (selectively) recognized them only in order to maximize profits. Either way, it points to management's instrumental interests in motivation; their interest is not in making work more satisfying for employees but in getting more out of them. It also suggests that much motivation theory can be seen as an 'ideology' that justifies hierarchy and inequality and presents the sectional interests of owners and their agents as if they were universal and shared. A real change in motivational practice would require a different structure of ownership and the power relations that this creates.

The second critical account of motivation draws upon ideas about the 'social construction' of the 'self', as well as the work of Michel Foucault and those who have been influenced by his analysis of what he calls the operation of 'disciplinary power'. As we have seen, over time mainstream motivation theory has come to emphasize the motivational importance of individual autonomy and self-management and used this to suggest that the exercise of management control has often been counter-productive and should be replaced by strategies of empowerment that promote employee commitment. Here power and individual autonomy are treated as opposites, as indeed they often are in classic Marxist accounts. But in this final section of the chapter we want to explore how power comes to shape the very ideals that we set for the exercise of individual autonomy. Our knowledge of the 'self' is socially produced, and as a result is never under my autonomous control. Motivation here is seen to be animated by the desire to fix and secure the very sense we have of ourselves as this is reflected in the attitudes of others' towards us. Many of the new motivational strategies involved in contemporary 'human resource management' can be seen to rely upon and play with these aspects of the ego.

Marxist analyses

'Men make history, but not under conditions of their own choosing.' *(Karl Marx)*

The profound creativity of human action Typically when we first join an organization it already exists – it has a history, buildings, rules that govern its operation, established procedures and systems. From this perspective it is as if our actions and thoughts and motives have nothing at all to do with the nature of the organization in which we work; the purposes of the organization and our purposes can be thought about in isolation from each other. Take university, for example. It is easy to see it simply as the context in which you can pursue your own individual goals of getting a degree, having a good time, etc. This sharp separation between subjective reality and the organization as an objective reality can encourage us to have a very limited view of work and the effects of what we do. It can lead us to ignore or deny the profoundly creative aspect of what we and others do.

For Marx, what distinguishes humans from other animals is that we do not have a biologically fixed or instinctually predetermined relationship either with ourselves or with the world. There is, therefore, neither a fixed human nature to which we might refer, or seek to discover, in order to understand human motivation; nor is there a fixed structure of external determinants of human responses. Instead, human nature is itself only shaped and reshaped through work and the consciousness that arises through such work. Work or labour then becomes a central explanatory concept – it is not to be understood as an aspect of a person's life alongside leisure, family, sport and so on, but rather as an historical process through which we humans create and recreate ourselves and our world. Moreover, work organizations cannot be understood in isolation from the social and political relationships in which they are embedded. Nor can the present social or organizational reality be treated as if it is somehow 'natural' and not itself the product of historical forces and itself subject to change and further development.

The process of production Let's take a closer look at what is involved in action / work / labour. Work can be thought of as a relationship between us and the world, or as our way of relating to the world. It involves a moment of **conception** in which we draw upon all our existing tacit knowledge and understanding to conceive of what we will do. For the most part we act habitually, doing what we have always done through drawing upon the skills and knowledge that we have accumulated in the course of our lives. Look at an infant or a child and it is immediately obvious how much and how long it takes each of us to acquire even the most basic of skills.

The second moment involved in work is one of **externalization**. we combine our accumulated knowledge, skills and thought with materials to hand and produce something – this can be an idea, work, picture or other kind of object.

Finally what has been created becomes part of the external world – **objectification** – and is available for both ourselves and others, and for future generations.

While all labour involves such processes of conception, externalization and objectification, there are two further potentials – reification and alienation – that are important for our understanding of human motivation (see Box 2.5).

When you go to the library to find books to write an essay what is your sense of your relationship to these? Are they oppressive, non-human 'truths' that you must wade through simply to get your essay written. Here work, and its means of production – books and articles – are felt to have no relationship to you and your own thoughts and experience. Instead these objects dominate and oppress you. Alternatively, are the books merely the objectification of other people's thoughts – thoughts that were shaped by their own history and interests and reflections – upon which you can then draw in shaping your own thoughts and opinions. Here, writing becomes a creative relationship between yourself and the objective world through which both you and the world are developed and changed.

The contradictions of capitalism and alienation The story that Marx tells of human history is a story about the relationship between an evolving 'means of production' – the accumulating knowledge, skills

Box 2.4: Tacit knowledge

Tacit knowledge is a set of skills and ways of understanding that is so familiar that we take it for granted as what we know of how things are, and can only with difficulty explain or describe it. A good example is riding a bicycle. Like so many of the skills upon which we depend, riding a bicycle is something that we learnt, possibly with some difficulty. It took time and effort to coordinate our legs working on the pedals with steering. We fell off a few times before we learnt the basic skill and then refined it. We also had to learn the rules of the road so that we stop and give way at the right places, and ride on the correct side of the road and are not a danger to ourselves and others. But today we just get on a bike and cycle and do not even have to think about what we are doing deliberately. Despite our obvious 'practical' skill, however, when we try to teach someone else to cycle we are hard pressed to find the words that explain it. It's obvious, taken for granted.

Box 2.5: Reification and alienation

Reification: to treat something as if it has an independent existence of its own, rather than as the product of human thought or work.

Alienation: a reversal of the relationship between the producer and their product such that what is humanly produced comes to dominate the producer.

and artefacts through which we manage our relationship to nature – and the forms of social relationships or 'relations of production' that come into existence around any particular set of productive relations. Although he offered a broad historical sketch of these relationship starting with tribal society, then the ancient societies of Greece and Rome, and then an agrarian based 'feudal' society, Marx's key concern was with the emergence and dynamic of productive and social relationships under capitalism.

For Marx there is a contradiction at the very heart of capitalism. On the one hand the move from feudal to capitalist society involved a massive positive development in the means of production and, in this process, the emergent merchant class played a progressive role. In part this was achieved, as Adam Smith described, through an intensification of the division of labour, such that traditional craft skills were broken down into specialized tasks that could be carried out by a number of workers. But the success of the market also stimulated technological innovation and the huge increase in productive capability that industrialization allowed. In principle, such positive developments in the means of production should have been associated with the progressive liberation of humans from need. For Marx, however, the experience of work under capitalism turned into the exact opposite. Marx analysed these paradoxical effects of capitalism in terms of four forms of 'alienation'; four ways in which under capitalism what is humanly produced comes to impoverish the human producer.

ALIENATION FROM THE PRODUCT Under feudalism, although the worker would have had to give a proportion of what was produced to his lord, he was in other respects his own proprietor who was free to produce according to his own immediate needs and those of his family. Under capitalism this relationship to the land as a means of production is broken and, instead, increasing numbers of workers become entirely dependent upon the sale of their own labour on the market. Their labour becomes just like any other commodity, and what they produce is no longer determined by what they or others need but by monetary exchange driven by the search for profit and the accumulation of capital. For Marx, the key 'class' division emerges between those who must sell their labour in order to live and those who, by virtue of owning the means of production, are able to expropriate not only the surplus produced through their own efforts but also the surplus produced by others. This conflict of interest at the very heart of capitalism is expressed in the different meaning of wages; for the employee they are their only means of living, for the owner they are a cost to be minimized. The more the worker produces the cheaper labour becomes.

ALIENATION FROM THE PROCESS OF PRODUCTION Work does not allow the worker 'to develop freely his mental and physical energies'. Work can no longer be experienced as an end in itself but rather is just a means to ends that are external to work. Marx took as evidence of this the fact that 'as soon as there is no physical or other compulsion, men flee from labour like the plague'.

ALIENATION FROM OTHERS For Marx the 'individual' of economic theory was a peculiar invention of capitalist society. The person is fundamentally social and it is impossible to conceive of the person as somehow apart and distinct from the society and culture out of which he or she emerges. Yet under capitalism relationships between people come to be dominated by the logic of the market. Colleagues become rivals for jobs and for wages, as means or obstacles to one's own success. Others are seen solely through the calculative lens of profit or advantage.

ALIENATION FROM THE SELF Finally, and in a sense as an accumulation of these effects, Marx talked of capitalism as involving the alienation of both the worker and owner from themselves, from their own social nature. While an individual is always the product of the society in which he or she is born,

Box 2.6: The 'isolated individual'

'The "isolated individual" is a fiction of utilitarian theory; no human being exists who has not been born into and thus shaped by an ongoing society. Each individual is thus the recipient of the accumulated culture of the generations which have preceded him, and in his own interaction with the natural and social world in which he lives, is a contributor to the further modification of that world as experienced by other.' 'Individual life and species life are not different things;' Marx asserts. 'Though man is a unique individual he is equally the whole, the ideal whole, the subjective existence of society as thought and experienced' (Giddens, 1971, p. 13).

under capitalism awareness of this relationship is reversed and the social is subordinated to the pursuit of individual goals. We begin to treat the self and others like a market commodity.

It is important to point out that the alienation that is being talked of here is not from some ideal natural man; there is no such thing. Alienation arises instead from the contradiction between the socialized nature of production and the privatized ownership of the means of production under capitalism, which itself sets up a tension between the productive possibilities of capitalism and the experiences of those who produce within it. The solution, however, also lies within capitalism, for Marx believed that by bringing people together in large numbers – in cities and factories – there would be the potential for these contradictions themselves to be overthrown. To date, at least capitalism has proved remarkably adaptable.

Core assumptions of the Marxist perspective

- Man is a social animal rather than a self-seeking 'individual'.
- Production for exchange rather than use is a feature of capitalism rather than a universal of economic activity.
- Under capitalism, production is motivated not by the meeting of human needs but by the pursuit of profit and the accumulation of capital.
- The self-seeking opportunism that is the grounding assumption about the nature of human beings in neo-classical economics is better understood as historically specific to capitalism.
- There are different interests for different groups in organizations that are shaped not by 'individual' needs but by class position – whether one is an owner, or must rather sell one's labour in order to live.

If the interests of labour and owners (and their agents, management) are fundamentally opposed, then this suggests two things as regards motivation. First, it suggests that the problem of motivation is built into capitalist organizations. This explains why motivation has become a 'holy grail' of

CASE STUDY 2.4 A problem (of motivation) at PYT plc (4)

Emily had worked at PYT for the past eight months. She'd worked in a shop before that, but had not liked the weekend working. At least here her weekends were her own. She had got married last year and her and her husband, Robin, spent most weekends doing up the house they'd bought.

She enjoyed the training course that PYT sent her on when she first arrived and she'd been amazed to discover that the techniques they had taught her really worked. The trick seemed to be to get people talking after you'd told them that you were just phoning to check their entry in the directory. The 'open' questions she'd been taught to use – Where exactly is your shop? Have you been there long? What sort of area is it? – really did seem to get people talking and then she'd change to closed questions – Would you like a quarter or half page? Shall I go ahead and book that for you? – to try and make the sale. She was surprised how many people went along with what she suggested.

Sometimes she felt a bit guilty with the small businesses – she wasn't sure they needed to spend that much – but then, as they'd taught her, advertising is important if you want to grow your business. She liked working on Ruth's team and when she'd made her first sales Ruth had shouted it out and everybody clapped. The thing she still felt most uncomfortable about was some of the other people in the office. They were a bit posh and were always talking about the designer clothes they'd bought, the restaurants they'd been to and the expensive holidays they were going on. She and Robin barely had enough to live on, what with the new house. Emily had started taking a Selfridge's bag with her when she went shopping. She couldn't afford to shop there but at least they wouldn't know that she had to buy her clothes at cheaper stores. But Emily saw PYT as a place where she might be able to make something of herself. If she worked hard and was successful then perhaps she could get to be a manager in a year or so.

Question

Can you find examples of Marx's four versions of alienation in Emily's attitude to herself, her work and her co-workers?

management writers that has been pursued for over a century. Secondly, it suggests that the problem will never be solved within capitalism and so the managerial quest for performance and satisfaction will be endless, in part because it wants to solve the problem without addressing its root cause, which lies in the exploitation made possible by private ownership.

Rethinking motivation: Efficient and rational for whom?

MOTIVATION THEORY AS IDEOLOGY In whose interests are theories of motivation developed and whose interests do they serve? Marx argued that at any moment in history the dominant class would typically disseminate ideas that serve to legitimize its own position of dominance. He talked of this as 'ideology' – presenting the interests of a particular group as if they were universal interests. Take Maslow's ideas of a hierarchy of needs. How might the idea of a hierarchy of needs serve to justify and legitimize the current structures of hierarchy and power in an organization? Now it is clear that Maslow and McGregor were critical of the way organizations fail to meet human needs, but as their ideas have been popularized by management texts, these critical aspects of their ideas are typically edited out. Instead their ideas are read as if they offer a 'natural' justification for hierarchy. It is tempting to simply assume that those doing lower level, or menial work in an organization are somehow at a lower level of development, preoccupied with lower level needs, while those at the top have 'grown' and are (rightly) rewarded with the opportunity for 'self-actualization'.

MOTIVATION AND ECONOMIC INEQUALITY While knowledge of motivation might be said to have developed over the years, it is still up to management, rather than the employee, particularly at lower levels of an organization, as to whether these ideas are taken seriously. Motivation is in this sense an optional extra for management – they can always fall back on the force implicit in the employment contract to get people to do what is required. The fear of unemployment is all the motivation that most people need. The theories have not led management to address or change the structures of power in which they work. It is for managers to introduce empowerment – employee power on managers'

Image 2.5

CASE STUDY 2.5 A problem (of motivation) at PYT plc (5)

As Damian Rawls, the Sales Director, had feared, PYT was continuing to haemorrhage customers and Peter was becoming increasingly alarmed at the prospect of the office missing its half-year profit target. Damian was on the phone to him every week now to ask about how the office was doing and had just told Peter that he was going to visit the office next week to take a closer look at operations. Peter immediately called his section leaders, Mel, John and Ruth, into his office.

Perhaps Peter did not know how thin his office walls were, but staff heard him shouting at them: 'I don't care if the staff are under huge pressure, we've just got to meet these targets'.

Question

Are profits all that matter? If we need a job in order to live then why should managers give another thought to our motivation?

terms – rather than acknowledge a real dependence upon employees. All this means that a concern for motivation can be applied selectively and strategically. If you need a high level of commitment and loyalty, or if you fear the power of a union or a political shift of power towards the interests of labour, then perhaps we should invest in winning hearts and minds, or treat certain groups of employees very carefully. However, if unemployment is high and replacements easy to find, if the costs of motivation exceed the likely benefits, then there is no need to weigh employee needs against the interest in profit. The rhetoric changes but not the power structures.

THE POWER OF DIVIDING One final criticism of conventional theories emerges from a consideration of Marx's views on alienation. For Marx the contradictions of capitalism were likely to be removed by its own internal dynamics. As an unintended consequence of capitalist production, the organization of work would bring large groups of employees together in factories and offices, and as citizens. Given the conflict of interest around production between wages and profits he believed that people would begin to see their true interests. While as an 'individual' I might be weak relative to my employer, as a member of a trade union or a political party I could be powerful. While conventional theories of motivation acknowledge the 'social' needs for belonging, affection and recognition, these do not extend to the collective needs for concerted resistance or political action. But they also point to the political significance of what has been termed 'individualized' attention. By focusing on the 'individual' employee, by emphasizing the hierarchical differences between individuals, by keeping them absorbed with their careers and promotion prospects, a whole set of forces are set up that avoid or preclude collective action.

Important empirical studies

LABOUR AND MONOPOLY CAPITAL (HARRY BRAVERMAN) Braverman's reinterpretation of Taylor's scientific management in the 1970s draws its inspiration from Marx's analysis of the dynamics of capitalism. What Taylor suggested was the product of the application of scientific methods to the study and organization of work is seen by Braverman in terms of the logic of capitalism that sets the pursuit of profit on a collision course with the human importance of meaningful work. What Taylor offered as a rational separation of mental and manual work is seen by Braverman as a process of de-skilling, driven by concerns to reduce costs, intensify work effort and reduce the potential for worker resistance.

Braverman's starting point is the 19th century craftsman; the coherence, knowledge and skill embodied in craft work, and the relatively autonomous organization of craft labour within craft unions. The scientific application of seemingly neutral rationality to such work by proponents of scientific management can be seen to be driven by the logic of profit rather than a universally beneficial efficiency. The separation of mental and manual labour is from this point of view an act of theft in which management captures the skills and knowledge of skilled labour and on this basis is able to de-skill and fragment jobs, and in the process extract more output for less cost. Coherent jobs with their own intrinsic satisfactions are broken down into relatively meaningless fragments and these fragmented tasks can then be performed by unskilled labour that is both much cheaper and more easily replaced than the skilled craftsman.

Braverman's work was important because its focus on the labour process was an important antidote to the rather abstract and idealized images of employment coming from management writers. The early introduction of new computer-controlled technologies in the 1970s where skilled work was recorded on computer tape pointed to the continuing relevance of his critique of Taylor. Braverman's (1974) book inspired a host of critical studies of work but was itself criticized for its rather passive portrayal of the worker and the degradation of work under the relentlessly unfolding logic of capitalism. Workers are portrayed as the victims of strengthened management control.

MANUFACTURING CONSENT (BURAWOY) One of the difficulties Marxist accounts of work face is to explain why, given the conflict of interest between profit and wages, there is so little resistance on the part of organized labour to its own exploitation. Explaining this seeming paradox was the task that Michael Burawoy set himself in his 1979 study, *Manufacturing Consent*. Where Braverman explains work intensification in terms of increased management control achieved through the separation of conception from execution, Burawoy suggests that work intensification has been achieved through a management strategy of worker 'self-organization'.

What his empirical study observed was workers' enthusiastic participation in worker-led games of 'making out'; attempts by a host of means to maximize bonus payments. Playing such games,

Burawoy suggests, creates a sense of personal autonomy and choice, it relieves the boredom and drudgery of work and gives people a sense of accomplishment. While such games are played in the spirit of an assertion of autonomy against management, by playing the game people inadvertently come to accept the rules of the game; a logic of capital in which labour is systematically disadvantaged. The pleasures and apparent freedoms of the game ensure greater productivity. Importantly, Burawoy's study observes how the bonus system games, and the defence of wage differentials between different groups of workers, have the effect of separating people off from one another and encouraging workers to see work in the same instrumental terms as they themselves are viewed by management. The game gives us a sense of being in control, of being able to use the company rather than just being used, but the result is that we work ourselves hard.

Power and the 'self'

Marxist analyses focus on how ownership gives some the power to exploit others through creating economic insecurity. The second set of ideas that we will explore suggest that modern motivation techniques play not just on economic insecurity but a person's insecurity about the value of the self. These ideas involve questioning the very notion of 'individual' autonomy and raise the possibility that power works not to constrain this autonomy from the outside but instead by shaping our very notion of what it is to be an individual. It is here that notions of economic power associated with the private ownership of property can be seen to be intimately linked with personal concerns with self-identity and security. To begin to introduce these ideas we will in what follows look a little more closely at how a person's sense of self is developed and maintained, and then see how this becomes a key lever for motivating both ourselves and others at work.

The formation of the 'self' In everyday language we often talk about the self as if it were a something that we have. We treat the self as if it were the psychological equivalent of our bodies; something that is relatively fixed, stable and independent from the world. Although the self is unique to us, here it is being thought about as if it were indeed a 'something' – an object. Here we will look at some ideas about how such a sense of a solid self emerges.

How far back can you remember? Usually people have no memories that they can easily bring to mind much before the ages of three or four. Even then the memories are fragmented – a particular scene or taste or event – always laced with the doubt that it might be something that others have talked about rather than an actual memory. So why is there this critical gap in our memory and what does this mean for our understanding of what it is to be or have a 'self? Does it mean that early experiences are simply unimportant? This seems unlikely and here we will pursue an alternative explanation; that we are not born with a developed sense of self but instead 'self-consciousness' is the product of early experiences and development.

One of the most influential early accounts of this process comes from an American pragmatist, George Herbert Mead. In his book, written in the 1930s, called *Mind, Self and Society*, he drew a distinction between three aspects of the self – the 'I', the 'me' and what he termed the 'generalized other'. Mead suggested that we are not born with a developed sense of self but merely the potential for such 'self' consciousness.

Finding my self in the mirror of others' responses Mead argued that I come to my first sense of self, not through defining my own experience for myself but, instead, through 'taking over' the attitudes of 'significant' others towards me. So I can think of myself surrounded by parents, grandparents and siblings and finding my first sense of self as if in the mirror of how these people responded to me. But language can be deceptive here for this is the very foundation of these differentiations of the self as 'I', 'me', 'my', 'others'. Mead argues that I become aware of the self first as a 'me', as an object to/for others, and indeed as a child acquires language s/he typically refers to the self initially in the third person – as 'me'. My sense of self as an active agent, as an author or subject, as 'I', only comes after I have begun to organize a sense of 'me' as the 'object' I am for others. Mead talked about the relation between the 'me' and the 'I' in terms of *'the "I" of this moment becoming the "me" of the next'*. As an 'I' the self has to be understood as a continuous, active but endless process of becoming. As lived the self is in a 'constant transition from a now thus to a new now thus'. But I can also reflect on this active process of being and experiencing, and in doing so come to define the self as this or that, 'me' or 'not me'. What is important to note is that I cannot ever quite capture the self in reflection; I can never reduce the self to the status of a known object. Instead the mind is constantly moving very rapidly between engagement with the world, and reflection on this engagement.

The self as a synthesis of images Mead's account of the formation of the self allows us to differentiate between the active, engaged and reflexive moments of selfhood. But in his description of my first sense of self being acquired through 'taking over' the attitudes of others towards me he also allows us to see the social nature of the self, and thereby come to understand some of the difficulties of achieving and maintaining a sense of autonomous 'self-identity'. My identity is a set of ideas as to what defines me uniquely as a human being, but Mead's analysis suggests that this definition of self is always socially constructed.

'Taking over' has a rather mechanical tone to it but, in practice, this involves my coming to understand who I am through making sense of others' responses to me. In reality this can mean that our initial sense of self is in many ways more about others around us than it is about the self. As a child it is too easy for us to ascribe the other's response as being to do with who we are rather than what is happening to them. For example, a mother who is depressed can leave a child feeling as if they do not quite exist and a parent who is angry can leave a child feeling that they are bad. Alternatively, the very different needs, aspirations and expectations of parents can simply make it difficult for the child to synthesize into a coherent unity all the different experiences they have with their 'significant others'. Ideally, of course, the parents will have the psychological maturity and space to respond accurately, and with love to the child's own initiative and this then founds a strong positive sense of the goodness of the self as a resource for future life. What should be emphasized here, however, is that our initial sense of self as 'me', is made up of my *synthesis* of others' responses to me – it is this synthesis that actually constitutes or creates my founding sense of 'me'. These processes go hand in hand with the acquisition of language as a ready-made set of differentiations between self and other, past and present, me and not me.

Learning what the self must be (to be loved) Even in the most loving of environments, part of what the parents will be concerned to do is to introduce the child to the 'norms' or standards of behaviour of the wider society in which the child must eventually take their place. While initially some physical constraints may be placed upon the child, with the entry of the child into language and the formation of an early sense of self, then it becomes increasingly possible for the behaviour of the child to be influenced *symbolically* by the parents. The response of 'significant others' to the child is in part shaped by their sense not only of who the child is but of what the child must be. Here praise ('what a good girl, well done') as well as criticism ('don't do that, that's very naughty') as well as straight bribery ('if you do that then you can . . .') are all used to try to direct the child's conduct towards desired ends. So the sense of self that we acquire from others contains not just a sense of who we are, but also a sense of what we must be in order to be liked, loved, recognized or belong. Such is our dependence that, again, our very existence seems to depend upon our being able to be what the other wishes us to be (or at least what we imagine we must be to win their recognition and love).

Image 2.6 Acquiring a (guilty) conscience

Acquiring a (guilty) conscience Psychologists talk of two related processes that together further differentiate the psychological structure of the early ego – the formation of an 'ego ideal' and a 'superego'. Part of what is involved in 'taking over' the attitudes of others is what Freud calls 'identification'; the internalization of some aspects of another as a part of the self. The ego ideal involves the internalization of some idealized aspect of the parent, which then serves as an internal standard against which the self is measured. It has a double aspect. On the one hand, it is an ideal of what we can be or should be like. It is akin to the borrowing of another's power – a sense of what one also might become. But any ideal is also necessarily a description of what we are not, and depending on the gap between the self and ideal self it can become an internalized voice that constantly berates and criticizes the self for being less than perfect – for our inadequacy, incompetence and insignificance. Freud referred to this 'critical agency' as a 'superego' that turns its frustration and anger not out towards others, but back upon the self for being bad, inadequate or not good enough.

What has happened then is that an external relationship with a very powerful other – a parental figure – has been internalized as a relationship between two aspects of the self; what we are and what we must be (to be loved). Such internalized ideals can be motivating. Think of those inspiring figures – teachers, parents, heroes – who have become models of what you would like to be like. But it is important to remember that ideals can never be fulfilled. The self is always in the process of becoming and will never become a perfect 'something' whose value is established unambiguously once and for all. But the *pursuit* of such perfection is another thing, and perhaps precisely because the self is 'open' there is a strong desire to know, fix and secure the self.

Securing the self at work How then do these ideas about the formation of our early sense of self-consciousness help us to understand adult human motivation more fully, and in particular how power, self-identity and insecurity become linked? Although the force of our early experiences with others makes these founding experiences of the self highly consequential for how we think about ourselves for the rest of our lives, it would be wrong to imagine that once formed, our self actually becomes independent of others. If we have a good start in life then this gives us a certain basic security or confidence that allows us to more easily withstand negative experiences, but because the idea we have of the self or 'self-concept' is a 'synthetic' object, our sense of who or what we are (of 'me' in Mead's terms) is always vulnerable to the responses of others. We are all typically prone to treat the responses of others as if they were a mirror in which we see ourselves.

When we talk about 'self-identity' we are talking about the creation and maintenance of a certain synthesis of experiences; a sense of the continuity over time of our experience of being a self and of the coherence of our own and others 'objectifications' of the self. As a fundamental aspect of my knowledge of the world, my sense of self is obviously among my most precious possessions. But what if this knowledge is 'reified' – that is, treated not as an always partial and selective definition of me as 'this' or 'that', but rather as the 'whole' and 'objective' truth of who I am? This makes protecting my identity seem like a matter of life or death. I am therefore prone to be constantly comparing myself with others (am I better or worse than them) and alert to how they see me (do they like, admire, respect me, are they insulting me?). It is this vulnerability of the 'self' that is central to modern motivation techniques. In the mirror of the other's response I look both for confirmation/recognition and feel myself to be exposed to possible rejection or attack.

Exercise 2.4

I once visited a factory in the north-west of England. It was a plastics factory and the operators each worked at the end of a large moulding machine, pressing and abstracting mouldings for car bumpers. The factory was staffed largely by Asian immigrants but managed by white English managers. I was shown round the factory by a white manager, and we had a conversation about the production process across an employee as if he was not there. Later I went to talk to this man who turned out to be a university educated schoolteacher who had come abroad and found factory work only because he could find no work as a teacher at home in Bangladesh. What do you think it was like for him to be ignored in the way that he was by the manager? How do you think this may have fitted with his earlier experiences at university? Over time what effect do you think being ignored, overlooked and disregarded would have on his sense of himself?

That each of us is self-conscious, with a sense of our uniqueness and capacity for autonomous action, means that we are both aware and typically resistant to others' attempts to control us overtly. At least in the management literature, if not in practice, part of the history of ideas about motivation that we have traced is a grudging but dawning recognition that the exercise of control is often likely to have negative motivational consequences. As we saw earlier, Walton argues that controlling managers are likely to produce not discipline but adversarial employment relation. I am another person not an object to be used merely for management's purposes, and if I feel myself being manipulated in that way I am likely to resist. Management's seeming recognition in recent years of individual autonomy looks promising, as if enlightened managers have given up control and are now wise enough to simply try to encourage individual commitment.

Here management power and employee autonomy seem to be at odds. But in what follows I want to argue the exact opposite; that power works precisely, and much more efficiently, through shaping the exercise of individual autonomy. It does this in part through coming to shape the very ideals in terms of which I come to judge my own and others' actions. And as Luthans observed, selective recognition by managers is a very powerful way to influence this self-management. To develop this alternative view of power we will briefly look at some of the ideas of Michel Foucault, in particular his analysis of what he called 'disciplinary power'.

The power of being made visible and knowing it In his book *Discipline and Punish*, Foucault (1979) notes a shift in the late 18th century from what he calls a 'sovereign' view of power to what he terms 'disciplinary' power. We often locate power elsewhere with the 'powerful' – the boss, chief executive, prime minister, Queen – but Foucault argues that this idea merely conceals how, in fact, we practise power upon the self and upon each other. He offers a prison design by Jeremy Bentham, the 19th century utilitarian, as a model for this new form of the exercise of power. Cells in the prison were organized around a central tower, in which, behind blinds, a guard could watch over the prisoners. The key question to ask is what is the effect of the blinds?

On a railway station in central London a printed sign with a symbol of an eye tells me that I am being filmed by security cameras. As I drive back home later in the day, road signs tell me that there are speed cameras in operation. Again the question is why, if they want to catch me speeding or committing crimes, do they tell me in advance that I am being watched? Or closer to home perhaps, what is the effect of knowing that, at the end of the academic year, you are going to have to sit an exam?

It is because knowing that one is being watched, that what we do is visible, but not being able to know at any moment in time quite who is watching, changes our behaviour. Foucault suggests that in effect we can do away with the guards, at least for some of the time, since each of us prisoners will over time come to internalize the power relationship and will effectively watch over our own conduct, and those of others. As he puts it, we will 'simultaneously play both roles'. Foucault argues that a whole host of contemporary social technologies have similar effects. These technologies work through making us knowable and visible in certain ways, and through classifying, comparing, homogenizing, hierarchizing and excluding have the effect of both 'individualizing' and 'normalizing' people.

Let's explore what such processes might mean in the context of work and motivation. When Maslow and others began writing of basic human needs for belonging, for love and status, and recognition, they were exhorting managers to recognize employees as other human selves rather than just anonymous labour. Their intentions were no doubt humane, but given the 'synthetic' nature of the self and its vulnerability to others' responses, such *recognition* then becomes a powerful lever on conduct.

- At its simplest the adult relationship between boss and employee can have echoes of earlier power relationships; the boss can become the ideal around which I model myself, a person whom I want to please, for whom I want to be special.
- The hierarchy itself can also serve as a mirror of the value of the self. I can feel a failure when I compare myself to others higher up the hierarchy, and more successful compared to those 'lower' down. I can see promotion as an opportunity to 'make something of myself', and see my colleagues as competitors for such promotion.
- Through performance figures and accounting information the 'results' of my work are made visible to me and others. Praise and criticism, and the occasional dismissal or promotion, advertise what kind of employee I must be if I want to keep my job, if I want to be a success.
- In anticipation of desired recognition and feared blame I supervise my own conduct. Company standards over time become the lens through which I judge and supervise myself. I set myself targets and goals, I criticize my own performance and identify the strengths I need to build on and the weaknesses I need to work on.

SOURCE: © ISTOCKPHOTO.COM/CHRIS SCHMIDT

Image 2.7 The power of being made visible

- I come to view my 'self' as a project – as my own bit of capital, to be developed, marketed, packaged and sold.
- As Foucault puts it, I become 'the principal of my own subjection'.

Key studies

Reframing human resource management (Barbara Townley) Barbara Townley has drawn extensively on Foucault's writing to offer a very different view of human resource management. Her work picks up on a recurrent theme in this chapter – the indeterminacy or incompleteness of the employment contract – and offers a very different view of the history we have traced. One way to read this history is as a gradual and progressive 'uncovering' or 'discovering' of the truth of motivation – a cumulative knowledge of individuals and their responses to different kinds of job and management. We can see this knowledge as an objective, even scientific, fact that any 'rational' manager should be keen to use. But Townley questions this view of knowing; what if it is not so much an uncovering of some essential truths about the 'self' but rather a way of producing the 'individual' at a particular point in history.

Following Foucault she argues that ways of knowing are also always a form of power relationship. The progressive study of motivation is both stimulated by the desire to render the person controllable, and the knowledge that is produced then has important power effects in the way that it becomes embodied in techniques and practices of organizing the workforce. Part of human resource management involves what she calls 'dividing practices'; work is separated from home, and jobs are ranked in terms of skills, responsibility, experience, seniority and function. Similarly, the individual comes to be categorized in increasingly elaborate ways, as we have seen, in terms of needs, expectations, skills, attitudes, goals and ideals. This knowledge then becomes embedded in ways of *examining* the person in processes of selection, training and development, appraisal, feedback and surveys. It also becomes embedded in ways of talking and getting employees to talk about the self in mentoring and coaching, appraisal and development. The accumulation of knowledge about motivation in this way can be seen, over time, as providing a way of distinguishing 'myself' from others, as well as shaping the norms through which I will judge and appraise myself and others. In the context of work at least it becomes the very means through which we think about the self.

'Someone to watch over me' (Wilkinson and Sewell) Graham Sewell and Barry Wilkinson (1992) drew on Foucault's ideas in a study of shop floor work at a UK engineering firm they called Kays. They suggested that the new physical layout of the shop floor and use of electronic data associated with the introduction of total quality management and just-in-time stock control had greatly increased the visibility of shop floor work and greatly decreased the opportunity for workers to exercise discretion. The quality of what was produced could be traced to particular individuals, and was then reinforced by the public display of quality and productivity information that advertised both desired standards and individual deviations from this. All this was backed up with an emphasis on teams who were given responsibility for achieving targets and continuous improvement. Following Foucault, they suggested that workers were much more effectively controlled under the new production systems. Increased visibility, the knowledge that every aspect of work was being monitored and the likelihood that any failure would bring public humiliation to an individual were enough to ensure that individual employees managed themselves in line with management expectations.

Happy families at Hephaestus (Catherine Casey) Casey's (1999) study of culture change in a transnational company she calls Hephaestus adds a psychological dimension to our understanding of quite how effective new forms of management control can be. Casey suggests that employees typically embraced the values of a happy family that management advertised; they believed the story that management told them. In this way the values of the organization came to act as an ideal that informed individual conduct and the way that they judged themselves and others.

Her argument is that modern management techniques work in part through encouraging such identification with ideals. Whereas in former times employee aggression would be channelled outwards towards management, now she suggests it is channelled back on the self for failing to live up to the ideal of a competent, caring and committed employee. The problem at Hephaestus was that the organization was not quite like the ideal it claimed to be. Repeatedly, members of the family were 'killed off', and the emphasis on being a good team member also involved team attacks on those who had let them down, and rivalry for the recognition of the team leader. The results for employees were considerable levels of individual stress caused by concerns about their own competence, and confused and ambivalent feelings about the official rhetoric of their being all part of one big happy family. For the most part, however, people went along with the official story, and challenged and criticized themselves and colleagues rather than management, for the hypocrisy of saying one thing and doing something different.

Contributions and limitations of critical approaches

The principal contribution of the approaches informed by Marx's analysis of the dynamics of capitalism is to draw attention yet again to the inequalities of power relations at work and how these inform management's selective interest in theories of motivation. While many of the mainstream writers were informed by concerns to improve the human condition, their ideas arguably gained currency because it was hoped that they could help managers to bridge the gap between employing labour and turning that into effective labour power. Capitalist organizations had managed quite well without theories of motivation, and, like John at PYT, managers can still rely on the fact that people need a job as a powerful force for motivation. Changing political, educational and economic conditions have altered the nature of work and employee expectations such that brute force and coercion are less possible, and their negative effects more obviously counter-productive, but employees' calculation of self-interest still goes a long way in ensuring that, as individuals, they will be compliant with what is asked of them. Particularly at lower levels of organizations it is still easy to find all the abuses of economic power; low wages, poor working conditions, and coercive and arbitrary management practices.

But if economic exploitation is a reality then, as we have seen, this creates a puzzle as to quite why those who are disadvantaged by a system are so willing to cooperate in their own exploitation. Some of this, as Burawoy argued, can be seen as the unintended side effects of their own attempts at 'making out', but it is here that ideas about the social construction of the self and in particular Foucault's ideas are particularly helpful. If theories of motivation in the end become the very means through which we come to understand, think and judge ourselves, and if motivation involves self-management, a preoccupation with making something of ourselves, a competitive orientation to others, and a tendency to view failure as a failure of the self rather than the product of economic forces over which we have no control, then the aggression that Marx hoped might be turned outwards against the institutions of private ownership is instead turned inwards against the self.

But these later views of power also disturb some of the reassurance that comes from a view of the world where the worker is cast as the victim of external forces and relatively powerless, at least as an individual, to make a difference. Foucault's analysis of the 'micro-physics of power' robs us of the

SOURCE: © GETTY IMAGES/SIQUI SANCHEZ

Image 2.8 Exploitation: a thing of the past?

illusion of being victims, or of the hope that if only we can rid ourselves of the 'bad' other – bosses, owners, lazy workers – then all will be well. We practise power upon ourselves and each other – manager and worker are in this sense both subjects – and it is much more difficult to even conceive of resistance if the effects of power are to be discovered in the very ways in which we think about ourselves.

This section began with a quote from James Wolfensohn, the President of the World Bank, talking about global poverty and inequality. What the motivational emphasis upon individual autonomy and self-discipline ensures, perhaps, is that we are simply too preoccupied with ourselves to notice or feel part of such global processes, let alone to figure out the role that our own conduct has in both reproducing the problem and creating the solution.

Chapter summary and conclusions

This chapter began with the ideas of Frederick Taylor and his principles of scientific management. Motivation here was about money and the potential for the interests of management in profit, and workers in higher wages, to be reconciled through a division of mental and manual labour. Such ideas stand in sharp contrast to the earliest ideas that we have explored in this chapter; those of Marx, and his suggestion that there is a fundamental contradiction at the heart of capitalism. We produce together, but then some people, by virtue of being owners, can exploit those who have only their labour to sell. The owners' interest in maximizing profits is always at odds with the employees' interests in maximizing their earnings. Economic power gives owners and managers a powerful lever to dictate the terms on which others work – in this sense economic insecurity is all the motivation that many need. But then there is a huge difference between dull conformity under pressure of coercion and enthusiastic participation. The challenge for management has been to find ways in which they can turn labour into committed employees. It is not enough for employees just to turn up; what is wanted is their commitment and energy and the effort that goes with this.

Marx's ideas, and the associated fears of industrial conflict and political change, haunt the subsequent study of motivation. For the mainstream theories that we considered there was and continues to be a problem of motivation, but for these writers the problem is assumed to be solvable within capitalism if only they can understand the individual more thoroughly. The early content theories that we considered were those of Maslow, McGregor, McClelland, Herzberg and Hackman. Each focuses on a different dimension as the explanation of motivation. For Maslow, motivation was to be achieved through a better understanding of human needs and the integration of this understanding into the organization of work. Maslow suggests a hierarchy of needs from physiological, through safety and belonging, to status and recognition, and finally self-actualization. McGregor, drawing

CASE STUDY 2.6 A problem (of motivation) at PYT plc (6)

PYT ceased to operate as a company when its contract to manage the directory was not renewed. One of the factors involved in the decision not to renew the contract was the discovery of certain financial irregularities by PYT auditors in the previous year. The new incentive structure for sales people – under which they were to be paid commission only on net new business – had a fatal flaw. Staff in one office realized that if a single record card was removed from the office of the support staff all records of net customer losses attributable to an individual sales person were lost, and their commission earnings were thereby greatly inflated. The scam was only discovered after eight months, by which time it had spread to a number of offices and cost nearly US$1 million. In this case, then, the highly incentivized pursuit of self-interest had an unanticipated yet disastrous effect on the common interest in the future of the business.

Question

Is there such a thing as a common interest in work organizations? How could we arrive at a shared definition of such a common interest?

upon Maslow, suggests that the behaviour associated with theory X is easily discovered in work organizations but is to be explained not in terms of some truth about workers – they are lazy, will refuse responsibility, etc. – but rather in terms of the assumptions management make about workers and the effects of these assumptions on workers. The problem of motivation is in the manager not the employee. McClelland develops this thought further with his exploration of managers' motivation – their needs for achievement, power and to be liked. His finding was that the need for power is the best predictor of good management in terms of the climate such managers create among staff – as long as they have their own ego needs under control.

But then Herzberg enters with a different story. The focus on management–employee relations misses the point. The key drivers of motivation are intrinsic to the job a person does; the work itself and the opportunities it offers for achievement, recognition and responsibility, all of which allow individuals to grow psychologically. These factors produce positive satisfaction, and should not be confused with the factors that cause dissatisfaction, which include supervision, salary and security. Removing sources of dissatisfaction will not produce satisfaction but rather an absence of dissatisfaction. Hackman and Lawler pursued this thought that it is the work itself that matters with their assertion that 'internal motivation' depends upon work being meaningful, involving the experience of responsibility, and where there is knowledge of the results. These motivations in turn imply the need for jobs to have skill variety, task identity and significance structured into them.

The second mainstream set of theories that we explored are often termed 'process theories'. In their earliest form – Vroom's expectancy theory – it was argued that motivation is the product of valence (what I want and do not want), instrumentality (my expectations of what leads to desired outcomes) and expectancy (my expectations about how what I want and how to achieve it are related). Importantly, the employee is rediscovered here as an intelligent person, making sense of their experiences and then acting on the basis of the expectations that these experiences have created.

These process views were further developed in the 1980s and 1990s under the weight of renewed competitive pressure to solve the problem of motivation through a recognition of individuals' capacities for self-motivation. Reluctantly, it seems that managers have finally learnt the lessons of earlier studies. Management cannot control staff – pull their strings like puppets or rely on coercion. This will at best only produce dull compliance if not outright opposition. People need to motivate themselves and the manager's task is to create the conditions that support this. We looked at Levinson's argument that it is a person's own ego-ideal – what they aspire to achieve – that motivates. Locke and Latham relatedly argued for the importance of stretching goals for motivation; ideally these are goals that we set for ourselves and to which we are committed. Bandura, as a social psychologist, takes us further into the mysteries of self-motivation with his ideas about the importance of our own 'self-efficacy'. Past experience will have shaped a set of beliefs we have about what we can do and its likely success, and these will shape what we attempt and how strongly we pursue the goals we set for ourselves. Managers can support such self-motivation by creating empowering conditions that allow people to feel that they can make a difference. Luthans also suggests that ideals, goals and people's views of themselves can be influenced by the selective use of recognition by managers.

Now taken at face value this history of motivation theory suggests a progressive movement towards enlightened management conduct. It begins with Taylor stripping out the mental content of work and insisting that thinking and planning was manager's work, along with close control and monitoring of mindless staff. Then gradually what he had taken away is rediscovered in employees – the range of different needs beyond money, the damaging results of certain management assumptions, the importance of whole and meaningful tasks. Then, with the process theories, the rediscovery of the thinking self-conscious employee, who is as capable of autonomous action as the manager, and who must therefore be encouraged to manage themselves, with management in a supporting and enabling role. The theory is seductive. We would all like to think of ourselves as in control – as able to make a difference. We have all been taught to work upon ourselves, to improve ourselves and make something of ourselves. What could possibly be wrong about that?

For Marx and those influenced by his thought the problem of motivation needs to be understood on a wider canvas. Getting people motivated will always be a problem under capitalism because, although we depend upon each other to produce wealth, private ownership of the means of production allows owners to exploit those who must sell their labour in order to live. Though profits are only made through labour, the interests of owners diverge since labour is a cost to be minimized if profits are to be maximized. Either managers can rely on job insecurity to ensure compliance, or if it is cost-effective, they can invest in winning hearts and minds. But still the contradictions persist.

While Marx looked at the power effects of ownership and focused on economic insecurity, more recent theories have explored how insecurity about the self, and management's power to create insecurity about the value of the self, is used to motivate. The seeming celebration of individual self-management in empowered organizations is here recast as a more subtle and effective form of domination. Power works not through constraining us from the outside but through shaping the way we think about ourselves, the goals we set ourselves and the judgements we make about ourselves. Managers and employees are no different from each other in this respect; both are shaped as subjects by the new forms of organizational control. But while we are encouraged to become and remain pre-occupied with ourselves then all sorts of collective and political opportunities for resistance and change are foreclosed. Inequality and injustice remain but we are now prone to blame ourselves and our colleagues for failure. We are so busy making something of ourselves, so eager to compete with our colleagues for promotion, so keen to have the security of belonging to a happy family, that we cannot even think that things could or should be otherwise.

Motivation theorists set out to discover the secrets of human nature so that more could be got out of it. Others with more humane interests wanted managers to see the employee in more than economic terms but still believed that the interests of managers and workers could be reconciled within capitalism. Others have identified not with the organization and its goals but with those who suffer from being managed. Mainstream theory here reappears as an ideology that masks the conflicts of interest at the heart of capitalism, and in the recent recognition of employee autonomy has simply found a new object for more subtle forms of domination.

Discussion questions

1. How has our understanding of how to motivate ourselves and others developed since Frederick Taylor first introduced his ideas about scientific management more than a century ago?
2. Which of the ideas covered in this chapter did you find particularly helpful in thinking about your own motivation?
3. What are the key differences and similarities between content and process theories of motivation?
4. Can managers motivate or is motivation always self-motivation?
5. In what ways is it impossible to understand motivation without also thinking about how power works on the self and in relationships?
6. Is Marx's concept of alienation still useful in understanding the modern experience of working?
7. Why is personal autonomy so important to motivation? In what ways is the image of the autonomous self always something of an illusion?
8. What are the key lessons that managers should draw from the study of management over the last century and a half?

Further reading

Richard Sennett, *The Corrosion of Character: The Personal Consequences of Work in the New Capitalism*, Norton and Company, London, 1998.

This is a follow-up study to an earlier classic that Richard Sennett and Jonathon Cobb wrote called *The Hidden Injuries of Class*. It is based on interviews with the now grown-up child of first generation immigrants in the United States, and offers a compassionate view of how they make sense of their own experiences of failure and dislocation arising from the globalization of capitalism.

Peter Fusaro and Ross Miller, *What Went Wrong at Enron*, Wiley and Sons, London, 2002.

This is a very readable account of the recent collapse of Enron. It offers a description of the fatal consequences of economic incentives for senior executives, and the way in which the organizational culture – 'Rank and Yank' – helped to keep employees quiet as the company headed for collapse.

E. Locke (ed.), *'The Blackwell Handbook of Principles of Organizational Behaviour*, Blackwell, Oxford, 2000.

There are a number of good articles in this collection of current thinking about motivation. They are clear and easy to read but completely uncritical.

Tracy Kidder, *The Soul of a New Machine*, Allen Lane, 1982.

This is a great read and an exciting account of the development of a new computer. It is a story that illustrates both the frustrations of large organizations as well as the energies that can develop in a small group committed to a task they all believe in.

References

Bandura, A. (2000) 'Cultivate self-efficacy for personal and organizational effectiveness', in E. Locke (ed.) *The Blackwell Handbook of Principles of Organizational Behaviour*, Oxford: Blackwell.

Braverman, H. (1974) *Labor and Monopoly Capital*, New York: Monthly Review Press.

Burawoy, M. (1979) *Manufacturing Consent*, Chicago: Chicago University Press.

Casey, C. (1999) 'Come join our family: Discipline and integration in corporate organizational culture', *Human Relations*, 52(2):155–178.

Conger, J. (2000) 'Motivate performance through empowerment', in E. Locke (ed.) *The Blackwell Handbook of Principles of Organizational Behaviour*, Oxford: Blackwell.

Foucault, M. (1979) *Discipline and Punish: The Birth of the Prison*, London: Allen Lane.

Giddens, A. (1971) *Capitalism and Modern Social Theory: An Analysis of the Writings of Marx, Durkheim and Weber*, Cambridge: Cambridge University Press.

Hackman, J. R. and Oldham, G. R. (1980) *Work Redesign*, Reading MA: Addison-Wesley.

Herzberg, F. (2003) 'One more time: How do you motivate employees?', *Harvard Business Review on Motivating People*, Boston MA: Harvard Business School Press.

Latham, G. (2000) 'Motivate employee performance through goal-setting', in E. Locke (ed.) *The Blackwell Handbook of Principles of Organizational Behaviour*, Oxford: Blackwell.

Levinson, H. (2003) 'Management by whose objectives?', in *Harvard Business Review on Motivating People*, Boston MA: Harvard Business School Press.

Luthans, F. and Stajkovic, A. (2000) 'Provide recognition for performance improvement', in E. Locke (ed.) *The Blackwell Handbook of Principles of Organizational Behaviour*, Oxford: Blackwell.

McClelland, D. (2003) 'Power is the great motivator', in *Harvard Business Review on Motivating People*, Boston MA: Harvard Business School Press.

McGregor, D. (1989) 'The human side of enterprise', in H. Leavitt, L. Pondy and D. Boje (eds) *Readings in Managerial Psychology*, fourth edition, p.p. 314–324, New York: McGraw-Hill.

Maslow, A. (1989) 'A theory of human motivation', in H. Leavitt, L. Pondy and D. Boje (eds) *Readings in Managerial Psychology*, fourth edition, p.p. 20–35, Chicago: University of Chicago Press.

Mead, G.H. (1934) *Mind, Self and Society*, Chicago: University of Chicago Press.

Sewell, G. and Wilkinson, B. (1992) 'Someone to watch over me: Surveillance, discipline and just-in-time labour process', *Sociology* 26(12):271–289.

Thomas, K. and Velthouse, B. (1990) 'Cognitive elements of empowerment: An interpretative model of intrinsic task motivation', *Academy of Management Review* 15(4):666–681.

Townley, B. (1994) *Reframing Human Resource Management: Power, Ethics and the Subject at Work*, London: Sage.

Vroom, V. H. (1964) *Work and Motivation*, New York: Wiley.

Vroom, V. H. and Deci, E. (1992) *Management and Motivation*, Harmondsworth: Penguin.

Walton, R. (1985) 'From control to commitment in the workplace', *Harvard Business Review*, March–April:77–84.

3 Groups and Teams at Work

Alessia Contu

Key concepts and learning objectives

By the end of this chapter you should understand:

- The traditional and mainstream views of teams at work and why they are important for work organization.
- The main contributions to the subject, and their differences, drawing upon various theoretical contributions and empirical studies.
- Critical perspectives on teamwork, the political issues they highlight in terms of inequalities, identity and resistance, and the opportunities they offer for understanding the difficulties and challenges of organizational life.

Aims of the chapter

This chapter will:

- Explore the meaning of teamwork.
- Explain how and why teamwork is used in organizations.
- Highlight the problems, open questions and limitations of mainstream models of teamwork.
- Indicate the contribution of critical approaches to teamwork.
- Explain and illustrate the implications of power, insecurity, identity and knowledge for understanding teamwork.

Overview and key points

The first part of this chapter introduces mainstream views of teams at work. Referring to a case study of a new media company, it elaborates the assumptions held and the importance attached to the idea that teamwork is good for organizational performance, and that teamwork favours flexibility, motivation and learning. The text makes connections to contemporary ideas about teamwork, as well as referring to past studies that have been significant for our understanding of the ways teams, and their members, behave.

In the second part of the chapter, problems of mainstream thinking are unravelled and addressed by drawing upon the work of radical and critical studies of teamwork to show that:

- The categories we create can become prescriptions and lose their relevance for understanding the challenges and difficulties of organized life.
- Organizational life is complex, ambiguous and embedded in relations of power.
- Teamwork is neither intrinsically good nor new.
- Radical and critical views can enhance democratic debate by questioning taken-for-granted assumptions about teamwork.

Mainstream views of teams at work

Introduction to mainstream thinking on groups and teams

Most people assume the benefits of working in teams and many recognize the importance of belonging to a group, of whatever kind, to get a job done. There are many types of groups, including self-managing teams, task forces, 'hot groups', 'Japanese teams' and so on.

Many management gurus, and also many academics, would without hesitation justify the role of teams in creating and sustaining successful organizations. It is these justifications that are presented and discussed in the first part of this chapter.

Thinkpoint 3.1

Have you ever worked as part of a team in a company or similar organization? What explanation or justification was offered by managers or team members for the organization of workers into teams?

First, however, we need to consider the message presented by advocates of teamwork. The message is clear: 'if the organization is to perform it must be organized as a team' (Drucker, 1992). Others foresee that 'teams will be the primary building blocks of company performance in the organization of the future' (Katzenbach and Smith, 1993, p. 173). Data published for the Department of Trade and Industry in the United Kingdom, which forms part of the Workplace Employment Relations Survey 1998 (WERS – Cully *et al.*, 1998) reports that 65 per cent of workplaces have the majority of their employees working in teams. Other international surveys (see Cohen *et al.*, 1996; Waterson *et al.*, 1999) indicate that managers have acted upon this message. According to one estimate in 2000, 80 per cent of all Fortune 2000 companies had over half of their employees working in teams (Flores and Gray, 2000, cited in Thrift, 2001, p. 420).

The reasons given to justify why teams are important, if not fundamental, for organizational success are diverse. Summarizing the arguments of both popular and academic mainstream literature, we can suggest that teamworking ranks highly on three dimensions that are central for today's organization: flexibility, motivation and learning (see Figure 3.2).

Key problem: What is a team?

Work organizations seem to have discovered the importance of teams. At the same time teams, or group or 'groupings' of various kinds, are everywhere. We support, or play, in sports teams, we have groups of friends, we love or even play in music bands. At university, teaching activities are often accomplished by collaborating – working with others as a unit, rather than individually.

There is a certain confusion associated with groups and teams, given that we often use these words interchangeably and on different occasions and circumstances. What is the difference between 'teams' and 'groups'? In sociology, for example, a group is a social unit that 'sits' between the individual and the collective/institution/organizational. Psychologists suggest that a group is a socio-psychological dimension where each individual satisfies the need of affiliation – i.e. of being part of something bigger than him or herself.

Thinkpoint 3.2

In thinking of the social units you belong to, what would you describe as a group? What as a team? What do you think is the difference between a group and a team?

Perhaps you have a *group* of friends with which you go to the pub regularly and whose company you enjoy very much. You probably would not call this group of friends a team. Yet, you would describe as a *team* the same group when it enters the Monday evening quiz and competes against other teams at the pub. We are calling a 'group' an ensemble of people who share certain interests and passions, or perhaps simply enjoy each other's company. Even if they do not themselves view each other as members of a group, they may well be identified as a group. The quiz team is still a group, because it is still an ensemble of people that arguably share an interest – i.e. participating in a quiz. But they now have a specific purpose, or goal – namely taking part in a quiz, perhaps with the objective of winning it. They have a task that is clear: combine their knowledge to answer the most questions correctly. They must collaborate with each other to answer the questions correctly. So, we seem to have identified key differences in the meaning of the word 'team' and that of 'group'.

Sometimes we are assigned to groups or teams by default as we enter certain institutions, such as university. We do not choose the people, or the time/space of engagement, or the type of engagement. We call these *formal* groups. As a student you might be assigned to a seminar group, or, for your course work, you might be required to complete a team-based project. Perhaps this last example is the one closer to what you might experience in your future working life. In the team-based project, the team is responsible for the delivery of an outcome (presentation, research report), just as at work a team can be responsible for the management and delivery of a project, such as a new product or service. The key point is that the idea of 'team' implies collaboration between 'players' or members to undertake a task.

Management writers consider it very important to be precise and explicit on the difference between work groups and teams. For Katzenbach and Smith (1993) the orientation to the task and clarity of performance goals are the fundamental characteristics for understanding the difference between work groups and teams, which they define in the terms set out in Box 3.1.

Disciplines that have influenced the teaching, training and the implementation and management of teams at work include sociology, psychology and psychoanalysis. Understanding how teams work and the behaviour of teams and their members might be important in your everyday student life as well as for your future career. This is a point that career advisers often emphasize in their presentations to students! Schools and universities are 'invited' by policy makers and governors to train students in teamworking skills (see Flores and Gray, 2000, p. 24), which is both cause and effect of the sheer number of companies employing teams at work in one form or another. So, when being assessed for a job as a trainee, the selectors might well try to discover whether you are a 'team player'. Does your behaviour enable others to contribute to defining and accomplishing a task, or do you either dominate or withdraw?

Image 3.1 Undergraduate outdoor teambuilding events can be used as ice-breakers, and as a way to sensitize students on the importance/relevance of teamwork

Box 3.1: Work groups and teams: Definitions by Katzenbach and Smith (1993)

Work group: a small number of people working in a collaborative style with individual input and accountability. An example can be your seminar group at university.

Team: a small number of interdependent people with complementary skills who are committed to a common purpose, performance goals and approach for which they hold themselves mutually accountable. The team has joint, specific 'collective work-products' such as experiments, reports, products, etc. An example can be your course work based on a team-based project.

The photograph here was taken during a teambuilding event for undergraduate students. Teambuilding is constituted by a series of games and exercises through which the participants learn to become a cohesive team. These games are based on the understanding of the nature of groups, their processes and behaviours, which goes under the name of 'group dynamics'.

It was Kurt Lewin and his colleagues, mainly at the MIT Centre for Group Dynamics, who suggested (building on a series of experiments, an example of which is included on page 131) that a group is a particular psycho-social dimension distinct from the individual one. In other words, a group is more than the sum of the individuals comprising it, an aspect that is signalled by the sense of cohesion of the team. Lewin describes this as the 'we-feeling' or 'belongingness' exhibited by the members, which is what the teambuilding event is designed to create – build a team out of what starts as a mere collection of three to eight individuals. Reynolds (1994, p. 45) proposes a list indicating the 'group processes' one should be aware of, and suggests some questions you can use to investigate and understand the processes of the groups you belong to:

- *Communication*. Who talks to whom, who supports whom? Who seems actively involved? Who does not?
- *Decision making*. How are decisions and choices made? Who is involved in this and in what way?
- *Power and influence*. What seems to be the basis and pattern of power and influence in the group? Does it change over time?
- *Conflict*. How are conflicts of ideas, opinions or interests worked out within the group? Are they resolved and if so how?
- *Ethos*. What does it seem to be like to belong in this group? Are there accepted norms of behaviours? What roles or rules developed?

However, not everything that happens in groups is easily subjected to scrutiny. Psychoanalytic approaches have shown that group processes are not always conscious – i.e. they are not always intentional and guided by a known and linear rationality. In particular, the work of Wilfred Bion has identified the existence of specific 'group phenomena', which are unconscious responses to the group situation characterized by a high emotional content, be that hate, love, fear or anxiety. For Bion (1961), every work group activity, hence also the ones you are involved in, can be obstructed, diverted, and on occasions assisted by these powerful emotional drives that cluster in what he calls the group's 'basic assumptions'. These are instantaneous, inevitable and instinctive ways in which individuals in a group combine and associate unconsciously in specific ways. There are three fundamental basic assumptions:

- *Dependency*. When the group is completely dependent on a leader who is invested with all the powers, just like a god, for providing answers to the anxieties of the group, hence providing security.
- *Expectancy or pairing*. When in the group there are two people (or sub-groups) that focus the attention of everyone. These are invested by the group with the hopes that something great will come – a Messiah – be it a person, idea or utopia, which will solve all the problems/issues/anxieties of the group. It is the hope itself that provides security.
- *Flight/Fight*. When the group transforms the insecurity into a threat from a person or an object that needs to be fought or escaped. It is the action itself that keeps the insecurity at bay.

Non-psychoanalytic approaches, mainly in social psychology, have been the main sources for management theory and managerial practice regarding or involving groups and teams (for example, in training and development). This is because social psychology tends to share the same set of assumptions of mainstream management theory – that is, to enhance control and predictability.

To illustrate some of the insights of social psychology for understanding team behaviour, let's return to the example of the team-based project. As is often the case in this situation, the project report is marked for the team as a whole. Each student is not assessed individually: the mark for each individual is the team mark. A complaint is often made that some people in the team do not 'pull their weight' and a few members end up doing most of the work. In this case the team might be affected by the 'free-riding tendency' (see Albanese and Van Fleet, 1985) – that is, the tendency of some individuals to reduce effort and contribution in a team situation. This phenomenon in social psychology is called 'social loafing' and is mainly said to occur in situations, where, for example:

- The number of participants is very high, making it difficult to assess individual's contributions.
- The interest in the task is low and rewards are unclear or irrelevant.
- There are no systems in place for checking and improving individual's contributions.

This diagnosis also suggests that the free-riding tendency can be effectively managed by limiting the size of the group and by introducing rewards and control systems.

Team-based work (such as the project for your course work) can be an anxiety-provoking and unfair experience. But it may also be exciting for the possibilities it offers – for example, of actually sharing the workload, of creating new interpersonal relationships and learning new things. This excitement, social psychology tells us, can also be frustrated or perhaps taken too far. Groupthink (Janis, 1972, 1982) is a phenomenon whereby the team tends to search for, and reach, an immediate agreement. The explosion of the NASA Shuttle *Challenger*, 73 seconds after it launched in January 1986, is considered one of the clearest examples of groupthink. Even if the engineers working for NASA raised concerns on the readiness and safety of the Shuttle's structure in the conditions expected at the launch, those concerns, and the information they were based on, were silenced. The NASA team gave the 'go' signal, initiating a tragedy that killed the seven astronauts of the *Challenger's* crew. Groupthink, it has been suggested, distorted the decision-making processes of the small groups of people involved in taking these delicate decisions. Reaching a premature consensus halted the collection and open evaluation of information and the analysis of alternatives. Learning stopped as any further development was effectively frozen by a consensus that was more based upon insecurity than upon an open and considered assessment of diverse sources of information and possible options. Groupthink, therefore, is also involved in a 'risk shift': an illusion of invulnerability and enthusiasm for a certain action or decision that polarizes the group towards higher risk. The risk that the group takes is higher than what people would risk individually.

When the group is affected by groupthink the issues at stake are poorly discussed and examined, leaving many possible solutions or routes unexplored. Dissenting voices are often stereotyped and marginalized, or 'invited' to reconsider their position, as happened in the case of the engineers working for NASA. This, ultimately, may invalidate team performance (see page 132 for the importance of dialogue) and participate in creating disasters that, like in the case of *Challenger*, could have been easily prevented.

Janis argues that many important historical fiascos in US foreign policy (for example, the involvement of the United States in the war in Vietnam) were at least partially due to groupthink. It has also been argued that the current US administration is affected by groupthink (see Levine, 2004). The decision to start the war against Iraq, and the actual management of the war itself, is said to present all the characteristics that Janis considered important for identifying groupthink:

- illusion of invulnerability
- belief in inherent morality of the group
- collective rationalization
- out of group stereotypes
- self-censorship
- illusion of unanimity
- direct pressure on dissenters
- self-appointed mindguards.

'Real' teams at work Teams are not in themselves a panacea (Dunphy and Bryant, 1996) and are not infallible (Plunkett and Fournier, 1991, p. 32). Yet, mainstream management theory suggests that when teams are introduced in the right way and nurtured as part of a wider organizational philosophy and strategy, they outperform individuals and collaborative groupings. In the management literature there is a wide utilization of the word 'team' and almost a blind acceptance of the value of teams for organizational success. Many authors have tried to identify the factors that intervene in heightening team performance (see Hackman, 1987; Campion, Medsker and Higgs,

1993; Cohen, Ledford and Spreitzer, 1996; Tannebaum, Beard and Salas, 1992; West, 2004). These authors have ventured to explain exactly what teamwork is, and in what sense teams are important for organizational success.

For Katzenbach and Smith (1993), for example, the connection between teams and organizational success is performance. Teams, or what they call 'real' teams, should be understood as discrete units of performance and not, or not only, as examples of positive organizational values such as sharing, collaborating or listening to others. Katzenbach and Smith (1993) propose that the importance and the impact of teams at work is dependent on how much they are *not* a simple new label attached by senior managers (or by your lecturers) to old ways of working; they are *not* to be equated with well-intentioned teambuilding events proposed by management consultants and they are *not* the same as recipes presented in the popular management books making the best sellers list. Teams, rather, are identified as a distinctive form of organizational technology – i.e. a particular way of organizing work that is designed to achieve specific ends. As Katzenbach and Smith (1993) put it, there is a 'wisdom' related to teams at work. To create 'real teams' (i.e. teams that reach high performance) managers need to learn a proper *discipline* which requires application, time and commitment.

Features of team discipline are:

- adequate level of complementary skills
- truly meaningful purpose
- specific goals and performance objectives
- clear working approach
- mutual accountability.

The discipline needed to create a high-performance team is demanding for all those involved. It cannot be improvised or faked, and it is intrinsically connected to a clear strategic commitment to create a high-performing organization. So senior executives, warn Katzenbach and Smith (1993), need to be realistic and clear on what high performance means for their organization. Then, they need to implement it correctly. There can be resistance to real teams, but effective discipline erodes this resistance and prepares for the advent of 'real', high-performing teams. We shall now consider an example of a team at work in a new media company.

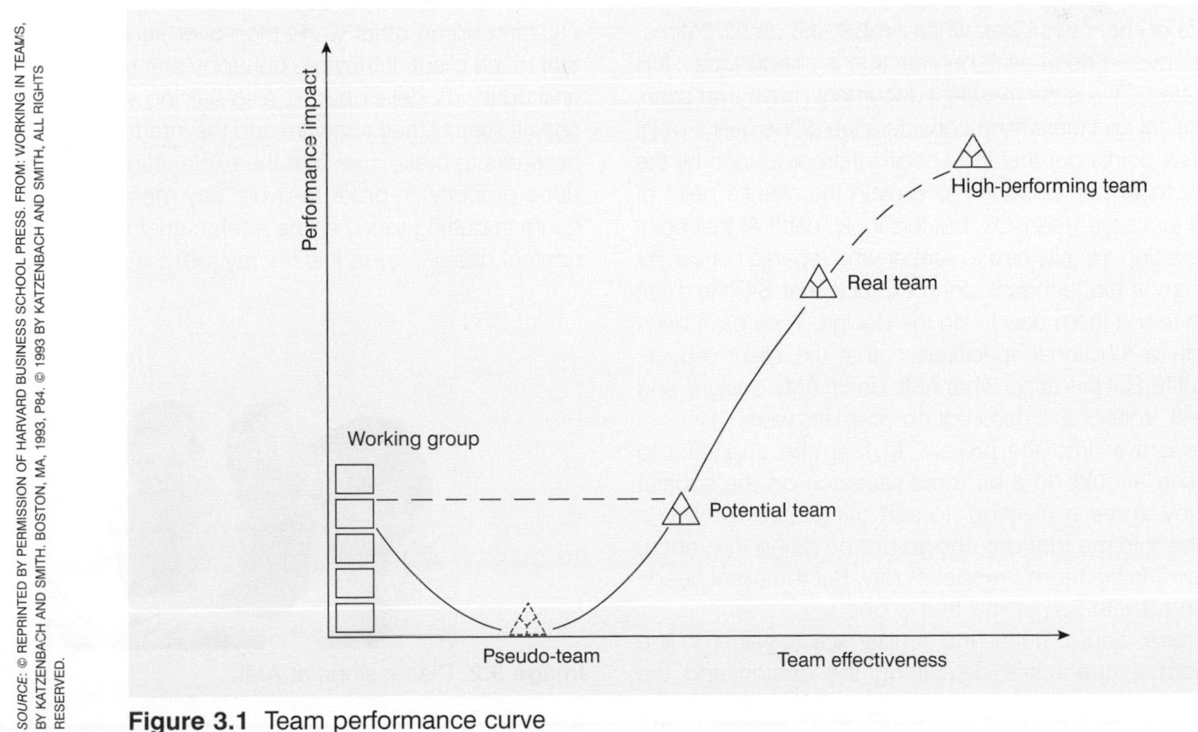

Figure 3.1 Team performance curve

Case study: AML, the digital media communication agency AML is a digital marketing and communication agency. Among its services, the company designs and builds websites, and it develops marketing campaigns using multiple digital platforms – i.e. the internet, mobile phones, CDs, etc. The philosophy of work of AML is that better digital solutions can be obtained by working in

CASE STUDY 3.1 AML (1)

When I arrive at AML on Monday morning in mid-July, I join a meeting with Laura, a junior content designer, Teresa the account manager/producer who's also an expert in content design, and John a technical developer. They are discussing a document that Laura has produced over the weekend, which was supposed to express the ideas and solutions they came up with on the previous Friday. They had a series of e-mail exchanges over the weekend and they are now going through the amendments to the document that Laura has written. Laura reads the document aloud. The discussion is rather careful and specific. John asks Laura if it is possible to explain in detail the diagrams in the document, and also if she can explain better the folder view. John is a developer in his late twenties. He is helpful in proposing changes, such as a drop-down folder, that are well received by Laura and Teresa. But John is also rather distant and annoyed. He leaves the meeting twice excusing himself but without explanation, and so leaving his fellow workers stunned and puzzled. Then I understand why he is behaving in this way. He is irritated by the fact that Laura has not followed faithfully the brief they discussed on Friday, which was put together in a series of pieces of paper. John asks Laura: 'Have you got it? It is very important, have you taken it home?'

Having made the corrections, Laura is left to make the further amendments on her own. Later, when Amber, the creative director, sees the revised document, her reaction is unequivocal: 'It is too complicated. This is the messiest document I have ever seen. It is too technical and there is no consideration of the user's point of view.' Laura points out that the specification produced by the client is very technical. She tries to explain the client's point of view. Amber just says 'yeah, Ok, but this looks naff!' At that point John comes along. He sits next to Amber who repeats her verdict that the design is too technical. John explains that S4 (the client company) is telling them how to do the design. They have been provided with a functional specification that the client expects AML to beautify. But this is not what AML does. AML designs and builds 'perfect' solutions. It does not do cosmetic work.

Amber is drawn into the project. In fact she suggests to Laura that she should do a bit more research on the subject and then they agree a meeting 'to sort things out'. Amber is unhappy. She told me that she should not be doing this, not at this stage, as it is the team's responsibility. But the client needs to be presented with something that is good.

Later, Teresa, Laura, John and Amber are together in the meeting room. Laura starts describing the design and the problems. They are not starting from scratch because they have the S4 specification and Laura's document. In a way, the atmosphere is rather playful with jokes and laughter, but the joke also alludes to subtle tensions. John offers to prepare tea. When he comes back, Laura who knows he knows how she likes her tea, finds he has put in sugar and exclaims 'Revenge!'.

The meeting is now very different from the one in the morning. Amber just asks 'OK what are we trying to do? What do we need to achieve? Everything that is needed becomes a specific feature, even if there is a long discussion on what the feature might look like. So, for example, they agree that in the address book there will be cartoon characters that can be associated with the names in the address book. They all participate in coming up with suggestions and ideas, and at the end of the meeting the room is wallpapered with sheets of drawings, sentences and navigation diagrams. Laura, as content designer, has to put everything together in a document that presents exactly what was agreed in this meeting: the detailed content design of the project. Laura returns to her workstation to start doing that even though she thought she had already done that during the weekend. She is still smiling and, looking at me, she says 'You are not going to stay are you? It is already five o'clock.' Teresa and John are staying too because they are catching up on other work. Moreover, Teresa is the direct contact to the client. If they are unhappy she has to deal with them, and John, as developer, is also liaising with the client on the specificities of their software and the interface needed with it, so he wants to make sure that the explanation of the navigation is done properly. In order to avoid any mess he decides to help Laura in putting together the artefact that specifies the detailed content design, 'even if is not my job!' he adds.

Image 3.2 Discussions at AML

teams made up of multiple, complementary skills. So, by putting together content, graphic and technical experts, it is possible to design and produce solutions that are neither over-designed nor too technical, but a 'perfect' balance. Case study 3.1 provides an example of a real life working situation at AML, involving a series of meetings for creating what they call 'the detailed content design' of an e-mail system for a product at the interface between the internet and mobile phones. In this vignette they are discussing specifically the design of the mailing system address book.

Here are a few questions that can help you to think about the case and the various issues involved in understanding teams at work:

- How would you describe AML's work organization?
- Is this a 'real team'? Can you identify and summarize the features listed in Katzenbach and Smith (1993)?
- Where do you think there are problems? What do you think they are due to?
- Do you think the team could improve their performance? How? What should the managers do in order to help the team?
- In what ways are the three dimensions we have signalled earlier of flexibility, motivation and learning activated and affected?
- How do you explain the fact that the workers stay at work even if their working time is over?

Perhaps one of the reactions to the AML case is that they seem to be very disorganized! Yet, they do have an organization – the team – which has all the characteristics indicated by Katzenbach and Smith (1993). The common purpose is to design the outline of the mailing system, which is the joint work-product. The members of the team need to collaborate in order to achieve this objective – they could not design it individually. They all have different, complementary skills (content designer, developer and graphic designer), and each of them is fundamental and necessary for realizing the design. Yet, everything is rather loose and unclear. There are no templates that specify what a detailed content design should look like, for example. They spend a lot of time discussing what should be in a detailed content design, and also how it should be presented, which does not seem an efficient utilization of time. As soon as they show the document/artefact they have produced to the creative director, she says 'it's too naff'. This does not strike one as a useful, constructive comment, and it does not give any clear direction. Then, when Amber gets heavily involved in the second meeting, things seems to be different. She does not tell them what to do but she facilitates their thinking, helping them to achieve a successful balance between the user point of view, creativity, usability and the constraints dictated by the client's specifications. You might have noted that there are no clear rules about how each person should participate, or what they should do. Everything seems to be left to personal interpretation and willingness. Yet they also seem highly committed. They work a great deal, including weekends via e-mail exchanges, and well beyond 'normal' working hours. Accountability is also shared. They are accountable not only to Amber, the creative director, but also to each other. In the vignette we see how individuals' contributions, suggestions and ideas are not only expected but closely monitored and judged by the team members.

Many characteristics of AML are often associated with post-bureaucratic organizational forms. In the following section we shall consider how teams connect to these 'post-bureaucracies' and enter into the details of the key ideas around teams at work. As indicated earlier, teams in the mainstream are said to activate/enhance three main organizational dimensions: flexibility, motivation and learning. We shall look at these dimensions and suggest why teams are considered to be involved in enhancing and activating these dimensions.

Key ideas and contributions to thinking and important empirical studies

Many popular and academic authors include 'teams' as a central feature of their favoured prescriptions for improved organizational performance. Teams, for example, are identified as essential components of the implementation of the principles of total quality management (Oakland, 1996). They are the building blocks of 'excellent organizations' (Peters and Waterman, 1982), key elements of the 'learning organization' (Senge, 1990) and they are critical components of virtually all high-performance management systems that build profit by putting people first (Pfeffer, 1998).

Despite having different accents and connotations, they share a common theme. Responsible teams or self-managing teams or semi-autonomous teams are some of the names given to the building blocks of new 'post-bureaucratic' organizational forms, which are comparatively flat and agile because they have few hierarchical layers (Peters, 1988). Teams tend to enhance organizational flexibility and learning as they can explore and react quickly to any problem or new challenge. Decisions can be taken at the team level and do not need to go through a long chain of command. Motivation is also greatly enhanced as teams are 'empowered' by bestowing upon the members responsibility and autonomy in performing organizational tasks, in contrast to traditional organizations with their tight rules of command, short span of control and coordination (Jenkins, 1994, p. 852).

The three organizational dimensions that teams activate and enhance are summarized below. The three dimensions are interrelated. The distinction between them is analytical. It enables us to distinguish theoretical resources and empirical studies for each of the dimensions that teams are said to activate and favour in organizations.

Teams for flexibility: Lean production 'Dynamic work teams are at the heart of the lean factory.' This is the way Womack *et al.* (1990, p. 90) put it when introducing their influential book, based on five years and US$5 million of research on the status of the organization of work in the automobile industry around the world. Lean design defies traditional criteria of organization of production and management thinking. Its aim is to avoid waste, slack and redundancies. It is in this sense that production is 'lean'. 'Just-in-time' is one of the principles that makes this process possible. In Just-in-time, every point in the chain, from the suppliers to the producers and distributors, only delivers on demand, so that capital is not tied up in stock, and product refinements that require new parts can be speedily introduced. The system must be fast and efficient, with few errors, and this is what lean design aspires to achieve.

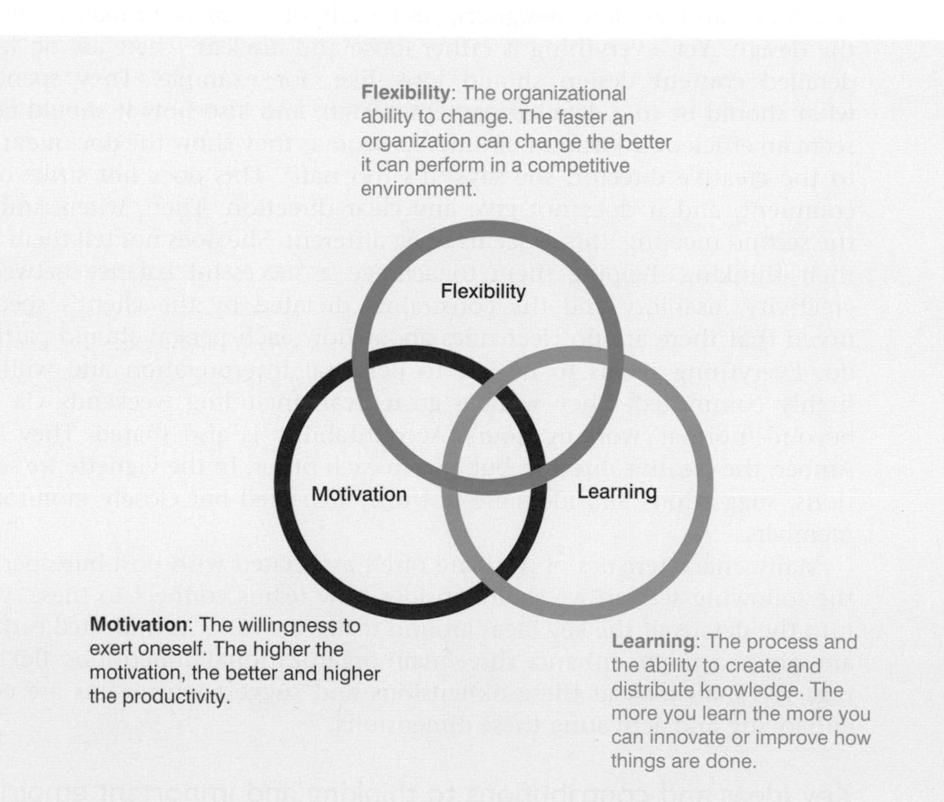

Figure 3.2 Organizational dimensions where teams intervene, according to mainstream literature

THE DIFFERENCES BETWEEN MASS AND LEAN PRODUCTION In traditional mass production, the assembly line is the place and the time where all the thinking and design behind the product – for example, a car – comes together in a predetermined and closely specified manner. The entire process is designed by industrial

SOURCE: © MINNESOTA HISTORICAL SOCIETY/CORBIS

Image 3.3 Ford car assembly line

engineers according to classical (e.g. Taylor's) principle of organization. This means that the engineers have conceived, at least in principle, the best way in which workers should assemble the thousands of parts necessary to make a complete car. There is a strict division of labour and allocation of specific roles. The production process is broken down into small operations, and each individual is required to perform a very narrow range of discrete tasks. Each action is studied in minute detail and prescribed in clear order. In the assembly line (see picture above) the workers are posted to different key points in the line. Their movements are prescribed in minute detail, and the pace of their action is established by the motion of the line. Foremen make sure that the workers follow the orders given to them. In this respect, humans perform the role of cogs in a wider organizational machine.

Lean production involves a very different approach to work organization. In lean production, work is organized around teams. We take the real example of NUMMI (New United Motor Manufacturing Inc.) to describe what this means in practical terms. NUMMI was, in origin, an assembly plant owned by General Motors (GM) and one of its worst in terms of productivity levels, quality and absenteeism. Case study 3.2 provides an account based on Adler (1993) and Womack *et al.* (1990).

Here are a few questions that can help you to analyse the case of NUMMI (overleaf) and explore the various issues involved in understanding teams at work:

- Can you summarize and explain the main differences between mass and lean production?
- What is the position of the workers in each of them?
- If you were a worker can you envisage any problem with working under the conditions of lean production? And if you were a manager?
- Can you explain in what way teams are enhancing flexibility, learning and motivation at NUMMI?

Commentators have questioned the simplistic connection that sees teamwork as exemplification of post-bureaucratic organizational forms. For example, Adler (1993) and Adler and Borys (1996) point out that NUMMI has clear hierarchies; it has standards and formalized procedures designed to achieve the best way operations can be realized. It also has structured flows of information/communication and control, just as the 'traditional' bureaucracy. More importantly for the discussion of the difference between Taylorism and lean production, these authors contend that NUMMI's organization of work cannot be considered in any way *beyond* Taylorism. Rather, they argue, NUMMI represents the perfecting of fundamental Tayloristic **precepts** of time and motion, and standardization, but these principles are inserted in a virtuous circle of continuous improvement, what we have said below is called *kaizen*. The system that makes this possible they call 'enabling' or 'learning bureaucracy':

> using learned analytical tools, their own experience and the expertise of leaders and engineers, workers create a consensual standard that they teach to the system by writing job descriptions. The system then teaches these standards back to the workers, who then by further analysis, standardisation, re-analysis, refinement and re-standardisation create an intensely structured system of continuous improvement. The salient characteristic of this bureaucracy is learning, not coercion. *(Adler, 1993, p. 104)*

CASE STUDY 3.2 NUMMI

NUMMI, a joint venture between Toyota and GM in Fremont, California, was formally established in 1984. It has approximately 350 teams in production made up of five to seven people and a leader. Small teams are supposed to encourage participative decision making and team bonding (Adler, 1993, p. 5). Each team is responsible for a different portion of the assembly line. Four teams form what is known as a group, with the first layer of management being the group leader. Each team has to coordinate its own work and the relations with other teams. Also, the cleanliness and tidiness of their workspace is the responsibility of the team. Team members are trained in all the tasks necessary to the team operation, and they can rotate when needed. Teams are responsible for quality checks and small repairs. Problems are solved when they occur. Any defective operation on the line is tackled immediately, rather than being pushed up to 'quality control' and being left to pile up for attention in a rectification section. In order to solve the problems when they appear, and even before they occur, workers must be able to do something that was unthinkable in the traditional production line, namely to stop the line.

Teams are also encouraged to utilize the 'Five Why's' – a questioning strategy designed to get to the bottom of the problem the team is facing. They are also asked to propose improvements to the system of production beyond immediate problem solving, through a system of suggestions or, for example, by joining **quality circles**. These are teams made up of workers as well as specialist engineers, looking at implementing suggestions and ideas with the goal of improving the system of production continuously.

Management's role in NUMMI, as in Toyota, is that of providing expertise to help production teams with problem solving. In order to compete with the performance gains – in quality as well as price – achieved by Toyota, other auto makers have followed their lead in introducing lean manufacturing methods. And the basic ideas of lean production have been applied in many other industries, with mixed results. The system organized around production teams has often proved to be extremely efficient, much more than traditional plants. The fact that teams are constantly attentive to the work and detect errors immediately reduces the rework needed at the end of the line. In other words, the essence of the teamwork in NUMMI is its flexibility because workers can do all the different tasks and are collectively responsible for improving their ability to work productively as a team. Each new idea, new successful implementation and new process is not only adopted by the team but is spread to the whole organization in a continuous race to improvement. This is known by the Japanese word ***kaizen***.

By the end of 1986 NUMMI's productivity was the highest in GM and was twice that of the old plant. More then 90 per cent of the workers declared themselves to be satisfied with their employment in NUMMI and absenteeism fell from 20–25 per cent to 3–4 per cent. Both in Toyota and NUMMI there are formal agreements in place that seal a true reciprocal obligation between workers and employers (Womack *et al*., 1990, p. 102). For example, there are agreements on a certain level of job security and policies, which avoid job cuts as a way out of financial crisis. The teams are part of a system in which the workers, the managers, the suppliers and the distributors are integrated and are said to share a common destiny, 'a community of fate' (Berders and Van Hootegem, 2000, p. 55). This is also obtained through the socialization of the employees into an organizational culture that values their work and their knowledge, putting them at the centre of the production process. Emblems of traditional differences in status such as different dress codes, different food facilities, parking spaces, etc. are erased in order to inspire a spirit of communality and equality. The main idea is that the whole organization shares the same values and same destiny, so everyone has to do their best to make the company succeed.

Teams for motivation: Participation, satisfaction and humane ways of working When teams are empowered to solve problems, to offer innovative solutions, all the workers become active participants in their work. They can shape the specificities of their working practices, and they can improve them, rather than being mere executors of managers' orders. In other words, employees' importance and value is recognized; and they are not considered as simple appendices of the machines or bureaucrats of impersonal organizations. The 'empowerment' of employees has become extremely significant in recent times. With the motto of 'people first', for example, Pfeffer (1998) proposes a seven point list for organizational success where enlightened 'people management' is at the centre of a profit-making organization that invests and treats its employees with respect, building up relations of trust and cooperation rather than relying upon expensive direct control systems. When people are empowered to work in teams they can manage themselves and develop real commitment and ownership of what they do. The autonomy and discretion that people enjoy in teams translates into intrinsic rewards and job satisfaction (Pfeffer, 1998, p. 74), which in turn has an impact on employee morale and productivity.

The assumptions underlying this view are part of an extended legacy that stretches back to the socio-technical tradition, the human relations movement, and the **quality of working life movement** (see Procter and Mueller, 2000; Buchanon, 2000; Huczynski, 1996). You can find some of these classical studies summarized at the end of this subsection. It is important to consider that this legacy emphasizes that:

- An organization is not only a technical system but also a **social system**; and both need to be managed.
- In social systems, groups are an important source of norms of conduct and informal rules.
- A democratic approach to a task, which favours participation and autonomy, enhances the quality and quantity of the output.

Scientific management considered material benefits primary for generating motivation in otherwise uninterested, idiosyncratic workers who require constant control and supervision to be kept on the task. In contrast, 'modern management thinking' maintains that social, psychological and moral factors also intervene in regulating workers' motivation and satisfaction. This is why many

Box 3.2: Learning and bureaucracy

For Adler there are three aspects involved in creating a 'learning and enabling bureaucracy':

1. The open, trustworthy and prompt relationship between management and workers' unions which 'on the basis of the recognition that job security is fundamental to an employee's well-being' agrees to a no-layoff policy and to a listening and prompt response on employees' demands.
2. Standardization of operation is a fundamental factor. This, in NUMMI, is extensive. NUMMI still uses the Tayloristic precepts of studying and defining procedures of time and motion. But these precepts, rather than being decided by some engineer detached from production and without any consultation with those on the shop floor, are actually devised by the workers themselves. In NUMMI, the workers 'hold the stopwatch'. The members of the team will observe and time each other, finding the most efficient and safest way to perform a certain operation. Then they break the work down into small parts and try to improve each of these parts. The team then compares the results with other teams on the same station during other shifts and the best one becomes the standard procedure for that particular operation in the plant. The workers become themselves work engineers. In this respect they are 'empowered' because, rather than being told what to do, they find out for themselves what is the best way of doing something. They are managers of their own activity. They are not alienated appendices of a machine or mere executors of someone else's design. Rather they execute their own design.
3. The other aspect, which is connected with standardization, is that it offers a basis for continuous improvement. The improvements of one team, in a particular shift, for example, become the benchmark to be improved upon by the other teams. This introduces the challenge that continues the virtuous circle of the learning bureaucracy.

commentators suggest that successful organizations are those able to fulfil the psychological and social needs of the employees, where personal growth and organizational growth are not in conflict, but fulfil and reinforce each other. A humane, motivating and respectful working life is regarded as fundamental for successful organizations both as a business solution, as well as the application of values of the democracies of the West to the workplace (Lammers and Szell, 1989; Heller, Pusic, Strauss and Wilpert, 1998; Plunkett and Fournier, 1991).

These ideas might seem more applicable to professional and services companies or the so-called 'knowledge intensive firms' (Alvesson, 1993). These are companies, of which AML is an example, where the products and services are the knowledge itself. Yet, Volvo is an example of a company that has implemented the ideas of employees' participation and autonomy in car manufacturing (see Case Study 3.3).

Classical studies

THE HAWTHORNE EXPERIMENTS: THE IMPORTANCE OF SOCIAL NEEDS AND GROUP NORMS AT WORK In 1927 Elton Mayo was commissioned to study the factors that intervened in the productivity of the workforce of the Hawthorne Plant of the Western Electric Company in Chicago. During the research process, the researchers manipulated the lighting level on the shop floor. The result was that, at every level, productivity unexpectedly increased.

The researchers then asked for volunteers to work in a room separate from the rest of their colleagues (the relay assembly room). A group of women accepted and their work was observed by a researcher who stayed in the room and interacted with them. Variables were manipulated such as pauses, working time and lunch breaks. The results again showed an increase in productivity regardless of the modifications.

The researchers inferred from these results that it was not the *working* conditions but the actual *social* condition of being observed and studied that had brought about the changes in productivity. The 'Hawthorne effect' came to be known as the phenomenon whereby observation interferes with what is studied. But an equally significant aspect of this result was the insight that, by working together and sharing the experience, the workers had created a wider unit, a *group*, which the researchers started thinking had something to do with the increase in productivity. After a long process of interviewing, the final part of the study was an observation of 14 male bank wirers. By

CASE STUDY 3.3 Self-managing teams at Volvo

In the 1960s Volvo started a series of experiments designed to improve on the repetitive, straining and alienating conditions of Tayloristic forms of work. These problems, as Bernstein (1992) suggests, were made more urgent by the lack of 'external labour' to cover for jobs that the Swedish workers did not want to do. Volvo experimented with a socio-technical work design (see Trist and Bamforth, 1951) and a participatory style of management. This resulted in a design of the Uddevalla plant that abandoned the assembly line altogether in favour of 'stand still' production stations. Multi-skilled self-managing teams work in parallel stations, each member acting as teachers, assemblers, inventory managers and quality controllers, entirely responsible for building a complete car.

These experiments have, however, almost been completely terminated and traditional assembly systems have been reintroduced in Volvo. Lower productivity is often indicated as the main reason for this. But empirical evidence in this respect is dubious and contested (Jonsson, Medbo amd Engstrom, 2004), and more complex explanations seem to be involved (see Wallace, 2004; Berggren, 1992) including, for example, changes in the economic situation in the early 1990s, with unusual levels of unemployment in Sweden. It has also been suggested that the 'Swedish model for work life development' brought into question sedimented power relations – for example, the differences in availability and ownership of symbolic and material resources for employers and employees, which was threatening traditional and established interests. This also explains the reassertion of traditional management control in the system of production (Jonsson, Medbo amd Engstrom, 2004).

studying their interactions the researchers realized that informal groups had emerged that did not coincide with the formal groups based on the spatial and sequential organization of work. These informal groupings were shown to have a leader who emerged in the process of interaction. The researchers found that these groups had informal norms and their members were strongly conditioned by these norms, which regulated the workers' general behaviour and also the pace of production.

TRIST AND BAMFORTH: AUTONOMOUS RESPONSIBILITY AND SOCIO-TECHNICAL SYSTEMS In 1951 Trist and Bamforth published in *Human Relations* the results of research on the working methods and conditions of miners in England in which the method of coal-getting had been changed from 'hand got' to 'LongWall'. The LongWall is a method that reproduces the mass production engineering method with rigid sequence, functional interdependence and spatio-temporal extension of the factory regime. This replaced the 'hand got' method based on small group work. In the 'hand got' system each member was self-selected, and consisted of a workers' pair to which often one or two external individuals were associated. This group was the primary unit responsible for the whole cycle of operation for getting the coal. They had an embodied knowledge of themselves, of each other and of the conditions and situations in which they worked, also because often there were ties of kinship between the members who all came from the close knit local community. This knowledge and the leeway in their action enabled the members to modulate their work as a whole, guaranteeing continuous coal-getting as well as safety for all in the harsh underground conditions. This situation of group leadership and self-supervision was called 'responsible autonomy'.

The LongWall system broke down the cycle, giving specific roles to each individual, effectively segregating the workers into the seven categories of skills, as well as pay, in which it was constituted. At the technological level a new integration was achieved by the introduction of a new task sequence. But this new method disturbed the existing social order and equilibrium and this was neither recognized nor addressed by management. Hence, new problems and issues emerged. For example, new informal groups substituted the ones based on the 'hand-got' system. But these were solely private arrangements without any institutional and mutual obligation that offered support to its members and were also open to anti-social behaviour, coalitions, etc.

KURT LEWIN: THE IMPORTANCE OF PARTICIPATION AND DEMOCRATIC STYLE In 1948 Lewin recounts the experiments with groups of children by Lipitt and by Lipitt and Whiye, at the Iowa Child Welfare Research Station. The children were divided into homogenous groups based on socio-economic characteristics, as well as according to the results of psycho-social tests. The aim was to create equivalent groups on such qualities as leadership and interpersonal relationships. The task of the groups was to make theatrical masks. The scientists kept activities and instruments of the groups constant while they varied the atmosphere of the groups with the help of a leader assigned to each group. The leaders created a group with a *democratic* atmosphere, a group with an *autocratic* atmosphere and a third one with a *laissez-faire* atmosphere. For the democratic group many paths of actions and behaviours were open; for the autocratic only one, namely the path determined by the leader. In autocracy the leader determined not only the kind of activity but also who should work with whom (Lewin, 1948, p. 77). In the *laissez-faire* atmosphere the group was left to its own devices. The results obtained showed a striking difference in the performance and quality of the masks: the democratic groups developed a wider sense of cohesiveness and sense of belonging, what Lewin calls the 'we' feeling.

Overall, the three experimental conditions proved that authoritarian groups are more productive at the beginning but soon are ridden by internal struggles and aggression among members. The scapegoat is a well-known phenomenon when one member is singled out and bullied by the others, and is an exemplification of group aggression in authoritarian group conditions. The *laissez-faire* atmosphere tended, instead, to create apathy.

This, and other studies, became important because they were considered to demonstrate that certain psycho-social needs, such as that of belonging and social acceptance, can be satisfied by groups that are managed in a democratic style. Groups can take some time to 'learn' democracy, as they need to learn how to take decisions out of the many alternatives, and how to accommodate differences. But, in the long run, the outcome of their work is higher both in qualitative and quantitative terms.

Teams for learning: Continuous improvement and innovation The issue of learning and knowledge creation and diffusion has increased in importance in recent decades, with many asserting that knowledge is the source of competitive advantage. A flourishing literature has developed that analyses, describes and often prescribes strategies, ideas and models for understanding, creating, facilitating and supporting organizations that learn, to improve or innovate by creating, transferring and managing successfully new and existing knowledge (Drucker, 1993; Senge, 1990; Nonaka and Takeuchi, 1995; Davenport and Pusak, 1998). The level and quality of creativity and problem solving required to innovate or improve on existing business solutions is very high. An individual working alone rarely produces the creative ideas or solutions required, for example, for complex or discontinuous innovation (Tushman and Nadler, 1998). If this seems blindingly obvious at an intuitive level, it should also be appreciated that theoretically the creation and transfer of knowledge – in the form of learning – has been increasingly recognized as a social phenomenon rather than an individual cognitive endeavour. This is why teams/groups, as a basic social unit, can be considered as media of knowledge creation and diffusion. Specifically, learning and knowledge creation occur:

- in the social context
- in interaction and participation in shared practices
- in processes of reflection and feedback
- in freedom to explore and implement new and daring concepts.

For all these reasons, many studies are concentrating on team learning and how this can be favoured and nurtured in organizations (Argote *et al.*, 2000; Wood and Bandura, 1989; Gibson and Vermeuler, 2003; Edmonson, 2002). As Peter Senge (1990, p. 236) puts it, 'there has never been a greater need for mastering team learning in organization than there is today'.

According to Senge, areas and issues that should be considered for facilitating team learning are:

- *Discussion and dialogue*. These are two different modes of communication, both important. Discussion enables members to dissect a topic or a problem from various points of view. Dialogue is a 'free flow of meaning' through which people can observe their own thinking, understand how it developed and enable it to cohere in a collective meaning.
- *Dealing with conflict and defensive routines*. Defensive routines are entrenched in often unacknowledged habits that we use to defend ourselves from the embarrassment and threat that comes with exposing our thinking. Reflection and mutual inquiry are skills employed for dealing with conflictual situations and defensive routines.
- *Practise team learning*. Create space and time (with specific sessions or learning laboratories) to practise discussion and dialogue and to develop skills for dealing with defensiveness.

Box 4.3: Peter Senge

Dr. Peter M. Senge is the founding chairperson of the Society for Organizational Learning (SOL) and a senior lecturer at the Massachusetts Institute of Technology. Dr. Senge is the author of *The Fifth Discipline: The Art and Practice of the Learning Organization*. He has lectured extensively throughout the world, translating the abstract ideas of systems theory into tools for better understanding of economic and organizational change. He has worked with leaders in business, education, healthcare and government. *The Journal of Business Strategy* (September/October 1999) named Dr. Senge as one of the 24 people who had had the greatest influence on business strategy over the last 100 years.

Image 4.4 Peter Senge, author of the *Fifth Discipline*

Source: http://www.solonline.org/aboutsol/who/Senge/

Exercise 3.1

You can engage with your seminar group in a 'learning laboratory' to improve your skills at dialogue and negotiation. Centre your discussion on the question: 'How do we deal with conflicts?'

The ground rules that everyone has to respect are:

- *Suspension of assumptions*. Do not hold on to your position at any cost but try to understand your own and all the others' views.
- *Act as equals*. There might be differences between you – some people have better marks than others, or are considered more knowledgeable. Suspend these differences for the time you are in this 'learning laboratory'.
- *Spirit of inquiry*. Try to understand what are the deep assumptions beyond the positions you and others hold. Probe by asking what is the evidence or reason that justifies the positions people hold. Ask the question how have we come to accept these views.

You might have already recognized the possibility that if a team can be a medium of knowledge creation, learning as a social phenomenon does not occur exclusively within the restricted, officially prescribed formal boundaries of specific, formal or functional team membership. There are some authors (Lave and Wenger, 1991; Brown and Duguid, 1991) who have suggested we should also concentrate on what they call 'communities of practice' (COPs), which are made up of people who cluster around a specific practice (such as the design of digital solutions as in the case of AML) they are involved in, and for which they often share a keen interest. Participating in these communities, people develop new ways of doing or improving on existing practice, and the activities comprising the practice itself. In this process of participation they develop a certain identity (in the case of AML as web designers, for example) and become active and recognized members of that wider community. Learning occurs in the participation in the practice, as members engage and develop a specific language, share stories that help make sense of the practice and produce artefacts that are meaningful for all the members. We can be members of many COPs. In some we might be at the periphery whereas in others we might be at the centre, recognized as competent members, even experts of that practice.

Thinkpoint 3.3

To which COPs do you belong? Can you identify the key aspects, such as specific language, stories and artefacts, of each of the COPs you belong to?

If learning occurs at various levels and dimensions and it is not restricted to specific business units like formal teams, then we need to consider the implications for organizations. One of these implications is that multi-membership (see Figure 3.3) should be noted and managed (Wenger, 1998; Wenger and Snyder, 2000; Wenger, McDermott and Snyder, 2002), for example, by identifying the existing COPs, and by fostering and nurturing COPs and the members' freedom and ability to tap into the different levels and dimensions of learning and innovation.

Exercise 3.2

Deploy the model of multi-membership and the concept of COPs to analyse the AML case study.

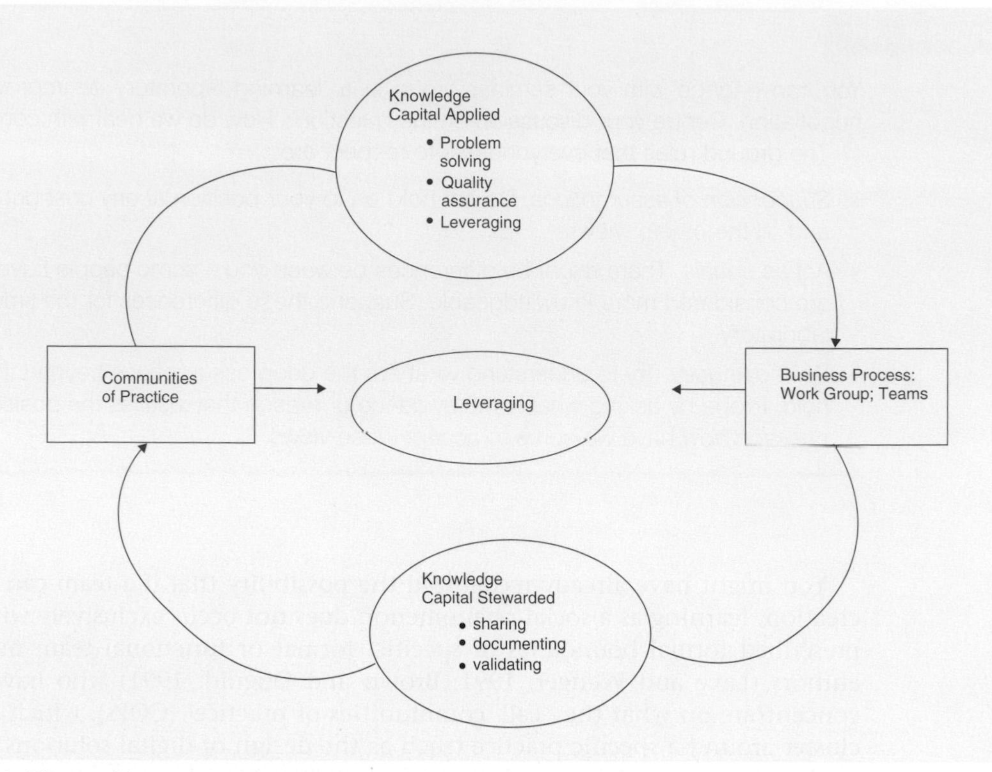

SOURCE: © REPRINTED BY PERMISSION OF HAFVARD BUSINESS SCHOOL PRESS. FROM: CULTIVATING COMMUNITIES OF PRACTICE, BY WENGER, DERMOTT & SNYDER. BOSTON MA 2002, P19. © 2002 BY ETIENNE WENGER, RICHARDR

Figure 3.3 The multimembership learning circle

Recap questions

1. Why are teams considered important for today's organizations?
2. What is a team? What is a group?
3. What are group processes and phenomena?
4. What are the organizational dimensions teams to activate and enhance?
5. Why are teams important for change?
6. Why are teams important for productivity?
7. Why are teams important for knowledge creation?
8. What are the main empirical studies that sustain and inform the mainstream view of teams at work?
9. What are their most salient theoretical contributions to our understanding of teams?
10. Do these ideas help you in making sense of your experience of teams?

Key problems and open questions

Much of the mainstream literature on teams at work has been dedicated to understanding how they behave and how they can be made more effective with a view to enhancing various aspects of organizational performance. In particular, team effectiveness has been studied in terms of productivity and members' attitudes and behaviours (Kirkman, 2000). Some research has substantiated the claims that teams increase productivity (Cohen and Ledford, 1994; Trist *et al.*, 1977; Wellins *et al.*, 1990). Other research has been less positive as the experiments have not demonstrated a correlation between teamworking and higher productivity (Wall *et al.*, 1986; Cordery *et al.*, 1991). This has resulted in a general ambiguity about teams at work. What makes them perform at their full potential is still an open question. Team effectiveness is said to be linked to elements such as team development, design, leadership and resistance. We shall look at each of these in turn.

How do teams develop? One of the oldest and better known models of how teams evolve and develop over time was proposed by Tuckman (1965) and slightly modified in Tuckman and Jenson (1977). These later stages are indicated in italics.

- **Forming**. This is the stage when people start to know each other and start understanding their activity and the task to be accomplished. A general consensus starts emerging, which is identified as the *conforming stage*.
- **Storming**. Conflicts among people emerge due to frustration or difficulties with the task and different personalities, styles of working and ideas.
- **Norming**. Norms and patterns of acceptable and recognized behaviour of conduct, work objectives and style emerge. A *reforming stage* sets in when people assess their behaviour according to the new standards established in the norming stage.
- **Performing**. This is the stage when team members as a team concretely engage with the task and the activities required for its accomplishment. (Two other stages – *adjourning* and *mourning* – have also been added. The first is the moment of concluding the task with the accomplishment of the team objectives. The second signals a certain reluctance to 'let go' of the team and engage actively with new activities and new tasks in new teams.)

This model of team development is based on stages that need to be completed before the group can pass to the next stage. It is therefore hierarchical and closed, even though it does not offer a specific time scale. As Reynolds (1994) points out, Tuckman has himself been very critical of the application of his model to all groups. But this is exactly what has happened. His model has become dominant. It is well known, and widely applied, particularly in management training and development.

As Poole (1983) put it, 'for 40 years researchers on group development have been conducting the same study with minor alterations' (cited in Gersick, 1988, p. 11) as they have been based on the idea that there must be a linear progression to teamwork, as assumed in Tuckman's dominant model. But many have become increasingly critical of the hierarchical ordering and strict division into stages. It was Gersick's (1988) research that finally challenged the idea that team development is only conceivable as a set of necessary stages the team must go through.

Gersick's (1988) qualitative study, which was part of wider research into team effectiveness, suggested that teams do not follow specific and necessary stages. Rather, they proceed in the accomplishment of their task by what she calls 'punctuated equilibrium'. This expression comes from biology and it is based on the observation of fossils, which indicate that, in nature, change (evolution) does not occur in long continuous processes of development. Rather, it is characterized by periods of relative stability (*equilibrium*) which are suddenly interrupted and disrupted (*punctuated*) by a revolutionary period where new forms emerge. Gersick observed the same type of development with her team experiments. Aspects she has found to be important for activating these key revolutionary moments were (i) the continuous relations with the external environment of the team and (ii) the constant awareness of time and deadlines.

Thinkpoint 3.4

Reflecting on your experiences of teamwork, which model seems more appropriate to you? Why? What issues are not considered in these models that you have come across in your experiences of teamwork?

How should teams be designed? Many authors point out how difficult, and delicate, the task of designing teams is. This also includes the problem of allocating and matching proper technical and problem-solving skills to the task (Katzenbach and Smith, 1993; Hackman, 1987; Hackman and Morris, 1975). Research has also been conducted on the issue of how to match demographic elements and tenure as this effects team effectiveness (Ancora and Caldwell, 2000). One of the most successful models of team design has been produced by Meredith Belbin. Belbin's model for team management concentrates on the importance of designing teams that are balanced in terms of personal characteristics and abilities of members. In a nine-year research project, Belbin and his research group identified nine 'roles' that are seen to be crucial for team effectiveness (see Table 3.1). A 'role' is defined as a tendency to behave, contribute and interrelate with others in a particular way. Each of these roles is considered significant for team effectiveness because it helps to provide a good balance for achieving the task.

Table 3.1 Belbin's model for team management

Rules and descriptions – team role contributions	Allowable weaknesses
Plant	
Creative, unorthodox, imaginative; solves difficult problems	Ignores details; too preoccupied to communicate effectively
Resource investigator	
Extravert, enthusiastic, communicative; explores opportunities; develops contacts	Over-optimistic; loses interest once initial enthusiasm has passed
Coordinator	
Mature, confident, a good chairperson; clarifies goals, promotes decision making; delegates well	Can be seen as manipulative; delegates personal work
Shaper	
Challenging, dynamic, thrives on pressure; has the drive and courage to overcome obstacles	Can provoke others; hurts people's feelings
Monitor evaluator	
Sober, strategic and discerning; seeks all opinions; judges accurately	Lacks drive and ability to inspire others; overly critical
Teamworker	
Cooperative, mild, perceptive and diplomatic; listens, builds, averts friction, calms the nerves	Indecisive in crunch situations; can be easily influenced
Implementer	
Disciplined, reliable, conservative and efficient; turns ideas into practical actions	Somewhat inflexiable; slow to respond to new possibilities
Completer	
Painstaking conscientious, anxious; searches out errors and omissions; delivers on time	Inclined to worry unduly; reluctant to delegate; can be a nit-picker
Specialist	
Single-minded, self-starting, dedicated; provides knowledge and skills in rare supply	Contributes on only a narrow front; dwells on technicalities; overlooks the big picture

Note: Strengths of contributors in any one of the roles is commonly associated with particular weaknesses. These are called allowable weaknesses. Executives are seldom strong in all nine team roles.

Source: Reprinted from team roles at work, Belbin (ed.), 1993, p. 23 with permission from Elsevier

Box 3.4: Research field

Researchers at Henley College studied teams involved in playing a business management game where each team played a 'company'. The game enabled the researchers to have an objective measure of team performance – i.e. the financial results of the 'companies' playing the management game. The researchers also measured and categorized the participants according to a set of broad human characteristics – mental ability, personality, character and orientation – via specific psychometric tests. They also closely observed teams during their activities. The researchers manipulated variables, one of which was the composition of the members of each team. The teams were then observed and scored on observation items. It is from an elaboration of these data that researchers identified nine roles that have proved to be significant, and that hindered performance when they were not taken up. Teams, for Belbin, are a matter of balance: 'What is needed is not well-balanced individuals but individuals who balance well with one another. In that way human frailty can be underpinned and strengths used to full advantage' (Belbin, 1993, p. 73).

The success of team roles could be explained by the fact that Belbin's model claims predictive capacity. This means that by applying the instruments provided to test and score people, it is possible to design the best team (in the given circumstances) to perform a specific task. Such a promise is very appealing and might explain the interest in Belbin's model shown by managers and students. Belbin's self-inventory is an easy test for students and managers alike. Managers can score themselves and their employees and apply what has come to be known as Belbin's method for designing teams. For £984 you could also participate in a two-day training course and become a Belbin accredited trainer or consultant (http://www.btinternet.com/~cert/accreditation.htm).

However, in organizational psychology the validity of Belbin's model and his team-role self-perception inventory has been questioned and retested, with mixed results. For example, Furnham, Steele and Pendleton (1993, p. 254) found that there is little psychometric support for the structure of Belbin inventories.

How do you make teams work?

ADDRESSING RESISTANCE Students and advocates of teams at work report that creating 'real teams' is difficult because there is often resistance to their implementation. Berneinsten (1992, p. 359), for example, reports that in the experiments at Volvo discussed earlier, 'to everyone's surprise some workers resisted changes because they preferred the traditional approach of doing a single task all day'. Weisbord (1992), in recounting his attempt to implement participative work design and teams in his company, points out that some ex-supervisors, as well as some workers, could not adapt to the self-managing teams: 'Sidney, our best shipper, a world class miracle of efficient distribution had about as much interest in participation as a gourmet chef would have in McDonald's. "I don't want more responsibility. Why can't I just pack orders?" ' (Weisbord, 1992, p. 98).

Do the quotes reported above signal a resistance to teamwork? This is anecdotal evidence, you might think, and you would be right. Mainstream researchers have rarely undertaken in-depth exploration of employees' experiences of teamwork. Some studies have attempted to identify the factors that intervene in producing resistance to working in teams. Kanter (1983), for example, considers that teams are not immune from organizational politics as people pursue personal agendas, internal competition, etc., resulting in a disruption of team cohesiveness and effective task accomplishment.

Some of the factors intervening in generating resistance that have been studied are: perceptions of fairness and trust; attitude towards change; and cultural values.

PERCEPTION OF FAIRNESS AND TRUST Some researchers have concluded that trust and fairness of treatment in the perception of employees is an important element in avoiding or engendering resistance to teamwork. According to Kirkman (2000), the aspects of work that have proven significant for employees' perception of fairness (Kirkman *et al.*, 1996; Jones and Lindley, 1998) are:

- pay
- distribution of workload
- criteria for decisions
- interpersonal treatment.

However, Kirkman (2000, p. 7) argues that one should not believe that fair management will *necessarily* reduce resistance. In the first place, there should be a desire of the worker to be self-managing or 'self-leading', as Manz (1990, p. 486) also stresses. There must be, these authors maintain, a certain philosophy held by the employees if they are to be willing and productive members of a team. It is a certain view and meaning of their work that makes working in teams personally meaningful and

Box 3.5: Definition of 'resistance'

Resistance in the mainstream literature is defined as any conduct that serves to maintain the status quo in the face of pressure to alter the status quo' (Zaltman and Duncan 1977, cited in Kirkman and Shapiro, 1997).

appealing for them. These non-fairness issues are related to **dispositional factors**, such as stable attitudes towards change and cultural values. These dispositional factors are clarified below.

TOLERANCE FOR CHANGE As Kirkman (2000) suggests, low tolerance towards change is negatively associated with the introduction of self-managing teams. People may well understand intellectually that change is required but they can have negative emotional responses that can be unconscious or conscious, such as a fear of not being able to develop the skills and behaviours required, or of not understanding the task. They can find it extremely difficult to cope with the novelty and ambiguity that self-managing teams might mean for them intellectually, physically and emotionally.

CULTURAL VALUES Hofstede (1980, 1983) has suggested that cultural values are based on durable, desirable conduct that is deemed proper, in particular, to certain societies (Kirkman and Shapiro, 1997, p. 11). So, values (e.g. shared problem solving rather than reliance upon a single authority figure) that facilitate self-managing teams may be resisted more in certain cultures than others. Yet, Kirkman notes that there can be variation in the values also within cultures. This model therefore, does not focus only on national differences (as was the case in Hoftstede's research) but also on individual differences within a national culture (see also Kluckhohn and Strodtbeck, 1961; Maznevski and DiStefano, 1995). This implies the possibility of investigating any prospective or established worker, and identifying how he/she scores on the following categories:

- *Collectivism–Individualism*. This is evident in the attitude towards teamwork as a process that requires interdependency. It regards how much a person finds it desirable to share, collaborate and depend on others for results, thereby valuing the benefit of the group (collectivism) over self-interest (individualism). Individuals embedded in a collectivist culture are understood to be less likely to resist teamwork than those steeped in a individualist culture.

The following considerations have a bearing upon the attitude towards self-management:

- *Power distance*. This is the level (high or low) of acceptance of an unequal distribution of power. Individuals with high power distance expect and respect managers to lead them. Those with low power distance are more comfortable with a high degree of autonomy and responsibility and are more inclined to by-pass bosses, status and formality in order to get the job done. High power distance is expected to create resistance to self-management.
- *Orientation*. Doing versus being. This is the orientation towards work and non-work activities. Being-oriented people have a tendency to emphasize non-work activities, while doing-oriented people emphasize the accomplishment of goals at work. The being-oriented people are expected to have a higher resistance to self-managed teamwork because this may require a continuous process of goal-setting, higher commitment and effort at work.
- *Determinism versus free will*. This concerns the belief of who or what controls one's life. Determinists believe that outcomes and life's difficulties are controlled by forces outside oneself (God, fate, management, etc.). They are thought more likely to resist self-management.

Limiting and containing resistance, for example by selecting the individuals with the 'right' dispositions is what Kirkman's work is designed to achieve. Another of the main aspects related to team effectiveness is that of leadership. We discuss next how this relates to teams at work.

Addressing leadership Should teams, and especially the so-called self-managing teams, have a leader? What type of leadership should be utilized in organizations based on teamwork? It is true that self-managing and self-leading teams would not require, in principle, a leader or supervisor because this role is internal to the empowered team? Research (Wall *et al.*, 1992) has shown that self-managing teams reduce cost by removing traditional supervisory hierarchical levels. Employees are empowered to be autonomous and responsible in how they organize, coordinate and improve their work. Yet, this creates strong demands upon managers who are under pressure to maintain systems of direction and control. As Manz (1990) argues, following a study by Mulder (1971), employees lack the managerial knowledge and education, and therefore lack the 'expert power' attributed to managers. Therefore many management writers point at the fundamental role of leaders in companies where work is organized into teams. Not only, as we have said earlier, does management need to provide clear performance goals for the team (Hackman *et al.*, 1989; Katzenbach and Smith, 1993; Lipman, Blumen

Table 3.2 Traditional versus 'SuperLeadership'

Traditional leadership	SuperLeadership
• Direction	• Encourage self-goal-setting
• Instruction	• Encourage self-evaluation
• Command	• Encourage high self-expectancy
• Assigned jobs/tasks	• Facilitate self-problem solving
• Assigned goals	• Develop self-initiative and responsibility
• Hierarchical conflict resolution	• Encourage within-group conflict resolution
• Reprimand	• Provide training
	• Encourage opportunity thinking

and Leavitt, 1999; Shea and Guzzo, 1987), but the role and the behaviour of managers external to the team – the 'external' leaders (Manz and Sims, 1987; Hackman, 1992; Glaser, 1992) – is also fundamental for the success of the team.

Hackman (1992), for example, has argued that team leaders should focus on critical aspects of the team performance: clear direction, enabling structure, supportive organizational context, available coaching and adequate material resources that the leaders must constantly monitor and take action as required. Manz and Sims (1987) delineate, more in depth, what is for them the actual role and specific behaviour in order for such leaders to be effective and useful to the team. They suggest that the 'external leader' is one who is able to make the team lead itself. They call this 'SuperLeadership' (Manz and Sims, 1993; Manz, 1992). They consider it ineffective, and even dangerous, for the performance of the self-managing team to have traditional leadership (e.g. a foreman) using a top-down approach. In Table 3.2 you can see the set of behaviours associated with traditional leadership and you can compare it with that of the 'SuperLeader' (Manz and Sims, 1993, p. 209).

Exercise 3.3

Using Table 3.2, analyse and discuss leadership in the case of AML. Who is leading the team? What type of leadership can you identify? Illustrate your arguments with examples from the vignette.

In SuperLeadership, external managers and superiors are supposed to facilitate the team to lead itself. But how does a team specifically develop leadership? Glaser (1992) suggests that self-leadership is obtained through a process of progressive empowerment of the team – a shift of power and authority from the supervisors to the team itself. Self-leadership is the last stage of a four-stage process:

- *Stage 1*. The team is unempowered. Glaser calls this an underdeveloped group. The groups follows the direction of the facilitator, who deploys a top-down leadership style very similar to the traditional one of planning, directing and controlling.
- *Stage 2*. The team starts questioning aspects of its work through dialogue and requests feedback. The role of the leader starts being more that of a coach, offering counsel and advice in a continuous, open communication with the team.
- *Stage 3*. The team is, as Glaser defines it, 'somewhat empowered'. This is a team able to contribute possible strategies and to engage in some critical thinking regarding the planning, controlling and directing of its work.
- *Stage 4*. An effective, self-managing team is established. It is 'fully empowered' as the team itself takes responsibility for planning, direction and control. The team leader has the role of a SuperLeader, facilitating the members of the team to lead themselves, while control of the teamwork is, for the most part, in the hands of the team.

Summary of key mainstream contributions and empirical studies In the first part of this chapter we have provided some definitions and discussed the distinction between *team* and *group work* as they are defined in management theory. We have also considered some of the insights developed in psychology and psychoanalysis for understanding the experience of being in a group. We have seen that there are many group phenomena and that some of them are not necessarily positive for performance, such as the free-riding tendency and the groupthink.

In mainstream management theory teams are considered fundamental for today's organizations. It has been suggested that teams are important because they activate/enhance three organizational dimensions that are considered central for healthy and wealthy work organization: flexibility, motivation and learning. We have analysed and discussed many different empirical studies that are important for studying teams at work in the mainstream management literature. These included traditional industries such as the automobile industry. With the case of NUMMI we illustrated teams working in regimes of 'lean production', 'learning bureaucracy' and 'continuous improvement'; with Volvo, we discussed participative work design and self-managing teams. We also presented a case of a knowledge intensive company, AML, which develops, designs and builds 'perfect digital solutions'. This helped us in illustrating what are often referred to as post-bureaucratic organizational forms, with only two organizational hierarchical layers, and where interdependent members working in self-managing teams are fundamental for getting the job done.

The notions that sustain the positive view of teams at work for increasing morale, flexibility and ultimately productivity, we have argued, are not entirely a new phenomenon but belong to a long tradition of studies that gave origin to the 'human relations school' (Mayo, 1933, 1945), the socio-technical tradition of work design (Trist and Bamforth, 1951) and studies in social psychology devoted to understanding and facilitating social change and democratization through groups (Lewin, 1948). The empirical studies we have referred to are summarized in Table 3.3, where it is indicated how each of

Table 3.3 Summary of empirical studies

Authors	Key concepts	Key contributions
Mayo (1933, 1945)	• Social needs • Group norms and rules	• Informal groups have an impact on motivation and conduct in organizations. They need to be managed
Lewin (1948)	• Group cohesion: we-ness	• A democratic participative atmosphere increases quality and quantity of output
	• Group dynamics • Group atmosphere	• Social relations can be changed and improved by intervening with/in group dynamics
Trist and Bamforth (1951)	• Autonomous responsibility • Socio-technical system	• Social systems can produce groups that show high levels of responsibility even when they have high autonomy • When introducing organizational change we need to intervene not only on the technical but also on the social system
Adler (1993) Adler and Borys (1996) Womack *et al.* (1990)	• Lean production • JIT • Learning bureaucracy	• Teams' responsibility for a practice increases flexibility, motivation and learning • Standardization, formalization and continuous improvement can be obtained also with team-based production
Berggren (1992) Bernstein (1992)	• Self-managing teams • Participative design and organization	• Democratic, participative design is feasible • Social and political factors intervene in favouring the success or failure of a new design

them has contributed to the debate on teams at work. Then we looked at aspects and issues that management theorists consider important for enhancing and perfecting team effectiveness and efficiency. Group development, roles design, resistance and leadership, it is suggested, are some of the areas that need to be attentively managed in order to obtain high-performing and successful teams.

Contribution and limitation of mainstream

Conceptual and methodological contributions and limitations One of the main contributions of the mainstream literature on teams at work is that it appears to offer a solution for everything: it explains how teams work, why they work and how you can make them work more effectively, and even how you can yourself become a successful team member. This can be useful in so far as it helps to reduce the anxiety of what to do when faced with a teamwork situation. Yet, if you have experienced it, team life is rarely as rosy as the mainstream literature seems to imply, and the prescriptions do not necessarily help in improving the situation. It is not always, or not 'just', a matter of 'wrong implementation' of teams at work. Too often, mainstream knowledge creates an overenthusiastic and simplistic view of organizational life that pictures teamwork as a **panacea** (Jenkins, 1996; Dunphy and Bryant, 1996; Sinclair, 1992). The categories and the prescriptions offered in the mainstream are often detached from the complexities and messiness of organizing people and resources. A list of bullet points that is mechanically applied without regard to the particularities of the situation can create more problems than it solves.

Much of the mainstream literature centres on the classification of what teams are and how it is possible to improve team effectiveness. The aim is to establish – by limited, often anecdotal and methodologically dubious studies – the basis for models that can establish conceptual differences (such as the distinction between 'real teams' and 'groupwork') and predict behaviours and results (for example, by limiting the number of individuals with cultural values that are not conducive to self-managing teams; or recruiting people to fill required roles). However, the possibility of finding comprehensive and universally predictive models is, as Berders and Van Hootegem (2000, p. 7) put it, a 'mission impossible'. Many have pointed out that when we leave the field of prescriptions (i.e. the magic bullet points) it is very difficult to make comparisons between different plants and experiences (Mueller, 1994; Berders and Van Hootegem, 1999, 2000; Van Amelsvoort and Benders, 1996; Buchanon, 2000). In the concrete experiences of work, the variances we can find are enormous and the issues at work numerous and awkward.

Thinkpoint 3.5

Can you employ any of the concepts of the mainstream to analyse and compare teams at work in NUMMI, Uddevalla and AML? What limitations do you find?

In the case of AML, many elements that are suggested in the mainstream, such as assessing employees for relevant roles and identifying resistances, and matching people to obtain role balance, are impossible given the resources available. Including the elements suggested in the literature in the recruitment and selection process could be a sensible thing to do, but it would be very costly – an aspect little considered in the mainstream literature where there is a silence on costs issues as well as the broader feasibility of introducing the prescriptions for 'proper' teamwork (Dunphy and Bryant, 1996; Sinclair, 1992). Their universal, one size fits all prescriptions do not take into consideration the specificity of the industry. In order to understand teams at work, we need to include a much wider set of issues based on a 'detailed examination of historical, technological and socio-political internal and external conditions of teamworking practice' (Knights and McCabe, 2000). Teamwork, in other words, should not be considered as a well-defined, fixed package but, rather, it is dependent upon, and influenced by a set of dynamic circumstances: 'issues of the extent and nature of delegated power, or whether socialisation of teams' members plays an important role, are contingent on a variety of national, corporate and local factors' (Thompson and Wallace, 1996, p. 105).

Specifically then, some of the suggestions given in the mainstream knowledge of teams at work, such as testing for roles and disposition to resistance, imply the existence of a labour market that contains a right balance in terms of roles, dispositions and skills from which the company can source workers. This is rather unlikely – a heroic assumption as it might be called. In AML, for example, given the particular and novel field of AML's business – digital marketing and communication – AML's owners and directors consider themselves lucky when they can recruit workers with even a minimum of experience and skills. Issues of costs and availability of basic as well as expert skills for an independent, small company operating in a new-forming industry are very significant and should not be underestimated for the impact they have on the work organization.

Empowerment, control and power relations Many authors, as we have seen, enthusiastically assure us that control is 'pushed down' to the workers; that with empowerment there is a power transaction from the management to the workers by means of letting the workers participate and make decisions regarding the planning, coordination and method of their work (Glaser, 1992; Manz and Sims, 1987). Yet some authors in the mainstream literature seem to be worried by this aspect of teams at work, signalling that, perhaps, this devolution would not be entirely desirable; at least if it happened to the extent that is often rather loosely advocated. The anxiety is due to the possibility that 'pushing down' responsibility and autonomy at work might be 'too literal' and, to a certain extent, 'too real'. For authors in the mainstream there is a danger of this happening as it could have undesirable consequences. Power devolution might result in loss of control, or in over-confidence and, in turn, misjudgements on the part of subordinates (Corger and Kanungo, 1988, p. 480). Others point to how empowerment can become an 'agency problem', which refers to the problem of reconciling loss of top-down control with the organizational requirement for goal congruence (Mills and Ungson, 2003). More simply, this means that there is a danger that empowered employees follow different goals and ends from those that are called 'organizational' ones. Then the question becomes, you might think, what are the organizational goals or ends? And also, who is to decide what they are and how to pursue them? If you are asking these questions you are entering the terrain of values, and who decides what the dominant values are to be. You are asking ethical and **political questions**.

Mainstream thinking refers to organizations (and teamwork) as neutral and apolitical entities with specific 'needs', just as if they were organisms. The term 'organizational need' is widely invoked as a

CASE STUDY 3.4 AML (2)

AML work organization seems to be centred around a team that participates in a community of practice designing 'perfect new media solutions'. This practice shapes their identity as new media designers. The directors, such as Amber, are some of the experts of this practice. AML, with its mixed-team organization, seems to favour organizational learning. But this explanation does not seem to tell us much of the situation, as Laura – a novice to the company and to the practice – found herself at the 'centre' of AML's practice of design, with much responsibility and unclear and ambiguous autonomy. You would have thought that, being a novice, she would be participating only at the periphery of the practice. In fact, Laura lacked the identity of a competent member, her colleagues did not recognize her as such. Yet the team *had* to work in this paradoxical situation: with spurious leadership, lack of guidelines or templates and with a key figure in the practice being a novice.

For the mainstream, this would be evidence of irrationality, or, at least, a lack of managerial knowledge. But this is a naive interpretation. The creative director intervenes in the practice in very effective ways to facilitate the team in achieving its task, when she sees fit or when she can. She is neither irrational nor lacking in managerial knowledge. The mainstream, in other words, does not offer us ways for studying such paradoxes and ambiguities. It is these points of paradox and ambiguity that critical perspectives can help us to understand. These are studied and elaborated as the means and effects of relations of power that shape and reproduce both the identities of those involved and the field of work, including what is possible and impossible to do and also not to do. So, for example, a critical understanding of this situation might explore how the relation of subordination upon which capitalist relations of production are f(o)unded make it possible for Laura to be employed at the very centre of the practice as cheap labour. This forces everyone else in the team to intensify and extend their effort – including working during the weekend and overtime – in order to get the job done and also maintain their own identity as expert designers of perfect new media solutions.

shorthand for the aims of owners (shareholders) and managers of an organized system of production. This system is not only (re)producing wealth, but it is also (re)producing (unequal) social relations. Some people, the workers, are subordinated to others – that is, to managers (and owners) who, it is suggested, are the ones who are 'supposed to know', as they have acquired a monopoly of expert knowledge. Manz, we have seen earlier, calls this 'expert power', which is what helps in guaranteeing the dominant position of management in the system itself. But, as we have seen, this is exactly what is potentially subverted if teams at work (with their autonomy, empowerment and learning) are taken too literally.

To summarize, mainstream knowledge is mainly an instrumental knowledge devoted to prescribing how to make teams more efficient and effective in search of higher productivity. This approach takes for granted that this end is right and universal. This knowledge has various consequences as it legitimizes shareholders' and managers' positions of authority, in particular of a masculine kind (see Metcalfe and Linstead, 2003, specifically on teamwork), and the social and material resources that these managers (particularly senior managers) enjoy in contemporary capitalist societies. Perhaps, it is in order to gain access to these positions and resources that you are now reading management at university, and studying this book.

Expert knowledge also helps in reducing the anxieties of managers (and management academics) in the face of the uncertain, open nature of everyday life. As the anxiety of losing control demonstrates, managerial identity and the knowledge and practices that support it, are not established once and for all. Managers depend on others, the subordinates, to continue to accept and reproduce their position of subordination. Hence, there is a continuous search for new ideas and new prescriptions that help this reproduction. But, at the same time, this relation is also constantly under threat. New practice, new relations and knowledge – such as team 'empowerment' – which are intended to improve and maintain the status quo can, if taken too literally, threaten the status quo itself, as Corger and Kanungo (1988), Mills and Ungson (2003) and Manz and Sims (1991) have all, with a degree of uneasiness, noted.

Some of the limitations of the mainstream literature are illustrated in Case Study 3.4 with reference to the AML case.

Critical perspectives on teams at work

Introduction to critical approaches to teams at work

Critical perspectives share and develop some of the considerations we highlighted earlier. They approach (and conceptualize) teams at work not as a neutral technology of work design, but as a practice that intervenes in creating, maintaining and reproducing unequal social relations. To signal this shift, we can now use the term 'teamworking' rather than 'teams at work', to emphasize that we are no longer talking about a neutral tool in pursuit of unproblematic and universal organizational goals. A critical view implies that the meaning, value and the existence of these social relations (work relations), the practice that sustains them (like teamworking) and the identities (such as 'team members', 'SuperLeader', etc.) they sustain (and by which they are sustained), are not 'naturally given'. They are not given by some external authority (God, the market, the state) or internal entity (human nature). Rather, they can be thought of as the result of 'sedimented power relations' (Laclau, 1990).

Box 3.6: Definition of 'sedimented power relations'

Sedimented power relations are decisions taken (and routinely reproduced) which establish what something is (and what it is not). They create a situation so normal, so constant, that we take it as natural – so much so that it becomes difficult to look at it as anything but entirely normal and 'given'. Situations that you might find difficult to consider as strange include the fact that you eat every day if you wish, that you have a family, that you are a woman or a man, that you have money to buy more or less what you want. You have money to spend either because you are a wealthy owner (of land or capital, for example), or you employ yourself in a company or in a profitable activity, or you beg or steal.

Critical writers contest the **idealized picture** of teamwork painted in the mainstream literature. This idealization can be seen in the somewhat benign nature of teamwork as creating a win-win work situation (Ezzamel and Willmott, 1998): employees are more satisfied and their work is 'smarter' because they have been treated like adult human beings with respect and they are given responsibility and autonomy. This makes it possible for the 'organization' to be more flexible, innovative and capable of sustaining and building its future.

The idealized, rosy picture is obtained by dismissing behaviours, ideas and issues that do not fit the creed sustained in the mainstream – what Sinclair (1992) calls the 'team ideology'. The mainstream promises a better organizational reality for managers and for workers alike. But, as we have seen, things often 'do not fit'. There are 'remains' – that is, elements that disrupt the nice, clear picture of teams at work.

Thinkpoint 3.6

How is the idealized picture sustained and maintained? Behaviours that 'do not fit' are quickly dismissed, if even noticed, in different ways in the mainstream. For example:

- *As irrational aberrations*, as in the case presented earlier of the Volvo operator who actually stated he preferred to be told what to do. The suggestion is that it is irrational to prefer the inhumane and alienating repetition of Taylorist organization to the empowering and democratic self-managing teams. What do you think?
- *As personal shortcomings or idiosyncrasies*, as in the example of the order filler (page 137) who was fantastic at his job but just could not understand how good and amazing the whole new system based on teamwork was.
- *As unfortunate individual/cultural predispositions*, as in the case of the Kirkman model (page 138) whereby if you are individualist and being-oriented and high in power disposition you are hopeless because the likelihood that you are going to be a bad team player is high!
- *As perceptions* of fairness, trust and justice, which makes these issues a subjective matter to be addressed and seemingly resolved by means of ethical codes of conduct and regulations.

Critical perspectives on teamworking question what, in the mainstream literature, are taken-for-granted 'truths' of teams at work, pointing out the contradictions of such teamwork theory and practice. First, we shall delve into contributions that aim to show another, arguably darker side to teamwork. This section is entitled 'The other side of the coin', which specifically highlights issues of inequality and autonomy/freedom. Concepts and ideas will be illustrated by reference to the NUMMI case presented earlier. As a significant part of the critical debate centres on the concept of control, a second section is dedicated to understanding teamworking by considering how issues of identity are of relevance for its critical analysis. Other empirical studies, including AML, will be used to illustrate these ideas.

The other side of the coin

Working smarter *and* harder One of the key considerations pointed out by critical writers is that teamworking is generally a top-down, management (or employer) driven process. As Procter and Mueller (2000) note, many of the original studies of teams at work, particularly those of the socio-technical tradition, were cases where employees had organized themselves in autonomous groups (see also Ezzamel, Willmott and Worthington, 2001), while today teamwork is introduced by management as part of a proper managerial strategy (Procter and Mueller, 2000, p. 8). This strategy has specific stated aims, one of the most important being to increase the efficiency of the workforce – as the slogan goes, 'by working smarter not harder'. Yet, many contend that often teamwork means working smarter *and* harder (Adler, 1993; Parker and Slaughter, 1988; Berggren, 1992; Garrahan and Stewart, 1992; McCabe and Black, 1996). In other words, teamworking can produce (and it often does) work intensification. Voices from the union movement have been extremely critical of practical applications of teamwork, specifically in regimes of 'lean production', so much so that it has been recast as 'mean production' (Parker and Slaughter, 1988; Grenier, 1989).

Production is 'mean' because of the negative effect upon the employees of minimizing stockpiles of parts and other forms of duplication in production. These are considered as waste in the lean, JIT design. Yet they function as 'buffers', which, Parker and Slaughter argue, make the system more bearable for the workers as they give them a breathing space that is lacking in the highly regimented lean design. Buffers also give managers a certain leeway, enabling them to keep things going, covering for problems or emergencies if they arise. CYA ('cover your ass'), by building in some elements of slack and redundancy, has often been considered a prudent operating procedure, as Parker and Slaughter (1988, p. 16) observe!

By aiming to eliminate waste of all kinds, lean production does not give any leeway and pressurizes all the 'components' of the system continuously, without any possibility of having a steady and tolerable pace. The pace of production is relentless and continuously stressed to higher and higher degrees, in many different ways, for example, by speeding up the line. Parker and Slaughter call this management-by-stress (MBS) as, when following the principles of *kaizen*, new standards are created that assign additional activities to the workers of a team that must also keep up with a faster assembly line. But higher stress is also felt every time there is an absentee from the team, or a new, novice worker is assigned to the team. Given that workers in the NUMMI teams are interchangeable, and a team is completely responsible for a certain area of work, then it is the team that is responsible for covering for slow workers, novices or absentees. Each worker has to continue with their normal tasks and all the team members are called to do a bit of the work of the novice or the absentee. In other words, the cost is on the team and the team leader and, as Parker and Slaughter (1988, p. 21) put it, 'no department's budget is hurt by absenteeism'.

Thinkpoint 3.7

What problems do you see with this system? Do you think this system ensures equality in the distribution of effort/cost? Do you think this system of work respects human dignity? What is human dignity for you?

Box 3.7: The meaning of 'human dignity' and inequality

Human dignity might appear an uncontested concept, but the example of what is understood by 'human dignity' in the context of the advocates of lean production is enlightening. Human dignity is central for the 'empowered' workforce yet, as Parker and Slaughter (1988) point out, the whole teamwork rhetoric employs a peculiar notion of humanity. They give the example of the answer given by Monden (1983), an advocate and popularizer of the practices of Toyota, to those who criticize the lack of buffers and slack. Monden suggests that allowing for slack 'does not give the opportunity for the worker to realise his [sic] worth. On the contrary, that end can be better served by providing the worker with a sense that his work is worthwhile and allowing him to work with his superior and his comrades to solve problems they encounter.' This example, apart from showing the gendered organization of work, also succinctly points out how human dignity and human fulfilment is defined within a mainstream perspective, namely, to exercise one's abilities to solve problems with others. This view is *defined by management*, and somewhat 'given', ready made, to the workers who simply have to accept and actualize 'this dignity' in the terms and in practices that are established by management. A narrow view of human dignity established by a particular section of the population, namely management, is taken to stand for a universal and necessary view of human dignity. This instrumental view of human dignity at once poses a particular view as universal and also reproduces and legitimizes the structured system of inequalities in wealth and status that are normal features of capitalist societies.

Parker and Slaughter (1988) contend that this intensification of work is less humane than traditional forms of work organization. In the name of empowerment, this system cuts the possibility of breathing space and personal autonomy that 'buffers' of different kinds made possible. Teams have an unprecedented level of responsibility but also a limited possibility of exercising genuine autonomy, since the main objective of the system is to develop higher and higher degrees of efficiency (and productivity). It, therefore, requires strict adherence to its own rigid methods and procedures (Klein, 1989, p.p. 60–61).

These considerations are important and represent a departure from the mainstream for two reasons. They point to the other, ugly face of teamwork as an intensifying and stressful practice of work, which does not really square with mainstream images of teamwork as a more playful and fulfilling cooperation in achieving harmonized organizational ends. More fundamentally, it puts into question who benefits from the work smarter and harder logic. For Parker and Slaughter, the workers are not necessarily benefiting from this process of intensification of their labour, which instead serves the ends of 'those' exploiting the workers' capacity for labour, as they get more labour for less money and less managerial overheads, in a regime in which 'participation' is on management's terms.

Teamworking as control and consent over labour effort and cost With the shift to a critical view of teamworking, we pay attention to its role in the perpetuation of a particular socio-economic order – that of liberal capitalist societies. In liberal capitalism, the owners of the business organization (the 'shareholders') and its controllers and enactors (management) are, broadly speaking, concerned to maximize profit at the minimum cost. This is obtained by dividing and coordinating a set of productive activities where the surplus (income minus expenditures) generated in these activities (which, as we have seen earlier, are made natural and normal by the use of comparatively impersonal organizational ends) is privately appropriated (by the owners themselves).

Karl Marx, a political thinker, developed the understanding that, in capitalism, the planning, division and coordination of work are intended to ensure control of the workers in a process that is alienating and exploitative. By 'control' is meant the mechanism of exploitation. While wages are paid for the workers' *capacity* to engage in purposeful activities, the transformation that adds value to a given process of work happens only in the moment of its actual application. *Without control, this application is at a discretion of the workers*, and that is why management is employed to control workers in order to get the maximum application at a minimum cost. Control is needed to make sure that workers submit to the logic of capital accumulation, so as to eliminate what are considered 'unproductive' time and practices – what we called 'waste' in JIT. This understanding of work organization – which highlights the role of management in controlling workers in order to produce a surplus that can be distributed to shareholders – questions something that for us all is entirely normal. It is so normal, infact, that we take it for granted as our existence is routinely seen within the coordinates that this system produces and maintains. We expect and also wish to enter wage relations with an employer, with the inequalities and the subordination to, or over, others that this relation implies. We generally regard this as an unexceptional, even natural progression in life, signalling independence and the entrance into adulthood.

Thinkpoint 3.8

Do you think there are alternatives to this organization and division of labour and resources? How could those alternatives be realized? What problems do you foresee?

In other words, critical perspectives suggest that even if teamworking moves away from the fragmenting, individualizing logic of Taylorism, it maintains the same fundamental logic of workers' exploitation. But it is accomplished in a different way as the workers are given the means to influence, within narrow limits controlled by management, at least part of how the application of their labour should be accomplished. The logic (and the power relations that are sustained by it) is much the same, as the coordinates are that of maximum application of labour at minimum cost for the owners. This, in the case of NUMMI, was accomplished by work intensification so as to achieve

SOURCE: © GRONK, 1997

Image 3.5 Consent

maximum input per unit of work. But it can be accomplished in different ways. In AML, we saw how workers 'feel responsible' for finishing the detailed content design of the e-mail system address book. They stay at work late to get the job done. This means that they continue to work beyond 'normal working hours' – a concept that has become almost obsolete in many (e.g. knowledge-intensive) firms – and far beyond the working hours for which they are paid. This effort, then, is literally (money) and figuratively (time that could be spent doing other things in their life) at the workers' expense.

This example of AML illustrates what Friedman (1977) calls control by 'responsible autonomy', in which workers are encouraged and rewarded by management to exercise their discretion in ways that are responsible for attaining management's goals (e.g. greater productivity). Teamwork is a practice that can help facilitate this feeling of involvement in the work they do, and a sense of ownership of their practice that increases the responsibility they have for their work. Through teamworking, they actively **consent** to furthering their own exploitation and further their subordination. It is in this sense that teamwork is considered a subtle form of control, not least because it is clothed in a rhetoric of participation and employee involvement. It is intended to enhance work effort, thereby increasing productivity but saving on labour cost (see Pollert, 1996; McCabe and Black, 1996; Buchanan, 2000).

Thinkpoint 3.9

Why do people consent to this form of control? How is it that teamworking facilitates this consent?

Some writers, such as Parker and Slaughter (1988), have argued that the utilization of the team concept – what, as we have seen, Sinclair calls 'team ideology' – is a manipulation that 'cons' workers. It cons them into believing that the managerial strategies for intensification and consent are good for them, desirable and serve their interests as workers and as individual human beings. In other words, teamwork is regarded as a managerial strategy that realigns (most of the time successfully) 'individual motivation' with 'organizational need' (see Mueller, 1994); it reduces conflict and resistance at work; and it marginalizes or neutralizes the need for, and the role of, unions, as the employees' material and psychological needs are met through their (managed) identification with their team.

One of the problems with this view is that it implies that that the workers are ignorant and blinded in understanding their own real interest, while there are others, arguably radical theorists or union leaders, who are knowledgeable about what these interests are, and uncover them for the workers. This essentialist view of the human subject also assumes that there is such a thing as a 'real' interest, where real is understood as a fixed and determined knot in our lives that if undone would 'sort' our lives forever, or, at least, release us from our delusions (false consciousness) so showing us our true interest.

A murkier picture of teamwork

Many critical writers suggest the picture is much murkier than the one presented above, given that the contradictions of teamwork are evident and available to workers, managers and students, making teamwork a 'contested terrain' rather than an encompassing ideology that is readily and effectively applied by a cunning management to a naive workforce. Garrahan and Stewart (1992) contend that at Nissan workers willingly consent to their own subordination and further exploitation. The workers know very well what they are doing, but nevertheless they still do it. In other words, they are not simply 'conned' and manipulated by managerial strategy and its ideology (teamwork). Research on teamwork implementation presented by Pollert (1996) and McCabe and Black (1996) suggests that teamworking can create a set of ambiguities for the workers, which does not necessarily lead to consent (see Ezzamel *et al.*, 2001). Managers themselves experience conflicting demands that make the contradictions of teamwork more evident and give reason 'for the union to retain a foot hold' (Pollert cited in McCabe and Black, 1996, p. 114). In the politics of production, teamworking reflects local dynamics where its principles are partially implemented, imperfectly adopted and inconsistently applied. However, we should avoid slipping into a form of 'contingency analysis': 'when faced with the grand claims of would-be gurus, the danger is that we slip into a form of contingency analysis where a detailing of the context displaces theoretical reflection altogether' (Knights and McCabe, 2000, p. 6).

We need additional theoretical resources to question teamworking and problematize the issue of consent and the reproduction of relations of inequality, which, it has been suggested, this practice perpetuates. Many authors (see for example Ezzamel and Willmott, 1998; Ezzamel *et al.*, 2001; Knights and McCabe, 2003; McCabe and Knights, 2000; McKinlay and Taylor, 1996; Sewell and Wilkinson, 1992; Sewell, 1998) have attempted to address these questions, in particular by considering how workers' *subjectivity* – their sense of self – is central to resistance and consent. These views draw upon theoretical sources that we explore and illustrate next.

Self-discipline and surveillance Detailed ethnographies can enable us to make sense of how it is that workers' sense of identity comes to be shaped in conduct that secures willing consent and compliance to work smarter and harder, as teamwork becomes a means for control that increases their productivity and exploitation. The main point conveyed by these studies is that teamworking itself is a social practice through which workers discipline themselves, and each other, by continuous surveillance and by creating, as well as enforcing on themselves and on others, the identity of 'team-mate' (see Barker, 1993, 1999; Sewell and Wilkinson, 1992; Sewell, 1998). This knowledge exerts power as it is also a self-knowledge, by which workers can talk about themselves and 'rationalize' their conduct, by considering what it means to be a team player, and what it takes to be a good team member. How is self-identity specifically conceptualized? A key to answering how it is that people consent and willingly subject to the working harder and smarter logic is embedded in a certain understanding of subjectivity – i.e. what we say we are and how we identify ourselves, most of the time, as free, autonomous and rational beings.

In the mainstream literature, people are considered 'essential beings' – i.e. they 'carry' a sense of self that can be classified and measured in all sorts of scales and categories. In the case of teamwork, people might be categorized for their orientation, for their locus of control, for their personality trait or IQ. Critical writers, in particular those influenced by the work of Michel Foucault, challenge this essentialist and psychologized view of identity. They consider how our 'subjectivity' – i.e. our own sense of self – is constituted and reproduced everyday by actively participating in social practices and in acquiring and reproducing the knowledge that sustains and explains these practices. This means that our subjectivity is not so much described, as it is constituted, for example, by a knowledge that tells us that we have an IQ of 120, have a 'being-orientation', and are high in 'power distance'. Foucault calls this complex set of practices 'power/knowledge', as knowledge itself is productive of relations of power.

Our sense of self is then constantly maintained and reproduced by participation in social practices, by our social relations in the family and friends, by what we read, the products we buy and so on. But this is counter-intuitive, you might think, as you are and always will be your 'own person'. You might 'change' or 'mature', but deep down you are always 'your self'. In other words, there is a sense of continuity about your self-identity that you might feel very strongly about. For critical writers the coherency of our sense of self is like a narrative (see Ezzamel and Willmott, 1998) that we keep on telling us and others – what 'we really are' – but also 'what we really are not' and 'what we really would like to be'. This narrative is continuously negotiated and often comes under threat with feelings of anxiety and insecurities engendered by 'things' that do not fit either with what we thought of ourselves or what we thought of as our reality.

Thinkpoint 3.10

Reflect on your own narrative and thinking of your life as a university student and other experiences you might be undertaking (such as part-time jobs or voluntary work). What is your sense of self? What experiences have challenged the view you have of your self? What experiences have reinforced your sense of self?

An example in AML In the case of AML, John's sense of self is narrated as a knowleadgeable tehnical expert, a 'wizard' in producing elegant and creative technical solutions. To sustain this sense of self he had to collaborate with others. Yet teamworking in AML calls for an involvement with others in phases of design that, for him, is, as he put it in an interview, 'far too much'. He finds himself working as a content designer, while 'my job is technical, I am a technical expert'. In other words, this practice threatens his sense of self as technical expert. Perversely, however, he knows that the final product, will be viewed and assessed by others (his colleagues, his managers, the clients, and the members of the community of technical experts, the internet and mobile users) not simply as a technical solution but as a complete whole. So he engages yet more actively and forcefully in the practice of work to make sure that this 'really is' the elegant and usable solution, which is what sustains the narrative of himself as a 'wizard' and expert.

Further illustrations of the importance of identity in understanding teamworking as a technology that fashions compliant subjects can be derived from the ethnographic work of James Barker (1993, 1998). Barker's study of ISE, a US electronic company, is exemplary of the set of practices that the introduction of the self-managing teams can engender to create a pattern of discipline and surveillance, what he called 'concertive control'. Barker calls it concertive control (see also Tompkins and Cheney, 1985) because workers act in concert to develop the means of their own control (Barker, 1993, p. 4).

What is fascinating about Barker's study of ISE (see Case Study 3.5) is that the final result of the team activity has a strong resemblance to the traditional bureaucratic form of control – i.e. the card checking and ranking of performance. Nonetheless, the source of authority and the enforcement of this control is not the abstract impersonal rule of bureaucratic order but a diffuse set of mechanisms devised by the teams themselves and sustained by the team power/knowledge. Teamwork power/knowledge is composed also of the rules identified and recognized by team members as establishing and summarizing the proper conduct of a rightful teamwork ethic. Self-discipline and surveillance of the concertive control produced an even tighter iron cage than the traditional bureaucracy. Some have called this type of control 'chimerical control' exactly because it is not traditional top-down but is diffused and has hybrid and monstrous characteristics (Sewell, 1998, p. 12). The team members daily constructed, reproduced and maintained a power/knowledge of what they are, and what their work is, that makes them their own masters and their own slaves: 'ISE team workers are both under the eye of the norm and in the eye of the norm, but from where they are, in the eye, all seems natural and as it should be' (Barker, 1993, p. 435).

As we shift to a critical perspective, we consider teamworking as a social practice that institutes, maintains and creates certain power relations by means, as Knights and McCabe (2000) put it, of constituting particular kinds of subjectivities – in short, transforming individuals into teamworking subjects who assume a self-identity as team-mates or face problems or expulsion. For example, Barker points out that 'uncommitted workers' – that is uncommitted according to the team power/knowledge – do not last in the concertive system: 'If they wanted to resist their team control, they must be willing to risk their human dignity, being made to feel unworthy as "team-mates" ' (Barker, p. 436).

Resistance is futile(?) We seem to have painted a rather bleak picture of teamwork. On the one hand, we have suggested that considering teamwork as (traditional) ideology was empirically unsustainable, and theoretically flawed (see page 148). Then the concepts of concertive control, surveillance and discipline were proposed, which, however, from a different theoretical route, arrive at the same conclusion. The bars of the cage are even stronger as people are entrenched in what makes them what they

CASE STUDY 3.5 Teamwork and concerted control: Self-discipline and surveillance

Barker's ethnography of an electronic board assembly factory started at the beginning of the 1990s and lasted two years. The CEO had read the popular management writers (such as Drucker), praising the importance of teamwork and the recognition of employees' participation. He was fascinated and persuaded by this knowledge. He studied the system based on self-managing teams, and then implemented a new organizational design.

First he conducted a limited experiment or 'pilot', and then the whole production activity was organized into self-managing teams. Each individual was assigned to a team that became responsible for the manufacture or configuration of two or three electronic boards. The teams had to decide how to share the work, how to assign responsibilities, what were the ground rules of their work, etc. The company offered training in teambuilding and interpersonal skills and provided supporting advice. They were never told what to do but were guided, notably by the mission statement that was prepared for them by the ISE president. This expressed the values that the company expected from the team, and from each individual as a self-manager: personal initiative, responsibility in doing the work, commitment to the team, quality of individual and team contributions. Barker describes how team members at first experienced confusion and uncertainties because they did not know what to do. Yet, they soon realized it was 'really' up to them to decide how to do the work!

In an impressive number of meetings, teams started discussing closely what their work meant for them, what good quality was, what they expected from each other and so on. Barker notes how the team members started to talk about a sense of ownership and extreme commitment to the work they were doing, feeling that delivering the product on time was their responsibility. For example, there was an incident where some material arrived late, which then required the team to stay late if they were to get the order out to the customer as scheduled. Lea Ann, one of the team members, called the team and put it to everyone that it would take two hours overtime to accomplish the task. Some people had various commitments, but they discussed the issue and eventually all agreed to stay. One of them, they agreed, could go at the normal time because she wanted to attend her children's play at school, but she promised that she would work late the next time it was required.

This is a compelling example of how a team translated into practice the values indicated by the company. The team acquired a set of values that became translated, particularly when new employees joined, in more and more visible signs of commitment. The teams created a series of mechanisms that facilitated and disciplined workers into forms of conduct that reproduced and reinforced their identity as proper, valuable and respected members of an effective and efficient team. Mutual surveillance was part of the conduct of team members. The rules of the team became progressively clearer and more explicit and were enforced in many different ways. For example, some teams had time set aside in their meetings to confront members whose behaviour did not conform to the team rules.

But there were also more subtle means of mutual surveillance – for example, in relation to lateness. Before teamworking, the supervisors might have turned a blind eye to lateness. But teams developed a zero tolerance for tardiness so that everyone's arrival was ranked everyday with a colour coded card system. If a worker collected too many red dots, this would call for a sanction. As one of the employees put it 'now the whole team around me is observing what I am doing'. The constant surveillance promoted self-discipline and compliance as it implied that to be a team member one has to follow the conduct expected, the standards of which are agreed and monitored by the team itself.

SOURCE: © JIMSIZEMORE/CARTOONSTOCK.COM

Image 3.6

are: their own self-identity as team members. Teamworking power/knowledge seems comparable to the technology of the Borg in *Star Trek*, the famous sci-fi series. The Borg pursues the quest for knowledge and for perfection by assimilating in the collective mind all the alien cultures encountered, so all the differences are maintained in a perfect whole. The collective changes all the time, but it always stays the same imperturbably, just like capitalism which has to change in order to avoid collapse. 'Resistance is futile!' states the Borg in front of the terrorized subject, to whom perfection and knowledge is given when the assimilation is completed. Are we all assimilated in a system that gives us a sense of self? Are the Borg right – resistance is futile?

Critical writers suggest that it is not futile. But, again, it is not a matter of finding or even proposing a single solution or recipe. The point is that making explicit the ambivalence and ambiguity of everyday working practices helps in making explicit the antagonism and negativity of social relations. This reminds us how much the sedimentation and taken-for-grantedness of these relations is the results of political acts. As such, these are not naturally given, can be changed and are constantly threatened at work.

As Garahan and Stewart (1992) note in their study of Nissan, not all employees totally identify with the 'team-mates' ethos and identity. There is resistance to practices that were intended to strengthen the Nissan culture and its values such as the sponsoring of sports events, family events and holidays for employees' children. Many employees would not, or could not, identify with such values, and many were cynical towards teamworking (see also Ezzamel *et al.*, 2001; Knights and McCabe, 2000, 2003). Some of the workers (but arguably also some of the managers) would consider themselves to have no alternative other than to 'shut up and put up' because losing employment was not considered a real option. Their sense of identity as providers for their own family or homeowners or consumers, etc. made it impossible for them to consider risking losing their jobs.

More broadly we should consider that for critical writers social practices (such as teamworking) never totalize or exhaust the field of possibilities altogether. In other words, it is impossible to ever determine the meaning, the results and the possibilities offered by a particular practice. This means and implies that teamworking as power/knowledge operates neither according to the aims of the managers nor workers but it establishes what the identities of both might be. Fundamentally the issue refers to the fact that binary logic – i.e. that teamwork either produces consent or produces resistance; or the logic that if it is a managerial tool then it produces only workers' exploitation – cannot be maintained. As the meaning of social practices (in this case of teamworking) is never determined once and for all, it is open to contestation and its closure is constantly under threat and open to rearticulation.

We can illustrate this openness and ambiguity of teamworking power/knowledge with reference to McKinlay and Taylor's (1996) study of Pyramid (see Case study 3.6).

In summary:

- As a social practice, teamwork is 'owned' neither by the managers nor by the workers. What is a 'manager' and what is a 'worker' is realized and reproduced in the teamworking practice, as well as by other practices, which create and maintain the meaning of self and the meaning of work in our lives.
- Teamworking as power/knowledge is not a monolith established once and for all at the service of management. But it is constantly open to rearticulation that can disrupt and subvert the status quo.

Recap questions

1. What is understood by teamwork in the critical tradition?
2. Why are teams said to be a managerial strategy for work intensification?
3. Can you illustrate these views?
4. In what ways does teamwork further inequalities and exploitation?
5. What are the problems with these views?
6. What is concertive control?
7. Why is teamwork considered a social form of what is called power/knowledge?
8. How does this critical understanding of teamwork reconceptualize identity?
9. How does this help us in conceptualizing consent and resistance?
10. What examples from your own experience can you use to illustrate the complex, contradictory, ambiguous and, in a sense, murkier picture of teamworking?

CASE STUDY 3.6 Resistance and teamworking

In Pyramid, a technological company, teamwork power/knowledge came to play a role that compromised the expected aims for which empowered teams were introduced. A clue to the role of teamworking in dislocating managerial expectations and design can be seen in the adoption of the system of peer review for the teams. This was introduced by the management as a way of obtaining knowledge about the shop floor, as well as a forum for the teams to reflect on themselves and their teambuilding processes. It was, in other words, a disciplinary mechanism.

This practice of peer review proved largely unpopular at first, and it was resisted by many employees, who, for example, started to use retaliatory scoring to get at each other. Eventually, however, the equalizing of scores became widespread, which, of course, made this technology useless. Interestingly, the equalizing was made possible by the mobilization of the team ethos itself. It was argued that if the team is reaching the target why should different people be scored more highly than others if the overall result was good? This makes explicit how teamworking as power/knowledge is open to constant rearticulation, which also establishes the interests it is serving and not the other way round. Rather than creating consent it created a sense of resistance to the scoring system and the differences this was designed to establish among workers. In other words, it shows us how the system of inequalities, on which capitalist work relations are based, are actually subverted by taking teamworking 'too seriously' as the workers did in this case, over-identifying with the team ethos.

As a disciplinary mechanism, the peer review was supposed to classify, divide and rank the workers so that bonuses could be allocated to 'deserving' workers. The fact that this was done by the workers themselves should have tied them to their own self-evaluation. This also would provide the effect of a 'consensual' basis for bonus payments. But the workers disrupted these intended truth effects of the self-assessment exercise. They subverted the idea of consensual ranking and classification, as well as that of 'bonuses'. Managers faced with the impossibility of equality – because if bonuses were paid equally the profitability of the operation would be hurt – assigned the bonuses randomly. This response became a nodal point for the constitution of a clear antagonistic move, with teams going on a silent strike – what the employees called three weeks of 'go slow' – and a devastatingly high number of complaints filed against the managerial decision. This occurrence was symptomatic of the inequalities on which such workplaces are based.

Summary of key contributions, empirical studies and limitations in the critical approach

In the second part of this chapter we have analysed critically the concept and practice of teamwork. We referred to a number of empirical studies that have approached teamwork from a critical perspective. These studies are summarized in Table 3.4 and their main contribution to the debate in questioning teamwork is highlighted.

We have suggested that teamwork is often considered an ideology that, under the seductive slogan of 'working smarter not harder', in reality forces workers to work both smarter *and* harder. In other words, there is another, darker side to the rosy picture we have seen presented in the mainstream literature. By revisiting the NUMMI case and the AML case we have discussed how teamwork is a process that increases work intensification and furthers workers' exploitation, participating in eroding workers' rights and conditions. We have considered how one of the limitations of this view is that it assumes that workers are 'conned' by management into believing that teamwork is good for them. This critical structuralists view implies that workers are determined in their conduct and their belief by the managerial strategies and the manipulations they are able to engender, while both managers and critical social theorists are able to see what the workers' real interest is or should be. For example, critical structuralists think that workers' real interests should be that of resisting teamworking practices. However, some critical writers suggest that this privileged insight cannot be justified because, empirically, we observe that production, including teamworking, is a very contested terrain, and not a monolithic, whole encompassing ideology. Workers and managers are ambiguous in their understanding of teamwork and the way they participate in these practices. It is suggested that we can understand and address better the complexities and ambiguities of the experiences in production if, theoretically, we move away from essential notions of subjectivity. One's sense of self is not determined by managers' strategies but is produced, maintained and elaborated in the many practices, diffused mechanisms and technologies in which we participate in and in which we are constituted as subjects, like in the case of teamworking power/knowledge where people develop a knowledge about themselves and their conduct.

One of the limitations of this approach is that it appears to create a bleak picture of working practices because disciplinary mechanisms seem to produce entirely consenting subjects; excluding any sense of resistance. However, we have suggested that these mechanisms of power, of which teamworking is an example, cannot be considered to be owned by anyone in particular and cannot ever be defined in their meaning and consequences once and for all. In other words, even if teamworking can be intentionally introduced in order to exploit teamwork power/knowledge and increase self control and discipline, that does not mean that it produces what top managers and shareholders desire. The practice of

Table 3.4 Summary of empirical studies

Authors	Key concepts	Key contributions
Parker and Slaughter (1988)	• Mean production • Management-by-stress	• Teamwork is a managerial strategy of work intensification
Barker (1993, 1999) See also Sewell (1998) Ezzamel and Willmott (1998) Sewell and Wilkinson (1992)	• Concertive control • Self-discipline • Surveillance • Consent	• Teamwork is itself a social practice that produces and maintains a self-identity • This enhances control and consent
MacKinlay and Taylor (1996) See also Knights and McCabe (2001, 2003) Ezzamel and Willmott (1998) Ezzamel *et al*., (2001)	• Openness of social practices • Resistance	• Teamwork as a social practice and its subject cannot be determined once and for all • Teamworking can also provoke resistance and antagonistic behaviour

teamwork can actually be disruptive of production for both managers and workers. This indicates that discipline and surveillance of teamworking power/knowledge can also be a subverting force. The case of Pyramid illustrated the fear of some of the mainstream management authors. In fact, workers over-identified with the teamworking ethos, thereby traversing the fantasy that teamwork sustains, namely the notion that contemporary workplaces are sites of social relation based on an equal and just exchange. This over-identification brought forth the inequalities on which the capitalist system of production is based and became a nodal point around which an antagonism against management was coagulated.

Final remarks

> Teams and good performance are inseparable; you cannot have one without the other. But people use the word 'team' so loosely that it gets in the way of learning and applying the discipline that leads to good performance. For managers to make better decisions about whether, when or how to encourage and use teams, it is important to be more precise about what a team is and what it isn't. (*Katzenbach and Smith, 1993, p. 163*)

Some of my students and I love this quote because it condenses the taken-for-granted truth about teams and teamwork in mainstream management studies. But there is another truth that oozes from this quote on which I want to concentrate.

Some of my students find the quote appealing because they want to become managers. Arguably, they believe that if someone tells them precisely how they are supposed to manage properly, they will get it right and will be successful managers. This belief is directly attended by Katzenbach and Smith (1993), who propose to 'repair' the shortcomings of woolly thinking and bring in the due precision that will lead to good performance.

Who would not like that? If there were clear, sure recipes telling us what to do and how; if there was something of an indubitable descriptive precision; if there was a natural Truth, we would all know what to do at all times. How great that would be! No more uncertainties and doubts, nor that stomach-turning anxiety we occasionally or often feel but rarely mention. A template would describe and dictate our behaviour, working life and even family life and leisure. It would all be perfectly determined and we would be living in a world of . . . automatons. Yes, with a template for everything, everything would already be decided so we would be like sophisticated robots. We would not decide anything as the decision would be dictated by principles – of teamwork or total quality management, etc. Actually we would not even think of such a thing/concept as a decision. A decision requires an utter not-knowing. A real decision is a crazy step because it is something we take out of undecidability. It is after we have taken it that we find reasonable motives for taking 'this' decision rather than 'that' one. In other words, always it is the present that gives us a sense of the past and the future and not vice versa.

Mind you, the whole point of much of what we call knowledge is about telling us what to do, when and how. Much of management and organization theory is about explaining how things are organized in systems and how these systems help us to predict and control what we do. In organizations there are job descriptions, financial charts, business plans, procedures and contracts. All these indicate and even prescribe the role and behaviour of managers, workers, customers, clients and suppliers, and what these 'stakeholders' are supposed to do. You are reading this book because most likely you are a student in a university and your lecturer said you should read it, and because you are a conscientious student or because your family expect you to do your best at university, and perhaps, because you want to get a good mark and get a top, highly paid job.

So much is directed, ruled, regulated, decided. Yet there are things (ideas, behaviours, elements) that do not fit. As we have seen earlier, if employees really followed completely their job description or the implications of things such as teamworking, probably their units would arrive at a standstill. And, yes, your family may want you to be a conscientious student; but they also want you to be a rounded person, and have friends and keep fit and eat well and be a good citizen. So they probably would not want you to be over-conscientious! But when is the line reached? So many things are often contradictory and, anyway, you do not only do what your family wishes!

It is because things never fit perfectly, because there are some remains of what we are supposed to be and do that there are so many different views on life and interpretations and theories and cultures. Procedures, templates, desires, etc. can never tell us 'the truth' of what we are and what the world is about. We are not automatons. This is the sense of freedom, that is at once appealing, seductive, chastening and terrifying. There are alternatives to the way things are; they are not naturally given; they are not written in stone. They are 'sedimented' constructions, so much so that too often we forget that they are constituted. They are sedimented power relations, and power is not 'natural' – power is 'social'. That, in a nutshell, is the fundamental assumption upon which critical power/knowledge is constructed.

Alternatives are possible. Suspecting and undermining those who claim to have the truth, those who do not even consider that 'truth' is problematic, and showing and proposing alternatives that mobilize the values of equality and freedom, is part of what a radical and democratic project is about. And this is what this chapter, in showing mainstream and critical views, has tried to do in relation to the meaning and valence of teamwork. This is a way of making sense of the politics of one arena of management knowledge, and, as such, this knowledge itself, and your reading of it, is a political act.

Further reading

Barker, J. R. (1999) *The Discipline of Teamwork: Participation and Concertive Control*, London: Sage.

Danaher, G., Schirato, T. and Webb, J. (2000) *Understanding Foucault*, London: Sage.

Foulkes, S. H. and Anthony, E. J. (1957) *Group Psychotherapy: The Psychoanalytic Approach*, London: Penguin Books.

Marx, K. and Engels, F. (1888/1985) *The Communist Manifesto*, London: Penguin Books.

Procter, S. and Mueller, F. (eds) (2000) *Teamworking*, Basingstoke: Macmillan Business.

Wetherell, M. (ed.) (1996) *Identities, Groups and Social Issues*, London: Sage.

Websites

Social psychology and cultural studies sources:
http://www.socialpsychology.org/social.htm#group
http://www.cultsock.ndirect.co.uk/MUHome/cshtml/index.html

Radical and critical sources:
http://www.marxists.org/index.htm
http://www.wsws.org/
http://www.workersworld.net/
http://www.forumsocialmundial.org.br/
http://foucault.info/
http://www.thefoucauldian.co.uk/

Examples of teams and COPs consultants' sites:
Belbin: http://www.belbin.com/game-co-operate.html
Katzenbach: http://www.katzenbach.com/
COPs: http://www.solonline.org/
http://www.ewenger.com/

Portals and sites with resources, games and exercises on teambuilding and development:
http://www.grouprelations.com/
http://www.wilderdom.com/games/InitiativeGames.html
http://www.queendom.com/tests/career/team_roles_access.html
http://www.hrgopher.com/category/377.php
http://reviewing.co.uk/toolkit/teams-and-teamwork.htm

References

Adler, P. (1993) 'Time and motion regained', *Harvard Business Review* 71(1):97–108.

Adler, P. S. and Borys, B. (1996) 'Two types of bureaucracy: Enabling and coercive', *Administrative Science Quarterly* 41(1):61–89.

Albanese, R. and Van Fleet, D. D. (1985) 'Rational behaviour in groups: The free-riding tendency', *Academy of Management Review* 10(2):244–55.

Alvesson, M. (1993) 'Organizations as rhetoric: Knowledge-intensive firms and the struggle with ambiguity', *Journal of Management Studies* 30(6):997–1015.

Ancora, D. and Caldwell, D. (2000) 'Compose teams to assure successful boundary activity', *Blackwell Handbook of Principles of Organizational Behavior*, p.p. 199–210.

Ancora, D. G. and Caldwell, D. F. (2000) 'Bridging the boundary: External activity and performance in organizational teams', *Administrative Science Quaterly* 37(4):634–655.

Argote, L., Gruenfeld, D. and Naquin, C. *et al.* (2000) 'Group learning in organizations', in M. E. Gurner (ed.) *Groups at Work: Advances in Theory and Research*, New York: Erlbham.

Argote, L., Ingram, P., Levine, J. M. and Moreland, R. L. (2000) 'Knowledge transfer in organizations: learning from the experience of others', *Organizational Behavior and Human Decision Processes* 82(1):1–8.

Barker, J. (1993) 'Tightening the iron cage: Concertive control in self managing teams', *Administrative Science Quarterly* 38(3):408–437.

Barker, J. (1999) *The Discipline of Teamwork: Participation and Concertive Control*, London: Sage.

Belbin, M. (1993) *Team Roles at Work*, Oxford: Butterworth-Heinemann.

Belbin, M. (2004) *Management Teams: Why They Succeed or Fail?* Second edition, Oxford: Butterworth-Heinemann.

Berders, J. and Van Hootegem, G. (2000) 'Team and their context: Moving the team discussion beyond existing dichotomies', *Journal of Management Studies* 36(5):609.

Berders, J. and Van Hootegem, G. (2000) 'How the Japanese got teams', in S. Procter and F. Mueller (eds.) *Teamworking*, Basingstoke: Macmillan Business.

Berggren, C. (1992) *The Volvo Experience: Alternatives to Lean Production in the Swedish Auto Industry*, Basingstoke: Macmillan Press.

Bernstein, P. (1992) 'The learning curve at Volvo', in R. Glaser (ed.) *Classic Readings in Self: Managing Teamwork*, Pennsylvania: Organization Design and Development, Inc.

Bion, W. R. (1961) *Experiences in Groups and Other Papers*, London: Tavistock Publications.

Brown, J. S. and Duguid, P. (1991) 'Organizational learning and communities-of-practice: Toward a unified view of working, learning and innovation', *Organization Science* 2(1):40–57.

Buchanan, D. (2000) 'An eager and enduring embrace: The ongoing rediscovery of teamworking as a management idea', in S. Procter and F. Mueller (eds.) *Teamworking*, London: Macmillan Business.

Campion, M. A., Medsker, G. J. and Higgs, A. C., *et al.* (1993) 'Relations between work group characteristics and effectiveness: Implications for designing effective workgroups', *Personnel Psychology* 46:823–850.

Cohen, S. and Ledford, G. (1994) 'The effectiveness of self-managing teams: A quasi experiment, *Human Relations* 47(1):13–43.

Cohen, S. G., Ledford, G. E. Jr. and Spreitzer, G. M. (1996) 'A predictive model of self managing work team effectiveness', *Human Relations* 49(5):643–675.

Cordery, J. L., Mueller, W. S. and Smith, L. M. (1991) 'Attitudinal and behavioural effects of an autonomous working group: A longitudinal field of study', *Academy of Management Journal* 34: 464–476.

Corger, J. and Kanungo, R. (1988) 'The empowerment process: Integrating theory and practice', *Academy of Management Review* 13: 471–482.

Davenport, T. H. and Pusak, L. (1998) *Working Knowledge: How Organizations Manage What They Know,* Cambridge, MA: Harvard Business School Press.

Drucker, P. (1993) 'Knowledge-worker productivity: The biggest challenge', *California Management Review* 41(2):812–856.

Drucker, P. F. (1992) 'The new society of organisations', *Harvard Business Review* Sept–Oct:95–104.

Dunphy, D. and Bryant, B. (1996) 'Teams: Panaceas or prescriptions for improving performance?', *Human Relations* 49(5):677–699.

Edmonson, A. C. (2002) 'The local and variegated nature of learning in organisations: A group-level perspective', *Organization Science* 13(2): 128–146.

Ezzamel, M. and Willmott, H. (1998) 'Accounting for team work: A critical study of group based system of organizational control', *Administrative Science Quarterly* 43(2):358–397.

Ezzamel, M., Willmott, H. and Worthington, F. (2001) 'Power, control and resistance in "the factory that time forgot" ', *Journal of Management Studies* 38(8):1953–1981.

Findlay, P., McKinlay, A., Marks, A. and Thompson, P. (2000) 'Flexible when suits them: The use and abuse of teamwork skills', in S. Procter and F. Mueller (eds.) *Teamworking*, London: Macmillan Business.

Flores, F. and Gray, J. (2000) *Entrepreneurship and the Wired Life: Work in the Wake of Careers,* London: Demos.

Friedman, A. (1977) *Industry and Labour: Class Struggle at Work and Monopoly Capitalism*, London: Macmillan.

Furnham, A., Steele, H. and Pendleton, D. (1993) 'A psychometric assessment of the Belbin Team-Role Self Perception Inventory', *Journal of Occupational and Organizational Psychology* 66:245–257.

Garrahan, P. and Stewart, P. (1992) *The Nissan Enigma: Flexibility at Work in a Local Economy*, London: Mansell.

Gersick, C. (1988) 'Time and transition in work teams: Toward a new model of group development', *Academy of Management Journal* 31(1):9–41.

Gersick, C. (1989) 'Marking time: Predictable transitions in task group', *Academy of Management Journal* 32(2):274–309.

Gibson, C. and Vermeuler, F. (2003) 'A healthy divide: Subgroups as a stimulus for team learning behavior', *Administrative Science Quarterly*, 00018392, June, Vol. 48, 2: 202–239.

Glaser, R. (1992) *Moving Your Team Towards Self Management*, King of Prussia, PA: Organization Design and Development Inc.

Grenier, G. (1989) *Inhuman Relations: Quality Circles and Anti-Unionism in American Industry*, Philadelphia: Temple University Press.

Hackman, J. R. (1987) 'The design of work teams', in J. Lorsch (ed.) *Handbook of Organizational Behavior,* Englewood Cliffs, NJ: Prentice Hall, p.p. 315–342.

Hackman, J. R. (1992) 'The psychology of self managing in organizations', in R. Glaser (ed.) *Classic Readings in Self: Managing Teamwork*, Pennsylvania: Organization Design and Development, Inc.

Hackman, J. R. and Morris, C. G. (1975) 'Group tasks, group interaction process and group performance effectiveness: A review and proposed integration', in L. L. Berkowitz (ed.) *Advances in Experimental Social Psychology*, 8: 47–100, New York: Academic.

Heller, F., Pusic, E., Strauss, G. and Wilpert, B. *et al.* (1998) *Organizational Participation Myth and Reality*, Oxford: Oxford University Press.

Hofstede, G. (1980) *Culture's Consequences: International Differences in Work-related Values*, Beverly Hills, CA: Sage.

Hofstede, G. (1983) 'National culture in four dimensions: A research-based theory of cultural differences among nations', *International Studies of Management and Organization* 13:46–74.

Huczynski, A. A. (1996) *Management Gurus*, London: Thomson Business Press.

Janis, I. L. (1972) *Victims of Groupthink*, Boston, MA: Houghton Mifflin.

Janis, I. L. (1982) *Groupthink: Psychological Studies of Policy Decisions and Fiascos*, Boston, MA: Houghton Mifflin.

Jenkins, A. (1996) 'Teams: From ideology to analysis', *Organization Studies* 15(6):849–860.

Jones, R. G. and Lindley, W. D. (1998) 'Issues in the transition to teams', *Journal of Business and Psychology* 13(1):31–40.

Jonsson, D., Medbo, L. and Engstrom, T. (2004) 'Some considerations relating to the reintroduction of assembly lines in the Swedish automotive industry', *International Journal of Operations and Production Management* 24(8):754–762.

Kanter, R. M. (1983) *The Change Masters: Innovations for Productivity in the American Corporation*, New York: Simon and Schuster.

Katzenbach , J. R. and Smith, D. K. (1993) *The Wisdom of Teams*, Boston, MA: Harvard Business School Press.

Kirkman, B. L. (2000) 'Why do employees resist teams? Examining the "resistance barrier" to work team effectiveness', *International Journal of Conflict Management* 11(1):74–93.

Kirkman, B. L. and Shapiro, D. L. (1997) 'The impact of cultural values on employees' resistance to teams: Towards a model of globalized self managing work team effectiveness', *Academy of Management Review* 22(3):730–757.

Kirkman, B. L., Shapiro, D. L., Novelli, L. Jr. and Brett, J. M. (1996) 'Employee concerns regarding self managing work teams: A multidimensional justice perspective', *Social Justice Research* 9(1):47–67.

Klein, J. A. (1989) 'The human costs of manufacturing reform', *Harvard Business Review* March April: 60–66.

Kluckhohn, F. and Strodtbeck, F. L. (1961) *Variations in Value Orientations*, Evanston, IL: Row, Peterson.

Knights, D. and McCabe, D. (2000) 'Bewitched, bothered and bewildered: The meaning and experience of teamworking for employees in an automobile company', *Human Relations* 53(11):1481–1517.

Knights, D. and McCabe, D. (2003) 'Governing through teamwork: Re-constituting subjectivity in a call-center', *Journal of Management Studies* 40(7):587–619.

Laclau, E. (1990) *New Reflections on the Revolution of Our Time*, London: Verso.

Lammers, C. J. and Szell, B. (1989) *International Handbook of Organizational Participation, Vol. 1 Organizational Democracy: Taking Stock,* Oxford: Oxford University Press.

Lave, J. and Wenger, E. (1991) *Situated Learning: Legitimate Peripheral Participation*, New York: Cambridge University Press.

Levine, D. I. (2004) 'The wheels of Washington: Groupthink and Iraq', *San Francisco Chronicle*, 5 February, A23 [sfgate.com/article.cgi?file=/chronicle/archive/2004/02/05/EDGV34OCEP1.DTL].

Lewin, K. (1948) *Resolving Social Conflicts: Selected Papers on Group Dynamics*, London: Harper & Row.

Lipman-Blumen, J. and Leavitt, A. J. (1999) *Hot Groups: Seeding Them, Feeding Them and Using Them to Ignite Your Organization*, New York: Oxford University Press.

McCabe, D. and Black, J. (1996) ' "Something's gotta give": Trade unions and the road to teamworking', *Employer Relations* 1992:110–127.

McKinlay, A. and Taylor, P. (1996) 'Power, surveillance and resistance: Inside the "Factory of the Future" ', in P. Ackers, C. Smith and P. Smith (eds) *The New Workplace and Trade Unionism*, London: Routledge, p.p. 279–300.

Manz, C. C. (1992) 'Beyond self managing work teams: Towards self-leading teams in the workplace', in R. Glaser (ed.) *Classic Readings in Self-Managing Teamwork*, Pennsylvania: Organization Design and Development, Inc.

Manz , C. C. and Sims, H. P. (1987) 'Leading workers to lead themselves: The external leadership of self-managing work teams', *Administrative Science Quarterly* 32(1):106–128.

Manz, C. C. and Sims, H. P. (1991) 'Superleadership beyond the myth of heroic leadership', *Organizational Dynamics* 19(4): 18–35.

Manz, C. C. and Sims, H. P. (1992) 'Becoming a SuperLeader', in R. Glaser (ed.) *Classic Readings in Self-Managing Teamwork*, Pennsylvania: Organization Design and Development, Inc.

Manz, C. C. and Sims, H. P. (1993) *Business Without Bosses: How Self-Managing Teams are Building High-Performance Companies*, New York: John Wiley & Sons Inc.

Mayo, E. (1933) *The Human Problems of an Industrial Civilization*, New York: Macmillan.

Mayo, E. (1945) *The Social Problems of an Industrial Civilization*, New York: Macmillan.

Maznevski, M. L. and DiStefano, J. J. (1995) *'Measuring Culture in International Management: The Cultural Perspectives Questionnaire'*, Working Paper, The University of Virginia: Charlottesville.

Metcalfe, B. and Linstead, A. (2003) 'Gendering teamwork: Re-writing the Feminine', *Gender, Work and Organization* 10(1):95–119.

Mills, P. K. and Ungson, G. (2003) 'Reassessing the limit of structural empowerment: Organizational constitutions trusts controls', *Academy of Management Review*, 28(1):143–151.

Monder, Y. *Toyota Production System*, Norcross: IIE Press.

Mueller, F. (1994) 'Teams between hierarchy and commitment: Changes strategies and the "internal environment" ', *Journal of Management Studies* 31(3):383–403.

Mulder, M. (1971) 'Power equalization through participation', *Administrative Science Quarterly* 16(1):31–40.

Nonaka, I. and Takeuchi, H. (1995) *The Knowledge Creating Company*, Oxford: Oxford University Press.

Oakland, J. C. (1996) *Total Quality Management: A Practical Approach*, University of Bradford Management Centre: European Centre for Total Quality Management.

Oakland, J. S. (1993) *TQM: The Route to Improving Performance*, Oxford: Butterworth-Heinemann.

Parker, M. and Slaughter, J. (1988) *Choosing Sides: Unions and the Team Concept*, Boston: South End Press.

Peters, T. (1988) *Thriving on Chaos: Handbook for a Management Revolution*, London: Pan Books.
Peters, T. and Waterman, R. H. (1982) *In Search of Excellence*, London: Harper and Row.
Pfeffer, J. (1998) 'The human equation: Building profits by putting people first', Boston, MA: Harvard Business School Press.
Plunkett, L. C. and Fournier, R. O. (1991) *Participative Management*, New York: Wiley.
Procter, S. and Mueller, F. (2000) *Teamworking*, London: Macmillan Business.
Pollert, A. (1996) ' "Team work" on the assembly line: Contradictions and the dynamic of union resilience', in P. Ackers, C. Smith and P. Smith (eds.) *The New Workplace and Trade Unionism*, London: Routledge, p.p. 178–209.
Poole, M. S. (1983) 'Decision development in small groups III a multiple sequence model group decision development', *Communications Monographs* 50: 206–232.
Reynolds, R. (1994) *Groupwork in Education and Training: Ideas in Practice*, The Educational and Training Technology Series, London: Kogan Page Limited.
Senge, P. (1990) *The Fifth Discipline: The Art and Practice of the Learning Organization*, New York: Doubleday/Currency.
Sewell, G. (1998) 'The discipline of team: The control of team-based industrial work through electronic and peer surveillance', *Administrative Science Quarterly* 43(2):397–429.
Sewell, G. and Wilkinson, B. (1992) ' "Someone to watch over me"; Surveillance, discipline and the just-in-time labour process', *Sociology* 26(2):271–298.
Shea, G. P. and Guzzo, R. A. (1987) 'Group effectiveness: What really matters?', *Sloar Management Review* 28(3):25–37.
Sinclair, A. (1992) 'The tyranny of team ideology', *Organization Studies* 13(4):611–626.
Starkey, K. (1996) *How Organisations Learn*, London: Thomson Business Press.
Tannenbaum, S. I., Beard, R. L. and Salas, E. (1992) 'Team building and its influence on team effectiveness: An examination of conceptual and empirical developments', in K. Kelley (ed.) *Issues, Theory, and Research in Industrial/Organizational Psychology (Vol. 82)*, Amsterdam: Elsevier Science, p.p. 117–153.
Thompson, P. and Wallace, T. (1996) 'Redesigning production through teamworking: Case studies from the Volvo Truck Corporation', *International Journal of Operations and Production Management* 16(2):103–118.
Thrift, N. (2001) '"It's the romance, not the finance, that makes the business worth pursuing": Disclosing a new market culture', *Economy & Society* 30(4):412–432.
Tompkins, P. K. and Cheney, G. (1985) 'Communications and unobtrusive control in contemporary organisations', in R. D. McPhee and P. K. Thompkins (eds.) *Organizational Communication: Traditional Themes and New directions*, Newbury Park, CA: Sage, p.p. 179–210.
Trist, E. and Bamforth, K. (1951) 'Some social and psychological consequences of the Longwall method of coal-getting,' *Human Relations* 4(1):3–38.
Trist, E. L., Susman, G. I. and Brown, G. R (1977) 'An experiment in autonomous working in an American underground coal mine', *Human Relations* 30:201–236.
Tuckman, B. W. (1965) 'Developmental sequences in small groups', *Psychological Bulletin* 63(6):384–399.
Tuckman, B. W. and Jenson, M. A. (1977) 'Stages of small group development revisited', *Group and Organization Studies* 2:419–427.
Tushman, M. and Nadler, D. (1998) 'Organizing for innovation', in K. Starkey (ed.) *How Organizations Learn*, London: Thomson Business Press.
Wall, T. D., Kemp, N. J., Jackson, P. R. and Clegg, C. W. (1986) 'Outcomes of autonomous workgroups: A long term field experiment', *Academy of Management Journal* 29: 280–304.
Wall, T. D., Kemp, N. J., Jackson, P. and Clegg, C. (1992) 'Outcomes of autonomous workgroups: A long term field experiment', in R. Glaser (ed.) *Classic Readings in Self-Managing Teamwork*, Pennsylvania: Organization Design and Development, Inc.
Wallace, T. (2004) 'The end of good work? Work organisation or lean production in Volvo organisation', *International Journal of Operations and Production Management* 24(8):750–753.
Waterson, P. E., Clegg, C. W., Bolden, R. and Pepper, K. *et al.* (1999) 'The use and effectiveness of modern manufacturing practices: A survey of UK industry', *International Journal of Production Research*, 37:2271–2292.
Weisbord, M. R. (1992) 'Participative work design: A personal odyssey', in R. Glaser (ed.) *Classic Readings in Self-Managing Teamwork*, Pennsylvania: Organization Design and Development, Inc.
Wellins, R. S., Byham, W. C. and Wilson, J. (1991) *Empowered Teams*, San Francisco: Jossey-Bass.
Wenger, E. (1998) *Communities of Practice: Learning, Meaning and identity*, Cambridge: Cambridge University Press.
Wenger, E. and Snyder, W. (2000) 'Communities of practice: The organizational frontier', *Harvard Business Review* Jan–Feb:139–145.
Wenger, E., McDermott, R. and Snyder, W. M. (2002) *Cultivating Communities of Practices*, Boston: Harvard Business School Press.
WERS – Cully, M., Woodland, S., O'Reilly A. and Dix, G. (1998) *1998 Workplace Employee Relations Survey*, London and New York: Routledge.
West, A. (2004) *Effective Teamwork: Practical Lessons from Organizational Research*, Oxford: Blackwell.
Wood, R. and Bandura, A. (1989) 'Social cognitive theory of organizational management', *Academy of Management Review* 14:361–384.
Womack, J. P., Jones, D. T. and Roos, D. (1990) *The Machine that Changed the World*, New York: Rawson Associates.

PART II
The Organizational Dimension

Part II covers a wide, though far from exhaustive, range of topics. Each chapter shows how they are examined in mainstream analysis, but also challenges the conventional assumption that organizations function as coherent and self-reproducing systems. In the mainstream, the consideration of politics, conflict or cultural diversity is fleeting and/or is seen as a disruptive element that needs to be cauterized or contained. More critical approaches explore the recurrence and proliferation of such disruptions and the integral nature of their relationship to organizational and technological life, and their significance for its continually changing forms.

4 Management and Leadership

David Knights and Hugh Willmott

Key concepts and learning objectives

- To show how ideas about organization, management and leadership are developed and applied in practice, with particular reference to a case study.
- To explore some of the tensions associated with managing and leading staff.
- To present and define a number of key concepts that are relevant to mainstream and critical analysis, such as types of leadership and styles of management.
- To develop an understanding of the assumptions and theories underpinning mainstream thinking on management and leadership.
- To understand some important concepts relevant to mainstream and critical analysis, such as effectiveness and efficiency, and performance and control.

Aims of the chapter

This chapter will:

- Introduce the nature and significance of management and leadership and explore the linkages between them.
- Identify the assumptions and values underpinning and framing mainstream thinking about management and leadership.
- Consider personal and impersonal modes of control, and the use of forms of 'mutual adjustment' within both.
- Provide an overview of the diversity of mainstream thinking about management and leadership.
- Explain and illustrate the basis of criticisms of mainstream thinking about management and leadership.
- Show how concepts of inequality, knowledge, power, freedom, identity, inequality and insecurity can provide a different way of considering issues of management and leadership.
- Examine different strands of a critical approach for analysing organization management and leadership.

Overview and key points

This chapter is concerned with an appreciation of the overlaps, interconnections as well as the differences between management and leadership in both a conceptual or theoretical and a practical or empirical sense. In everyday conversation, in the media, in workplaces and even among academics, the terms are often used interchangeably and this is acknowledged, but the chapter also documents their difference and distinctiveness. In developing this knowledge, we seek to understand the development of thinking about management from closed to open system theory and from the control of factors of production to the shaping of culture and values. By contrast, the chapter examines thinking about leadership where the emphasis is upon directing others through inspiration and motivation, rather than through hierarchical control. Leadership is understood in terms of personal(ity) qualities. In the second part of the chapter these mainstream views of both management and leadership are examined critically to reveal the assumptions that they take for granted.

Mainstream approaches to management and leadership

Management and leadership are central to studying behaviour in workplaces (see Box 4.1). Both concepts have been adopted and elaborated to make sense of, and also to control, what goes on in work organizations. As a concept, 'management' identifies responsibility for maintaining the division and coordination of tasks, often through the development of a hierarchy to regulate the allocation and flow of work. Leadership is concerned less with allocating work tasks than with energizing staff with a sense of direction and commitment. It promotes a collective sense of purpose to which members of the organization commit their 'hearts and minds'. The role of management in organizing and controlling the labour of others is said to account for 'the proportion of output that cannot be explained by the growth of input' (Chandler, 1977, p. 490). 'Management' supplements and may even replace 'leadership' to the extent that a hierarchy, whether formal or informal, develops. Responsibility then passes from the founder or leader to a group of 'professional' managers who sustain the continuing division and coordination of productive effort.

Box 4.1: The importance of management

Management has been celebrated as a modern invention whose importance and impact is equivalent to the most influential of world-changing technologies: 'What were the most important innovations of the past century? [Make your own list – antibiotics, contraceptives, computers, etc.]. All of these innovations transformed our lives, yet none of them could have taken hold so rapidly or spread so widely without another. That innovation is the discipline of management, the accumulating body of thought and practice that make organizations work. When we take stock of the productivity gains that drive our prosperity, technology gets all of the credit. In fact, management is doing a lot of the heavy lifting' (Magretta, 2002, p. 1). In short, it can be claimed that management is crucial in turning gizmos into gadgets, inventions into necessities, or innovations into taken for granted everyday realities.

Distinctions have their limits. At what point does black become white? In the case of management and leadership, it might be argued that the 'leader' who founds an organization probably exercises some 'management' skills, such as the ability to plan effectively. Equally, management involves some of the skills associated with 'leadership', such as the capacity to inspire respect. It would be a mistake to think of 'leadership' as *simply* coming before 'management'. Following the introduction of more management and the formalization of procedures, the initial sense of direction and inspiration may diminish – something that makes 'leadership' a recurrent concern (see Box 4.2).

It has become fashionable recently to elevate leadership over management. An interest in, and preference for, 'leadership' often indicates a desire to move away from 'bureaucratic', command-and-control approaches associated with 'management' (see Chapter 14). Leadership is therefore linked with a process of organizing in which (in principle) greater emphasis is placed on inspiring, listening, facilitating and involving people, rather than instructing them to act. Leadership is linked to communication and innovation. Grint (2005) has associated management with the solving of 'tame' or routine problems, whereas leadership is required for more difficult, 'wicked' problems that defy any

Box 4.2: Management is 'Out', Leadership is 'In'

'. . . the world's most admired manager, GE's legendary leader Jack Welch . . . consciously rejected the word *manager*. It carried too much bad baggage. It smacked of control and bureaucracy. Welch was on a crusade. His call for *leaders* struck a responsive chord' (Magretta, 2002, p. 5). What might Welch do with managers who were unresponsive to this call?; and what does that tell us about the standing of most managers in such organizations? For those of you who may be interested in reading more about Welch and GE, see N. M. Tichey and S. Sherman (1993), *Control Your Destiny or Someone Else Will*, New York: Doubleday.

clear-cut solution. An example of a comparatively tame problem, which can also be complex, is teaching a young adult to pass the driving test. Being a good or 'successful' parent of this young adult is, in contrast, an ill-defined and recurrently tricky endeavour. 'Management might be focussed on solving complex but essentially tame problems in a unilinear fashion: applying what worked last time; but leadership', Grint suggests, 'is essentially about facing wicked problems that are literally "unmanageable" ' (Grint, 2005, p. 9).

There is, of course, a difference between preaching an approach to leadership and practising it. As we shall suggest when considering more critical studies of management, what accounts for this difference is the politics of organizing (see Chapter 8) where issues of identity, inequality, power and insecurity are entangled in the advocacy of leadership (and management) as well as resistance to its realization. A self-aware, facilitative approach to leadership may sound like a good idea, only to be rejected by managers who have invested their careers, and their very selves, in a 'bossier' kind of relationship with their 'subordinates'. Or these managers may be deeply sceptical about the value of a participative style in highly demanding and contradictory contexts where it is difficult to maintain a consistent approach, and where greater participation seems to risk loss of control. They may believe that effective leadership demands a more 'hard-headed', aggressive and coercive approach – one that has been emphasized in a number of recent business-related TV shows, such as *The Apprentice* (http://www.bbc.co.uk/apprentice/) where Alan Sugar celebrates an autocratic style that scores points at the expense of his subordinates. In the United States, where the show originated, it was Donald Trump who took on the role of the business 'master' (see http://www.nbc.com/nbc/The_Apprentice/).

Those wedded to an autocratic style are likely to experience great difficulty in shifting from a 'hire and fire' mentality to one in which 'coaching' and engaging staff is seen as more appropriate to the idea of leadership. At best, the security provided by charisma and charm may make bullying tolerable. And, in the effort to 'change their spots', autocratic managers may lose their capacity to lead. That is because their ability to provide a degree of certainty and security in confusing and contested situations is what, despite their bullying tendencies, can make them seductive, if not necessarily particularly attractive, figures of authority.

Fuzzy boundaries: Management and leadership

We have noted how definitions of, and boundaries between, management and leadership can be useful but also somewhat loose, arbitrary and potentially misleading (see Box 4.3). Each tends to be defined in relation to the other, and a notion of 'good management' may well incorporate leadership skills. There are further complications. 'Management' is a term used to describe a comparatively privileged (in terms of pay and status) occupational group or elite, as well as an organizational function or role. This not only adds a layer of complexity in terms of developing an analysis but also it creates difficulties in practice, as the issue of privilege can undermine the 'legitimacy' of management decisions. However, the meanings attributed to the concepts of management and leadership are fluid, and vary with the contexts in which they are used and, indeed, the terms may be used almost interchangeably, as in the lament or exhortation: 'There is a need for better management/leadership around here'.

A recurrent complaint of senior executives is the lack of 'leadership' in middle and supervisory levels of management. Because they are judged ultimately on the basis of their subordinates' performance, executives generally want to see more productivity, effectiveness and innovation within 'their' organizations; and they often regard 'better leadership' from their subordinates, including middle managers, as the key to such change (see Chapter 11.) This desire is understandable but it fails to appreciate how identification with, and commitment to, the organization often declines lower down the hierarchy.

Box 4.3: Manager or leader?

At DipPep (a pseudonym), the meanings of 'manager' and 'leader' were virtually interchangeable. Leadership was regarded as an integral and essential element of management (even if, in practice, the motivation and scope for 'leading' was restricted by the manager's position in the hierarchy). At BoxCo (a pseudonym), in contrast, the CEO repeatedly emphasized the difference between management and leadership in order to highlight what he perceived to be missing (i.e. 'leadership') from his management team.

Securing commitment is by no means straightforward. Lower levels of staff are generally much less well paid and provided for; they also lack any direct accountability to the owners or senior executives Whether the organization performs especially well is of limited consequence to them, in terms of their sense of self-esteem, career prospects or returns on stock options. Employees may therefore be rather unresponsive to calls to exercise greater leadership (for example, in teams, see Chapter 4), or to commit themselves beyond the call of duty (i.e. to do more than is formally written into their job description). Where employees are fearful of losing their jobs, they may comply superficially with new expectations without being committed to them. In conditions where staff lack a strong identification with the organization for which they work, qualities characterized as 'leadership' are less likely to emerge among them. Here managers may also find it more difficult to be effective leaders. In other words, issues of power, inequality, identity and insecurity (i) shape how we organize, (ii) stimulate calls for and (iii) prompt different responses to, demands for more or better 'management' and 'leadership'.

To summarize:

- 'Management is associated with the maintenance of existing organizational arrangements, whereas 'leadership' is associated with their establishment, revitalization or transformation.
- The meaning of the terms 'management' and 'leadership' is often fluid – for example, the latter may be incorporated into the former.
- Issues of inequality and limited commitment to the organization can frustrate as well as stimulate efforts to improve management and/or leadership both among managers and staff.

Thinkpoint 4.1

Management and leadership: Your experience Think of an example of leadership drawn from your own experience – perhaps a job you have worked in, participating in a collective activity, playing a sport, or simply going out with mates.

- Can you identify elements of this experience that comprise some part of 'management'?
- What singled out certain people as 'leaders' or distinguished their behaviour as having the characteristics of 'leadership'?

Reflecting upon your experiences of leadership (see Thinkpoint 4.1) has probably shown you how ideas about leadership, and what we think of as management (and organization), overlap. For example, a person identified as a leader, or as exhibiting leadership behaviour, may also be regarded as a good organizer or manager – someone who is able to 'pull together' or harness the diverse skills of a group. Without this leader, the group may become 'dis-organized', perhaps resulting in the quest for a replacement leader. Or the failure of a particular leader may demand a different way of organizing that reduces the risk of dependency upon a single leader. One way to limit this risk is for rules and routines of organization to emerge, and for a managerial hierarchy to be created, whereupon conformity to the bureaucracy substitutes for leadership (see Chapter 10). Behaviour is then organized without such heavy reliance upon leadership that recurrently provides inspiration and direction, but with possible adverse consequences for harnessing the energies of those involved.

Exercise 4.1

Identify some of the different ways in which management and leadership overlap, interconnect, or are substitutes for each other.

Needless to say, activities identified as management and leadership extend well beyond the world of work. In other spheres – at home or in leisure pursuits – we often find ourselves being 'managed' by, or we end up 'managing' others, such as our partners, close relatives, friends and acquaintances. We also identify, and perhaps more readily admire, 'leadership qualities' in others and occasionally have these qualities attributed to our own actions. On reflection, we recognize that management and leadership connote prized qualities in modern organizations and societies, often because they are associated with individual or organizational performance or are attributed to different ways of organizing our activities. Not surprisingly, then, they are found to connect to each other, with management often signifying more structured, interpersonal aspects of organization and leadership pointing to the importance of nurturing interpersonal relations as well as a shared sense of purpose.

CASE STUDY 4.1 Bar Mar

In the previous chapter, we introduced the case study of Bar Mar. It will be recalled that Margaret was the owner-manager of the first Bar Mar who, before it had expanded to become an international chain of multi-award winning bar-bistros, controlled key decisions, such as the nature and pricing of drinks and food, opening hours, working hours, furnishings and so on. One of the things that had appealed to Margaret about running a bar was the opportunity to create a total experience for her customers, a key part of which involved the interaction with Bar Mar staff, herself included. She liked the idea of working with a small number of staff – co-workers and friends, as she thought of them – with whom she could provide and develop a distinctive atmosphere and range of drinks, snacks and light meals.

Margaret hand-picked her initial trio of staff by 'poaching' them from other local bars in which she drank and ate regularly, partly in order to develop her thinking about Bar Mar, but also to identify prospective staff. She successfully tempted them away from other bars by enthusing them with her concept for a new kind of bar, and also by offering them better pay. Working closely with them, Margaret found that she was able to run Bar Mar highly successfully with the very minimum of formal instructions or communications. Whatever issues came up were quickly resolved through a process of discussion or 'mutual adjustment' (see Box 4.4), albeit one in which it was understood and accepted that Margaret would always have the final word.

Margaret had the final word as a consequence of her legal position as the owner of Bar Mar, a position that also underpinned her authority on the premises, and not as a result of her considerable charisma, or her reputation as a minor pillar of the local community. It is this relationship of control to other members of her staff that lends plausibility to the pyramid shape of the organization chart (Figure 4.1). Margaret's position as owner-manager also allowed her to determine how and when her own labour was flexibly deployed – in the bar or in the kitchen, depending upon the demand for drinks or food. And if she felt like taking a break to do some shopping, or to see what was happening in other bars in her neighbourhood, she just informed her staff that she was going out for an hour or two.

The situation has now changed substantially. Today, Margaret is CEO of what has become an international chain of bar-bistros but she owns only 10 per cent of the shares in the business of which she was once sole owner. Funding for the ambitious expansion of the business came primarily from venture capitalists who, in return for their investment, secured a 51 per cent stake in the company, thereby giving them ultimate control. They were attracted to Bar Mar's proven business model. Its uninterrupted growth had demonstrated a capacity to manage relationships with all the key stakeholders – suppliers and employees as well as customers. The highly successful operation of Bar Mar in a competitive market-place had demonstrated the robustness of its distinctive formula, or strategy, for delivering greater (perceived) value to its customers than its direct competitors.

A substantial string attached to the venture capital funding, however, was the imperative to strengthen Margaret's management team by recruiting a group of senior managers

Box 4.4: The widespread operation of 'mutual adjustment'

'Mutual adjustment achieves coordination of work by the simple process of informal communication . . . Because it is such a simple coordinating mechanism, mutual adjustment is naturally used in the very simplest of organizations . . . it is also used in the most complicated, because it is the only one that works under extremely difficult circumstances. Consider the organization charged with putting a man on the moon for the first time. Such an activity requires an incredibly elaborate division of labor . . . But at the outset, no one can be sure exactly what needs to be done . . . the success of the undertaking depends primarily upon the ability of specialists to adapt to each other along their uncharted route . . .' (Mintzberg, 1979, p. 3).

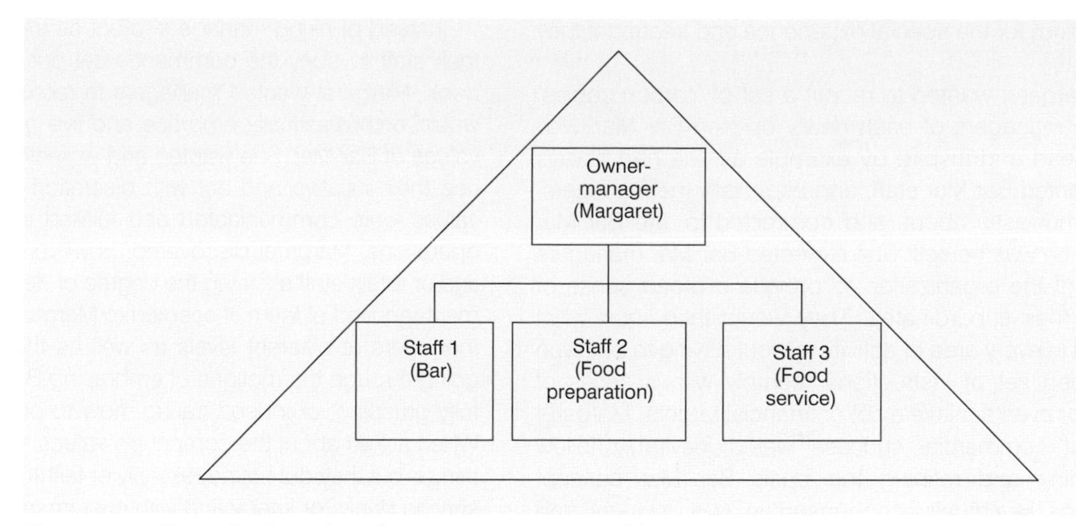

Figure 4.1 Organization chart for an owner-managed bar

with expertise in key functional areas (e.g. operations, finance, human resource management, etc.), and a proven track record in taking businesses through a period of rapid growth. Management expertise was the area where the venture capitalists identified the greatest challenge and risk. The creation of an experienced senior management team was identified as the way to manage the risks associated with sustaining the Bar Mar's strategy, and associated position of competitive advantage, during a potentially turbulent and disruptive process of rapid expansion. In common with her fellow directors, Margaret's authority as CEO is now effectively delegated to her by Bar Mar shareholders, who, legally, are in a position to replace her and any other members of the board of directors if they fail to manage this risk. However, Margaret has become so identified with the Bar Mar brand, and is so respected in financial circles for her flair for anticipating trends and ceaselessly innovating, that her immediate future looks pretty secure.

Privately, however, Margaret considers that her position as CEO is vulnerable. This is not least because any faltering of the company's peerless performance may be attributed to the lack of a 'professional' manager at the helm of the company. Not infrequently, she has felt out of her depth, and only her disarming willingness to admit her ignorance, her humour, and ability to learn quickly from others has saved her from more critical and potentially damning scrutiny; and one or two of her newly appointed senior executive team have made no secret of wanting her job.

Thinkpoint 4.2

Is Margaret a leader? Would you describe Margaret as a leader? Where and how does she 'lead'? What attributes of Margaret prompt you to think of her in this way? Do you think she would be identified as a leader in many different situations?

Reflecting upon her 20 years at the top of Bar Mar, Margaret takes satisfaction from how her methods of managing the company have adapted to its growth. When she was owner-manager of the first Bar Mar, she relied upon a personal relationship with her three staff. There was little need for formal rules and procedures as she could easily guide and coach them by word of mouth. Frequently, she was working alongside them and could readily see how they were performing and offer encouragement and 'advice' about how to do things better. As these staff told her, they tended to regard her more as a colleague than a boss, and were particularly impressed by her willingness to listen to their suggestions, as well as to their occasional grievances. What they perhaps did not realize, and this is something that Margaret did not share with them, is the extent to which they taught her about how to manage successfully as she carefully observed and reviewed their responses to her interventions and prompts as the owner-manager.

As Bar Mar expanded and additional bars were added to the chain, Margaret reluctantly discovered that she had to rely increasingly upon more impersonal methods. For she could no longer keep a direct eye on Bar Mar staff, yet she was determined to ensure that all Bar Mar employees maintained and continuously improved the standards that she had set in the first Bar Mar. The problem was that she feared that introducing rules and procedures – for preparing food and interacting with customers, for example – would undermine the spirit of continuous improvement and friendly, up-beat ambience that she wanted to nurture in the bars. This ambience, above everything else, is what she wanted to preserve and enhance. Not only was it what she wanted to create when opening her first Bar Mar, she also believed passionately that it is what would differentiate Bar Mar from its competitors, and would enable better staff wages and conditions, as customers would willingly pay a slight premium for the special experience and treatment they received.

Ideally, Margaret wanted to recruit a set of 'carbon copies' of herself as managers of each newly opened Bar Mar, who would then lead and inspire by example as she had always done She wanted Bar Mar staff, and especially the managers, to be as enthusiastic about, and committed to, the Bar Mar concept as she was herself. She expected Bar Mar managers at all levels of the organization to provide a broad sense of direction for their subordinates. They would then know what was required in every area of activity without having to be given a very detailed set of instructions, comply with a series of procedures or even achieve a set of financial targets. Margaret believed that commercial success would inevitably follow from upholding and refining the basic Bar Mar concept and ambience, eventually condensed in two, low-key and somewhat up-market slogans: 'Meet, Absorb and Recharge' and 'Lively Ambience, Exciting Food, Affordable Prices'.

Instead of hiring managers to act as trainers who would drill their staff to obey the commands set out in the corporate rule book, Margaret wanted managers to recruit and train staff who would enthusiastically embrace and live out the basic, guiding values of Bar Mar. She wanted and expected all Bar Mar staff to use their initiative and act with discretion to ensure that these values were communicated and fulfilled in every aspect of its operations. Margaret discovered, however, that it is not easy to find or retain staff showing the degree of dedication and commitment required of them. It seemed to Margaret that Bar Mar staff – managers at different levels as well as their staff – were often going through the motions of embracing Bar Mar values without fully grasping, or indeed caring, how to put them into practice. When asked about the company's values, they said 'all the right things' but they did not necessarily or faithfully act them out when serving drinks or interacting with customers. Instead of showing that they could not be more concerned for the customers, they unintentionally communicated an attitude of not caring less.

Thinkpoint 4.3

What dilemmas is Margaret facing? As Margaret expands the Bar Mar chain, she encounters a number of unforeseen difficulties of organization, management and leadership. How would you describe and diagnose these problems? What remedies would you consider in similar circumstances?

Margaret believed that more careful selection and training of staff could solve the problem. The human resources (HR) budget in these areas was substantially increased. This had mixed but generally disappointing results, however. According to reports from 'mystery shoppers' who regularly visited each Bar Mar, little difference could be detected between the experience of visiting bars where staff had been given additional training compared to staff in bars who had yet to receive it.

Thinkpoint 4.4

The limits of training Margaret believed that training would solve what she identified as a key problem for the reputation and future of the Bar Mar chain. What might have led her to place her faith in this remedy? What might explain its limited success? What solutions would you suggest?

Margaret was reluctant to abandon her faith in the Bar Mar concept. She believed that there must be some way of managing the staff that would enable them to 'do things right'. She continued to give much thought to this issue but, at the same time, she conceded that an alternative approach was required if the standards she had set for the company were to be realized and, ideally, surpassed. Against all her instincts, Margaret accepted that exemplary leadership was insufficient, and that it would have to be supplemented, and perhaps partially displaced, by a closer specification of requirements, more effective forms of surveillance and ultimately by disciplinary procedures for staff found breaching company rules. She comforted herself with the thought that this was simply a 'stop-gap' measure that could be dropped, or at least trimmed back, once the HR specialists identified a more effective way of training staff to embrace Bar Mar's defining values. But, half-consciously, she had her doubts about whether a 'magic bullet' would ever be found.

Thinkpoint 4.5

Additional information required? In considering this case and the series of 'thinkpoints', what additional information or knowledge about Bar Mar did you feel you needed? How might this have influenced or changed your views or assessments?

The mainstream agenda

The mainstream agenda is preoccupied with how to manage and lead in order to maximize performance; and it tends to assume an underlying consensus of values and objectives between members of society and organizations. Where there are some difficulties of alignment, it is assumed that a technical remedy, such as improved staff selection or training, will resolve the problem. Organization, management and leadership are conceived as three distinct but interrelated elements of a system that is routinely and legitimately treated as an object of manipulation and control. The mainstream is 'managerial' in the sense that it *assumes* the legitimacy of management and is focused on how to help managers in organizations meet their existing goals rather than reflect critically upon how these goals are identified and pursued. This is typically the *exclusive* focus of management textbooks, such as Laurie Mullins's *Management and Organizational Behaviour* (see Box 4.5).

In common with other chapters of this book, the first part of this chapter presents an overview of key elements of the mainstream approach before complementing this with a more critical approach in the second part.

Box 4.5: The purpose of mainstream thinking

'This book presents a managerial approach to organizational behaviour . . . The underlying theme of this book is the need for organizational effectiveness and the importance of the role of management as an integrating activity.'

Source: Laurie Mullins (1999) *Management and Organizational Behaviour*, fifth edition, London: Financial Times, p. 4.

Management: Discipline, function, social group As a discipline, the term 'management' is used to indicate a measure of responsibility, deliberate planning and control. This discipline was developed in work organizations – church, army, factory, etc. – but has increasingly become an integral part of modern everyday life. For example, the idea of self-management suggests the acquisition of a discipline that enables the individual to take responsibility for their own life (e.g. career choices and development), which they plan, review and control. Margaret's decision to establish the first Bar Mar and her continuing efforts to retain her vision during its expansion into an international chain requires considerable skills of self-management, such as allocating her time and focusing her effort. This effort to manage activities and processes occurs at all levels within organizations. The shop floor worker or the clerical assistant may have minimal formal authority and exercise little discretion, but they have some involvement in managing themselves and others to perform tasks that have been identified, but not exhaustively specified, by superiors within the hierarchy. Today, management as a discipline has been disseminated into almost every institution (e.g. charitable foundations, voluntary groups, personal health, etc.) in advanced capitalist societies. As a discipline and way of thinking, management is advocated to deal effectively with all kinds of personal and social problems, including the control of scientific work (see Box 4.6).

As a function, management is conceived in relation to an understanding of how collective forms of activity are organized. 'Management' is thought of as an essential and necessary component of such activity. Without this function, there is the prospect of chaos or, at least, a sub-optimal use of

Box 4.6: Management to control science

'Keith Waldron of the Institute of Food Research suggests a more balanced approach to managing research establishments could be developed through a closer relationship with business schools . . . Dr Waldron writes that the expertise to tackle the problem [of performance] could be found in business management schools. "Perhaps now is the time to exploit these with a view to clarifying the roles and responsibilities of scientists in relation to organizational management and strategic intent." '

Source: *Times Higher Educational Supplement*, 30 January 2004, p. 6.

Table 4.1 Summary: Three common meanings of management

Management as discipline	Practices directed to increasing output for a given input. Employed by many people but institutionalized in work organizations
Management as function	Conceived as an essential and universal component of organized activity
Management as a social group or elite	A social and organizational stratum that is positioned between a small number of major owners of property and land and a mass of comparatively unqualified and unskilled employees

resources involving unnecessary wastage of human and/or material resources. The function of management is understood to ensure effective forms of division and integration of tasks among elements – people and technologies – that comprise organization. It may be identified as a function for which there is collective responsibility (e.g. through mutual adjustment or a democratic election of managers) but it is more often conceived as an area of specialist expertise to be undertaken by those with relevant qualifications who are appointed by an elite. In the Bar Mar example, the management function was assessed to be weak by the venture capitalists who made their investment conditional upon the recruitment of senior executives with specialist knowledge of key areas.

Finally, management is conceived of as a social group that acquires and applies specialist expertise, and to which differential power and privileges are often attributed. The term 'management' is used to identify a stratum of people who occupy positions of comparative seniority and advantage within work organizations. Initially, Margaret was the sole member of this group, though she was reluctant to identify herself as hierarchically distanced from 'her' staff. Later, as the chain expanded, more managers were appointed (by Margaret) and eventually an elite group of executives joined the business as a condition of obtaining the financing for further expansion (see Table 4.1).

Thinkpoint 4.6

Consider the case of Margaret, the founder of the Bar Mar chain of bar-bistros. In what ways does she embody management as a discipline, function and social group?

In what ways does 'management' as a discipline shape your experience and how you act? Consider, for example, how notions of 'planning', 'budgeting' and 'scheduling' influence your everyday behaviour.

Exercise 4.2

Work in a small group to construct a table in which you list and illustrate some key elements of management as a discipline, as a function and as a social group.

Central to the mainstream view on management is an assumption that, as a function, as a discipline and as a social group, management plays an essential, impartial and legitimate role in improving human welfare. Those who are most closely identified with 'management' – as a discipline, function and/or social position – are understood to apply their specialist expertise in an impartial manner for the common good. Disciplined expertise is a hallmark of their functional contribution that is manifest in the strategies, structures and systems devised by them to transform raw materials and human labour into needed outputs (see Chapter 6); and it is the scarcity of this expertise that accounts for their formation as an elite social group. A rather different view of management is explored in the second half of this chapter, where we suggest that their expertise is shaped and applied in specific ways that are valuable for maintaining capitalist enterprise and/or the comparatively privileged place of managers within it.

Management as ever-present? The capacity to 'manage' – to plan, review and control – *may* be seen as a universal human capability that has been applied, more or less systematically and widely, in all societies. In pre-modern societies, however, other influences, notably, the weight of tradition or the dominance of myth, were more powerful in directing and legitimizing human behaviour. An acceleration of the discipline of management, involving the spread of calculating, secular, this-worldly reasoning, occurred during the 19th and 20th centuries when it was harnessed to the development of capitalist organizations (see Box 4.7).

Prior to the emergence and consolidation of capitalist economic organizations, management as a discipline had been developed, in comparatively embryonic form, in religious, military and governmental forms. It was then augmented, further rationalized and embroidered in the process of developing and governing commercial as well as public sector organizations so that, today, it is a pervasive discipline that extends well beyond work organizations and into everyday life (see Box 4.8).

CLASSICAL THINKING ABOUT MANAGEMENT We have noted how, in mainstream considerations of management, there is an assumption that the objectives or 'goals' of organizations are readily identified, understood and shared; and that the responsibility of management is to establish a framework of policy and practice that ensures their effective realization. Mainstream knowledge of management also assumes the value and legitimate place of management as a social elite. We will consider an alternative, more critical view of management, summarized in Box 4.9, on p. 268 of this chapter, but it is worth bearing it mind as we consider the mainstream approach.

Box 4.7: Management in modern society – what's new?

'Like generals of old [managers in 18th century Britain] had to control numerous men, but without powers of compulsion . . . Again, unlike the builders of the pyramids, they had not only to show absolute results in terms of certain products of their efforts, but to relate them to costs, and sell them competitively. While they used capital like the merchants, yet they had to combine it with labour, and transform it first, not merely into saleable commodities, but also into instruments of production embodying the latest achievements of a changing technology. And about it all there lay the heavy hand of a hostile State and an unsympathetic legal system, which they had to transform, as they had to transform so much of the rest of their environment, in the process of creating their industrial capitalism.'

Source: S. Pollard (1965) *The Genesis of Modern Management*, London: Edward Arnold, p.p. 6–7.

Box 4.8: The development of management in capitalist economies – a two-stage process

Historically, owners of capital – in the form of buildings, tools and machinery – emerged as a distinctive group who used skilled labour that previously worked in guilds and owned their own means of (craft) production but did not employ it directly. These owners developed and applied some basic management disciplines as they decided which tools and raw materials to purchase, what outputs would be required and where these would be sold. But these owners did not hire labour directly or take responsibility for how it was organized. Instead, they paid 'gang masters' who gathered together groups of workers. The gang masters were paid by the owners for whatever output they produced that met the agreed standard. In effect, during this first stage, owners 'outsourced' responsibility for work organization to the gang bosses. There was minimal direct intervention by owners in the organization of production, largely because this was contracted out to an external supplier of labour.

During the second stage, owners took a closer inerest in how production was organized. The owners employed their own staff – managers – to undertake the task of deciding when, where and how labour was to be deployed, in an effort to improve its reliability and productivity. Employees were hired directly by managers who decided how their effort was to be deployed and rewarded. Today, this second stage has become so institutionalized as to be largely taken for granted. Increasingly, this system of 'managerial capitalism' (Chandler, 1977) renders the owners almost invisible, in part because ownership has been extended through wider participation in savings and pension schemes. Despite their withdrawal from day-to-day management, the interests of owners has rarely suffered partly due to managers' legal obligations to shareholders but also because profit is the clearest measure of managerial competence.

A distinguishing feature of 'classical thinking' in management is its belief in the possibility of specifying a single way of organizing, managerial style or mode of leadership that would have universal efficacy. Conceived as a system of expertise that is technically adept, politically neutral and morally benign, classical thinking about management assumes the existence of a set of principles whose application will ensure the smooth operation of any collective endeavour. The possibility that management could be, like anything else, a manifestation of its time and place – a product of struggles between those who believe in, and value, its claims and those who are neither convinced nor seduced – is unacknowledged or brushed aside. Instead, it is assumed that more management – as discipline and/or function – inevitably produces a better world. With extraordinary self-confidence, its champions have urged its adoption in every sphere of human activity.

One of the most celebrated efforts to catalogue its constituent parts was produced by Henri Fayol (see Table 4.2); and versions of this list have reappeared in numerous guises (e.g. Barnard, 1936; Drucker, 1974; Koontz *et al.*, 1984) since its publication in *General and Industrial Administration* (1916/1949).

Table 4.2 Fayol's principles of management

	Principle	Description
1	Division of work	Reduces the span of attention or effort for any one person or group. Develops practice and familiarity.
2	Authority	The right to give orders. Should not be considered without reference to responsibility.
3	Discipline	Outward marks of respect in accordance with formal or informal agreements between firm and its employees.
4	Unity of command	One man, one superior!
5	Unity of direction	One head and one plan for a group of activities with the same objective.
6	Subordination of individual interests to the general interest	The interest of one individual or one group should not prevail over the general good. This is a difficult area of management.
7	Remuneration	Pay should be fair to both the employee and the firm.
8	Centralization	Is always present to a greater or lesser extent, depending on the size of company and quality of its managers.
9	Scalar chain	The line of authority from top to bottom of the organization.
10	Order	A place for everything and everything in its place; the right person in the right place.
11	Equity	A combination of kindliness and justice towards employees.
12	Stability of tenure of personnel	Employees need to be given time to settle into their jobs, even though this may be a lengthy period in the case of managers.
13	Initiative	Within the limits of authority and discipline, all levels of staff should be encouraged to show initiative.
14	*Esprit de corps*	Harmony is a great strength to an organization; teamwork should be encouraged.

Box 4.9: Thinking critically about management

Critical analysis questions how institutions become established, and are maintained, through the exercise of power and everyday acts of domination. Its analysis of management focuses upon fundamental conflicts of interest or paradoxes that recurrently undermine efforts to 'police' delegation, while mainstream analysis examines the obstacles in terms of personal foibles ('I know best') and interpersonal tensions ('let the boss carry the can'), and assumes that difficulties can be overcome by building confidence, and learning to trust and support others who will inevitably make mistakes and undertake delegated activities in a way that departs from the approach taken by the manager. The question, from a critical perspective, is whether the very organization of modern organizations – in terms of the divisions between ownership, management and subordinates – is conducive to establishing enduring relationships of trust and confidence; or whether such relations are repeatedly eroded by pressures that recurrently disturb and disrupt their formation.

Classical theory presupposes that any institution can benefit from attaining its objectives by identifying and enhancing its methods in five respects – planning, organizing, coordinating, commanding and controlling. The discipline of management subject the five components to systematic analysis so as to pinpoint current deficiencies and devise a remedy for their imperfect design. The role of management, as a discipline, is to identify and rectify weaknesses – influences and limited effectiveness – in institutions, and thereby secure their productive operation. Fayol and other 'classical' theorists believed that the application of universal principles of management would serve to transform institutions based upon custom, prejudice and favouritism into rational, balanced, well-integrated entities from which unproductive frictions, misunderstandings and conflicts are progressively eliminated.

Thinkpoint 4.7

Consider again the case of Margaret, the founder of the Bar Mar chain of bar-bistros. In what respects does her work illustrate Fayol's basic components of management? Are any aspects missing from Fayol's overview of components?

One absentee from Fayol's catalogue of components of management is any direct reference to motivation and to related, human aspects of work organization. Motivation is something that more recent management writers have repeatedly considered; and which is central to the study of leadership (see Chapter 2) where the focus shifts from functions to relationships. In Fayol's thinking, motivation is apparently assured by the smooth operation of the five components. He commends forms of 'good practice' that may be associated with the positive motivation of staff, such as equality of treatment and developing an *'esprit de corps'* so that strife and division is minimized. Other related elements marginalized by Fayol, though emphasized by later, 'modern' thinkers, include the development of staff, the importance of communicating with them and, finally, the wider social responsibilities of management. (See Chapters 10 and 14.)

Of the classical theorists, Mary Parker Follett was more conscious of the human dimension of management and how, at least within her own US culture, subordinates dislike being 'bossed about'. She proposed that management and leadership should be depersonalized so that authority is related to its context, and compliance is contingent upon what she represents as *the demands of the situation*, not of a manager or leader. As we shall see later, modern management and leadership has sometimes achieved this state of affairs – for example, by securing consent to some activity or set of symbols, such as achieving a bonus or identifying with the culture, thus obscuring the management control that lies behind them.

MODERN THINKING ABOUT MANAGEMENT More recent thinking emphasizes the particular circumstances (of culture, technology, history, etc.) in which management disciplines and functions are applied. Notably, open systems thinking (see Chapter 6) indicates, for example, that a style of leadership that 'fits' and performs well with one particular combination of people and technologies will not necessarily succeed when applied in a different context. There is greater attentiveness to how cultural differences and established ways of doing things – comprising practices of organizing, managing and leading considered 'normal' and 'acceptable' within particular environments – exert an influence upon people as they work. Employees are recognized to bring diverse elements of their 'environments', such as their habits, prejudices and expectations, to work; and open systems thinking suggests that such elements have to be managed in ways that are sensitive to, and appropriate for, the particular organization. In this way, open systems thinking can, in principle, incorporate some awareness of the 'importation' and influence of norms and values within organizations – ways of thinking and acting that can enable, but also may constrain, efforts to impose universal, formal rules and procedures.

Thinkpoint 4.8

Think of an occasion on which a person in authority (e.g. a teacher or manager) was insensitive to the particular circumstances of their actions. How was their behaviour received? What difference might appropriate preparation or skills 'training' have made?

In lay terminology, open systems thinking prompts consideration of a wide range of factors that interact to influence the situation and, therefore, the rational choice of 'strategies', 'structures' and 'processes' for managing it. Open systems thinking may extend to include 'flexibility' in which certain teams or players are managed and led, depending upon variations in the way in which they respond to different approaches. Simultaneously, it attends to the negative effects upon morale if such flexibility is interpreted as favouritism or inconsistency rather than an effective means of improving performance. It commends the scanning of environments to select a philosophy and design that matches what the environment has to offer (e.g. technologies, levels of skill) with what is demanded by it (e.g. speedy responses, reliability). So, even when a generic formula or prescription is embraced – such as 'strong corporate culture' (Chapter 9) or 'lean production' (Chapter 14) – modern thinking stresses how the particularities of the context should be taken into account and the formula thereby adjusted or modified to fit with the specific conditions in which it is being applied. But, at the same time, modern management thinking continues to hanker after guidelines that are conceived to have widespread efficacy, sometimes described as 'best practices'.

Modern management guidelines include being attentive to customers and anticipating, or even initiating, shifts in demand (e.g. through branding and associated customer loyalty schemes); paying attention to current and potential competitors so as to establish a distinctive market position where better profits can be made; attending to costs through careful monitoring and control (e.g. by harnessing the power of information and communication technologies), contracting out activities that can be done more cheaply elsewhere and establishing closer relationships with suppliers. It also involves attending to processes as much as outputs so as to achieve continuous improvements in quality and productivity; and paying attention to staff (e.g. by fostering greater openness and trust) especially in knowledge-intensive industries where their knowledge and skills are critical to performance. While these guidelines do not necessarily depart markedly from classical principles, they suggest a more holistic approach that is simultaneously mindful of the immediate (business) and wider contexts of its operations. Such 'modern' thinking has been applied in the private sector but is increasingly being introduced into public sector organizations – in the form of 'new public management' where 'business disciplines' drawn from the private sector are applied in an effort to 'modernize' and 'streamline' what are viewed as inefficient, excessively labour-intensive, customer-unfriendly and inflexible practices (see Box 4.10).

Major issues/controversies in this field: Mainstream debates

The human dimension of work Classical thinkers paid minimal attention to complex issues of motivation. They focused upon structures and systems (see Chapter 6) without much consideration of how employees would respond to such methods and measures. It was believed that a positive – cooperative, productive – response would follow naturally from the application of classical principles of 'good management'. In Frederick Taylor's *Principles of Scientific Management*, for example, it was assumed that better pay would compensate for the imposition of narrowly drawn and repetitive tasks. Taylor believed that economic reward is the primary, if not, sole purpose of going to work. From this

Box 4.10: Modernizing manufacturing – from mass to niche production

[A Japanese] company had realized by 1984 that demographic changes would soon fragment its market into niches. That implied a need to switch from producing a few washing machine models in high volumes to making a broad selection of models, which would sell at lower volumes. The challenge was to accomplish that without threatening profits. The company created a flexible production system designed to respond directly to the ebb and flow of sales. In five years it tripled the number of new washer models it introduced. The washer factory became accustomed to 11 model changes per day, versus 2.5 daily in 1985. Spending only US$2 million to US$3 million per year to make all these changes, the business doubled both its manufacturing capacity and the dollar amount of sales per employee. At the same time, quality dramatically improved.

Source: N. M. Tichy and S. Sherman (1993) *Control Your Destiny or Someone Else Will*, New York: Doubleday, p. 206.

assumption it followed that any change in working practices would be accepted as long as earnings increased as a result. It is questionable, however, whether Taylor's assumption about work and industrial workers' purely economic interest in wages is universally correct or merely a 'self-fulfilling' prophecy in the sense that more money is what workers demand if there is no other available means of compensating the deprivations experienced at work (see Box 4.11).

Box 4.11: Self-fulfilling prophecies

The notion of the self-fulfilling prophecy applies to large parts of human behaviour where those exercising power strongly condition the framework of meaning by their decisions. When managers believe that workers are only motivated by money, they devise the workplace in such a way as to virtually remove any other possible meaning or interests (e.g. planning the work, innovating methods, social recognition, camaraderie between workers) such that only the size of the wage can matter. Lo and behold, the assumption about economic interests is confirmed. But this is a self-fulfilling prophecy because scientific management has generated the conditions through which it would become true. Of course, an understanding that the prophecy is self-fufilling does not make the basic belief incorrect, but, rather, suggests that its effectiveness depends upon the situation that acts either to confirm or to deny its claims.

That said, it should be noted that Taylor, in common with Fayol and others (e.g. Urwick), believed that employees should be treated 'decently' by training them to acquire the work methods that were 'scientifically proven' . They were adamantly opposed to reliance upon some arbitrary (e.g. personal threat) basis for giving instructions. This, of course, placed a significant burden of responsibility upon those managers who had previously relied upon their power to hire and fire to simply pressure and coerce (i.e. bully) employees to 'work harder "or else" '. Not surprisingly, there was considerable resistance from managers to Taylor's principles. Applying the principles placed new demands upon them. Previously, they had not been burdened by the responsibility of introducing new methods but, instead, habitually relied upon personal (e.g. favouritism) and despotic (e.g. punishment-based) ways of securing employee productivity.

Largely absent from both despotic and 'scientific' approaches to management was any careful or close consideration of employee psychology. When Taylor challenged custom and practice, he did so by assuming a direct relationship between productivity and reward, in the form of payment by results. It did not occur to him that employees might place a greater value upon other concerns, such as solidarity with their fellow employees, their dignity or the comforts of habitual ways of working. Resistance to classical methods of organization, and especially to the demands (and privations) of scientific management, resulted in this assumption being questioned.

Thinkpoint 4.9

If Taylor were considering the work of students, how might he seek to apply his principles? To what extent do you think that academic credentials (i.e. degree results) have a tendency to perform the same function in university as money in scientific management? Can you identify areas of higher education that have been 'Taylorized' (some commentators have described contemporary universities as McUniversities)? Why might Taylor's ideas have limited application in this context? Can you identify areas in which Bar Mar has tended to become 'Taylorized'? In what ways has Margaret sought to resist this tendency?

Resistance to the application of the principles of scientific management was both individual and collective. As individuals, many workers disliked and resented the redesign of their jobs, which removed any scope for imagination or personal identification with the task. They often experienced the uniformity of the new methods as alien and degrading as these sought to eliminate all individuality and differences between workers and to minimize the scope for exercising discretion or creativity. Employees may have strongly disliked the 'irrationality' of 'unscientific', tyrannical bosses who managed according to personal whims and arbitrary prejudices, rather than by the seemingly impartial logic of 'scientific' principles. However, their disinclination to manage consistently and closely always creates space and scope in which employees can more readily develop and control meanings about their work (that is 'sub-cultures') that are not reducible to a calculation about output and wages (see Chapter 6).

Collectively, workers subjected to classical principles of management became homogenized and fragmented as their jobs were mechanized and de-skilled through a process of specialization that made each task narrower and more repetitive. A sense of control over the nature and pace of work was lost as 'scientific' experts applied the new disciplines of management. In addition, workers feared that increases in productivity arising from the implementation of forms of scientific management would result in major lay-offs. By design, its 'scientific' principles exclude workers from involvement in the development and application of this instrument of management control. They are entirely its targets or objects, not its architects or subjects. Not surprisingly, then, for many workers, the classical principles of management were not experienced as a neutral and progressive technology but as a political and socially divisive instrument that posed a threat to their sense of identity, solidarity and interests. To the extent that forms of scientific management encountered increasingly organized resistance, it had the effect of provoking opposition to its aim of rationalizing the workplace rather than exposing and removing irrational deviations from it.

THEORIES 'X', 'Y' AND 'Z' Throughout the history of management thinking and practice, there have been recurrent efforts to understand and manage the 'softer', more complex aspects of organizational behaviour. The emphasis here is upon getting employee motivation right. The underlying assumption is that properly motivated staff, from the bottom to the top of an organization, will develop the most appropriate and effective ways of organizing, including the appropriate use of 'harder', more rational and quantitative methods of assessing and rewarding staff. It is believed that the complexity of human motivation can, if managed effectively, enable organizations to be more productive as well as less heartless.

Thinkpoint 4.10

In what ways did Margaret attempt to manage the 'softer' aspects of the Bar Mar operation?

The introduction of more 'enlightened' or 'humanistic' management is understood to require a deep appreciation of individual and especially group psychology. It necessitates, for example, an understanding of how the norms of work groups can exert a stronger influence upon worker identity and behaviour than the rules and incentives imposed by managers. This is the central message of human relations thinking popularized by Elton Mayo, a Harvard academic, who studied the influence of social factors, such as recognition of contribution and the operation of group norms (e.g. the socially acceptable level of effort and cooperation) upon the productivity of factory workers (see Box 4.12).

Box 4.12: Mayo's human relations thinking

'Human collaboration in work . . . has always depended for its perpetuation upon the evolution of a non-logical social code that regulates the relations between persons and their attitudes to one another.'

Source: E. Mayo (1933) *The Human Problems of an Industrial Civilisation*, New York: Macmillan, p. 120.

So, even when there is a strong material incentive to produce more (e.g. payment by results), Mayo observed that the effectiveness of such inducements may be dampened by the strength of a group norm about the acceptable level of output. In such circumstances, the material incentive does not elicit a high level of productivity if there is a strong desire to avoid being excluded or stigmatized by fellow workers. Instead of operating against the grain of such work group norms and values – a stratagem that is seen to risk a loss of morale and/or increased opposition to management – the 'humanizing' approach pays close attention to employees' 'non-logical' or 'irrational', psychological 'needs'.

They are termed 'non-logical' or 'irrational' because, in purely economic terms, they are seen to obstruct the individual's maximization of earnings. Instead of ignoring or dismissing such 'needs', managers are encouraged to acknowledge, address and, indeed, 'exploit' the 'need to belong' – for example, by making the organization, and not the work group, the primary source of satisfaction of workers' 'irrational' needs (e.g. by developing schemes and styles of management that demonstrated how the corporation and their supervisors were taking care of their psychological as well as their material welfare). Human relations thinking suggested that while economic incentives could not be ignored, employees also seek to have their sense of identity developed and confirmed at work. For the advocates of human relations thinking, worker resistance to management control is surmountable by training managers in interpersonal, leadership skills. To put this another way, employees were no longer to be treated as mere 'hands' but were complex elements within an 'open system' – elements that imported values into the organization that managers would ignore at their peril, but, with the benefit of social science, might harness to their advantage.

Building upon the insights of human relations ideas, 'modernist' thinking shifts from a model of the worker as an appendage to the machine – writ large in Fordism (see Chapter 6) where the pacing of the assembly line was deployed to dictate the speed of each worker's task (see Chapter 11) – to an idea of the worker as a more complex creature who is malleable and, returning to our point about the self-fulfilling prophecy (see Box 4.11), comes to resemble how s/he is treated. That is to say, the worker is a person with diverse needs who, if treated like a machine, will tend to feel frustrated and resentful, and therefore become the mulish, inflexible individual who is motivated to work harder only by the incentive of more pay. Conversely, if the complex and diverse character of workers' interests, motives or orientations is recognized and met, the worker feels appreciated, grows in confidence and self-esteem, becomes more cooperative and therefore more productive.

McGregor (1960) summarized this difference between classical and modern thinking about management by coining the terms 'Theory X' and 'Theory Y' (see Table 4.3). Common to variants of Theory Y is the understanding, or assumption, that the need to belong enables the integration of individual and organizational goals; and that organizations can be managed in ways that motivate individuals by providing opportunities to fulfil their other needs, such as self-esteem and self-actualization (see Box 4.13).

Table 4.3 Comparison of Theory X and Theory Y

Understanding of	Theory X classical	Theory Y modern
Human nature	Lazy. Must be induced or coerced into productive activity	Potentially self-motivating. Will respond positively to opportunities to take responsibility and exercise discretion
Employee's attitude towards work	Negative. Extrinsic rewards (money) compensates for effort expended	Positive. Intrinsic rewards (enjoyment, fulfilment), such as the opportunity to learn and develop, are important
Role of management	Supervise and direct to ensure that work is done	Support to enable learning and development

Box 4.13: Theory Y in practice: 'Management by objectives'

Management by objectives (MBO) is a widely used technique in which common goals and targets are mutually agreed between superior and subordinate, and then subsequently reviewed to assess performance and identify changes (e.g. in systems or personnel) necessary to make further improvements. This is consistent with Theory Y insofar as subordinates are not given detailed instructions for performing their tasks but, rather, are permitted to use initiative and discretion to achieve the agreed goals.

Only then, advocates of Theory Y contend, is it possible to design the content of jobs and the activities of work groups, as well as relevant systems of reward, that harness human potential to the realization of organizational goals. In effect, a psychological remedy is advocated, which, it is claimed, can reconcile the 'needs' of the individual worker with the 'needs' of the organization. We have placed these terms in inverted commas because it is far from clear that needs can be so readily identified or taken for granted – an issue to which we will return in the second part of this chapter.

Exercise 4.3

Complete the following table by listing some of the key differences between 'X' and 'Y' theories of management

Table 4.4 Differences between X and Y theories

	Theory X	Theory Y
Challenges the idea that		
Focuses upon		
Assumes that		

Theories X and Y have their parallels in management styles. A 'managerial grid' (see Figure 4.2) constructed by Blake and Mouton' (1964; see also Blake and McCanse, 1991), which takes as one of its axes the results-orientation, is largely indifferent to human psychology and therefore a variant of Theory X but combines it with a people-centredness approach that is very reminiscent of Theory Y. This grid produces five distinctive styles and, of course, numerous less extreme mixes of them:

- low X, low Y = impoverished management
- high X, high Y = team management
- high X, low Y = country club management
- low Y, high X = authority-compliance management
- medium X, medium Y = middle-of-the-road management.

Management is described as 'impoverished where there is a lack of attention both to people and production. In effect, management is 'hands off'. Both managers and workers exert the minimum of effort to sustain the organization. 'Team management' combines maximum concern with employees and production by ensuring that individual needs and organizational goals are fully integrated. There is an emphasis upon building trust and mutual respect. 'Country club management' describes an approach where there is much attention to employee needs, but limited attention to production. The atmosphere is relaxed, and maintaining harmonious relationships is more important than raising output. Finally, high concern for production combined with minimal concern for people is described as an 'authority-compliance' approach. It is a form of management associated with arranging work in ways that are designed to minimize human intervention.

Not surprisingly, the 'team management' combination of concern for people with a concern for production is viewed as the most desirable. Blake and Mouton's 'team management' is similar to Likert's 'System 4' (see Table 4.5) where management develops and welds the contributions of individuals into an effective, mutually supportive and productive (synergistic) group.

For champions of modern Theory Y, the primary task and responsibility of managers is to enable and educate employees into seeing how the desire to satisfy their own needs can be aligned with the attainment of organizational goals. Managers might be invited, for example, to locate their 'style' on the axes of the 'managerial grid', and then to reflect upon how they can develop themselves to move in the direction of the optimal 'team management' approach. Blake and Mouton developed their grid in the early 1960s but it took another 20 years before the value of 'teamworking' became widely applauded and applied in forms of leadership (see below), total quality management (TQM), business process re-engineering (BPR) and culture management (see also Chapters 2, 4 and 7).

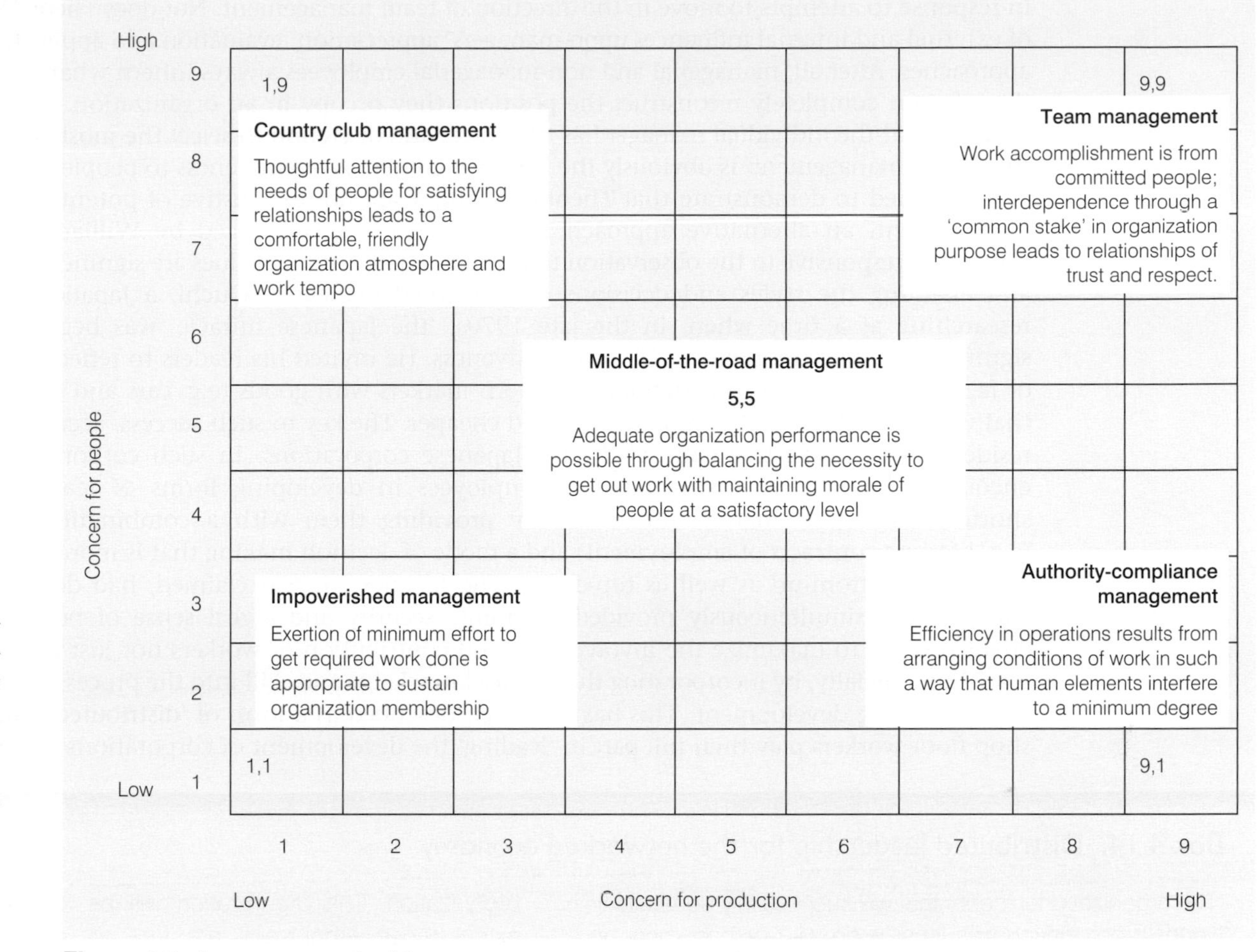

Figure 4.2 A management grid

Table 4.5 Likert's 'System 4' approach to management: Key features

Management characteristic	Management behaviour
Share knowledge and insights	Be attentive and approachable
Acknowledge and reward success	Provide guidance and coaching
Recognize and address personal issues	Support career advancement

Source: Adapted by the author from Likert, 1961.

Thinkpoint 4.11

- How would you describe Margaret's changing approach to management, using the categories developed by Likert?
- What limitations do you detect in the Theory Y prescriptions for improved employee motivation and productivity?

One limitation of a focus upon the needs of individuals as the key to motivation is the scant attention paid to the wider context of managing people in organizations. It does not consider, for example, how national culture or dominant organizational values may strongly condition not only the response of employees to different styles of management but also to the very construction or development of those styles in the first place. So, for example, employees who are used to 'authority-compliance management' may simply be less productive and/or less disciplined (i.e. 'slacken off'; 'take advantage') in response to attempts to move in the direction of team management. Nor does Theory Y take account of external and internal influences upon managers' appreciation, evaluation and application of different approaches. After all, managerial and non-managerial employees always inherit what has gone before – they do not completely reconstruct the positions they occupy in an organization. The theory simply assumes that the individual manager has the power and discretion to select the most effective style, and that 'team management' is obviously the best as it combines attentiveness to people and production.

Concerned to demonstrate that Theories X and Y are not exhaustive of potential philosophies of management, an alternative approach, labelled Theory Z, advanced by William Ouchi (1981) is somewhat responsive to the observation that wider organizational values are significant in constraining and enabling the styles and decisions of individual managers. Ouchi, a Japanese American, was researching at a time when, in the late 1970s, 'the Japanese miracle' was beginning to make a significant impact upon global US competitiveness. He invited his readers to reflect upon the success of Japanese companies in penetrating Western markets with goods (e.g. cars and electrical products) that were of better quality, more reliable and cheaper. The key to such success, according to Theory Z, resides in the distinctive culture of large Japanese corporations. In such corporations, the culture encouraged the active involvement of employees in developing forms of lean production and shortened design-to-manufacture times by providing them with a combination of job security (e.g. lifetime contracts of employment) and a mode of decision making that is more inclusive by being somewhat bottom-up as well as top-down. The Japanese, it was claimed, had developed corporate cultures that simultaneously provided economic security and a real sense of belonging. This had enabled them to maximize the involvement and contribution of workers not just through their hard work but, crucially, by incorporating their ideas, knowledge and skill into the process of innovation and manufacturing development. This has also been described as a form of 'distributed leadership' where shop floor workers play their full part in 'leading' the development of corporations (see Box 4.14).

Box 4.14: Distributed leadership for the networked economy

'The organizational theory that will successfully dominate the world of networking has less to do with management and more to do with leadership – not leadership in the charismatic sense that comes from the top, but leadership that exists and operates all throughout the organization. Such leadership is frequently not "scientific," nor the result of a formal planning process, but more results from a "hands-on" relationship with particular work processes – what Shoshana Zuboff has called informating the workplace.

The information age demands, and will enforce, a transition to empowered employees all throughout the organization. The organization will be successful to the extent those employees are free to, and capable of, exercising leadership. The organizations faced with the most difficult transition to the information age are likely to be those that never really bought into the industrial age management paradigm – the public sector, with higher education and health care being the two most obvious examples . . . they tend to be far more inertia-bound than their aggressive private sector cousins, particularly than the high-tech industries that currently drive the economies of developed countries.'

Source: Robert C. Heterick, *Getting Organized* (http://www.educause.edu/pub/er/review/reviewArticles/31260.html).

Theory Z suggests the importance of the context of management. The limited duration of the Japanese success story and its subsequent 'unravelling' also confirms the view that any 'best way' is limited by time as well as place. 'Fordism', founded primarily upon Theory X with a gloss of paternalism, is another example. Fordist manufacture, which was adopted by all the mass automobile manufacturers, combined Taylor's philosophy of job specialization and simplification with an automated line that effectively paced the work (see Chapter 11). This proved to be a highly successful approach until the system developed by Toyota, which unified elements of Theory Z with a greater responsiveness to consumers' developing interest in greater customization and better quality, demonstrated that Fordism was not, or was no longer, the 'one best way'.

Thinkpoint 4.12

Consider a situation in which you have been strongly motivated to perform a task or achieve a goal. How might Theories X, Y and Z be applied to account for the strength of your motivation?

It was not just Theory Z but a whole range of management thinking – including innovations such as culture management, teamworking, the learning organization, TQM, BPR and knowledge management (KM) – which embraced and promoted the view that employees responsible for daily production have numerous skills and tacit knowledge. These largely discounted by Theory X mass assembly automation, although could, in principle, be transformed into a resource for improving productivity and achieving greater profitability. In a market for mass produced goods that was reaching saturation point, it is also becoming increasingly important to develop ways of differentiating products in terms other than mere functionality. It was recognized that cars and other consumer goods could be a status symbol – an expression of one's place in the social order (see Exercise 4.4) or a statement of a particular lifestyle; and it also has became clearer that product competition is less likely to be successful if customer service fails to be of a high standard.

Exercise 4.4

Take a car manufacturer like Mercedes or some other of your choice and note one of its models that appeals to you, and how it differentiates itself from the equivalent models of other manufacturers. In the case of Mercedes, explore how surveys of reliability and customer satisfaction compare with the image projected by the manufacturer and reflect upon how any discrepancies are managed.

Technological developments in general, but information communication technology in particular, have also created the conditions in which the advantages of mass production can be combined with making products unique to individual, or groups of, customers (see Chapters 11, 12 and 14). Tailoring products to niche markets and 'mass customization' offer ways of combining economies of scale (thereby minimizing unit cost) with economies of scope (by enabling the same production line to create different models).

In *The Art of Japanese Management*, Pascale and Athos (1982) present a '7-S' framework, devised by the consultants McKinsey, that combines elements of Theories X, Y and Z. The '7-S' framework retains a classical emphasis upon structure, systems, skill and strategy but incorporates, and makes central, an attentiveness to staff, style and, most importantly, shared values. As with Theory Z, the focus in the '7-S' framework, which is also central to Peters and Waterman's (1982) highly influential *In Search of Excellence* (see Box 4.15), is upon developing a strong organizational culture. As we have seen, Theory Y anticipates that individual and organizational needs will be reconciled if individuals are given the opportunity to fulfil their needs. Theory Z, and especially *In Search of Excellence*, makes no such assumption. Instead, management is urged to 'create a broad, uplifting, shared culture' (Peters and Waterman, 1982, p. 51) where 'the real role of the chief executive is to manage the values of the organization' (ibid., p. 26), and where employees 'either buy in to their norms or get out' (ibid., p. 77). While some might want to describe the ideal Theory Z worker (see Box 4.15) as displaying obsessive behaviour that requires psychiatric attention, advocates of strong cultures seek to make all workers as devotional and obsessive about their companies as cult members are about their values.

In a chapter entitled 'Man Waiting for Motivation', Peters and Waterman (1982) contend that the key to delivering 'better relative performance, a higher level of contribution from the "average" is to establish a "strong culture" reinforced by "transforming leadership" '. It is this combination of culture and leadership that, according to Peters and Waterman, differentiates the 'best-run companies' from the also-rans. Their claim is that a strong culture provides the final solution to the long-lamented

Box 4.15: The ideal Theory Z worker

'One of our favourite stories is about a Honda worker who, on his way home each evening, straightens up windshield wiper blades on all the Hondas he passes. He just can't stand to see a flaw in a Honda! Now, why is all of this important? Because so much excellence in performance has to do with people being motivated by compelling, simple – even beautiful – values.'

Source: Peters and Waterman (1982), p. 37.

problem of motivating employees as it demonstrates that what (classically trained) managers 'have been dismissing for so long as the intractable, irrational, intuitive, informal organization *can* be managed' (ibid., p. 11). Contemporary thinking about management provides a linkage to identify and connects the basic sequence of managerial work where, in the case of Theory Z, objectives and policy are gathered around a few core values.

A NORMATIVE ORIENTATION Common to the variants of classical and modern thinking summarized above is a *normative* orientation. That is to say, there is an enthusiasm or impatience to prescribe – to say what *ought* to be done – in advance of any sustained effort to detect or diagnose what *is* being done.

Associated with this drive to prescribe is a tendency to identify simplistic, universal remedies, such as 'one best way' solutions or 'best practice' guidelines. These may be attractive to practising managers, and, indeed, to students, because they may seem to provide an authoritative, comforting answer to the bewildering, 'wicked' difficulties of managing unpredictable and awkward 'human resources' in dynamic and uncertain conditions. Such solutions appeal to a so-called 'need' for security that has been a recurrent theme of management thought. However, the relevance and adequacy of any prescription is dependent upon the quality of the diagnosis. Instead of concentrating upon solutions that can be sold to 'needy' managers, some researchers have emphasized the importance of first investigating and seeking to understand what managers do.

What do managers do? Behavioural approach To move beyond approaches that prescribe methods and styles of management, some researchers have undertaken observational studies of managers in order to investigate what they concretely do. On the basis of such a study where he observed the activities of senior management, Mintzberg (1973) concluded that their activity could be described in terms of the performance of three major, overlapping roles that comprise diverse forms of activity. These three roles are 'interpersonal', which includes liaison and figurehead activities in addition to general leadership; 'informational', which embraces the tasks of disseminating information, monitoring activity and acting as a spokesperson; and, finally, 'decisional' roles, which include those of negotiating, dealing with conflicts, allocating resources and taking entrepreneurial initiatives. In short, Mintzberg's study shows managers to be undertaking a number of key roles that frequently overlap in the manner of a venn diagram (see Figure 4.3). So, for example, activities as a

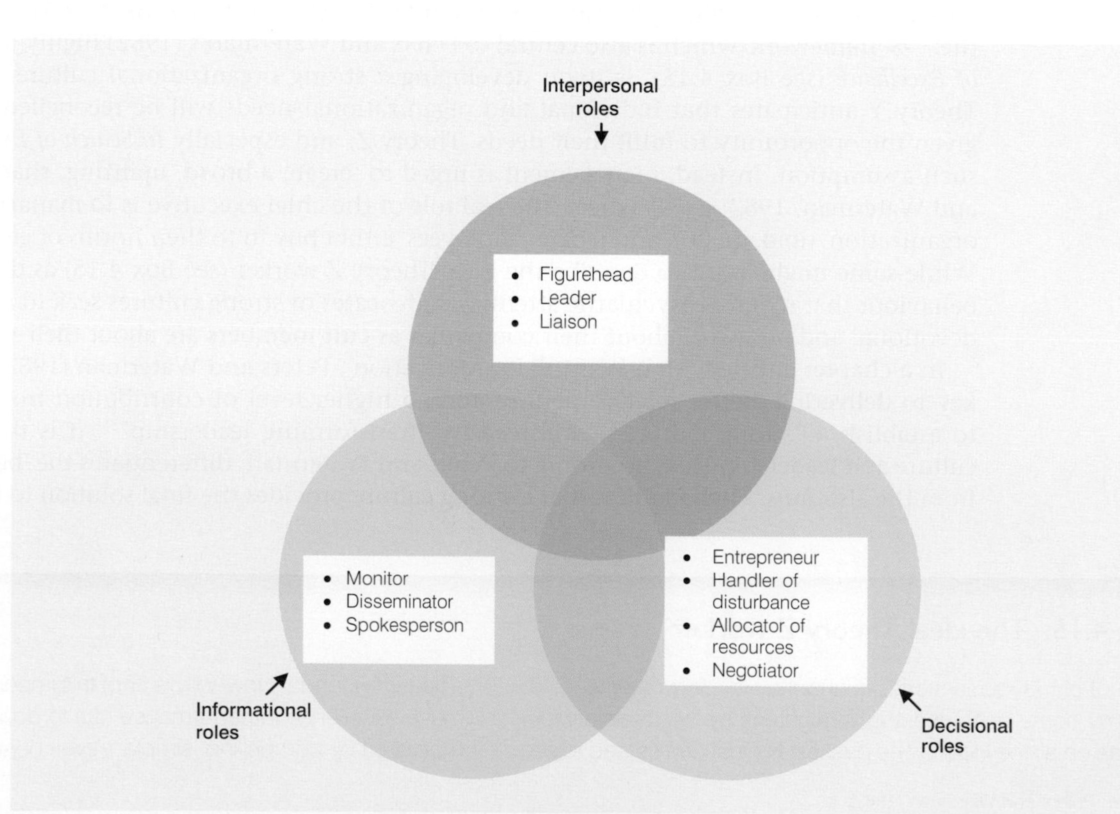

Figure 4.3 The roles and activities comprising managerial work

SOURCE: MINTZBERG, HENRY, *THE NATURE OF MANAGERIAL WORK*, © 1980, P. 59, FIG. 8. ADAPTED BY PERMISSION OF

"I heard you spent half the day looking for someone to process a file that would've taken you five minutes to do yourself. You sir, are management material."

Image 4.1

SOURCE: © RON THERIEN/CARTOONSTOCK.COM

figurehead may involve the dissemination of information about how resources are to be allocated; or processes of negotiation may involve liaison and the monitoring of others' performance and/or stance.

In addition to identifying the breadth of activity undertaken by managers and its conceptualization as the performance of three major roles, Mintzberg's analysis paints a picture of managers rapidly shifting between activities, operating as 'disturbance handler' one moment, then acting as a 'spokesperson' or playing the role of 'ceremonial figurehead' the next. In the process, they are seen to manage boundaries within organizations and with their environments. The proportion of time spent playing the different roles is said to depend largely upon the position occupied by a manager: s/he may be required to play one or two of the roles more frequently than some of others. Some managers may be centrally involved in monitoring, disseminating and prioritizing information, while others are primarily engaged in the entrepreneurial activity of initiating change and developing innovative solutions to problems. The key point to be appreciated, nonetheless, is that the practicalities of managerial work are more *complex, contingent and dynamic* than is implied by both classical and modern prescriptions for management. Managerial work, according to Mintzberg, is often fragmented, with much time being devoted to immediate concerns and problems, and rather little time being devoted to broader strategic issues. That said, it is also important to recognize that it was not the intention of classical writers, like Fayol, to describe how *individual* managers fulfil their responsibilities but, rather, to specify what components comprise the *collective* function of management.

Common to Fayol and Mintzberg's analyses, nonetheless, is a formulation of managerial work that associates it only with functions and roles that are seen as independent of the demands upon their time and attention – for example, from subordinates and superordinates, suppliers and customers. Their focus is upon either the components of management as a function or upon the activities of individual managers. Neither considers managerial work as a medium and outcome of wider institutional and politico-economic forces.

Other observational studies of managerial work suggest that interactions with other people are not only often brief but also charged with many multiple, cross-cutting issues and agendas (Kotter, 1982) that are rich in both local knowledge and political 'baggage'. Managers are seen to be involved in a process of continuously making sense of what is going on and what implications it has for themselves. They are also seem to be engaged in deliberately shaping the sense-making of their staff, but not necessarily in ways that are consistent from one day to the next, or that suggest a conscious and/or sustained attempt to 'manage culture'. Instead, managers are shown to be continuous 'scanners' of their work context, seeking out information that is valued for providing a *richer*, real-time picture of the threats as well as opportunities that are posed for their tasks and career prospects. Much managerial work is also shown to be about 'influencing' others in ways that are expedient and pragmatic. In this process, activities uncharted by Fayol or Mintzberg, taking the form of bantering, swearing and joking, form part-and-parcel of the process of forming and maintaining alliances as well as attaining some degree of personal popularity (Collinson, 1988; see also Chapter 10).

Such contemporary understandings of management are equivalent of the 'kitchen sink' drama that cuts through images of how managerial work 'ought to be' as it explores some of the practical complexities, contrariness and even absurdities (see Table 4.6). Politically charged expediency and opportunism are seen to be central to management in practice, as managers wrestle with numerous competing demands, multiple uncertainties, and endeavour to communicate, network and motivate simultaneously but often inconsistently (see Chapters 9 and 10). While Theories 'X', 'Y' and 'Z' each seek to identify a 'one best way' of managing, these empirical studies endeavour to provide a window upon what management actually does, serving to show how difficult, and perhaps even inappropriate,

Table 4.6 Key findings of contemporary empirical studies of managerial work

Character	Behaviour
Frenetic, fragmented and disjointed	Reactive rather than initiating
Preoccupied with ad hoc, immediate matters	Much negotiating and bargaining
Decisions and plans emergent in process of dealing with immediate matters	Preference for working with practicalities rather than abstractions

Source: Adapted from Hales, 1993, p. 14.

it is to manage using any single formula as, in practice, any consistent approach is routinely compromised by pressures to act in ways that contradict it.

Recent empirical studies show how normative theories of management tend to be highly idealized. That is to say, they abstract 'management' – as a set of principles, functions or roles – from the specific context in which the practice of management occurs. Even when they stress the importance of taking account of context, they underestimate the importance of the institutions and sets of relations that have been both a condition and consequence of the development of management and which continue to compel and shape the ongoing process of its operation and transformation. These institutions are also downplayed in studies that directly address the question of 'what managers do'. In the studies of Mintzberg and Kotter, there is little consideration of the wider context – politico-economic as well as cultural – in which, and through which, managerial work is undertaken. These studies do not, for example, consider how the very meaning of 'management' and aspirations of 'managers' have emerged through struggles to establish their credibility and exert influence in the teeth of opposition – for example, from owners who have been reluctant to trust them; from employees who have been unwilling to obey them; from politicians who think they fail to deliver on expectations for the economy; from regulators who seek to constrain them; and from a wide range of commentators, such as journalists, academics and various special interest groups, who alternatively idolize or harass them.

Thinkpoint 4.13

Consider the work of a CEO like Margaret at Bar Mar. In what ways would you expect their activities to illustrate the findings of studies undertaken by Mintzberg and Kotter?

Key ideas and contributions on leadership

We noted earlier how the idea of 'leadership' is distinguished from 'management' by a greater emphasis upon directing others through inspiration and motivation, rather than command-and-control reliance upon hierarchical position. Leadership also tends to be associated with personal qualities, such as drive, determination, focus, dedication, etc.; but it has also been associated with ruthlessness, obstinacy, autocracy and obsessiveness. In any event, ascribing the virtues of leadership to an individual suggests that their influence or capacity to 'get things done' does not depend purely, or even primarily, upon the occupancy of (managerial) position but, rather, upon qualities summed up as 'leadership' that may take a variety of forms and 'styles'.

Thinkpoint 4.14

Identify a person whom you have known and you regard as a leader. Attempt to create a list of characteristics that distinguish this person from other people. Would *anyone* exhibiting these characteristics be viewed as a leader? Can you think of situations in which such characteristics would be viewed negatively rather than positively?

Classical thinking about leadership

Leadership as a personality trait The traits approach to leadership concentrates upon identifying the qualities attributed to individuals who are widely viewed as leaders. Traits of leadership have included such qualities as initiative, intelligence and self-assurance. The difficulty is that few leaders have been found to share many of these traits and/or non-leaders are also deemed to possess them in equal measure. Such traits do not appear to discriminate sufficiently between leaders and non-leaders to be of analytical use. Nonetheless, a variant of the traits approach has resurfaced in the form of 'transformational' leadership (Burns, 1978; Bass, 1985) – a kind of leadership capable of meeting the challenge of re-energizing or reinventing organizations or departments during periods of turbulence and uncertainty. 'Transformational leaders' are conceived to possess the qualities needed to inspire and redirect staff to solve problems and attain ambitious objectives – objectives that are rarely achieved by relying upon a 'transactional' approach where cooperation relies upon narrow calculations of self-interest ('if you do/don't do this, you will/won't get this', as exemplified by bonus schemes, promotion systems, etc.). In contrast to mere managers who lack transformational traits and, as a consequence, fall back upon more mundane, transactional techniques to secure compliance, transformational leaders are seen to exhibit behaviours that energize and enthuse others so that their followers come to care as much and more about realizing the visions or mission of the leader as they do about any personal gain that they may derive from their fulfilment. Key features attributed to transformational leaders are set out in Table 4.7.

In common with trait theories of leadership, the idea of transformational leadership assumes that exhibiting its key features delivers the intended results irrespective of the circumstances, such as the nature and scale of the task at hand, the established systems and culture of the organization, or the readiness of followers to respond to the calls of a leader who aspires to be transformational.

We can conclude that classical approaches perceived leadership broadly to be an attribute of the individual – an individualized and therefore bastardized version of the ancient Greek image of leadership as honourable and heroic, so well represented by Odysseus in Homer's narratives. By contrast, modern approaches begin to see leadership more in relational terms and in the context of followers or with respect to the contingencies that are the medium and outcome of its impact.

Modern thinking about leadership In modern, contingency thinking, leadership is a product of an interaction between a number of variables. Contingency thinking also allows for the possibility that leadership is a function of collective activity comprising diverse elements that may be shared by, or passed among, various people at different times, rather than a role that is played by individuals who possess the appropriate traits or display the relevant behaviours. When leadership is conceived of as a function that occurs within any group engaged in a task, it is no longer seen as the preserve of a single individual but, rather, may be spread across a number of group members or simply executed as part of a group process. Numerous components of leadership as a function have been suggested (see Table 4.8), many of which bear a marked resemblance to the set of roles ascribed by Mintzberg to managers (see Figure 4.3), except that they are conceived as

Table 4.7 Transformational leaders

• Clear and compelling sense of vision	• Admiration and/or respect from followers	• Ability to communicate and persuade
• Capacity to provide and stimulate creativity and innovation	• Clear linking of strategies to vision	• Engendering of confidence and optimism

Table 4.8 Elements of the leadership function

• Father-figure	• Opinion shaper	• Planner
• Role model	• Policy maker and implementer	• Anxiety absorber
• Expert	• Arbitrator and mediator	• Figurehead
• Purveyor of rewards and punishments	• Distributor of tasks and responsibilities	• Scapegoat for failure

Source: Adapted by the author from Krech, Crutchfield and Ballachey, 1962.

a property of a group and may therefore be undertaken by one or more individuals at different points in time.

Situational theories conceive of different elements or aspects of leadership – such as the provision of expertise or the implementation of policy – shifting between individuals over time. Considered in this way, a person who emerges as a leader, and may be identified by the group as their leader, is the one who is perceived by others to perform the most significant of these elements or to be the best exponent of key leadership tasks, the importance of which may itself shift with changing circumstances. In short, leadership needs to reflect the situation in which it finds itself.

According to Adair (1979), the function of leadership, whether undertaken individually or collectively, involves not only the achievement of tasks but also the maintenance of group processes (e.g. building morale, maintaining focus) and addressing the particular needs of group members (e.g. self-esteem). Individuals are understood to exhibit leadership characteristics whenever they take

CASE STUDY 4.2 Cornerville street-corner society

In his classic **participant observation** study of street corner gangs in Cornerville (a pseudonym – an American slum), Whyte (1943/1993) demonstrated the centrality of leadership and organization regardless of whether the activity has a purpose in relation to work or the formal economy. The study concentrated on one of the gangs and discovered that unemployment, poverty and marginality were no obstacles to a highly organized life based on hanging around with the gang. These gangs were formed on the street where they can be found almost every night of the week. Membership continued well beyond teenage life into adulthood, even after marriage. Doc, the leader of the gang with whom Whyte spent most of his time, was either more proficient in all the activities (e.g. alley bowling, fighting, gambling, womanizing) or at least made to appear so. For he would promote those activities where he excelled and discourage those in which he was less skilled. Whyte (ibid., p. 23) found a 'very close correspondence between social position in the gang and bowling performance': bowling had become the main activity of the gang and, more importantly, the vehicle for maintaining, gaining or losing prestige. Several other social psychological regularities or norms were discovered relating to group behaviour. Among these were that: the leader spends more money on his followers than they on him; the gang has little collective coherence in the absence of the leader; the leader is more decisive and his decisions are more satisfactory to the group and therefore usually considered 'right'; and he is better known and more respected outside his group than any of his followers, and is expected to represent the interests of the group externally whether in conflict, competition or cooperation (ibid., p. 260). Whyte concludes that a major benefit of his study is to help inform social workers about leadership. Rather than relying on the so-called leading figures in the community – those middle class 'respectable business and professional men' – Whyte recommends that social workers mobilize the informal leaders in street-corner gangs that Cornerville people recognize. Potentially, these leaders could be harnessed to forms of community development – an orientation that has its parallels in the appropriation of informal shop floor behaviour for managerial purposes.

opportunities to practice the skills associated with delivering the elements of the leadership function. This understanding challenges the view that leadership is a manifestation of personality traits possessed by individuals. Instead, it is seen to be an outcome of opportunities, willingness and capacity to master its constituent elements. In this sense, leaders like Doc in Case study 4.2 are considered to be made in this process of 'mastery', not born.

Leadership *style* characterizes differences in how elements of leadership are undertaken. One possibility is for all members of a group to refuse to take responsibility for the leadership function such that no single leader arises – in effect, the style of 'abdication'. Another possibility is for the group or a leader to decide that each member will assume responsibility for all elements of the leadership function. Rather confusingly, this has been described as '*laissez-faire*', which implies that each individual is left to 'do their own thing', whereas it is clear that very considerable responsibilities are imposed upon each individual by a leader or actively embraced by all members of a group.

Leaving aside the rather rare and exceptional options of abdication and *laissez-faire*, a basic division in styles of leadership is generally between those that are consultative or participative (widely described as 'democratic'), and others that are imposing and dictatorial (widely called 'authoritarian'). A dictatorial style generally relies exclusively upon personal conviction, the force of personality and the power to favour, or to dispense with, followers. This may be accompanied by giving trusted lieutenants considerable discretion to act in ways that realize the broad direction and goals set by the leader as well as unqualified confidence in the ability of the mass of followers to excel in their work. Churchill, and more especially Hitler, provide examples of what House (1971) terms a 'path–goal theory' of leadership in which the central function of leadership involves identifying a route to the achievement of desired goals but does not necessarily include any detailed specification of how the goals are to be realized. While authoritarian leaders may not always be 'control freaks', they often get by with a minimal degree of cooperation from followers. Unconditional commitment may be the desired outcome but lip service rather than active consent or devotion to the leader may be sufficient to sustain their leadership. An authoritarian style is, however, more vulnerable to disenchantment and rebellion if the leader's grip on power is seen to slip – ironically in Churchill's case by his strategic role in winning the war and in Hitler's case by losing it (see Box 4.16).

Box 4.16: Hitler and Churchill: Born leaders?

The association of inspiration and direction with leadership explains why Hitler and Churchill are widely identified as leaders. Were Churchill and Hitler born leaders or did they learn to master key elements of the leadership function? Would they have emerged as leaders at any time or place, or did circumstances 'conspire', as it were, to identify them as popular, and seemingly 'natural', leaders? Especially through their speeches, each articulated a set of beliefs and policies that served to remove doubts and establish resolve in the masses who became their followers. Churchill and Hitler depended upon the cooperation of others – not only for the organization and management of the political and military apparatus they commanded, but also for a continuing belief in their leadership capabilities – something that was greatly tested when war propaganda was unable to conceal defeats and setbacks. In Churchill's case, qualities of leadership that were an inspiration to most of the population during a period of national crisis (i.e. the Second World War) were shown to lack popular appeal and relevant direction during the subsequent period of reconstruction, as evidenced by the rejection of his party at the general election of 1945. Hitler was seen as a charismatic leader but chose to consolidate his power through totalitarian methods intended to scare any doubters into submission. Yet had he not entered political life at a time of economic crisis due to hyperinflation in Germany, his message would probably have secured support only from a fringe of ultra-nationalists and racists. Followers can readily destroy as well as make leaders, since each process is dependent upon the situation or circumstances that render ideas (e.g. fascism) credible or at least supportable, and thereby confer leadership upon their most articulate and persuasive champions.

Thinkpoint 4.15

How would you characterize Margaret's style of leadership at Bar Mar?

A consultative style or mode of leadership necessitates a process of discussion in which followers participate in shaping opinions, making policies and making decisions about the distribution of tasks and responsibilities. In principle, the consultative style harnesses the collective wisdom of the group, rather than assuming that an individual leader possesses a monopoly of truth and good judgement. The consultative style risks paralysis induced by endless discussions resulting in costly delays, procrastination and compromises. Discussion may ensure a degree of harmony, but at the expense of dealing effectively with issues faced by the group. Styles of leadership can be related and contrasted by considering the extent to which group members take responsibility for the leadership function and the extent to which they rely upon a leader to perform this function.

Exercise 4.5

Above we have discussed the various approaches to leadership. Respectively, leadership is seen as consisting of:

- personality traits
- transformational capacities
- functions and styles.

In a seminar or tutorial group divide into three groups each of which is required to support and defend the merits of one of the three approaches. Each group should elect a spokesperson at the beginning of a discussion in which you seek to develop arguments to defend the approach designated to you. This is a role-play exercise so you do not necessarily have to be actually committed to the approach you are supporting, except for the purpose of this exercise. It will help to support your arguments with examples of leaders from the case studies of Bar Mar and Cornerville, the world of politics, sport, the media, soaps, history or whatever else may help to render your case more convincing. When you return to the whole seminar group, the spokesperson should present the defence after which there will be space for questions and comments from the group as a whole.

Leadership and contingency Contingency theories relate the effectiveness of leadership behaviours to the demands and possibilities presented by a specific situation or context. The success of a leader or leadership style is understood to be contingent upon the circumstances that support its effectiveness. Hickson *et al.* (1971) found that the power of a leader increases in direct proportion to their indispensability (difficult to replace) and their ability to manage uncertainty (see also Chapter 9). Other aspects of the situation that are regarded by Fiedler (1967) as influential include the nature of the task, the make-up of the followers including their assessment of the leader, the culture of the group and the formal position occupied by the leader. Fiedler's contingency model of leadership suggests that the effectiveness of a leader depends upon the adoption of a style that is appropriate to (i) the status of the task – is it structured or unstructured?; (ii) leader–member relations – is the leader trusted and respected? and (iii) position power – does the leader occupy a formal position of authority? (See Table 4.9.)

Table 4.9 Fiedler's contingency model of leadership

Style of leadership	Leader–group relations	Task	Position power
Authoritarian	Good	Structured	Strong
Authoritarian	Bad	Unstructured	Weak
Participative	Mixed: Not consistently or unambiguously positive or negative		

Fiedler distinguishes between styles of leadership that are more or less participative. A directive style, he contends, is more effective when there is little inconsistency and ambiguity about these three contingencies: they are either highly positive or completely negative. A directive, authoritarian style is said to deliver results in situations where the task is either highly structured or completely unstructured; where the leader is highly respected or totally disparaged; and where there is very strong or very weak position power. Conversely, where there is greater ambiguity or inconsistency in the contingencies – for example, where position power is high and the task is structured but trust in leader–group relations has not been fully established – then a more participative style is conceived to have a better chance of success. In turn, this suggests that for maximum effectiveness, the selection of a leader by an organization or a work group should be made on the basis of the contingencies of the situation. For example, only where there is ambiguity and inconsistency is it recommended that a person with a participative style be selected.

Thinkpoint 4.16

On what basis is Fiedler's assessment and recommendation of the appropriateness of different leadership styles being made?

A recurrent theme of contingency theories of leadership is the relationship between the leader and the group, and students of follower behaviour take up this aspect. They focus upon the readiness of followers to be led – are they willing, able and/or confident in their leader? Hersey and Blanchard (1993) suggest that the effectiveness of a leadership style depends critically upon its compatibility with followers' preparedness to accept and respond to it (see Table 4.10).

When followers are unable, unwilling or insecure about the task, then 'telling' by giving strong guidance on tasks is the most effective style. This coincides with the view, sketched earlier, of a leader being more powerful when s/he demonstrates an ability to manage uncertainty (see Chapter 9). At the other end of the continuum of 'follower readiness', 'delegating' is most likely to succeed when followers are able, committed and confident. In between, there are followers who have the ability to follow (e.g. to perform a task) but are unwilling or insufficiently confident to have the task delegated to them, and who therefore require support through 'participating' but need little guidance on the task. Another group in the middle are those with low to moderate readiness but lack the ability to perform a task independently of the leader. Nevertheless, they are willing and (over)confident so that 'selling', in the form of guidance on the task, justifying the instruction and providing support for its accomplishment, is advised.

Major issues/controversies in this field: Mainstream debates

Contingency theories of leadership, including Fiedler's, are based upon matching a style of leadership to the demands attributed to the current situation – in respect of the task, the relations with the group, the environment and so on. Vroom and Yetton (1973) and Vroom and Jago (1988) develop the contingency model to incorporate a consideration of the future consequences of adopting a particular style – an approach that extends beyond an assessment of its probable effectiveness in

Table 4.10 Hersey and Blanchard's contingency model of leadership style

Followership readiness	Leadership style
High (able, willing, confident)	Delegating
Moderate to high (able yet unwilling; able but insecure)	Participating
Low to moderate (willing and confident yet unable)	Selling
Low (unable, unwilling, insecure)	Telling

Exercise 4.6

What are the key similarities and differences between Fiedler's and Hersey and Blanchard's ideas about leadership?

achieving a current goal. The choice of leadership style, this theory suggests, should take account of its longer-term effects upon the motivation and commitment of individual employees and/or group members (see Chapter 2), such as the development of competencies and capacities to undertake future tasks. Balanced against this, the theory includes consideration of the time available to address a problem, which may, for example, make a more consultative approach untenable. Different types of problems are conceived to be best addressed with different leadership styles – autocratic, consultative or 'group', the latter being descriptive of a style where the leader acts as a chairperson or facilitator of a group discussion in which the objective is to achieve consensus among its members (see Chapter 4).

Vroom and Jago's (1988) contingency approach seeks to link particular styles of leadership (revolving around the autocratic–democratic polarity) to different contexts (see Table 4.11). Three kinds of context have been discussed:

1. Where democratic/participatory styles of leadership are presumed appropriate, there is generally uncertainty and ambiguity regarding relations with the led, the task structure and/or the power of the leader. An autocratic style is suited to all other situations, where the dimensions are clear-cut either in a positive or negative direction.
2. Followership studies concentrate more on the relations with the led, simply providing more detail as to the capability, willingness and confidence of followers to carry out tasks independently of the leader. These should inform the selection of the style of leadership.
3. Attention to personal and organizational development extends consideration of the context beyond the present to anticipate the consequences of a style of leadership for the future motivation, commitment, capability and competence of followers.

Table 4.11 Vroom and Jago's (1988) contingency model of leadership style

Type of problem	Leadership style
Principally affecting a single individual: tough time constraints	Autocratic Leader makes decision for subordinate or obtains information from subordinates and provides a solution
Principally affecting a single individual: manager wishes to develop employee	Consultative Problem explored with individual subordinates: decision taken by leader which may reflect influence of subordinates
Principally a group-level problem: tough time constraints	Autocratic Leader makes decision for subordinate or obtains information from subordinates and provides own solution *or* Consultative Problem explored with subordinates as a group, then takes decision
Principally a group-level problem: manager wishes to develop employees' capabilities	Group Problem explored with subordinates, with leader facilitating this exploration to achieve consensus

CASE STUDY 4.3 Management and innovation

Burns and Stalker (1961) conducted empirical case studies of management and organization. One of these concerned a rayon factory and the other an electronics company. In the rayon factory formal bureaucratic rules and relationships were dominant, interactions tended to be vertical and decision making was also strictly hierarchical – a method of organizing that, in the authors' view, is somewhat discrepant with modern thinking about management. Much to their surprise, however, the company was efficient and successful and appeared not to generate dissatisfaction or protest on the part of employees. By contrast, the electronic company exhibited what the authors called an organic system of highly informal and non-hierarchical procedures where face-to-face interpersonal relations rather than formal rules and methods determined working practices.

Since the 1950s, Peter Drucker (1974), the celebrated management guru, had criticized bureaucratic organization for its mechanistic, over-prescription of work processes where managers are reduced to mere administrators rather than 'dynamic, life-giving elements' (ibid., p. 3), stimulating businesses to creative growth. In common with other gurus, Drucker's prescriptions are an expression of his beliefs: for him, management is not a science or a technical and professional skill but, rather, a creative practice. Managing organically is, for Drucker, an imperative for all modern organizations. However, Burns and Stalker's research suggests that it is effective in some (comparatively uncertain and turbulent) environments, and for certain technological processes, but perhaps not for others. Their findings suggest that organic systems of management are best suited to situations of environmental and/or product market instability where a speedy and flexible response to change is critically important. Where the technology and the market for products are stable and more predictable, as in the case of the rayon factory, a mechanistic system of management is seen to work perfectly well.

Exercise 4.7

Return to the management Theories X, Y and Z discussed earlier and apply them to this case study. Which of the theories is most appropriate to managing an organization in a stable environment and which in a turbulent environment?

CASE STUDY 4.4 Qualbank (adapted from Knights and McCabe, 1999)

In 1989 operating costs were rising rapidly and rising faster than income. Between 1986 and 1989 the cost/income ratio for Qualbank, a leading UK bank, had risen from 65.5 per cent to over 75 per cent. The CEO described the organization at that time as having a 'many-layered management' that was in need of substantial rationalization. A strategy was put in place in 1989 to 'drive costs down and increase quality and sustainable income'. Between 1990 and 1995, 8500 jobs were removed following substantial restructuring. The company closed 19 per cent of its branches between 1989 and 1994 against 16.8 per cent for all banks; the company lost 37 per cent of its 1989 staff complement against 20 per cent for all banks (source: *Annual Abstract of Statistics*, British Bankers' Association). As well as downsizing, this entailed removing 15 per cent of in-branch work from the branches to back-office processing centres.

Homeco was a wholly owned but comparatively small subsidiary of Qualbank specializing in mortgages and had a staff of 320 organized around teams of workers each headed by a team leader. Alongside the rationalization of the bank, Homeco was also centralized and was expected to deliver a 25 per cent improvement in productivity in three years assuming no investment in technology. It was decided that the customer interface would remain at the branch level of Qualbank and therefore Homeco would regard the branch as its customer. With the principle of 'customer service' it was felt important that customers (branch staff) contacting Homeco should be able to fulfil all their requirements through a single communication. Productivity at Homeco for application processing increased by 103 per cent from 1990 to 1993 with a policy of fixed staffing levels. Under the regional structure, mortgages often took five days to be offered following receipt of an application. Now Homeco provides service levels of the same day issue upon receipt. However, there were considerable tensions if not ill will between Homeco and the bank branches of Qualbank.

'Partnership' meetings were introduced so as to reduce these tensions, which related largely to mortgage applications and processing. The basic objective was to encourage Homeco to be less restrictive in its lending policy and more flexible in administering mortgage business so as to enable the bank to reverse the loss of business to competitors now the market had moved against them. The Partnership had been initiated by three senior branch representatives and they attended alongside two less senior team leaders nominated by a Homeco senior manager whose absence reflected his belief that the issues were relatively trivial, not a view shared by the branches. In addition, there was a facilitator from the quality department of the bank, who established the purpose of the meeting as one of 'agreeing and prioritizing an internal customer/supplier improvement plan'. The facilitator continued to establish the ground rules as follows:

- participation on the basis of equality, not rank
- be objective rather than subjective
- it should be fun
- there should be no personal attacks.

Without questioning the validity of some of these ground rules, at a common-sense level many of them were breached within a very short period of time. While criticisms about Homeco from the branches may not have been directly personal, they did appear to be taken so. The opening discussion revealed that some managers in the branches felt that a polarized attitude of 'us' and 'them' had arisen between the branches and Homeco. These branch managers believed that Homeco followed a 'narrow interpretation of quality'. For example, they complained that under the auspices of the TQM programme, Homeco had instigated a scheme whereby 'junior' staff were measuring the errors on mortgage applications and, as a result, applications were being rejected. Complaints from branches particularly focused around being appraised by 'lowly' clerical workers at Homeco, the pedantic approach towards measuring errors, and also the loss of business due to mortgage delays.

Participation was very hierarchical throughout the meeting in that the more senior branch managers tended to dominate while aggressively outlining the problems and concerns as they saw them. Certainly, the meeting did not seem to be much fun, and did not come alive until the group moved outside of the highly mechanistic framework created by the facilitator. This framework involved each member listing the services that they believed themselves to provide for their 'internal customers'. These were then listed on a flip chart and everyone was asked to rank them in terms of importance and how well the service was performed. When this rigid framework for participation broke down, Homeco staff began to retaliate and defend themselves against the criticisms of the branch members. The initial and ongoing passivity of Homeco staff, however, seemed to reflect their junior status as team leaders vis-à-vis the more senior branch managers. But while junior, because of their power of veto, they were still in the driving seat.

Three areas of importance for improvement were eventually agreed upon:

1. *Decisions on mortgage applications*. The branches suggested that decisions were often arbitrary or certainly not sensible in terms of the current competitive market for loans. For this reason the second area of importance was
2. *Appeals*. Here branch personnel considered that anomalies were occurring that did not secure adequate treatment in appeals.
3. *Telephone communication*. Homeco required accurate mortgage information from the branches, and the branches needed to be kept informed as to the progress of applications.

Analysis

The Partnership was both a consequence and occasion for the exercise of power as well as generating certain resistant responses. One example of this exercise of power was the way that the branches largely set the agenda, despite apparently following the equal participation procedures laid down by the facilitator. In the Partnership, the facilitator stressed that he should be acting 'very much as an observer and allowing for far more autonomy within the group'. At one point, he noted that he was actually steering the group more than he should (understatement). But had he not done so, it seems unlikely that the Partnership would have progressed. Individuals were so preoccupied with their own idiosyncratic problems and anxieties that they were unable, or unprepared, to set them aside. The Partnership members looked for guidance, structure, motivation and leadership from the facilitator. Yet in terms of the philosophy and spirit of empowerment, this should have been continuously refused, thus encouraging the members to take full ownership of the problems they were attempting to handle, including those of how to work together in resolving them. This, of course, ignores the threat that such an approach would pose to the individual career identities of the Partnership members, for 'failure' of the Partnership could reflect badly on them, especially those branch managers who had initiated its development. Moreover, this empowerment would have more than likely increased the tensions between Homeco and the branch management. At the end of the second meeting the 'decision-making' team proposed that an agreement-in-principle (AIP) form be designed so that speedy acceptances of mortgages could be offered to clients at the branches. After a couple more meetings, however, the Partnership collapsed due to the failure to secure a response to a summary of the AIP problem (i.e. a single page of A4 which was little more than a record of what had been decided) that had been distributed to the Partnership members.

The person who had originally proposed establishing an AIP form commented on the Partnership's failure:

We've had to re-look at the Partnership because of the people we've got involved from the Homeco side . . . we're pulling together a more high-powered meeting. They're looking at bringing on board the Homeco general manager . . . the decision maker . . . the meetings have very much been going round in circles, and I was a little bit frustrated because I had done about a three-page document . . . and I discovered that that hadn't gone up the line to the regional director. So straight away, you know, I flagged up – things aren't happening . . . we need more senior people . . . it's purely the bureaucracy and the structure, through no fault of our own.

Another branch representative commented upon the failure of the Partnership and, regarding Homeco, he remarked:

They seem a bit intransigent or reluctant to change . . . There are still major problems . . . I found it incredible that the facilitator sat-in on the meeting where they started doing these AIPs, and then at the next meeting said that 'this is wrong, why didn't you measure the problems first' . . . why didn't he say that the first time? . . . we can do our part in this . . . but we're getting inconsistencies within Homeco . . . in terms of how they respond . . . we've done our bit.

Exercise 4.8

Examine this case from the point of view of the leadership studies discussed above. Which of the theories is most appropriate in seeking to understand the events of this case? Explain how the theory you have selected provides insights into the case.

Contribution and limitations of the mainstream approaches

The mainstream approaches to management and leadership are extremely varied and provide numerous insights. We can summarize our review as follows:

- 'Management' and 'leadership' are often used interchangeably and their meaning changes in accordance with circumstances and fashion. Currently leadership has had a new lease of life among both practitioners and theorists, which we will examine in the second part of this chapter.
- Management is generally associated with the maintenance of existing organizational arrangements whereas 'leadership' is more linked to change, innovation and transformation.
- Management can be seen as a discipline of modern society, an organizational function and a privileged social group, whereas leadership is seen either as an individual attribute, or a style appropriate to particular contingencies or contexts.
- While management is associated with planning, administrative coordination and control, leadership is linked with inspiring and motivating people, whether by autocratic or democratic means, to develop and realize their individual and collective capabilities.
- Most modern approaches to management and leadership have drawn on some variant of open systems or contingency theory.

The limitations of the mainstream approaches to management and leadership stem from taking for granted the prevailing form, structure and knowledge of organizations. The sense that mainstream thinking makes of management and leadership tends to assume and reinforce ways of organizing that have developed within this structure, even when they aspire to challenge them.

For example, more participative styles of management and leadership may be prescribed but basic inequalities of earnings are maintained or increased. Hierarchies are preserved even if they are de-layered. Leadership is associated with preserving, or bringing reform to, established forms and structures, not with their transformation in any radical sense. Managers are largely unaccountable to their subordinates even if subordinates are 'empowered'. The very term 'transformational' when applied to leadership (or management) is an oxymoron as its intent is to renew or streamline established practices, not to transform them. While democracy in society is trumpeted as a defining feature of modern, civilized societies, democracy in organizations is usually absent from the agenda. Forms of participation and involvement that operate within the framework of prevailing hierarchies, with management at the helm, effectively displace their substantive realization. In short, mainstream thinking implicitly endorses and legitimizes the values of the status quo and the distribution of material and symbolic (e.g. status) goods that flow from it. It plays upon, rather than addresses the roots of, the insecurities that are engendered by patterns of domination – with regard to gender and ethnicity as well as wealth.

We have noted how modern thinking about management and leadership is inclined to favour an open systems or contingency approach. By conceiving of organization, management and leadership in such terms, the existence and necessity of the 'system' and its sub-systems is taken for granted. The challenge is to control or manipulate its elements in ways that achieve existing objectives and priorities even more effectively. Disregarding the presence of inequalities and power in the formation of practice and theory, consensus is assumed, and attention is concentrated on adapting the organization to its environment. The problems with it are numerous. It assumes, for example, that:

- Managers or leaders are rational actors effectively applying their knowledge of the organization and its environment in pursuit of a consensual set of goals, yet knowledge is not only imperfect but often unavailable, behaviour is diverse and unpredictable and goals are variable and often conflicting between different members of an organization.
- Managers or leaders possess the power to implement their decisions and have them executed by lower hierarchy staff without leakage or even disruption, yet these staff frequently have a very low regard for the competence and integrity of their subordinates.
- Managers or leaders focus exclusively upon the goals of the organization and not upon their own personal interests in power and identity, or a concern with freedom and/or security that might conflict with such goals.
- Managers or leaders tend to adopt a linear causal understanding wherein one or a small number of determinants of desired behaviour can be discovered. This relies upon sharp boundary distinctions between so-called independent variables (e.g. managers or leaders) and dependent variables (e.g. the managed or led) since these are necessary if one factor or variable is seen to cause another. Yet this can presume the knowledge that there is a clear-cut boundary between the organization and the environment rather than understanding both as constructions that reflect and reinforce the power, interests, knowledge and identity of those that construct them.
- Managers or leaders need not concern themselves with a whole range of 'environmental', social and other interests and pressures that might conflict with the straightforward preoccupation with the economic goals of performance, productivity and profit.

Critical approach

Introduction: Overview of a critical approach to management and leadership

Critical analysts are sceptical about the assumptions upon which mainstream accounts of management and leadership are based. Major parts of the critical analysis of management were covered in the chapter on structure and design (Chapter 6) so here we will concentrate primarily upon the area of leadership. In any event, as we noted earlier in this chapter, there is considerable overlap between 'managing' and 'leading', with the term leadership being used to identify the more dynamic and innovative features of management.

The assumptions made in mainstream leadership and management literatures are generally so taken-for-granted that they are not explicitly made. Take, for example, the assumption of consensus. Few, if any, mainstream thinkers directly acknowledge that they assume consensus in organizations. They simply proceed as if this is the case. How do we know that? We deduce it from the fact that little attention is given to conflicts; and when conflict is addressed it is analysed as something pathological or attributed to something like 'resistance to change'. The possibility that there might be underlying, endemic conflicts, associated with inequalities of wealth, status or power or the incorporation of managers to deliver what is expected of them, is simply not contemplated.

The assessment of critical analysts, in contrast, is that organizations may *appear* to be consensual but this is because managers occupy positions in the hierarchy that enable them to suppress conflict and/or because subordinates have a 'realistic' understanding that compliance or consent is in their own 'best' interests. In other words, the absence of overt conflict is a consequence of relations of *dependence*. Subordinates are usually dependent on managers for a variety of workplace terms and conditions – for example, retaining their jobs, the allocation of tasks and responsibilities, increments in pay, overtime, promotion, future employment references, etc. Given this relative dependence, it is perhaps surprising that there is ever any conflict, especially of the kind that directly challenges management.

Thinkpoint 4.17

Think of an occasion – at home or university – where conflict has been suppressed; that is where a potential antagonism has not surfaced or been expressed. Does that mean that it does not 'come out' in other ways? Think of examples of how 'buried' conflicts are articulated, more or less consciously, in a covert or subtle manner.

The suppression of something does not mean that it is eradicated. Instead, it is driven 'underground' and manifests itself in acts of more or less subtle subversion. Often dissent and opposition are expressed in the form of humour directed at management practices. In 'Bullshit Bingo' (see Figure 4.4), it is the very basis of managerial expertise that is challenged. Management's self-importance – manifest in the obsession with holding meetings that often make little contribution to productive activity – is lampooned by redefining the content of its communications as 'bullshit'. Managers are seen to be slaves to, and mindlessly dependent upon, demonstrating their credentials as managers by puffing themselves up with self-serving platitudes and vacuous catchphrases.

At the very least, 'Bullshit Bingo' offers a form of tension release from the boredom and hypocrisy of routine managerial work where managers often either fear to say what they think, deliberately

Do you keep falling asleep in meetings and seminars? What about those long and boring conference calls? Here is a way to change all of that!

How to play: Check off each block when you hear these words during a meeting, seminar, or phone call. When you get five blocks horizontally, vertically, or diagonally, stand up and shout **BULLSHIT**!!

Synergy	Strategic fit	Gap analysis	Best practice	Bottom line
Revisit	Bandwidth	Hardball	Out of the loop	Benchmark
Value-added	Proactive	Win-win	Think outside the box	Fast track
Result-driven	Empower [or] Empowerment	Knowledge base	Total quality [or] Quality driven	Touch base
Mindset	Client focus[ed]	Ball park	Game plan	Leverage

Figure 4.4 'Bullshit Bingo'

mislead or are highly selective in what they communicate in order to gain some kind of tactical, competitive advantage. Problems of management are frequently described and diagnosed in terms of 'poor communication'. Yet communication is so often poor because there are games being played (i.e. monopolizing information; keeping others in the dark because they 'don't matter') and other priorities being pursued. Critical analysis assumes that conflicts of priority and 'interest' are endemic and deeply engrained, not sporadic or superficial. Forms of humour and gossip frequently are understood to expose the underside of organizational life by articulating a sense of grievance or absurdity that is felt but unexpressed on a day-to-day basis. Humour – notably, irony and satire – can be a comparatively subtle and ambiguous way of signalling issues and grievances that are otherwise difficult or dangerous to express. They are difficult and dangerous precisely because of relations of dependence that make the anticipated sanction or punishment following an overt challenge (in terms of employment prospects or reputation) too great. In effect, there is a climate of fear, often masquerading as one of openness (e.g. the 'open door' policy that no one dare take up) that operates to suppress dissent, and thereby produces the impression that no significant conflict exists.

A critical analysis of management and leadership also assumes that manifestations of conflict cannot be adequately explained away in terms of awkward, militant or pathological 'personalities'. Individual differences (see Chapter 3) are not denied, but their 'positive' (e.g. 'Sam(antha) is a brilliant, charismatic leader/manager) or 'negative' (e.g. 'Sam(antha) is an incompetent, indecisive manager/leader) evaluation is related to the particular social situations in which such differences are shaped (socialization) and assessed (organizational setting). From a critical analytical standpoint, Sam(antha) is not essentially 'charismatic' or 'indecisive' but is understood to have developed ways of interacting with other people (i.e. she has been socialized). And, *in the present context*, mainstream thinking often equates such ways of interacting with personality differences. This kind of thinking is itself a potent way of glossing over social differences and conflicts by attributing them to *essential* personality differences. In doing so, it takes for granted and acts to solidify and sanctify the *particular*, circumstances that, in principle, could be changed.

Yet, despite the best efforts of managers to suppress tensions, remove 'troublemakers' and placate dissenters, collective industrial action occasionally erupts as employees withdraw their labour or refuse normal cooperation in attempts to have grievances settled. Or, more frequently, individuals simply decide to seek employment elsewhere or become self-employed. For employees, the existence of a trades union can provide a degree of legitimacy and some protection against managerial victimization of activists. One task for the critical researcher is to expose the extent to which an apparent consensus conceals or diverts attention from seething discontent, dissent and disarray that bubbles beneath the surface of organizational serenity. This is to express the point rather colourfully. Yet most of us would recognize that organizations breed forms of antagonism, resentment and fear that are either unknown to, or are ignored or exploited by, management. Mainstream analysis is, of course, not unaware of imperfections of morale and motivation in the informal system of organizations. Efforts to build 'strong cultures' (see Chapter 9) or 'cohesive teams' (see Chapter 4) are responses to this. But the response is limited to developing 'better' styles of 'professional' management (as designers of effective cultures and teams) that, in principle, remove the sources of disaffection (e.g. by eliminating favouritism, bullying, sexism, racism, etc.). The critic, in contrast, is more likely to interpret conflict as an indication of employees' capacity to challenge, or at least subvert, the imposition of self-serving management control, including its seemingly benign forms (e.g. programmes of 'empowerment') rather than seek instantly to repair or eliminate it.

Thinkpoint 4.18

Think of your experience of working in an organization or simply being a student. How often have you been (or have you noticed others being) polite and cooperative to your (their) 'boss' or your teacher, and thought secretly – 'what a "bastard"?' Reflect on what made you or others have thoughts that were inconsistent with your (their) actual behaviour. What were their source – were they related to problems concerning managers as people, inadequate leadership, inequality at work, the nature of authority or something else?

CASE STUDY 4.5 Strife at the Dog and Duck

Conflict that is evident in organizations is often a reflection of the inequalities of income, status, hierarchical position and gender, ethnic or other diversities (see Chapters 2 and 7), but this is not always obvious. To illustrate this, we will return to our introductory chapter and the case of Jackie and Christine falling out behind the bar at the Dog and Duck. Jackie a student, is asked by the landlord to act as manager for an evening. This upsets Christine because she has worked at the pub for much longer and regards Jackie as an upstart. In everyday language, Christine feels snubbed. Feelings of injustice and resentment boil over into overt conflict between them.

Someone coming into the pub for the first time that evening who witnessed the dispute between Jackie and Christine may have reasonably concluded that this was a conflict between staff of similar status. Yet, as we know, Christine was angry with Jackie having been given the temporary management position when she felt that her experience and career ambitions in bar work qualified her better for the role. The situation was clearly explosive, just waiting for an 'accident to happen', and the ensuing row could have been anticipated, assuming knowledge of the background. Without this knowledge, it would be easy to describe this, and many other disputes, as just personality conflicts and therefore relatively trivial. Such descriptions are often favoured in mainstream thinking because they do not represent a threat to the often taken-for-granted presumption of an underlying consensus within organizations. In these accounts, conflict is represented simply as a clash between individuals that is seemingly unrelated to differences of values, priorities, politics and so on. Analysis of this kind pays limited attention to the social context of a behavioural event, such as the conflict discussed here.

Thinkpoint 4.19

Do you think it would have made any difference if Jackie had been Jack or Christine had been Christopher? What if Jackie and Christine had been from very different ethnic backgrounds? Would such differences have been irrelevant, or would they have made the conflict less or more likely, or take a rather different form? Of course, we cannot know. But such questions can encourage us to reflect upon how everyday working relationships are conditioned by wider social contexts, expectations, 'prejudices' and power relations.

What do you think a mainstream management view would be of this conflict, and of the landlord's decision to ask Jackie to manage the pub? Is it possible to act objectively or impartially in such situations?

CASE STUDY 4.6 BoxCo and leadership

Here we return to BoxCo (pseudonym) presented briefly earlier in this chapter. At BoxCo, the CEO emphasized the difference between management and leadership in order to highlight what he perceived to be missing (i.e. 'leadership') from his management team. He subscribed to a view of leadership that he had learned on a management course in which leadership was understood to be synonymous with personality traits or qualities, which though possible to improve, are broadly inherited characteristics. Consequently, most attention had to be focused on recruiting 'good' leaders – that is, people who were assessed to have natural talent as leaders.

Some more junior managers whose management training was more recent were highly sceptical of this approach to leadership. They recognized that the trait approach produces an almost endless list of leadership characteristics (e.g. extraversion, vision, initiative), which have little correlation with one another or with 'successful' practice. The trait approach attributes essences to individuals, thus ignoring the social context and the importance of followers in any leadership practice. Being convinced of the correctness of his views, the CEO as the leader of BoxCo was in a position to ignore the views of his subordinates. Fear of contradicting their 'leader' led the junior managers to comply with his views, thereby confirming the CEO's false belief that consensus prevailed. The cartoon here illustrates both the normality and absurdity of claims that difference of pay and status are largely irrelevant because each person has an equally important role to play in ensuring the success of the organization (see Box 4.17).

"Now, Dan, we're all equals here. Have a seat."

Image 4.2

Box 4.17: Blurring any distinction between self and organization

'. . . more leaders are attempting to bind employees to the corporate ideal, while curtailing forums of debate. They project an image of charismatic leadership, stress a compelling vision, depict their companies as surrogate family and attempt to blur any perceived difference between the interests of managers and non-managers . . . Such approaches seek to re-engineer the most intimate beliefs of employees, so that they are aligned with whatever the leader deems is helpful to the corporate enterprise. It makes it even less likely that employees will ask awkward questions of their leaders, and so be capable of correcting their inevitable misjudgements. These may constitute fertile conditions for the emergence of other Enrons in the future.'

Source: Tourish and Vatcha, 2005, p. 476.

A critical perspective on leadership

Before he became an academic, Keith Grint (2000) was a senior representative of a trade union. In that capacity, he had been practising leadership at least 10 years before he began studying it. His conclusions, after some 14 years of study and having written many books and research articles on the subject, was that his understanding had 'decreased in direct proportion to his knowledge' (ibid., p. 1). The more he read, the less he felt he understood. Instead of enriching or extending his insights, the literature was dulling and diffusing them. In this assessment, Grint echoes sentiments that had been expressed almost half a century earlier by Warren Bennis (1959), one of the top researchers in leadership studies. He suggested that 'probably more has been written and less is known about leadership than any other topic in the behavioural sciences' (ibid., p. 259). Having become critical of the mainstream approaches, Grint offers an alternative, constitutive approach. This approach contrasts with the three mainstream approaches – trait, contingent and situational – each of which is understood to have a distinctive identity in relation to whether leadership was *essentially* an individual matter or one that was *essentially* determined by the context (see Figure 4.5).

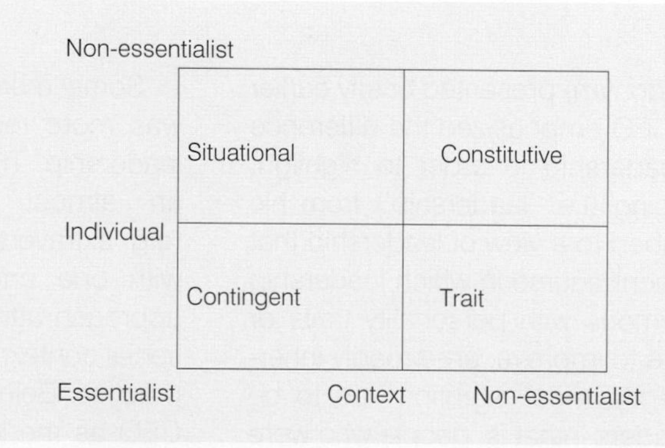

Figure 4.5 Essentialist and non-essentialist leadership

SOURCE: FIG. 1.2 (P. 2) FROM *THE ARTS OF LEADERSHIP* BY

Before discussing these approaches from a critical perspective, the term 'essential' is in need of clarification. In essentialist thinking, it is assumed that the world comprises a series of 'essences', and that the purpose of reflection is to discover the fundamental or universal aspects of whatever is being examined. So, for example, it would seek to identify what is *essential to human nature* as the basis of all human and social life. Take the phrase 'its just human nature'. It is frequently used as an explanation of a person's behaviour when nothing more specific comes to mind. It may, for example, be used to excuse a person or an action of which you disapprove, often because they behave in a way that is irresponsible or is seen to exhibit extreme self-interest. The excuse is built into a notion that it is natural, and therefore perfectly normal if not necessarily commendable, to look after yourself first. It is clearly a universal explanation. But it is developed within a particular context. In other words, its plausibility as a universal explanation is context-dependent but it is precisely this dependence that is unacknowledged by such explanations. That is why 'it's just human nature' can appear to be a self-evident truth when, arguably, it is a *claim* that acquires the status of truth only because it resonates with deeply ingrained, individualistic and Judeo-Christian attitudes. Such attitudes are tied up with notions of original sin and Darwinian ideas about the survival of the fittest. They take no account of either the awesome openness of human existence (as the New Testament puts it: the birds have their nests but the son of Man has no place to rest his head); and, relatedly, they disregard the deeply social quality of human development.

Exercise 4.9

The following questions could provide a focus for discussion in a small student group:

- If self-interested behaviour is 'human nature', does it mean that someone who sacrifices their own interests to the interests of others is not human?
- Would it ever be possible to disprove an explanation of behaviour that resorts to the notion of human nature?

Hint: There is always a danger of replacing one essentialism (human nature is 'X') with another essentialism (human nature is 'Y'). Think for example of McGregor's distinction between Theory X and Theory Y conceptions of management. Is there a way of avoiding such essentialist thinking?

COMPARING APPROACHES TO LEADERSHIP When we revisit the trait approach in the light of our reflections upon essentialism, we can better see how the context is ignored in favour of a more universal individual 'essence' – a personality or character that is seen to be the foundation of their leadership and/or transformational powers. The trait approach emphasizes selection as most crucial since if you get it wrong at that stage then there is no escape short of dismissing the leader. By contrast, the situational approach perceives the context as essential. It assumes that there are no universal modes or styles of leadership but only ones appropriate to different contexts or situations. The situational approach commends the training and development of leaders by developing and applying the appropriate skills for the specific context in which they lead. It assumes that the characteristics of the context can be pinned or boiled down into their essential features. Managers or leaders 'grow' into the job when they make a competent analysis that discloses the essence of the situation and act accordingly. Wherever an essence is sought – whether it be in the person or in the context – a deterministic stance is implicitly taken. That is, leadership is seen to be caused or determined by some essential factor – the personality (trait approach) or the environment (situational approach) (see Box 4.18).

Box 4.18: From traits to control reluctant followers to contexts to create willing followers

'Whereas the leader-centric perspective favours the rather direct control of followers . . . this (m)anipulation of contexts and constructions, rather than of leader behaviours, would, in a sense, constitute the "practice" of leadership. Rather than searching for the right personality, one would search for the opportunity to create the right impression.'

Source: J. P. Meindl (1995) 'The Romance of Leadership', *Leadership Quarterly*, 6(3):329–341, p. 333.

SOURCE: © FRAN/CARTOONSTOCK.COM

Image 4.3

The contingency approach seeks to combine both the trait and the situational approaches in one position and thereby believes both individual characteristics and the context are equally important elements of an adequate explanation, and associated technology, of good leadership. Here, certain types of leaders are appropriate to certain contexts and it is just a matter of matching the two. A major limitation of mainstream thinking is its reliance on open systems or contingency theory where a number of assumptions go unchallenged. For example, as we noted earlier, a linear conception of causation is favoured where one, or at least a small number, of prime determinants of the object ofstudy can be established. In order to deliver on this model of causation, hard-and-fast distinctions – between say leaders and the led and between the organization and the environment – are sustained so that clear-cut causal relationships can be made between them. So, in contingency approaches, the environment is depicted as the source of uncertainties, the reduction of which determines the effectiveness of leadership. Yet the environment, let alone the uncertainties that it is seen to create, is not a self-evident, transparent or readily accessible entity. Rather, its existence is defined, described or constructed by members of organizations and therefore the uncertainties are not independent of the interests, identities and politics of those that mobilize them as resources in their organizational pursuits. The same point is illustrated in the 'Small Cog' cartoon where the subordinate is encouraged or instructed to think of himself in a distinctive way – not as someone who occupies a small but key part in the bigger machine but, instead, as someone who costs the organization and therefore is a key, 'important' target of cost reduction. Here it is the worker rather than the environment that is being assigned an identity. In this case, the message is intended to concentrate the minds of employees to demonstrate how their production of benefits, or value, is at least equivalent to the costs, or drain, they impose on the organization.

This takes us to a more recent 'constitutional' approach (see also Knights and Willmott, 1992; Knights and Morgan, 1992), which not only questions the idea of essential leadership qualities or traits but also the idea that the context or environment is a self-evident, readily accessible truth or 'objective' reality. Both are understood to be constituted socially. What is seen as a 'good leader', or what the context or environment is, is conceived to be unavoidably open to interpretation, and any shared view, or 'consensus' about this is not independent of the exercise of power. Crucially, those who fill leadership positions or functions are expected to provide definitions of the context – indeed that is one of the common sense tests of a 'real' leader – and therefore have the opportunity to exert greater influence over others, including others' propensity to accept, in public at least, that they are suited to lead. From this standpoint, 'leadership' is less a matter of matching a style with a context than about 'the management of meaning' (Pfeffer, 1981; Smircich and Morgan, 1982) – of educating potential followers about (the 'real' or 'objective' naming of) the context so that they accept this definition of the situation and therefore, come to identify its author as their leader. The constitutive approach suggests that the very acquisition of positions of leadership involves managing others' definitions of reality, particularly those of potential and existing followers. Gaining the support of followers is about power and identity but this is often presented in the language of leadership.

If a manager can mobilize resources (e.g. finance, material artefacts or other organizations) and enrol people (e.g. politicians, celebrities or the public), s/he is likely to assume a leadership position but is also better placed to sustain this position once it is attained (the actor-network perspective discussed in Chapter 12 shares this view). Interpretations of reality tend to be more appealing and convincing when they facilitate people in maintaining their identities or making them feel free, less insecure and more respected (less unequal).

Exercise 4.10

Identify examples of leaders that you know, and examine them in terms of the four approaches discussed above. What is distinctively critical about the constitutive approach?

So far we have sought to elaborate the distinction between a critical and a mainstream approach. In the process, we confess to having committed one of the sins that critics often direct towards the mainstream. For we have tended to treat complex, diverse and multiple forms of knowledge (of leadership, for example) in a universal fashion as if all studies converged upon the four, readily identifiable conceptions of leadership – trait, contingency, situational and constitutive. But it would be more consistent with our critical thinking to conceive of the division of research on leadership into four types of approach as *itself* constitutive. Like any other schema, it is inviting you to adopt its definition of the situation. It is asking you to see the world through this lens. Implicitly, it is encouraging you not only to think about leadership in a particular way but also to engage in the practices associated with leadership in a different way as a consequence of being subjected to this knowledge. This process of influence forms part of what Gramsci (1891–1937) called 'organic' intellectual leadership, which is where thinkers do not simply describe social life in accordance with scientific rules, but rather 'express', through the language of culture, the experiences and feelings that others (who do not have the education, time or inclination) are unable to articulate for themselves. Critical scholarship offers an alternative to the content and form of intellectual leadership supplied and supported by those who are wedded to the status quo.

The example of ethics and leadership Various corporate scandals and disquiet about the trustworthiness and propriety of top corporate leaders has stimulated interest in the relationship between ethics and leadership. The mainstream response to major scandals such as Enron in the United States, where corrupt accounting practices led to the collapse of the corporation and the imprisonment of its chief executive, has sought to combine literatures on leadership traits and transformational leadership with those mainstream literatures on business ethics (where the latter is invariably perceived as a competitive, brand-image management tool) (see Chapter 15). Minkes *et al.* (1999, p. 328) argue that conformity to ethical requirements is a responsibility of, and depends on, leadership in the organization[1]. Drawing on the case of the Salomon Brothers, Sims and Brinkmann (2002) blame the leader John Gutfreund for moulding an organizational culture that resulted in unethical and illegal behaviour by its members. The focus of their research is on the character of Gutfreund, his absolute attention to a short-term business focus, his alleged willingness to cover-up illegal behaviour and the ease with which he allegedly betrayed his mentor in his rise to power.

A basic assumption of such contributions is that 'poor leaders' are a primary cause of current problems and therefore that better leadership will restore confidence. Treviño *et al.* (2003) are also concerned at the absence of empirical studies of ethical leadership and are critical in the sense that they wish to understand how ethical leadership is 'perceived and attributed to executives' (ibid., p. 7). But their concerns are voiced from within a taken-for-granted, common-sense notion of leadership. They favour an attribution theory approach that seeks to show how the qualities of ethical leadership are defined and attributed to managers by other members of the organization. This may *reveal* the dependence of such attributions on common-sense reasoning but it fails to problematize this dependence, as would a critical perspective. A main problem is that it tends to attribute leadership to managers of organizations that are deemed to be conventionally successful, and a lack of leadership to organizations that fail in some way. In other words, if an organization is deemed to be successful in common-sense terms, then it is conceived to be 'well led'. You may see parallels here with the mainstream systems approach discussed earlier in the chapter, where parts of an organization were explained in terms of their consequences for, or function in, maintaining its stability. It fails to focus on how the very topic of leadership and methods of researching it are socially constituted.

Feminist scholarship and leadership What is meant by the topic of leadership and methods of researching it being 'socially constituted' has been explored by feminist scholarship. Sinclair (2005, p. 1), for example, contends that there is a 'close connection between constructs of leadership, traditional assumptions of masculinity and a particular expression of male heterosexual identity'. The basic idea here is that what we understand as 'leadership' is deeply conditioned by its development over the past several hundred years in patriarchal societies where (commonsensically identified) positions of leadership have been occupied by men. Indeed, the very identification of only some positions (those generally occupied by males, such as president and CEO) as exhibiting qualities of 'leadership' downplays the possibility of women being leaders (e.g. in the domestic sphere). This effect is illustrative of how leadership has been socially constituted. Conversely, the very possibility of women, such as Amanda Sinclair, assuming a position of authority/leadership as a business school professor indicates that the-times-they-are-a-changing. That is to say, women are assuming positions in which they are able to give voice to alternative conceptions of management.

For Sinclair, an alternative way of 'doing leadership' involves an avoidance or renunciation of a 'macho' view of leadership, where the leader feels compelled to be 'hard' and 'controlling' so that respect is based upon fear and blind loyalty rather than a sense of mutual valuation and trust. This 'macho' approach, Sinclair suggests, is not only often counter-productive in terms of winning the trust and full cooperation of subordinates. It is also damaging, emotionally and spiritually, for the leader who is obliged to repress or hide those impulses and aspects of identity that are incompatible with being, or at least giving the appearance of being, 'macho'. And, of course, this applies as much, if not more, to women who feel pressured by the dominant expectations of leaders to be tough, combative and 'Thatcher-like' in their relationships with subordinates. Interestingly, leaders may often be gentle, subtle and even seductive, but it has been suggested by Marta Calas and Linda Smircich (2001) that such features are often made to appear invisible in the literature on leadership since they are rarely discussed. Their suggestion is that acknowledging the presence of seduction, for example, can facilitate the development of innovation in leadership theory – something that is evident in Sinclair's theory of leadership and sexuality (2005, Chapter 9) where she explores the varied ways in which sexual identities are brought to leadership.

Doing leadership differently

> For men and women in organizations, being different as leaders means asking what their leadership work is for. It involves standing up for work that is valuable and important, and insisting on doing it in a reflective and compassionate way, not simply capitulating to the imperatives generated by an overpowering boss, truculent client or invented sense of urgency. Leadership of this kind risks the individual being used as a scapegoat, being singled out as 'not a team player' or not 'on board' with the interests of the organization. Yet, in a wider sense, taking such a position is exactly what leadership is often about. *(Sinclair, 2005, p. x)*

Sinclair cautions about the appropriation of elements or trappings of this alternative conception of leadership to 'strengthen the status quo'. She foresees the way in which people, especially men, who are captivated by the idea of '*life as a contest*' will mouth 'the language of care and consultation' in order to sound fashionable and/or advance their careers. This is a manipulative use of the alternative conception of leadership as a weapon for managing a favourable impression so as to secure or advance their position.

More generally, as individuals, managers (men or women) may privately harbour doubts about the moral value and integrity of their actions. But, in order to hold down their jobs and/or meet their family responsibilities, they tell themselves and others, with greater or lesser conviction, that it is necessary to dilute or suspend personal values. They are encouraged in this by the tendency of corporate managers to punish those who take issue with their corporate practices, such as 'whistle-blowers' who are instantly removed and disowned.

Exercise 4.11

Can you think of people or occasions that illustrate an alternative form of leadership? Were there 'risks' and how were these dealt with?

CASE STUDY 4.7 Leadership at the Football Association

In 2004 the football governing body for England, the FA, went through a major crisis when the Chief Executive, Mark Palios and the England team manager, Sven Gŏran Erickson were discovered to have both had an affair with the same FA secretary, Faria Alam, who subsequently appeared on *Celebrity Big Brother*. Later, at a tribunal held to consider if her dismissal from her job had been unfair, she recalled how she had sat between her two suitors as they vied for her attention at the office Christmas dinner.

For the England manager, this was the second occasion that he had been caught up in a 'sex scandal'. That alone might have been sufficient reason to cast doubt upon the manager's leadership qualities or, at the very least, his judgement and character. The context of the England's team disappointing performance in the Euro 2004 tournament was the touchpaper for favouring such an interpretation, and critical elements in the media were not slow to play this card. However, an unexpected, and arguably more scandalous turn of events came to Sven's rescue. First of all, the FA denied that any affair had taken place and then, when this seemed implausible, the public relations people tried to protect their Chief Executive by promising the full detail on Sven to the *News of the World* in exchange for silence on Palios. The *News of the World* reported that 'The men who run football were even ready to bully top FA secretary Faria into giving details about her affair with Eriksson just to save Palios's neck.' Alam was reported to have refused to cooperate with the FA plan, so the *News of the World* ran its story exposing Palios's fling (see Box 4.19).

Box 4.19: Profile of Mark Palios (on the eve of becoming Chief Executive of the Football Association)

'As a restructuring expert, Palios understands the financial aspects of running a business and has experience of getting a troubled business out of the red. And as a football player, he has a deeper insight than most into the problems facing football.

Originally from Birkenhead, Palios joined Tranmere Rovers at the age of 16. During the 1970s and early 1980s, he was one of the club's best players, playing in mid-field and scoring 33 goals. He was also Tranmere's representative at the Professional Footballers' Association.

Palios joined Price Waterhouse Coopers in 1989 as a partner from Ernst & Young. He worked his way through the ranks and is currently a business regeneration leader, which many believe is exactly what the FA needs at the moment.'

Source: http://www.accountancyage.com/accountancyage/features/2040141/profile-footballer-turned-accountant-mark-palios.

Not surprisingly, given this revelation, Palios resigned. In the meantime, Sven's position hinged on whether or not he had lied about the affair with Alam. His position was that he had neither confirmed nor denied the affair. An FA investigation concluded that he had no case to answer. He retained his job as manager of the England team and it was the FA as an organization that was heavily criticized by the media. Management experts called upon by the media declared that the FA needed both reform and strong leadership. The irony of this suggestion was that prior to the 'sex scandal' Palios – the footballer turned accountant – had been widely praised for his reforms and strong leadership.

Thinkpoint 4.20

Do you think that reform and strong leadership would have been the answer to these problems or is there something else that might have been needed?

Leadership and management development One area in which management and leadership come together is in the sphere of management development where good management is conceived to rely upon the honing of interlinked mindsets. Jonathan Gosling and Henry Mintzberg (2003, p. 2) suggest a framework of management development that comprises five interventions that are necessary for improving the leadership of managers and the managing of leadership:

- Managing self: the reflective mindset.
- Managing organizations: the analytic mindset.
- Managing context: the worldly mindset.
- Managing relationships: the collaborative mindset.
- Managing change: the action mindset.

The identification of five mindsets emerged mainly through the authors' own practice in developing and delivering management programmes and it is not intended to be exhaustive. The emphasis upon managing rather than leading is intended precisely because 'nobody aspires to be a good manager anymore, everybody wants to be a good leader' (ibid., p. 1). Echoing our earlier discussion of how the meanings of management and leadership are differentiated, Gosling and Mintzberg argue that management without leadership is uninspiring but that leadership without management produces a disconnected style. This view of leadership nonetheless is somewhat unconventional as they believe that 'leaders don't *do* most of the things that their organizations get done, they do not even make them get done. Rather they help to establish the structures, conditions, and attitudes through which things get done' (ibid., p. 7, original emphasis). In other words, what they are suggesting is that leadership comprises that element of management which is concerned with establishing and enabling ways to get things done – with respect to creating 'structures', nurturing conditions and shaping attitudes. This requires the interlocking of the various mindsets. The action mindset is alert to, and facilitative of, change. In order to develop an effective patterning or structure of activities or to manage change, contexts and relationships are examined analytically. Finally, Gosling and Mintzberg's framework recalls that every intervention by the manager/leader is contingent upon the managing of self, which involves a reflexive mindset capable of reviewing, challenging and developing the other mindsets.

This is a potentially useful way of framing key aspects of activities identified as managing and leading. It locates these activities in a wider context that is attended to by the worldly mindset. It also appreciates that leading and managing in the context of organizations involves collaboration that necessitates the managing of relationships. But perhaps the key question concerns the boundaries of the knowledge that inform this process. Does the 'analytic mindset', for example, encompass the kinds of critical ideas about leadership and management that have been discussed in this and other chapters? To return to Amanda Sinclair's assessment of the boundaries of mainstream thinking about leadership, does the Gosling and Mintzberg framework itself exemplify a rather masculinist, if not macho, approach? How far does their reflective mindset stretch – just as far as is thought functional for getting the job done, or does it allow for the possibility, even if it does not commend it, of reflection resulting in the rejection of mainstream thinking and methods of leading and managing?

Exercise 4.12

Returning to Case study 4.7 on the English Football Association, do you think these five mindsets could help us to understand the problems that were experienced?

To take up the focus of the reflective mindset, it is relevant to acknowledge how managers are not unaware or unreflective about the pressures and contradictions of their work (Watson, 1994). Notably, they detect the tensions between the official, formally stated objectives and policies of their employing organization and the demands and evaluations of them from those immediately above them in the hierarchy. Needless to say, the obvious way to survive and succeed is to pay closest attention to the immediate priorities, expectations and criteria of evaluation applied by superiors (see Jackall, 1988; Dalton, 1959), and not to risk the emotional and financial penalties of being scapegoated or ostracized for 'rocking the boat' and failing to be a 'team player'. Here is another instance of how conflict is suppressed through self-censorship occasioned by reflection upon the likely consequences of being genuinely open and communicative. Not surprisingly, managers frequently feel frustrated and abused by the systems that they supposedly control, and bemoan the difficulties encountered in gaining unequivocal cooperation and commitment from their staff.

Managers routinely experience these contradictions and problems, but mainstream knowledge provides them with very limited resources for making sense of their situation. Management education and development tends to substitute prescription for diagnosis. That is to say, it rushes to provide a five bullet point plan of action without first examining in depth the nature of the problem for which the plan is presented as a solution. Such lists may supply managers with some reassuring prescriptions as well as a comforting sense of their own importance. They may even believe that, on the basis of this knowledge, they can develop or enhance a mindset for (strategically) analysing contexts or (operationally) managing change. Insofar as mainstream thinking marginalizes or trivializes discussion of the complex politics of managerial and leadership work, however, the consumers of mainstream knowledge are denied access to critical thinking that, arguably, would enable them to make more incisive sense of their predicament. In particular, it would challenge the tendency to diagnose difficulties in terms of personal failings (for which attendance at management development seminars is the recommended solution), and place in doubt any inclination to address these difficulties by redoubling their efforts (e.g. by becoming even more calculating or macho). In general, a major problem with management development courses that are intended to improve managerial or leadership skills is that they do not adequately address the conditions that impede their development and application. Their contents may be plausible enough in principle, but within a couple of weeks of taking the course, the pressures of work frustrate or overwhelm any good intentions to put them into practice.

Managers find themselves juggling competing demands for resources (e.g. jobs) and recognition – demands that come as much from other managers as from their subordinates. In mainstream thinking (e.g. Kotter, 1982), this is interpreted as inter-group politics as if such conflicts are unrelated to deeper social divisions, which include those of gender and ethnicity as well as those between employers and employees and managers and workers. It makes *ideological* sense to exclude from critical scrutiny the view that managerial authority is firmly founded upon objective expertise that is uncompromised by a concern to maintain the status quo and the distribution of privileges associated with it, including the lack of accountability of the managers to the managed. In this way, management is sanitized as it is distanced from the political conditions of its own formation and development (see Chapter 6).

CASE STUDY 4.7 In search of critical reflection

Tony Watson (1994) studied a group of senior managers. Following interviews with their new Managing Director, Paul Syston, these managers suspected that Syston had been hired as a hatchet man and feared for their jobs. In principle, such unsettling situations can stimulate a process of reflection on the conditions that make such episodes and responses possible. The managers might have reflected upon the rationality of an economic system that results in its participants, even its more privileged members, feeling deeply mistrustful and threatened. However, for this process of reflection to develop, there must at the very least be access to a (critical) theory that provides an interpretation of such episodes that gets beyond the personalities involved and the probable consequences for the individuals concerned, significant as they may be (see Willmott, 1997). Given their lack of access to such knowledge, it is understandable that the managers concerned were exclusively preoccupied with discussing Syston's motives, his personal style and inclinations, and were uninterested in analysing the conditions that make it possible for a boss to treat subordinates in a distant, intimidating manner. Had they avoided personalizing the problem – in terms of Syston's distant personal style or his appearance as 'a bit of a miserable sod' (Watson, 1994, p. 103) – they might have reflected on how the hierarchical relationship between managing directors and senior managers as well as between managers and their subordinates tends to produce such disorientating and demoralizing encounters.

Syston's coolness might be read as the nervousness or defensiveness of an outsider who is brought in by his own superiors, perhaps against his own preferences, for such a job but in order to secure his position or fulfil his ambitions. In other words, Syston's distant, non-communicative style can be interpreted as symptomatic of how the wider system of employment relationships is organized. By declining to enter into any kind of personal relationship with his senior managers, Syston minimized his moral relationship to them. It was probably this impersonal distance, above all else, that made the senior managers anxious as they experienced Syston as a cold fish and a closed book; and they anticipated that they would encounter great difficulty in exerting any personal influence over such a 'miserable sod'. The outcome of this anxiety was inaction, rationalized by the comforting idea that perhaps Syston would be willing to listen to them and therefore that they would 'wait and see' rather than, say, resolve collectively to defend and develop more open and democratic processes of corporate governance where, in principle, those occupying positions of authority, such as Syston, would be under much greater pressure from below to communicate the plans of the company with regard to job losses.

The prerogative and politics of management These observations call into question the legitimacy of managerial prerogative – that is, the right of management alone to manage, to make the key decisions so that all other stakeholders, including employees, have no voice in decision-making processes. In the mainstream literature, Child (1984, p.p. 15–16) offers the following assessment when commenting upon the issue of managerial prerogative. Problems arise, he suggests, when how the organization is structured 'becomes a victim of politics [because] it does not reflect political forces within the organization'. The implication is that politics are present *only* when the established political forces are disrupted – for example, when managerial prerogative is challenged or undermined.

An unfortunate consequence of this narrow sense of politics – as pathological with regard to the status quo – is that any structural design (see Chapter 8), however oppressive or coercive, is understood to be legitimate or apolitical. 'Politics' arise only when dissent is expressed or is ineffectively silenced. Such accounts of management soft-peddle on any sustained critical scrutiny of the conditions and consequences of management theory and practice. An image of the manager as a dispassionate technocrat is preserved. There is a failure to register how managerial work is politically charged on a continuous basis because, in capitalist work organizations at least, managers are *socially* distanced from, and are largely unaccountable to, those whom they manage, even when they succeed in deploying their charm and skills of communication to encourage a strong identification of employees with the corporation.

Acting as dispassionate technocrats does not protect managers from the vulnerabilities of their position. The logic of neutrality 'demands' that managerial work be subjected to the same rationalizing processes that it has visited upon less powerful groups. Even without the development of information technologies that threaten to automate the work of many supervisors and managers, employee involvement and corporate culture programmes promote the internalization of supervisory responsibilities among multi-skilled, self-disciplined operatives, and thus reduce the ranks of supervisory staff and middle management (see Chapters 10 and 13). Middle and junior management are increasingly the targets of de-layering in 'lean', 're-engineered' organizations. When they endorse technocratic ideology, they are not well prepared to make sense of, let alone resist, the contradictory operation of dominant 'logics' that pose a threat to their very existence. As employees, managers too are expendable. Managers, as Anthony (1977, p. 310) has observed, are likely to find themselves being treated as 'the unwitting victims of reorganization' as they are transferred, trained or dismissed at the behest of more senior managers who frequently employ consultants (arch-technocrats) to guide and/or justify their decisions. Like other employees, they find themselves subjected to the indignities of being 'regarded as human resources, shuffled and distributed by specialists in management development and planning' (ibid.). Increasingly, managers are the victims and not just the perpetrators of a rationality that inhibits reflection upon, and transformation of, a design and structure of organization that impedes efforts to develop more ethically defensible and morally sound forms of management theory and practice (see Box 4.20).

We now turn to a small selection of empirical case studies that reflect a critical approach to understanding management and leadership.

Selection of important studies within the critical approach

Doing managerial work In the following extract from Theo Nichols and Huw Beynon's (1977) study of an ICI plant, Colin Brown, a comparatively young and inexperienced manager describes how he

Box 4.20: Management knowledge and self-image

'It is certainly much more noble to think of oneself as developing skills toward the more efficient allocation and use of resources – implicitly for the greater good of society as a whole – than to think of oneself as engaged with other organizational participants in a political struggle over values, preferences . . . '

Source: Pfeffer, G. (1981) 'Management as symbolic action: The creation and maintenance of organizational paradigms', in L. L. Cummings and B. M. Staw (eds.) *Research in Organizational Behaviour, Vol. 3*, Greenwich, CT: JAI Press, p. 12.

uses a case of poor time-keeping to manage his relationship with a shop steward:

> Every man is born to do something and my function in life is to manage. I think this is a problem that most managers have failed to get to grips with. Now take an example. As far as I can see, any man who takes on the job of shop steward wants his ego boosting. But you've got to boost his ego in the proper manner. Now, if I get a bit of trouble – now take an example, perhaps of a serious case of a man who has been perpetually late. Now, I'm the manager, and it's my function to manage. It's my function to discipline this particular man. But I have to deal with the steward. So, what do I do? I take the shop steward aside and tell him that in half an hour's time this man Smith is going to walk into this room. That I'm going to stamp and bang the table and tell him that I'm going to put him out on the road with a caution. Then I'll say to the shop steward, 'and what you can do will be to intervene at this time. Make a case for the man. And we'll agree to let the man off.' Now the man comes in and I bang the table and the steward says 'Come on, Mr. Brown. Couldn't you give him one more chance?' I relent. The shop steward gets out of the meeting and says to him 'I've got you off this bloody time but don't expect me to do it again'. You see the shop steward gets his ego boosted. He gets what he wants and I get what I want. That's what good management is about. *(ibid., p. 122)*

Colin Brown begins by employing the notion that everyone is born to do something, and that his predetermined mission, for which he is naturally fitted, is to manage. This (essentialist) view includes the understanding that in any organization there will be a separation between managers (who are born to manage or trained to be managers) and those who are managed. It is this inevitable fact, Brown suggests, that most managers have 'failed to get to grips with'. Brown's belief in the division between managers and managed within the natural order of things is also reflected in his view that shop stewards aspire to quasi-managerial positions because they have a need to get their egos boosted. This, Brown observes, presents the manager with a challenge: to boost the steward's ego in a way that is 'proper' for the effective execution of the management function. The notion of 'proper' reflects Brown's view that good management is about the calculated contribution and negotiation of situations in ways that produce the maximum benefit for the minimum cost.

It is views like this that enable Brown to make sense of, and to organize, his work. They underpin and are supported by his skilful management of the interaction with the steward and Smith, the poor time-keeper. He takes the steward aside in order to rehearse his performance and generally stage-manages the disciplinary scene. Brown makes the most of his apparent capacity to put Smith 'out on the road': he identifies a low-cost opportunity to reinforce the relationship of domination over the steward. Brown stage-manages the situation so that, in the process of getting his ego boosted, the steward becomes both incorporated into the management process and indebted to Brown for enabling him to play out his (managerially defined) role as shop steward. And at the same time, Brown enjoys the game that demonstrates to himself as well as to others how he can move these pieces around the board.

On this occasion, the steward seemingly accepts the right of the manager to discipline Smith. And Brown 'recognizes', and indeed exploits, the right of the steward to make out a case for his union member. The positive sanction of the ego boost is used by Brown to ensure that the steward follows his script to the letter, and with gratitude. As long as it works – and this depends appreciably upon the interpretation(s) that the steward invokes to make sense of the situation – the asymmetrical relationship of power between the manager and the steward is hegemonically maintained and concealed in the very process of its reproduction.

Thinkpoint 4.21

What gives Colin Brown the right to discipline Smith? Why might managers find it useful to deal with a unionized workforce?

Leadership processes in a financial services company This study (Knights and Willmott, 1992) took place in the early 1990s when the UK financial services industry was experiencing a revolution in its markets due to major regulatory changes. This resulted in the CEO at Pensco (pseudonym) seeking to change the leadership style of his senior management team. In writing up this study, we were concerned to step outside of the orthodox paradigm, where the objective was to identify effective leadership in terms of specific traits, styles or contextual factors. Instead we observed senior executives in board meetings seeking to construct their own reality but often having their reality constructed for them by the CEO. We drew on different analytical frameworks to examine leadership practice as a lived-experience but one that is embedded in the CEO's construction of reality. To sustain this reality the CEO stigmatized any signs of divergence as evidence of individual incompetence, if not disloyalty. The CEO made effective use of his structural position at the apex of the hierarchy to assert his definition of the situation and to undermine the identity of anyone who sought to challenge it. Take the following extract from a board meeting where the Assistant General Manager of Customer Services (CS) challenges the CEO:

> CS: 'I think the point that I would like to make is that I think that one needs to distinguish between direction, which is clearly your prerogative and the more detailed decision-making, and I've felt that there's been a tendency to move down to a more detailed decision-making . . . '
>
> CEO: 'Oh, certainly, I think the idea of being in the City office and taking everything that is going just isn't on. Not with me and my temperament. I intend to be right there and I will stay there as long as I find, taking New Business as an example, that there have been "hot line" cases for two and half weeks and they still haven't left the office. That sort of thing will just drive me mad. And if anybody wants to get rid of me on jobs like that, there's a simple answer: don't let me see . . . '

In this transcript, the CS finds himself reprimanded for his rather mild attempt to persuade the CEO to focus less on the detail and more on the bigger picture of overall 'direction'. In response, the CEO picks on precisely a weakness in the area that the CS is responsible for – processing New Business so that clients have their policies speedily. He argues afterwards that while he is prepared to listen to those who think he is interfering too much (yet clearly he was not prepared to listen to the CS), 'my interests are quite calculated. They're not random.' But there is a broader context to the CEO's interventions, which is his concern to make decision making more sensitive and responsive to its strategic significance for the company's competitive position. That is why he is unwilling to tolerate New Business taking more than two and a half weeks to process.

Mainstream analyses of traits, styles or the characteristics of followers have proven less than informative since they fail to capture the lived experience and the politico-economic and cultural contexts of leadership as a practical accomplishment. A more critical approach is less concerned with providing technical prescriptions of leadership than highlighting some of the hidden processes to show how leadership is accomplished in daily encounters such as the brief excerpt illustrated above.

'Making out' We examined in Chapter 6 the ways in which productivity targets and bonus schemes were transformed by shop floor engineering workers into a competitive game whereby their function as a management control was obscured (Burawoy, 1979, 1985). Of course, management designed the bonus scheme with its targets and rewards for achieving them and did not anticipate how it could provide a framework for a game called 'making out'.

> 'Making out' can be seen 'as comprising a sequence of stages – of encounters between machine operators and the social or nonsocial objects that regulate the conditions of work. The rules of 'making out are experienced as a set of externally imposed relationships. The art of making out is to manipulate those relationships with the purpose of advancing as quickly as possible from one stage to the next'. . . 'The games workers play are . . . played within limits defined by minimum wages and acceptable profit margins. Management, at least at the lower levels, actively participates not only in the organization of the game but in the enforcement of its rules' (Burawoy, 1985, p. 80). Much of the stimulus to engage in such games 'derives from the inexorable coercion of coming to work, and subordination to the dictates of the labor process once there' (ibid., p. 81). In short, turning work into a game relieves workers of the numbing routine and the indignity of subordination; it almost becomes fun. It is also what best accounts for the huge amount of humour and practical joking that occur in factories (Collinson, 1992).

In short, game-playing displaced the need for managers as leaders because the workforce led itself – there was a kind of collective self-discipline that removed any necessity for management or leaders to intervene. According to Burawoy, the significance of creating a game out of the labour process extends well beyond the particularities of making out: 'The very activity of playing a game generates consent with respect to its rules' (Burawoy, 1979, p. 80). Management no longer needed to be visible as leaders or as the embodied manifestation of control and direction for the workforce. Involvement in the competitive game of achieving targets and bonuses meant that the workers managed themselves, thus removing what the classical writer Mary Parker Follett (see page 269) saw as the greatest vulnerability of managers – having to tell employees what to do. The case study demonstrates how the 'trick' of management or leadership is to dissolve into the background as those whom it seeks to manage are enabled to become self-managing.

Gideon Kunda (1991) also advances a thesis about how management seeks to develop a culture in which the workforce become self-disciplining because of having internalized the values of the company. In the company he studied, there was a comprehensive system of 'normative control' wherein employees were symbolically entrapped within the reality defined by management in terms of the corporate interests (ibid., 219–20). Management recognizes the importance of identity for employees and thereby seeks to map these concerns onto a sense of the organization as a community. Management and leadership is focused on managing identity through sustaining a strong organizational culture (see Chapter 9) whereby the norms and values are deeply internalized. However, Kunda finds that employees remain fairly ambivalent and relate to these attempts at internalizing an identity tied to the company with some irony and symbolic distance. But, of course, this can also be a safety valve or a means of boosting the egos of staff who consider themselves smart enough to see through, and poke fun at, the corporate culture. The generation of a corporate culture that seeks to secure the commitment and loyalty of employees through appropriating their identities can, argues Kunda (ibid., p. 222), also create the very conditions of its own demise. That is to say, by providing the conditions through which employees generate a sense of community, such solidarity can in principle be turned against the corporation and management interests just as easily as in support of them.

Contributions and limitations to thinking about the field

Contributions Critical thinking is concerned to link larger social and political issues with the theory and practice of managing, leading and organizing. It also focuses more directly on human, political and process dimensions of management and leadership. While the mainstream has recognized these aspects of life in organizations, the human, political and process dimensions of organization are domesticated by treating them as an informal system either to be manipulated to secure more effective management control, or, if this proves too difficult or costly, to be viewed as an aberration to be eradicated. By contrast, critical studies see human and political processes as integral to the 'lived reality' of organizations and view attempts to eradicate them as self-defeating.

Critical analysis of management and leadership may provide practitioners with insights into how management and leadership are possible since it is only through their acceptance as legitimate activities by the managed and the led that they can be in the least effective. In particular it:

- Gives close consideration to the political and processual character of (practices that are identified as) 'management' and 'leadership'.
- Applies a number of key concepts, including identity, inequality, insecurity and freedom to explore management and leadership as problematical *social* phenomena rather than taking them as self-evident objects of examination and improvement.
- Gives attention to the historical formation of management and the way leadership involves the management of meaning, including the meaning of management.
- Moves away from knowledge of management as assuming the adequacy of common-sense thinking and the legitimacy of the status quo.
- Invites a more sceptical assessment of the claims made in the name of management and leadership and thereby opens up a space for different notions of what they could mean.

In mainstream thinking, 'management' and 'leadership' tend to be widely viewed as unquestionably valuable and therefore desirable. Leadership, in particular, has a very seductive appeal. It is assumed to be something that is obviously 'needed' and, in principle, easily identified and improved. Books and courses on leadership instantly attract attention and gain a large audience. Critical analysis contributes to a stripping away of the gloss and hype that surrounds leadership. In this chapter we have concentrated on issues less connected with productivity, performance or profitability than is usual in the mainstream. Critical approaches, we believe, can provide managers and leaders with knowledge and insights that they would not secure elsewhere. This is particularly relevant when there is a proliferation of stakeholders making demands on organizations. Organizations exist within society and increasingly managers find themselves harried by predatory competitors, let down by unreliable suppliers, rebuffed by discriminating customers and deserted by footloose staff, not to mention pressured by fund managers who demand the impossible of 'above average' performance from all companies. And a parallel picture applies to public and not-for-profit sector managers who are under relentless pressure to introduce changes that promise to produce more for less. Today, managers probably have less discretion to pursue a narrow range of interests, especially as the media will expose any management that is discovered or deemed to behave dangerously or without due care and attention. Many organizations are caught up in increasingly global relations (see Chapter 12) where an apparently insignificant local action can have massive worldwide repercussions, much like a whisper turning ultimately into a hurricane. This goes for academic analyses every bit as much as practitioners, since actions and words are always affecting the actions of others and this can multiply into global proportions.

While we cannot ultimately control for the unintended consequences of our actions, we can endeavour to think ethically and to be as responsible as possible for what we say and do. It is clear from critical research that organizations are much more complex than the mainstream literature, in its search for 'quick fixes' or simple causal patterns, presumes. Understanding, for example, what part that identity plays in managers' and employees' lives, or how some level of insecurity can be productive yet incapacitating if excessive, is of greater value than fantasies about perfect leadership or profound management. Since organizations are dynamic, it makes sense to challenge conventional thinking about them. While the direct relationship between theory and practice or ideas and their adoption is not always obvious, academic research and writing indirectly and perhaps quite slowly filters into the consciousness of those we study. At the time of writing, there has been a fashion for leadership, and this is why we have sought to question and counter any tendency for management to become neglected. A critical approach tends to foster scepticism about panaceas or fashions, which is no less relevant to the fashionable advocacy of 'leadership' than it is to the longer established preferences for 'one best way' approaches to management, such as Theories X, Y and Z.

Limitations One of the strengths of a critical approach is that it is self-reflexive as well as reflexive about broader relations both internal and external to organizations. It follows that it is self-critical about critical approaches as well as the mainstream both in terms of the value of our theory and its implications for practice. We offer the following limitations of critical approaches, which are often excessively centred on managing people and may, as a consequence:

- Neglect the global nature of capitalism.
- Neglect the domination of financial power.
- Be theoretical and idealistic rather than practical and applied/pragmatic.

Insofar as we compensate for the domination of concerns with productivity, performance and profitability in the mainstream, one problem of the critical approach is to be over-concerned with issues of managing people or, to be more accurate, managing relations between people. Also we should beware believing that relations can be managed or controlled since that is rarely the case. Managing or leading is about facilitating the conditions that enable people to manage their own relations in ways that benefit one another and ultimately the productive power of an organization, but in ways that are responsible and ethical for others (e.g. customers, the public, environmentalists, the developing world, minorities or government) who are not direct stakeholders. Of course, the focus of this chapter on management and leadership necessarily means that we cannot avoid a strong focus on the human dimension as it is impossible to manage and lead without inspiring, engaging, motivating or driving human beings to pursue their tasks creatively, collaboratively and competitively.

The human dimension outside of organizations might lead us to focus on the broader structures of power such as global capitalism, international regulation and finance capital, particularly given the success of recent protests about global capitalism that have captured media attention. It is interesting to note how radical movements have made as much use of global telecommunications as have the corporations and the international institutions that they seek to criticize for their exploitation of developing countries, labour and the environment. Not only are the global corporations and the finance capital that sustains them exploitative of the comparatively weak, but also they tend to dominate other organizations, especially suppliers and distributors. Their power as both buyers and providers can force suppliers and distributors into uneconomic exchanges that render them ultimately vulnerable to cheap takeovers.

Finally, despite what has been claimed above regarding the indirect and often unintended, benefits of critical analyses to practitioners, much of it remains abstract, idealistic, and over-theoretical. For example, many critical theorists are prone to draw on esoteric theories drawn from philosophy partly perhaps to display their intellectual credentials and scholarly credibility. Whereas the mainstream justifies itself on claims to advancing a science of behaviour, the critics seek a philosophical self-justification.

Synopsis and conclusion

Theories of 'leadership', it is believed, enable us to identify 'leaders' and perhaps train them and others to become better leaders. For many practitioners and theorists of leadership, this way of understanding leadership makes good sense. The challenge is to develop or identify a way of conceptualizing and studying leadership (or management) that detects its existence and, if possible, enhances it. This process of detection and prescription necessitates developing a view or concept, or *theory*, of leadership (or management) that accurately reflects the realities of leadership 'out there'.

Can 'leadership', etc. be understood in another way? Attempting to do so is not easy as it necessitates some bracketing or suspension of belief in common-sense ways, or habits, of thinking. How else might 'leadership', etc. be understood, if not as an effort to capture and upgrade the realities that it aspires to reflect? To develop a different understanding requires the questioning and abandoning of the assumption of a neat *separation* between, on the one side, thought (or theory) and, on the other side, the reality (or practices) that concepts of organization, etc. are assumed to reflect, more or less adequately. For it is on this basis that established thinking, and knowledge, about organization, management and leadership is founded. If an alternative approach is to be advanced and appreciated, then the assumption of this separation must be set aside (see Box 4.21).

Rarely do we find organizations, other than families and friendship groups, not organized through a division of labour in which managers and leaders are in the senior hierarchical ranks enjoying the power to allocate scarce rewards and resources (e.g. wages, bonuses, promotions, status, etc.). In

Box 4.21: Disrupting the theory–practice division

If the separation between thought and reality is rejected, and the 'acid test' of an independent reality against which to assess competing theories is denied, how are we to assess the credibility of different theories, except against the claims of other theories?

In response to this concern, it can be suggested that the difficulties associated with rejecting the thought-reality separation are not a compelling reason for continuing to harbour the illusion that reality exists in an external relation to thought, and that reality can be reflected, rather than constructed, through theory. Accepting this argument does not mean that reality ceases to exist. It means, instead, that claims about 'knowing' this reality must be treated sceptically and *viewed as political rather than as disinterested (or 'scientific') claims*. Such claims are neither provable nor falsifiable by testing them against reality because access to this 'reality' (practices) is inescapably mediated or interpreted by value-based thought (theories).

This perspective, which itself should be treated as comprising a number of political rather than disinterested claims, or assumptions, has a number of implications:

1. Theories in management and organization studies are understood to be embedded in, and indelibly coloured by, the practices that they endeavour to represent. They do not stand apart from those practices. Nor can they ever reflect these practices, or even capture some element of them. They simply offer competing ways of making sense.
2. Theories should be viewed as comprising truth *claims*, the plausibility of which depends not upon their approximation to workplace reality, since this is inaccessible in any unmediated way, but upon how these claims are accepted and legitimized by different practitioners.
3. Truth claims in certain management theories (e.g. popularized accounts of Maslow's hierarchy of needs or notions of democratic leadership) may be enthusiastically received by managers while they are treated with extreme scepticism and even disdain by many management academics. Their credibility does not depend upon the accuracy of such claims but, rather, their plausibility, as interpreted within competing (discursive) frameworks of meaning.
4. When truth claims are endorsed, they are then actively drawn upon by those seeking to construct or define reality for others (e.g. the CEO in the Pensco example discussed above). In short, truth claims are an inescapable part of, or serve to construct, the very same reality that we claim to know.

addition, these managers and leaders enjoy several of their own material (economic) and symbolic (status) privileges associated with their position. We live in a hierarchical and competitive society that is grounded in an ethic of success and achievement. In Chapter 6 the ideology of equal opportunity was critically challenged as providing legitimacy to existing inequalities and a faith in *reason* for the mainstream simply to take them for granted. In this chapter, we have focused more on the difficulties that managers and leaders have in securing the consent or compliance of employees that are partly a result of major inequalities. While the mainstream takes this consent and compliance as unproblematic, the critical literature has sought to demonstrate how it may be secured by management appearing *not* to manage and lead as then, the extent to which they coerce and control employees is obscured. Sometimes this occurs accidentally as when employees become preoccupied with achieving their bonuses as a competitive game; at other times, managers foster and facilitate forms of employee collective and individual self-discipline as the most effective managerial and leadership strategy. Conditions are created in which subordinates find their work sufficiently meaningful for the sense they have of themselves (i.e. their identity) as to secure a self-disciplined commitment in fulfilling their tasks that displaces feelings of subjugation and grievances associated with exploitation.

Management and leadership are discussed in mainstream texts predominantly through the lens of a systems model where the parts of an organization are seen as similar to the parts of a body or a machine and/or through individualistic conceptions of the leader who possesses appropriate personality traits, is constrained by the situation or adapts to contingent factors. The organic or mechanical analogy largely remains unquestioned in the mainstream despite the fact that the parts of an organization are human beings who think for themselves, interpret their experiences and may challenge or contest, just as well as collaborate and comply with the demands made of them. Similarly, the ways in which the context and attribution of leadership are both constituted through relations of power and knowledge is not considered by the mainstream. Of course, these critical ways of understanding management and leadership completely undermine any possibility of there being a 'one best way'. Consequently, management and leadership have to survive and thrive as untidy and unpredictable activities within uncertain and continually changing circumstances. By focusing on power, knowledge, identity, insecurity, freedom and inequality, we are continually confronted by the precarious and unpredictable aspects of management and leadership. This makes it all but impossible to accept the mainstream in its presumptions of a general consensus regarding managing and leading members of their organization.

The critical approach does not follow the mainstream in legitimizing the status quo or providing managers with ready-made solutions designed to make organizations more efficient or profitable. This is what throughout this book we have called a narrow managerialism in the approach to studying organizations. Rather, the critical analyst is concerned to incorporate consideration of much broader issues in society such as equality, justice and freedom and the extent to which managers, leaders and their work organizations contribute to, or constrain and deflect attention toward, such ideals. It has to be said, however, that even though it is not their direct intention, critical studies of organization can be beneficial to management in providing alternative insights and visions that would be unlikely to arise from the mainstream. Indeed, an unintended consequence of critical work may be that it helps managers pursue their performance and/or profit objectives more effectively than the mainstream if only because its examination of issues – from motivation to governance – provides managers with a broader and fresher perspective that enables them to develop innovative approaches and/or avoid self-defeating methods of management control. Its effect may be to enable managers to think beyond the current conventional wisdom.

Discussion questions

1. How do managers and leaders make a difference to organizations?
2. Are the main assumptions underlying a mainstream approach to management and leadership valid?
3. Is management likely to be effective in the absence of leadership, and vice versa?
4. What are some of the contingencies that managers and leaders have to consider in carrying out their work?
5. What are the main differences between a classical and an open systems approach to organizational design and structure?
6. What does a critical view of management and leadership add to our understanding of organizations?

Further reading

Empirical studies

Burawoy, M. (1979) *The Manufacture of Consent*, Chicago: Chicago University Press.
Burns, T. and Stalker, G. (1961) *The Management of Innovation*, Oxford: Oxford University Press.
Collinson, D. (1992) *Managing the Shopfloor*, Berlin: de Gruyter.
Kanter, R. M. (1977/1993) *Men and Women of the Corporation*, New York: Basic Books.
Kidder, T. (1981) *The Soul of the New Machine*, Harmondsworth: Penguin.
Knights, D. and McCabe, D. (2003) *Organization and Innovation: Gurus Schemes and American Dreams*, Milton Keynes: Open University Press/McGraw Hill.
Kondo, D. (1990) *Crafting Selves: Power, Gender and Discourses of Identity in a Japanese Workplace*, Chicago, IL: University of Chicago Press.
Kunda, G. (1991) *Engineering Culture*, Philadelphia: Temple University Press.

Annotated readings

Yukl, G. (2002) *Leadership in Organizations*, Upper Saddle River, NJ: Prentice Hall.

Presents a comprehensive review of mainstream approaches to leadership in organizations. Also includes a chapter on the nature of managerial work and a final chapter that overviews a number of 'biases' and 'controversies' in the field. For students who want to gain a close understanding of what 'mainstream analysis' looks like, this is to be strongly recommended.

Grint, K. (2005) *Leadership: Limits and Possibilities*, London: Palgrave.

A text that takes a more critical approach to the claims made by theories of leadership.

Sinclair, A. (2005) *Doing Leadership Differently*, Melbourne: Melbourne University Press.

Takes an explicitly feminist line on leadership. Connects with mainstream preoccupations but addresses them in a more critical way. Provides something of a bridge between mainstream and critical approaches. Written in a more personal and engaging manner.

Alvesson, M. and Willmott, H. C. (1996) *Making Sense of Management*, London: Sage.

Reviews critical contributions to the study of management including its specialist areas of activity such as marketing and accounting. Illustrates how critical analysis can be applied to develop an alternative way of making sense of the development of management.

Anthony, P. (1986) *The Foundations of Management*, London: Tavistock.

An accessible and thoughtful reflection upon the basis of management's claim or prerogative to manage. Pays close attention to the morality of management.

Parker, M. (2002) *Against Management*, Oxford: Polity Press.

An entertaining polemic that draws together the numerous strands of criticism that can be levelled against management. Includes a critique of 'critical management'.

More general reading

Academy of Management Executive (2003) 'Retrospective: The practice of management', 7(3):7–23.
Ackroyd, S. and Thompson, P. (1999) *Organizational Misbehaviour*, London: Sage.
Bryman, A. (1999) 'Leadership in organizations', in S. R. Clegg, C. Hardy and W. R. Nord (eds.) *Managing Organizations*, London: Sage.
Burnham, J. (1941) *The Managerial Revolution*, Harmondsworth: Penguin.
Casey, C. (1995) *Work, Self and Society: After Industrialism*, London and New York: Routledge.
Fulop, L. and Stephen Linstead, S. (eds.) (1999) *Management: A Critical Text*, London: Macmillan Business.
Hales, C. (1993) *Managing Through Organization*, Routledge: London.
Harding, N. (2003) *The Social Construction of Management: Texts and Identities*, London: Routledge.
Jackson, N. and Carter, P. (2000) *Rethinking Organizational Behaviour*, London: Financial Times/Prentice Hall.
Knights, D. and Morgan, G. (1992) 'Leadership and corporate strategy: Toward a critical analysis', *Leadership Quarterly* 3(3):171–190.
Pollard, S. (1965) *The Genesis of Modern Management*, London: Edward Arnold.
Rhodes, C. (2002) 'Coffee and the business of pleasure: The case of Harbucks v. Mr Tweek', *Culture and Organization* 8(4):293–306.
Shotter, J. (1992) 'The manager as a practical author: Conversations for action', in J. Shotter (ed.) *Conversational Realities: Constructing Life Through Language*, London: Sage.
Willmott, H. C. (1984) 'Images and Ideals of Managerial Work', *Journal of Management Studies* 21(3):349–368.

References

Adair, J. (1979) *Action-Centred Leadership*, Aldershot: Gower.
Anthony, P. (1977) *The Ideology of Work*, London: Tavistock.
Barnard, C. (1936) *The Functions of the Executive*, Cambridge, MA: Harvard University Press.
Bass, B. (1985) *Leadership and Performance: Beyond Expectations*, New York: Free Press.
Bennis, W. G. (1959) 'Leadership theory and administrative behaviour: The problem of authority', *Administrative Science Quarterly* 2:42–47.
Blake, R. R. and McCanse, A. A. (1991) *Leadership Dilemmas: Grid Solutions*, Houston, TX: Gulf Publishing.
Blake, R. R. and Mouton, J. S. (1964) *The Managerial Grid*, Houston, TX: Gulf Publishing.
Burawoy, M. (1979) *The Manufacture of Consent*, Chicago: Chicago University Press.
Burawoy, M. (1985) *The Politics of Production*, London: Verso.
Burns, J. M. (1978) *Leadership*, New York: Harper & Row.

Burns, T. and Stalker, G. M. (1961) *The Management of Innovation*, Oxford: Oxford University Press.

Calas, M. and Smircich, L. (2001) 'Voicing seduction to silence leadership', *Organization Studies* 12(4):567–602.

Chandler, A. D. Jr. (1977) *The Visible Hand: The Managerial Revolution in American Business*, Cambridge, MA: The Belknapp Press of Harvard University.

Child, J. (1984) *Organization*, second edition, London: Harper and Row.

Collinson, D. (1988) ' "Engineering humour": Masculinity, joking and conflict in shop floor relations', *Organization Studies* 9(2):181–199.

Collinson, D. (1992) *Managing the Shopfloor*, Berlin: de Gruyter.

Dalton, M. (1959) *Men Who Manage*, New York: Wiley.

Drucker, P. (1974) *Management: Tasks, Responsibilities, Practices*, London: Heinemann.

Fayol, H. (1916/1949) *General and Industrial Management*, London: Pitman.

Fiedler, F. E. (1967) *A Theory of Leadership Effectiveness*, New York: McGraw-Hill.

Gosling, J. and Mintzberg, H. (2003) 'The five minds of a manager', *Harvard Business Review*, Nov., 1–9.

Grint, K. (2000) *The Arts of Leadership*, Oxford: Oxford University Press.

Grint, K. (2005) *Leadership: Limits and Possibilities*, London: Palgrave.

Hersey, P. and Blanchard, K. H. (1993) *Management of Organizational Behaviour: Utilising Human Resources*, sixth edition, Englewood Cliffs, NJ: Prentice Hall.

Hickson, D., Pugh, D. and Pheysey, D. (1971) 'Operations technology and organisation structure: An empirical appraisal', *Administrative Science Quarterly* 14:378–397.

House, R. J. (1971) 'A path–goal theory of leadership effectiveness', *Administrative Science Quarterly* 16:321–338.

Jackall, R. (1988) *Moral Mazes: The World of Corporate Managers*, New York: Oxford University Press.

Knights, D. and McCabe, D. (1999) 'There are no limits to authority?: TQM and organizational power relations', *Organization Studies* 20(2):197–224.

Knights, D. and Morgan, G (1992) 'Leadership as corporate strategy: Towards a critical analysis', *Leadership Quarterly* 3(3):171–190.

Knights, D. and O'Leary, M. (2006) 'The possibility of ethical leadership', *Journal of Business Ethics*, forthcoming.

Knights, D. and Willmott, H. (1992) 'Conceptualising leadership processes: A study of senior managers in a financial services company', *Journal of Management Studies* 29(6):761–782.

Koontz, H., O'Donnell, C. and Weihrich, H. (1984) *Management*, eight edition, Tokyo: McGraw-Hill.

Kotter, J. (1982) *The General Managers*, New York: Free Press.

Krech, D., Crutchfield, R. S. and Ballachey, E. L. (1962) *Individual in Society*, New York: McGraw-Hill.

Kunda, G. (1991) *Engineering Culture*, Philadelphia: Temple University Press.

Likert, R. (1961) *New Patterns of Management*, New York: McGraw Hill.

Magretta, J. (with N. Stone) (2002) *What Management Is*, London: Profile.

McGregor, D. (1960) *The Human Side of Enterprise*, New York: McGraw Hill.

Minkes, A. L., Small, M. W. and Chatterjee, S. R. (1999) 'Leadership and business ethics: Does it matter? Implications for management', *Journal of Business Ethics* 20:327–335, cited in Knights and O'Leary (2006, op. cit., p. 12).

Mintzberg, H. (1973) *The Nature of Managerial Work*, New York: Harper and Row.

Mintzberg, H. (1979) *The Structuring of Organizations*, Englewood Cliffs, NJ: Prentice Hall.

Mullins, L. J. (2002) *Management and Organizational Behaviour*, sixth edition, London: Financial Times/Prentice Hall.

Nichols, T. and Beynon, H. (1977) *Living with Capitalism*, London: Heinemann.

Ouchi, W. (1981) *Theory Z*, Reading, MA: Addison-Wesley.

Pascale, R. T. and Athos, A. G. (1982) *The Art of Japanese Management*, Harmondsworth: Penguin.

Peters, T. and Waterman, R. H. (1982) *In Search of Excellence*, London: Harper and Row.

Pettigrew, A. (1973) *The Politics of Organizational Decision Making*, London: Tavistock.

Pfeffer, G. (1981) 'Management as symbolic action: The creation and maintenance of organizational paradigms', in L. L. Cummings and B. M. Staw (eds.) *Research in Organizational Behaviour, Vol. 3*, Greenwich, CT: JAI Press.

Pfeffer, J. (1981) *Power in Organizations*, Massachusetts: Marshfield.

Sims, R. and Brinkamann, J. (2002) 'Leaders as role models: The case of John Gutfreund at Solomon Brothers', *Journal of Business Ethics* 35:327–339, cited in Knights and O'Leary (2006, op. cit.).

Sinclair, A. (2005) *Doing Leadership Differently*, second edition, Melbourne: Melbourne University Press.

Smircich, L. and Morgan, G. (1982) 'Leadership: The management of meaning', *Journal of Applied Behavioral Science* 18:257–273.

Tourish, D. and Vatcha, N. (2005) 'Charismatic leadership and corporate cultism at Enron: The elimination of dissent, the promotion of conformity and organizational collapse', *Leadership* 1(4):455–480.

Treviño, L. K., Brown, M. and Pincus, L. (2003) 'A qualitative investigation of perceived executive ethical leadership: Perceptions from inside and outside the executive suite', *Human Relations* 56(1):5–36.

Vroom, V. H. and Jago, A. G. (1988) *The New Leadership: Managing Participation in Organizations*, Englewood Cliffs, NJ: Prentice Hall.

Vroom, V. H. and Yetton, P. W. (1973) *Leadership and Decision-Making*, Pittsburgh: University of Pittsburgh Press.

Watson, T. (1994) *In Search of Management*, London: Routledge.

Whyte, W. F. (1943/1993) *Street Corner Society: The Social Structure of an Italian Slum*, fourth edition, Chicago: University of Chicago Press.

Willmott, H. C. (1997) 'Critical management learning', in J. Burgoyne and M. Reynolds (eds.) *Management Learning*, London: Sage, p.p. 161–176.

Note

1 The following paragraphs draw heavily on Knights and O'Leary (2006).

5 Culture

Joanna Brewis

Key concepts and learning objectives

By the end of this chapter you should be able to:

- Outline the origins of the interest in organizational culture.
- Understand the 'culture is something that an organization has' perspective.
- Critique the central link this mainstream perspective makes between the 'right' culture and high levels of organizational performance.
- Understand the 'culture is something that an organization is' perspective, and the important ways in which it challenges the orthodoxy.

Aims of the chapter

This chapter will:

- Identify the origins of organizational behaviour's interest in culture.
- Outline the mainstream perspective on culture.
- Identify the extent to which the key claim of this perspective stands up to empirical and conceptual scrutiny.
- Outline the critical perspective on culture, and the ways in which it departs from its mainstream counterpart.

Overview and key points

Organizational behaviour (OB) as a discipline, as should be fairly obvious by now, seeks to understand why people behave as they do in organizations. The literature on **culture** is no exception. Borrowing from anthropological studies of societal cultures, the study of organizational culture focuses on the values, beliefs and norms about what is important and how things should be done in a particular organizational setting. Culture is seen to represent some kind of shared commitment to particular ways of relating to the organization, to superiors, to colleagues and to role.

For example, you (hopefully!) share a certain kind of organizational culture with your fellow students. You might share, to some degree, a belief that higher education is important, that your university will deliver the best kind of education for the future you have planned, that your tutors are qualified to deliver such education, that your task is to participate in lectures and seminars, study independently outside of these sessions, abide by course work deadlines and so on. And you will undoubtedly be expected to comply with such beliefs even if you are not committed to them. The key argument here is that values like these influence behaviour in organizations and so are worthy of study in their own right.

This interest in organizational culture emerged in the late 1970s as a result of a series of challenges facing Western management practitioners and theorists at the time. These have been said to include the following:

- *A general decline in religious belief.* This can be linked to the longstanding claim that modern society is alienating – as discussed in preceding chapters. Westerners, it seemed, therefore began to look to work as a source of 'identity'. Organizational culture became seen as a way for them to find answers to questions like 'Who am I?' as well as 'What is my job for?', 'What is my organization for?' and so on (see also Chapter 2).

- *The expansion of highly technical work and the growth of service industries.* These developments meant that workers required more skills and expertise (and therefore could not be managed using the traditional authoritarian approach) but also needed to behave in 'customer-pleasing' ways. The emerging **New Right** politics also emphasized individualism (e.g. Thatcherism in the United Kingdom and Reaganomics in the United States), and workers were becoming more educated and demanding more autonomy as a result. Again, culture here can be understood as a way to give employees more day-to-day discretion or freedom – the idea being that there is no need for strict rules and/or management surveillance if workers already have the 'correct' values, such as 'the customer is always right'.
- *The limitations of a mechanical, 'Theory X' approach to managing people.* The 'management science' approach, which dominated theory and practice during the 1960s and 1970s, had become discredited because employees could not in fact be managed purely through 'objective' and mathematical analysis of organizational operations. This led to a renewed focus on the 'soft', 'human' elements of organizations. The culture literature represents part of this backlash in its emphasis on what Peters and Waterman (1982, p. 11), as we shall see later, call 'the intractable, irrational, intuitive, informal organization'.
- *Innovative production methods.* Techniques like 'just-in-time' were making organizational operations more efficient (see Chapter 4). But this required increased flexibility and therefore greater commitment from workers. Given that culture supposedly provides a reservoir of meaning for the individual worker and also enhances a sense of collectivity among workers, a strong set of shared cultural values should – it was argued – enhance their commitment.
- *The 'Japanese miracle'.* The emergence of Japan following the Second World War as a world economic power was seen to have something to do with the cultural values informing Japanese management techniques. **Globalization** – the breaking down of economic, political, cultural and technological barriers between countries (see Chapter 12) – meant that the West was paying more attention to other countries. And if Japan could create such dramatic success through underpinning its economic activities with a strong value system, why couldn't this also work elsewhere?

In this chapter we will discuss both mainstream and critical approaches to organizational culture. First we review the mainstream perspective, which sees culture as something that an organization *has*, as something that managers can shape and modify. It also dominates the literature. This 'has' perspective urges managers to make every effort to ensure that employees have the 'right' values, beliefs and norms. Creating culture 'at the top' in this way is said to engender harmony and stability in the organization, as well as ensuring that employees behave in the 'appropriate' ways. 'Has' theory therefore draws a strong link between the management of culture and organizational success, but there is controversy as to whether there is 'one best culture' for all organizations or whether culture is in fact a matter of contingency. In this part of the chapter we also review some of the (many) mechanisms that the mainstream approach suggests can be used to manage culture, and end with a more critical look at the empirical and conceptual support for its key claim – for instance, whether a strong culture always leads to excellent organizational results.

In the second part of this chapter we discuss the critical alternative, which argues that culture is something that an organization *is*: in other words, everything in the organization, from the market segment it targets to the number of people it employs, speaks in some way of underlying values, beliefs and norms in that environment. Culture here is also seen to emerge organically as workers learn together to cope with what their jobs require of them. Plus, because workers differ both in terms of what they face within the organization and their experiences outside work, 'is' theory argues that any one workplace is likely to house a number of potentially antagonistic *sub*cultures. For these reasons, this perspective is much more sceptical about the management of culture and argues that such initiatives will either be resisted by employees anyway, or that they come close to an attempt at brainwashing – an unethical use of management power.

Introduction

> [A]nyone who has spent time with any variety of organizations, or worked in more than two or three, will have been struck by the differing atmospheres, the differing ways of doing things, the differing levels of energy, of individual freedom, of kinds of personality. For organizations are as different and varied as the nations and societies of the world. They have differing cultures – sets of values and norms and beliefs – reflected in different structures and systems. *(Handy, 1993, p. 180)*

Despite OB's relatively recent interest in culture, it has nonetheless become a major, perhaps *the*, focus of attention in the area. We already know broadly speaking what culture is – shared organizational values, beliefs and norms – but it is worth breaking the concept down a little before we embark on the chapter proper. Aspects of organizational culture might include some or all of the following:

- Mission and goals: what is the organization aiming towards? – e.g. to be the UK market leader in a particular product, or to expand into markets in other parts of the world.
- The **psychological contract**: what employees can expect of the organization beyond the formal employment contract (e.g. job security, exciting work) and what the organization can expect in return (e.g. long hours, customer responsiveness).
- Authority and power relations: these are not the same thing. Someone can have formal authority but no real power to influence what others do, and vice versa (see Chapter 8). This is nicely illustrated in Ackroyd and Crowdy's (1990) study of abattoir workers, where the authors suggest that teams in this environment were formally led by chargehands, but in reality the chargehands were often fairly low down in the informal hierarchy that had developed.
- The qualities or characteristics that members should have (or not have): some organizations for example stress innovation, initiative and risk-taking, others emphasize caution, conservatism and attention to detail. (Dembrow, Markow and Thompson Inc. is probably an example of the latter.)
- Communication and interaction patterns: do staff address managers by their first names? Do they see colleagues as competitors or collaborators? Do they see co-workers in the evenings or at weekends?
- Rewards and punishments: how is 'good' behaviour rewarded – praise or something more tangible like a bonus or a promotion? What kind of sanctions are available for 'bad' behaviour? Is it OK to be late three days in a row? How far does an employee have to go to get the sack?
- Ways of dealing with the outside world: how committed is the organization to protecting environmental resources? Are recycling schemes, electricity saving policies or car sharing arrangements in place, and how seriously are they taken? Moreover, is information shared with competitors or are all organizational processes shrouded in a veil of secrecy?

Image 5.1

Organized activity demands that people work together in coordinated ways, whether they are in a university, a shop, a factory, a call-centre, a publishing house or wherever. So it would be impossible if the individuals concerned did not agree to some extent on issues like those identified above. Culture therefore provides a source of organizational 'common sense' upon which members draw when deciding where, when and how to act. And if organizational structures, strategies, regulations and policies frame the possibilities for behaviour formally and explicitly, culture could be argued to bring the organization to life. In other words, much of what is outlined above will already be spelt out in written documents like strategic plans, job descriptions and disciplinary procedures. But if cultural values, beliefs and norms in any way contradict these documents then members will probably subvert or ignore the formal rules in their real-life workplace activities – as we have already seen in the abattoir example.

Thinkpoint 5.1

How do some of the questions on p. 346 relate to your university? For example, what do lecturers guarantee to students – prompt feedback on assessed work, perhaps, or maybe they have an open door policy so you can see them whenever you want to? What do they expect in return – essays always being handed in on time or thorough preparation for seminars maybe? Do you ever socialize with your lecturers? To what extent are you encouraged to work with other students on assessed essays or presentations? How would your department deal with plagiarism? And what might the answers to these questions say about the values, beliefs and norms that exist at this institution?

Thinkpoint 5.2

Can you think of instances in your university where what happens in practice goes against institutional rules? For example, perhaps extensions are sometimes granted over the phone when the rules state that forms must be filled out in order for students to make such a request, or attendance registers are not always kept for seminars.

Moreover, because organizational culture consists of values, beliefs and norms that exist in people's heads, we can only actually identify it at the level of what Schein (1992) refers to as **cultural artefacts**. These are tangible phenomena that embody organizational culture, such as types of people employed (personalities, levels of education, etc.), traditions and rituals, technology, architecture, logos, heroes, stories, myths and so on. Schein argues though that there are in fact three levels of culture, and that, as Figure 5.1 suggests, artefacts represent the tip of an iceberg in the sense that the other two levels are hidden from view.

Values incorporate answers to questions like 'What are we doing?' and 'Why are we doing it?': they involve ethical statements of 'rightness'. So an organization's values might include a commitment to equality of opportunity, to solving human problems through the application of technology or to profit maximization for shareholders – but these can be brought to light only through careful and directed questioning.

Basic assumptions on the other hand are almost impossible to surface. These are unconscious and taken for granted ways of seeing the world and are *the source of values and artefacts*. They concern questions about:

- Our relationship to our environment (should we seek to master nature or to live in harmony with it?) and to each other (should our prime orientation be to ourselves as individuals, or is it more important to be a member of and offer loyalty to a group?).

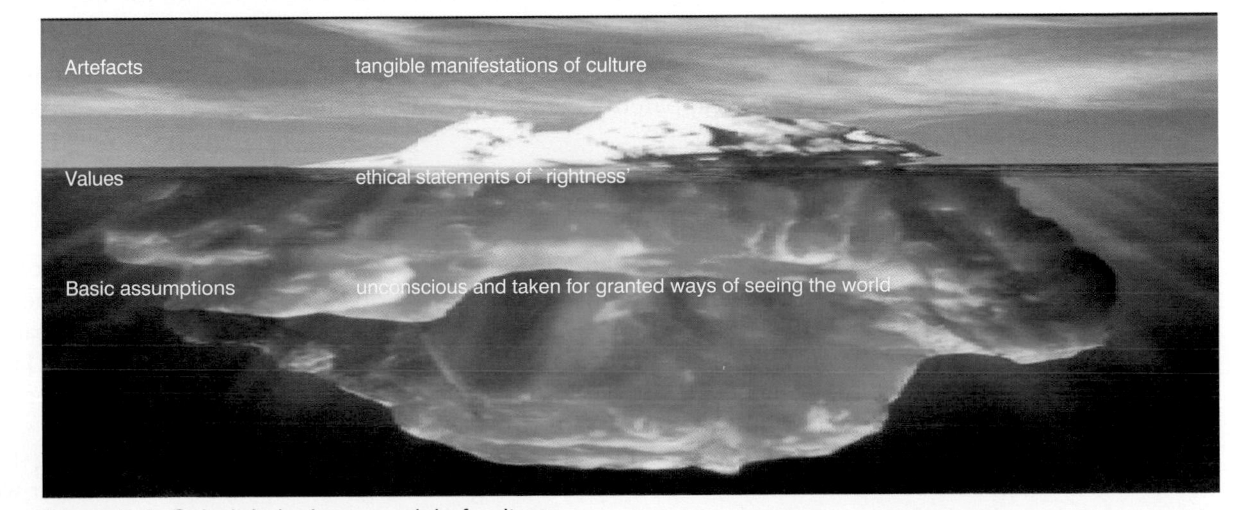

SOURCE: © SCHEIN. COPYRIGHT © (2006) JOHN WILEY & SONS INC.

Figure 5.1 Schein's iceberg model of culture

- Reality and truth (is there such a thing as a universal, timeless human truth or reality or do we live in dynamic worlds that are largely of our own making?).
- Human nature (are we essentially good, bad or a mixture? Is it appropriate to place our trust in others or do we need to take steps to avoid being exploited by them?).
- Human activity (should we focus on measurable achievement and see our activities as a means to an end, or is it more appropriate to live for the moment and enjoy the actual process of our activities?).

With the context for the chapter now established, we turn to the mainstream perspective.

Mainstream perspective on organizational culture

Introduction to the mainstream perspective, AKA culture is something that an organization 'has'

Most of the relevant literature views organizational culture as, in Smircich's (1983) words, something that an organization *has*. From this perspective culture is understood to be:

- *A variable*. Like capital or other assets such as information technology, culture – how employees think and feel – is something that can be manipulated by managers.
- *Integrating and stabilizing*. Because culture is shared between organizational members, it is seen to provide a '"natural" force for social integration' (Meek, 1988, p. 455). Culture brings people together: it ensures that they all think, feel and act in relatively similar ways, that they all develop similar workplace identities. Thus it creates consistency and reduces conflict. The 'has' theorists suggest that culture simplifies people's choices about how things work, what is important and how to behave in organizations.
- *Created at the top*. Culture is set by senior management and disseminated downwards throughout the organization. This can be referred to as **cultural engineering** (Jackson and Carter, 2000, p.p. 27–28) – creating the 'right' kind of organizational culture such that management-imposed values rule out particular courses of action or narrow the range of options for a decision.

Culture here then is understood overall as a management 'lever', a means of ensuring that employees direct their efforts towards organizational goals. Peters and Waterman (1982, p. 11) sum the 'has' perspective up neatly in their suggestion to managers that:

> All that stuff you have been dismissing for so long as the intractable, irrational, intuitive, informal organization *can* be managed. Clearly, it has as much or more to do with the way things work (or don't) around your companies as the formal structures and strategies do . . . you [are] foolish to ignore it.

So what might cultural engineering look like in practice? Case study 5.1 describes one of the best known examples of an apparently successful cultural change, which took place at British Airways between 1982 and 1996.

Key issues and controversies

In the BA case, we see fairly striking evidence to suggest that the 'has' theory account of organizational culture is plausible in terms of the link it forges between the management of culture and organizational effectiveness. Indeed, this claim – that 'a culture has a positive impact on an organization when it points behavior in the right direction . . . [a]lternatively, a culture has [a] negative impact when it points behavior in the wrong direction' (Kilmann *et al.*, cited in Alvesson, 2002, p. 43) – is probably the most important one that it makes.

As already suggested, 'has' theory sees the 'appropriate' culture as leading to organizational effectiveness in two ways: first, by providing meaning for employees so that their work makes some kind of sense to them, which can be seen as motivating; and, secondly, establishing particular ways

CASE STUDY 5.1 Cultural engineering at British Airways, 1982–1996

SOURCE: © REPRODUCED BY PERMISSION OF BRITISH AIRWAYS

Image 5.2

British Airways was produced by a 1974 merger between British Overseas Airways Corporation (who offered long-haul flights) and British European Airways (specializing in flights to continental Europe). In its early years, BA was very bureaucratic and rules-oriented (see Chapter 13). It is described as having an introspective, inflexible culture where over-staffing was routine, hierarchy was all-important and little attention was paid to customer service, employee opinion or profitability.

There were also substantial cultural differences post-merger. BOAC staff tended to look down on their BEA counterparts, believing they provided flights for 'tradesmen' whereas their own services were for 'gentlemen'. BEA employees on the other hand regarded the BOAC staff as snobs who had no real sense of the cut-throat world of commercial competition. The result was disastrous in terms of performance – indeed in 1980 BA was voted the airline to avoid at all costs and, at the time, was also the most unpunctual European carrier flying out of the United Kingdom.

When John King was appointed by Prime Minister Margaret Thatcher as BA Chairman in 1981, he saw a need for drastic action because of the huge losses the company was making. His 'survival plan' created nearly 20 000 staff redundancies, closed routes and disposed of BA's cargo-only service. By the time Colin Marshall took over as CEO in 1982 an operating surplus had been created for the first time since the merger. Marshall's objective was to build on this by encouraging all BA staff to take responsibility for customer satisfaction, and also to develop a more holistic outlook on the company, bridging functional and cultural divides. An extended training initiative was therefore developed. Marshall was quoted at the time as talking about 'designing' BA staff to deliver good service, just as BA already designed the seats on its planes, its inflight entertainment and its airport lounges to do the same.

The first of these training events was launched in 1983. Two days long, it was called 'Putting People First', and was eventually attended by 40 000 staff. The course focused on encouraging effective personal relationships, the idea being that if staff felt good about themselves they would also feel good about interacting with customers. A senior director was present for question and answer sessions at each of these events and Marshall himself frequently attended. Other programmes followed, including 'Managing People First' for BA's 1400 managerial and supervisory staff, launched in 1985. Its objectives were to foster a more caring and trusting relationship between managers and their teams, and to improve communication and staff motivation. Another – 'Day in the Life' – was introduced in the same year to improve cooperation and break down barriers between BA's various functions.

At the same time other more tangible changes were afoot, including privatization in 1987 and a takeover of British Caledonian Airways in 1988. Both marked how much progress BA had made towards becoming a market-oriented, customer-facing organization. The organization's structure was also changing – Marshall revamped BA into 11 profit centres, streamlining its bureaucracy and allowing for greater cross-functional communication and cohesion. Executives who he felt weren't up to the changes were removed and performance-related pay, linked to the new BA values, was introduced.

But the developments didn't end there: in 1987, 'Awards for Excellence' were brought in to recognize high levels of performance among staff, and the suggestion scheme 'Brainwaves' was introduced. In 1988 BA began to offer an in-house MBA in conjunction with Lancaster University; and the initiative 'Winning for Customers', consisting of a training event to signal that every staff member makes a difference to the customer experience, and an associated course for supervisory and managerial staff, was launched in 1992.

All in all, this lengthy and expensive programme seems to have transformed a loss-making public organization colloquially known as 'Bloody Awful' into a profitable private company, which won the *Business Traveller* 'World's Best Airline' award for seven years up to and including 1995. Indeed, former CEO Bob Ayling (who took over from Colin Marshall in 1996, when Marshall became Chairman) suggested in a BA magazine that the organization 'has been one of the great turnaround stories of the late twentieth century. The image this airline has built for itself in the past 14 years has stood it in great stead' (*Business Life*, 1997, p. 45). The BA example therefore suggests that culture can indeed be engineered, and that a substantial hike in performance can be achieved by managers embarking on this kind of initiative.

"It's just a familiarity we like to go through with new employees."

Image 5.3

to think, feel and act, which are linked to the achievement of organizational goals. The 'has' theorists believe that the strength of an organization's culture – the extent to which employees buy into management-directed values, beliefs and norms – has a direct impact on its performance, however that is measured. The basic 'guarantee' of this literature is that, properly managed, culture can help to build employee commitment, convey management philosophy and legitimate their policies, motivate staff and facilitate socialization of new employees.

The 'swearing in' cartoon pokes gentle fun at the socialization of new staff into a particular company's culture, suggesting that this amounts to asking them to swear an oath of allegiance to hard work, turning up on time and putting in extra hours as and when required. But the 'has' literature takes these possibilities more seriously. As established in the chapter overview, it believes that, once employees have taken on board the 'right' values, these will guide their behaviour without the need for costly and demotivating direct supervision. Indeed Deal and Kennedy (1988, p. 15) go as far as to claim that it is possible to increase every worker's productivity by one or two hours a day if culture is managed effectively.

'Has' theorists, then, are functionalist and technical in their outlook. Their **functionalism** can be seen in the claim that culture performs a function in its maintenance of organizational equilibrium and consensus. The 'has' perspective is also **technical** because it seeks to develop knowledge about organizations which enables managers to manipulate specific variables (workers' values, beliefs and norms) in order to achieve a specified outcome (organizational effectiveness). And of course the suggestion that culture might be the solution to the age-old problem of getting employees to work hard because they enjoy it and feel fulfilled has a broad populist appeal among organization theorists and managers alike – perhaps this is why there are so many contributions to the 'has' camp.

Exercise 5.1

Going back to your university, try to identify the ways in which academic staff endeavour to

- Encourage you to commit to your studies (e.g. by emphasizing the reputation of the university and its good graduate employment record).
- Convey their philosophy (e.g. my institution believes in encouraging students to critique everything they are exposed to and bases all teaching on offering several sides of the same theoretical or empirical story).
- Justify practices like a plagiarism policy or the rules that govern how your degree grade is calculated (e.g. by suggesting that plagiarism policies protect students against others who cheat and thus gain higher grades by unfair means).
- Teach freshers or direct entry students 'the rules of the game' (e.g. by holding social events at the beginning of each year or operating a student mentor system).

How successful are they in these endeavours, in your opinion?

But its suggestion that getting the culture 'right' results in high levels of performance aside, there are two areas on which there is disagreement in the 'has' literature. The first of these is the question as to whether there is one culture, which, if implemented in any organization, will result in high performance (the 'one best culture'/'one size fits all' argument) or whether the right kind of culture is actually a question of the variables affecting the organization (the contingencies/'horses for courses' argument). So that you can get to grips with this debate, this section begins by reviewing the two sides, identifying the best known contributions to each and suggesting that the second is probably more plausible in common-sense terms.

The second 'has' theory controversy surrounds the mechanisms that should be used by managers to change, consolidate or establish organizational culture. Again, the central points of this discussion are rehearsed here, to draw your attention to the many cultural tactics that managers might have at their disposal, and to focus on some of the key decisions that 'has' literature suggests they need to make in this regard. We end the section by acknowledging that, although 'has' theorists are not universally optimistic about the end result of cultural management strategies, this has not had any noticeable impact on wider public demand for its prescriptions and advice – perhaps because of the aforementioned attractiveness of the primary link it makes between culture and organizational performance.

In terms of the 'one best culture' argument, Peters and Waterman (1982) – whose work is discussed in more detail in the 'Important empirical studies' section later in this chapter – and Ouchi (1981) are probably the most notable proponents. Their position suggests a kind of magic formula for organizational success. Peters and Waterman identify eight cultural values that they say exist in America's best performing companies, and which should be introduced into all organizations to ensure 'excellence'. Indeed the subtitle of their best-selling text *In Search of Excellence* is *Lessons from America's Best-Run Companies.*

Similarly, Ouchi analyses what he sees to be a distinctive form of culture in Japanese organizations – in fact his work is an example of OB's 'Japanese turn' as described in the chapter overview. Ouchi calls this approach Theory Z, after Maslow's claim that type Z is the highest form of self-actualization (see Chapter 2). It is based on the assumption that, instead of the competitive ethos of the 'market' organization or the rules-driven bureaucracy, workers in a Theory Z organization behave in appropriate ways because they share a commitment to the same value system. This also helps them to counter the apparently alienating characteristics of the modern world – something we have already touched upon. Ouchi recommends that US managers should try to socialize their employees into just such a culture – and the subtitle of his book (*How American Business Can Meet the Japanese Challenge*) once again makes his message very clear.

More common in 'has' theory, however, is the contingencies/horses for courses argument. These theorists pick and mix a range of different internal and external variables to which, they argue, managers should attend when deciding what kind of culture best fits their particular organization. The best known of these writers are Deal and Kennedy (1988) and Handy (1993), who borrows extensively from earlier work by Harrison (1972). Deal and Kennedy (whose ideas are also developed in the 'Important empirical studies' section) identify a four-fold 'typology' of organizational culture, where the suitability of each cultural type depends on the level of risk involved in an organization's activities and how quickly it receives feedback on those activities. Handy, similarly, identifies four key categories of culture to fit a range of organizational situations, as follows:

1 *The power culture (represented by a web)*
   - Depends on a central power source, usually the founder or owner.
   - Trust between centre and 'outlying' staff is key to effectiveness, as is personal interaction.
   - The central figure needs to select staff who have similar ways of thinking so they can be left to get on with their work: thus members have a lot of freedom.
   - Few rules and routines; decisions depend on balance of power rather than procedure.
   - A strong, cohesive and flexible culture where politically minded risk-takers thrive.
   - Centre's influence declines as organization grows bigger (and the web weaker), which may prompt break-up into smaller divisions or a shift towards role culture (see below).
   - Tough and competitive, possibly causing low morale and high labour turnover.
   - Replacement of the centre at the end of their career is a key challenge because 'a web without a spider has no strength' (Handy, 1993, p. 184).
   - Likely to be found in small entrepreneurial organizations such as trading, finance or property companies, new businesses and/or family firms.

SOURCE: © ISTOCKPHOTO.COM/JESSE YARDLEY

Image 5.4

2 *The role culture (represented by a Greek temple)*

- Reason and logic are key values here.
- A bureaucratic and highly structured organization; temple's pillars are specialist departments like marketing or production, and roof is senior management team.
- Organizational operations controlled by job descriptions, reporting procedures, communications policies, etc.
- Staff are selected on basis of capability/expertise and are not required to do anything more than their roles require.
- Power comes from hierarchical position, not personal charisma.

SOURCE: © ISTOCKPHOTO.COM/BART PARREN

Image 5.5

- Works well where the market is predictable or a **monopoly/oligopoly** exists.
- Provides security and predictability for workers, who are able to climb the 'career ladder'.
- 'But Greek temples are *insecure* when the ground shakes' (Handy, 1993, p. 186 – emphasis added): they do not respond quickly to changing circumstances, and can be frustrating for those who seek freedom.
- The civil service, car manufacturers, oil companies, life insurance companies and high street banks are all likely to be role cultures.

3 *The task culture (represented by a net or a matrix)*

- Centres on getting the job done, bringing the right people and resources together at the right time to work on a project; staff may be simultaneously involved in several different projects.
- Key values are expertise and teamwork.
- Overall control maintained by central allocation of resources and people to projects.
- Suited to competitive and volatile markets with short product cycles, where responsiveness, cooperation and creativity are vital.
- Project teams can be formed and abandoned rapidly and decision making is often faster, being devolved to team level.
- But no real attention to economies of scale and staff may have little opportunity to develop expertise when working across a range of projects (can also generate confusion and insecurity).
- May be found in venture capital firms, management consultancies and advertising agencies.

SOURCE: © ISTOCKPHOTO.COM/JIM JURICA

Image 5.6

4 *The person/cluster culture (represented by a galaxy of stars)*

- Key value here is individuality or freedom.
- Organization exists only for its members' benefit; it comes into existence when people find that sharing office space, desks, an IT network, etc. helps them, but there are no collective goals as such.
- Overall control is only possible by mutual consent, and power is shared.
- Tends not to last: 'Too soon the organization achieves its own *identity* and begins to impose on its individuals.

SOURCE: © ISTOCKPHOTO.COM/JUSTIN HORROCKS

Image 5.7

It becomes, at best, a task culture, but often a power or role culture' (Handy, 1993, p. 191 – emphasis added).
- Unusual but may be found in barristers' chambers or architects' partnerships, or in small organizational enclaves like consultants in an NHS hospital.

Handy, as we can see, stresses size, market and individual worker preference as the key variables in identifying the best culture for a particular organization. Other contingencies that have been identified as important include:

- National culture – see, for example, Hofstede's (2001) discussion of differences between IBM subsidiaries in various parts of the world.
- Political environment – such as Tayeb's (1988) comparison of industrial relations legislation and government attitudes to market regulation in the United Kingdom and India.
- Founder/leader – like Henry Ford, whose approach to management is discussed by Corbett (1994, p.p. 123–132), and Konosuke Matsushita of the Matsushita Corporation, analysed by Pascale and Athos (1981).
- Technology – Anthony's (1994) discussion of production processes in coal-mining, for instance.

Our intuition should tell us that the contingency stance is a more sensible position to adopt when organizations vary so widely in terms of size, sector, ownership, location, staff and so on, especially given the advent of the so-called 'global village'. As Handy (1993, p. 183) points out: 'It must be emphasized that [any culture] can be a good and effective culture; but people are often culturally blinkered, thinking that ways that worked well in one place are bound to be successful everywhere. This is not the case.'

Exercise 5.2

If you are a student who is studying abroad, think about how educational practices in universities at home differ from those in the country where you are doing your degree (you might have to e-mail a friend at home for information). If you are a 'home' student, ask a friend who comes from elsewhere. Some examples might be:

- How essays are marked (some higher educational cultures typically award much higher marks in general than others).
- How degrees are graded (some use grade point averages, others prefer 'bands' like the British class first upper second/lower second/third system).
- How students treat academic staff and vice versa.
- The extent to which you are expected to write in your own words or submit course work as part of your assessment, and so on.

The contingency literature also acknowledges that organizations may house **subcultures** because of the particular circumstances facing different departments or functions. This **cultural differentiation** requires that managers work to integrate these various groups of employees, to encourage them to understand each other despite their differing values, beliefs and norms. Typologies – such as the four cultures identified by Handy – might therefore be best understood as **ideal-types** for benchmarking real organizations, indicating the dimensions that could be important in understanding why particular values exist and whether these values come together to 'form a coherent [organizational] . . . whole' (Brown, 1998, p. 72).

Thinkpoint 5.3

Think about the different departments or functions in a 'typical' manufacturing organization – marketing, R&D, production, finance, human resources and so on. Using Handy's typology, identify the kind of culture you would expect each department to have and suggest why this might be.

The second controversy in the 'has' literature centres on the most appropriate ways to manage organizational culture. These discussions tend to focus on changing an existing culture – as in the BA case study. But it is worth remembering that cultural initiatives may also involve managers trying to preserve the status quo, which can be particularly challenging in the face of large numbers of staff leaving or joining the organization. Alternatively, they could be trying to build a specific type of culture in a new organization. Daymon (2000), for example, discusses efforts to encourage commercial values around high profit and low costs as opposed to 'traditional' broadcasting values of creativity, artistic merit and production excellence among incoming staff at Countrywide Television.

However, it is also true to say that the **cultural transmission mechanisms** (CTMs)[1] used are broadly speaking the same whether managers are trying to change, maintain or build a culture. Also, change is probably more difficult than the other types of cultural engineering, '[b]ecause it entails introducing something new and substantially different from what prevails in existing cultures' (Trice and Beyer, 1993, p. 393). For present purposes, therefore, we will concentrate on cultural change.

As implied above, although there are many different explanations available, there is no real agreement in the 'has' literature as to the best way to change a culture. It has been argued in fact that the approach management chooses to shift employees' values, beliefs and norms ought to be based on criteria such as how many people need to change and how much of their behaviour needs to change; how different the new culture is from what exists at the moment; and whether people either inside or outside the organization already espouse the new values, so that they can be used as role models.

Exercise 5.3

Evaluate the BA case study in terms of what it suggests about how many people and how much of their behaviour needed to change in this organization; how different the new culture was from the old; and whether there were any external or internal role models for the new ideas and behaviours. How might it have felt to be an employee experiencing this series of interventions?

There are also many empirical examples of the CTMs managers have deployed to change (or maintain or build) a culture. These have been claimed to fall into two main categories:

- Devices that are the responsibility of the human resources department and focus on employee resourcing (getting the 'right' people into the organization and ensuring that they perform in a particular way once there, as well as 'disposing' of the 'wrong' people), employee development (training staff in 'appropriate' ways) and employee relations (encouraging 'suitable' forms of communication between management and staff).
- 'Symbolic leadership' devices – the ways in which senior members of the organization go about managing the rank-and-file employees and how these tactics embody various values, beliefs and norms to those employees.

These measures are also said to be more effective when used in a kind of cultural package, as on their own they are unlikely to have much impact. Moreover, a 'consistent cues' approach is said to be necessary such that 'all aspects of every . . . programme must unequivocally promote the desired state culture' (Brown, 1998, p. 166).

We have already seen a very good example of the use of human resource devices to change a culture in the British Airways case study – where employee resourcing, employee relations and employee development tactics were all used to shift the prevailing values towards an emphasis on customer service and internal staff cooperation.

Thinkpoint 5.4

Can you classify the various CTMs used at BA into the categories of resourcing, relations and development? Some may fall into more than one.

In terms of symbolic leadership devices, on the other hand, **management by example** (MBE) is probably the epitome of such techniques. It involves, quite literally, 'walking the talk', acting out the organization's cultural vision because, in the old adage, actions speak louder than words. Indeed, according to the 'has' theorists, managers should 'be seen as spending a lot of time on matters visibly related to the values they preach' (Deal and Kennedy, 1988, p. 169). After all, management talk begins to sound like so much hot air after a while if it is not backed up by behaviour.

There are some very evocative examples of such 'embodiment leadership' in cultural change projects, including Lee Iacocca's refusal to draw more than US$1 a year salary until he got General Motors on its feet again and Colin Marshall of British Airways (them again!) assisting check-in staff on the first day of the company's Super Shuttle service when they were overrun with customers. We have also seen other BA instances of MBE in senior directors always being present for Q&A sessions at the 'Putting People First' events and Marshall himself frequently turning up into the bargain.

Thinkpoint 5.5

Which values do you think Iacocca, Marshall and the latter's senior BA colleagues are trying to embody to staff in the MBE examples discussed above?

In sum, then, 'has' theory disagrees on (a) whether one culture fits all organizations, and (b) how managers ought to go about changing, maintaining or constructing cultures – in other words, no clear message emerges here about the appropriate combination of cultural transmission mechanisms.

But to conclude this section we should also note the cautionary tales that appear periodically in the 'has' literature with regard to the realities of managers embarking on a cultural intervention. For example, it has been suggested that many initiatives of this kind fail because any initial enthusiasm on the part of staff fades and training is not used to properly support the changes. Another recommendation is that sufficient time and space is given to employees to voice their resentment about the changes and 'grieve' for what has been lost (rituals, heroes and so on).

Managers contemplating changes of this kind are also counselled to attend to organizational **multiculturalism** – i.e. not to assume that the organization has one culture through and through. They should allow for the fact that different groups of workers may have different sets of values (as we saw above in the discussion of cultural differentiation) and thus could respond to a cultural change programme in varying ways. The UK National Health Service is a particularly interesting example here. In the wake of the Griffiths Report and the importation of managers with no medical expertise, there was an attempt by the new incumbents to impose a culture of efficient use of resources. This led to clashes with clinicians, who argued that patients simply needed the best care regardless of cost. Such debates persist to this day, but here the *managers* were the *minority subculture* trying to impose their values on a *dominant* culture – as may often be the case when a new management team arrives in an organization.

Overall, then, it would be unfair to say that the 'has' literature necessarily sees cultural change as a 'quick fix' or a panacea for all managerial problems. As Deal and Kennedy (1988, p. 163) have it, 'let us summarize the dismal economics of effecting real and lasting cultural change: it costs a fortune and takes forever'. They suggest that achieving even half the change in values, beliefs and norms that management propose in any one initiative necessitates spending between 5–10 per cent of the salaries of the staff being targeted, and so strongly recommend that managers ask themselves whether embarking on cultural change is either necessary or worth it.

However, the above warnings (which certainly emphasize the possibility of cultural change but also alert managers to the potential pitfalls along the way) seemingly do little to sap the enthusiasm of the corporate market in particular for 'how to' texts on organizational culture. Indeed, one of the best selling books in this area – Deal and Kennedy's (1988) *Corporate Cultures* – also issues, as we have seen, a clear warning about the economic and temporal costs of trying to change culture. It is to two such texts – the key empirical contributions to the 'has' literature – that we now turn.

Important empirical studies

In this section we will briefly review two of the central empirical texts in the 'culture is something that an organization has' school in order to draw out their central lessons. These are Peters and Waterman's (1982) *In Search of Excellence: Lessons from America's Best-Run Companies* and Deal and Kennedy's (1988) *Corporate Cultures: The Rites and Rituals of Corporate Life*. They have been chosen because there exists 'something of a consensus that [they] were central to stimulating the growth of popular managerial interest in organizational culture', along with Ouchi's (1981) *Theory Z* (Parker, 2000, p. 10). As we know already, Peters and Waterman fall into the 'one best culture' camp, whereas Deal and Kennedy prefer to argue for cultural horses for organizational courses.

Peters and Waterman gathered their data by interviewing managers in 43 top performing US companies, all Fortune 500 listed. They began with a list of 62 of McKinsey's[2] 'star' clients and subtracted 19 – including General Electric – on the basis of specific performance measures. The organizations left included Hewlett Packard, McDonald's, Procter and Gamble, and Disney. Peters and Waterman's conclusion, as we have seen, was that these 'best-run' companies operated on the basis of eight cultural tenets that were at the heart of their performance. These constitute the authors' recipe for success: they argue that every organization needs to live by the same tenets in order to create excellence. The eight tenets outlined in the book are as follows:

- *A bias for action*. Instead of discussing and planning everything in minute and pernickety detail, go out and make things happen – use the trial and error approach.
- *Close to the customer*. Listen to what the customer wants and tailor business activities accordingly.
- *Autonomy and entrepreneurship*. Empower employees and encourage innovation, creativity and risk-taking.
- *Productivity through people*. Regard employees as the organization's most important resource and the source of quality goods and services.
- *Hands-on, value-driven*. Managers must get involved in the work that their staff do as well as demonstrate their own commitment to the central corporate values (referred to above as management by example).
- *Stick to the knitting*. Stick to producing whatever it is that the organization is good at; don't be tempted by diversification.
- *Simple form, lean staff*. The organization's structure should be as flat and flexible as possible; top-heavy bureaucracies are inimical to excellence.
- *Simultaneous loose–tight properties*. Employees should have a great deal of discretion all the way down to the shop floor (loose properties), as management exercises control through a strong set of centralized values (tight properties).

Of course this list sounds almost commonplace now – we would expect that the majority of businesses would seek to operate on the basis of such values. But *In Search of Excellence* is probably also the most prominent management book of recent times, having sold millions of copies worldwide and been translated into many different languages. It would be surprising, then, if it had not had some effect on managerial thinking. And in the early 1980s it was certainly heady stuff, given the aforementioned backdrop of management-by-numbers (Parker, 2000, p.p. 10, 12, 16).

Recap

Peters and Waterman's key message is 'My way or the highway' – i.e. there is 'one best way' to business excellence via cultural management.

Deal and Kennedy, in a text originally published around the same time as *In Search of Excellence*, similarly stress that 'people make business work' (1988, p. 5). Their research encompassed 80 US companies, 18 of which had strong cultural values and were all high performers. The latter group included DuPont, the chemical, energy and materials giant, and vehicle component manufacturer

Dana Corporation. But unlike Peters and Waterman, Deal and Kennedy argue that the type of culture that is most likely to breed business success depends on particular features of that business's environment – specifically the level of risk that the business faces and the speed of feedback it receives. On this basis they develop a four-part typology, similar in form to Handy's, which unfolds as follows:

SOURCE: © GRANADA

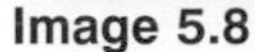
Image 5.8

1 *Tough-guy culture*
- Key values are speed (making decisions quickly) and emotional resilience (living with the consequences).
- A high-pressure, individualistic, all-or-nothing culture, nicely illustrated by 'rogue trader' Nick Leeson's claim that he needed 'balls of steel' to survive the Baring's Bank trading floor; it respects risk-takers and mavericks.
- Suits organizations, particularly new ones, where operations are risky (e.g. millions of dollars invested in a film) and feedback rapid (e.g. when using dynamite to explode the last stretch of a tunnel under construction).
- But has a short-termist outlook, plus there is little cooperation between members and no real incentive to learn from mistakes.
- Constant pressure also makes employee burnout likely.
- Those who thrive are tough and competitive, want to do well on their own merits and prefer to work alone.
- The police force, construction companies, management consultancies, advertising agencies, television, film and publishing companies and sports teams might all be tough-guy cultures.

2 *Work hard/play hard culture*
- Values customers, trying to meet their needs and solve their problems.
- Also emphasizes action, or what Deal and Kennedy (1988, p. 114) call the 'try it; fix it; do it' ideology, and teamwork.
- Performance measured by results, such as sales generated.
- As its name suggests, a friendly culture where having fun (e.g. staff parties) is as important as hard graft.
- Suited to organizations where the risks are small (e.g. no one sale makes or breaks a retail organization like Tesco, Marks and Spencer or Next, a car salesroom or an estate agency) but feedback is quick (e.g. you either close the sale or you don't).
- Manufacturing companies may also fall into this cultural category: workers here know when mistakes are made but checks along the production line mean no single error is a disaster.
- Good for extraverts.
- But emphasis on volume can override attention to quality, not always adaptive to change and has a tendency to prefer quick fix solutions.

3 *Bet-your-company culture*
- Attention to detail and precision are key values here.
- Has a long-term orientation and believes in giving a good idea the chance to work.
- A relentless 'drip drip' pressure culture where technical expertise is emphasized because errors are costly.

- Knowledge is shared and staff interdependence seen as important.
- Suitable for high-risk, slow-feedback environments where running a business 'means investing millions – sometimes billions – in a project that takes years to develop, refine, and test, before you find out whether it will go or not' (Deal and Kennedy, 1988, p. 116), and a quick fix ideology could be disastrous.
- Produces high-quality inventions and breakthroughs.
- But vulnerable to short-term fluctuations: always waiting for the 'pay-off'.
- Survivors have character, confidence and the stamina to 'wait it out'.
- Oil companies, the nuclear arms industry, mining corporations, investment banks and the forces (who spend considerable time and money preparing for wars they may never have to fight) could all exhibit this culture.

SOURCE © CROWN COPYRIGHT 2005 REPRINTED WITH PERMISSION

Image 5.9

4 *Process culture*

- Very bureaucratic; the emphasis is on caution and getting processes right.
- Status-oriented and formal; hierarchy is visible in artefacts like size of desks, office space, etc.
- Suited to low-risk, slow-feedback environments: 'This lack of feedback forces employees to focus on *how* they do something, not what they do' (Deal and Kennedy, 1988, p. 119).
- Organizes and routinizes work when required, and may allow other sorts of organizations to survive.
- Survivors are orderly, attend to detail and work by the book.
- But an inflexible and potentially stifling culture.
- May be found in insurance companies, government departments, public utilities and highly regulated industries like pharmaceuticals.

Exercise 5.4

Compare Deal and Kennedy's cultural types to Handy's. Where are the similarities and the differences?

Recap

Deal and Kennedy's key message is 'It depends' – i.e. there are several different routes to excellent performance via cultural management, according to the circumstances that organizations face. The challenge is to match the culture to the circumstances.

Despite their differences, these key contributions to the 'has' perspective both make fairly unequivocal and empirically grounded claims about the connection between culture and organizational performance. Rather than just accepting these claims, however, we should subject them to scrutiny. Before we do so, we will briefly revisit the British Airways case, because developments following Colin Marshall's apparently successful re-engineering of culture in this organization foreshadow both this and later critical discussion of the 'has' perspective.

CASE STUDY 5.2 Cultural engineering at British Airways: What happened next?

Although BA had apparently been 'turned around' in the 1980s and early 1990s, there were during this period also several warning signs that all was not entirely well. In 1993, for example, Richard Branson of Virgin Atlantic won a libel case against John King and Colin Marshall. This arose from Marshall's claim that Branson had lied in alleging that BA was engaging in 'dirty tricks' (i.e. forms of unfair/illegal competitive activity). Branson's accusations included the suggestion that, after Virgin relocated from Heathrow to Gatwick in July 1991 and thus began to compete directly with BA, BA sought to steal Virgin customers by encouraging their staff to pose as Virgin employees. He also said that BA had gained access to confidential Virgin files, and that the BA public relations guru Brian Basham had been deliberately spreading detrimental stories about both him and Virgin in the City and the British media. Branson was eventually awarded £500 000 in damages, Virgin won £110 000 and BA were also held liable for some £3 million in legal costs as well as being forced to publicly apologize.

In addition, there was conflicting evidence regarding just how far the customer service ethos had been taken on board. Heather Höpfl's anecdote about a BA flight attendant who offered passengers six leftover cartons of milk after a flight could be seen to suggest that this employee was going out of her way to 'delight' customers, even though her actions were in fact against company rules. On the other hand, Bob Ayling claimed in the aforementioned *Business Life* (1997, p. 47) interview that:

I believe we already have a caring team working for us . . . who make every effort to make our passengers feel as comfortable and as at home as possible. But somehow we haven't been able to communicate that properly and I don't know why . . . Perhaps because, up to now, we've concentrated on projecting the more macho side of the company, how strong we are, how powerful and business-like.

These are fascinating claims from the Chief Executive of a company that had spent the previous 15 years or so (and enormous sums of money) trying to promote customer care in all aspects of its operations! But, then again, perhaps Ayling's comments can be read as reflecting back on the dirty tricks episode?

Ayling himself was to create his own controversies during a stormy four years at the BA helm. After a very healthy first 18 months, the June 1997 announcement of a new corporate identity caused a not-so-positive stir. The changes included a brand new livery for BA, dubbed World Images and to appear on plane tailfins, cabin crew scarves, business cards and ticket jackets. World Images featured 50 new designs commissioned from artists all over the world to replace the traditional red and blue BA logo. The key intention was to revamp BA (yet again) into something more cosmopolitan, diverse and friendly, to reflect its growing numbers of both overseas staff and customers and play down the potentially offputting associations of the organization's 'Britishness'. But shareholders called the rebranding unpatriotic and extravagant and Margaret Thatcher demonstrated her own feelings when she draped a hanky over a model BA plane tailfin featuring a World Images design at a Tory party conference.

Moreover, the announcement of this initiative coincided with two ballots on strike action by BA staff. One, concerning the sale of the inflight catering division, was resolved without industrial action being taken. The other related to an aspect of Ayling's cost-cutting Business Efficiency Programme (BEP) which meant that cabin crew stood to lose out financially. This ballot – for a 72-hour strike – was successful by a majority of 3 to 1. In the event, and arguably due to what was widely regarded at the time as intimidation by BA management,[3] only 300 staff went on strike but a further 1500 called in sick. The action ended up costing the airline £125 million. In the aftermath of the strike, Ayling did however began to put restorative measures in place, such as an internal task force focusing on staff motivation and patching up relations with customers.

1998 also proved to be somewhat of a curate's egg for Ayling and BA. It featured, among other things, the decline of the 'Asian Tiger' economies, rising levels of customer dissatisfaction and more legal action by Branson, this time alleging that BA had no business using their 'World's Favourite Airline' slogan. Although the Advertising Standards Authority found in BA's favour in the end, a Consumers' Association survey published at the same time suggested that they had lost considerable ground in terms of being an airline that people recommended to each other. By late 1998 Ayling had had to declare BA's first ever third quarter loss.

In 1999 an internal opinion survey entitled 'It's Your Shout!' proved rather damning – staff apparently did not believe BA directors could cut costs and still maintain quality, were cynical about their commitment to honest and straightforward communication with employees and also did not believe that the board cared about them. 'Putting People First' was

SOURCE: © SAM SMITH/CARTOONSTOCK.COM

Image 5.10

therefore rejuvenated as 'Putting People First Again', involving all 64 000 staff. BA's financial performance began to improve after the announcement of a six-year low in annual profits in May, but was not helped by the decision in June 1999 to cease using the World Images designs on planes – Ayling's claims that the movement away from the traditional BA logo had been welcomed notwithstanding.

In August 1999, Ayling was forced to announce 1000 job losses. However, things started to look up again later in the year as new service innovations (such as flat beds in business class) and an e-commerce initiative to increase online sales were publicized. Customer satisfaction measures began to improve and BA's low-cost airline Go was also doing well – somewhat ironically when its parent company was moving strategically away from the economy end of the market and focusing its attentions on 'front cabin' passengers.

Nonetheless, a further 6000 job losses were made public in February 2000 and the BA share price then nosedived as part of wider market trends. By March Ayling had been forced to resign. The charismatic and charming CEO had apparently failed to persuade BA customers or staff of the viability of his vision. Even his planned alliance with American Airlines, which would have given the two airlines joint control of over 60 per cent of transatlantic flights, was eventually diluted into a marketing agreement after regulator objections – and one that did not permit the partners to work together to set prices.

On top of the difficult task of continuing to cut costs whilst simultaneously improving staff morale, Ayling's Australian replacement Rod Eddington also had his fair share of additional turbulence to negotiate. This included the grounding of all Concordes in August 2000 following the Paris air crash in which 113 people lost their lives,[4] the UK foot and mouth crisis of March 2001, which had a substantial impact on British tourism, and of course the horrific events of 9/11. A total of 7000 redundancies were made as a result during 2001, followed swiftly by the announcement of 5800 additional job losses in the following February. BA also declared its worst annual losses since privatization later in the spring. However, things were improving by September, with the airline netting seven awards from *Business Traveller*, including Best Business Class and Most Innovative Airline.

But a further round of industrial action – this time unofficial – caused more havoc in July 2003. Some 500 flights were cancelled as BA check-in staff protested about the introduction of electronic swipe cards for clocking on and off, because of their concerns about possible changes to staff rosters as a result. Despite a fairly speedy resolution, these events again had a very negative impact on service and were also disastrous in PR terms – indeed BA issued both televised and newspaper apologies to its customers as a result.

Then there was the announcement that, from August 2004, all UK staff would be subject to drug and alcohol testing under certain circumstances. This policy was developed, say management, for safety reasons and it came in the wake of several controversies involving the use of alcohol by BA staff. Although unions agreed the move, it was publicized just as major research findings suggested such testing is likely only to have a small effect on numbers of accidents, productivity, etc. This research also argued that it could also be very expensive, not to say divisive, if introduced across the board in an organization. While the researchers accepted that testing may be worthwhile in occupations where safety or public trust are of paramount concern (as of course is the case with many jobs at BA), the jury may still be out as to whether it is justified for *all* BA employees.

At the time of writing, the latest development in the BA saga, at the height of the August 2004 holiday season, was chaos at Heathrow created by a shortage of check-in staff. Many flights were either cancelled or delayed as a result, meaning hundreds of travellers having to camp overnight at the airport and losses running to millions of pounds for the company. The cause was a combination of factors including delays in taking on replacement staff and sick leave. Ironically, only days earlier, BA had narrowly avoided strike action over pay planned for the English bank holiday weekend by hammering out a last-minute deal with unions.

Recap

Before we move on to examine some of the limitations of the 'has' perspective on organizational culture, remember contributors to this body of thought agree that culture:

- Is an organizational variable that managers can manipulate.
- Integrates and stabilizes organizations because it ensures that everyone thinks, feels and acts in the same way.
- Is created at the top and disseminated down through the organization.
- If properly managed, generates excellent organizational performance.

They disagree, however, on:

- Whether there is 'one best culture' for all organizations.
- The best way to change, maintain or build a culture.

Limitations and contributions

One area of contention over whether the claims made by the 'has' perspective stand up to scrutiny is the issue of whether *strong* cultures are always *good* cultures. Here we could note, for example, the argument that while strong cultures enable stability, coordination and rapid decision making they may also encourage complacency, lack of creativity, inflexibility and **groupthink** (see Chapter 4). So a strong culture might actually harm performance. Indeed, work by Kotter and Heskett (1992) suggests organizations with strong cultures are no more likely to perform well than organizations whose value systems are relatively weak. 'Strong culture' organizations which performed poorly during the US economic boom years of 1977–1988 include Sears, General Motors and Goodyear, whereas some of their 'weak culture' counterparts – such as GlaxoSmithKline and McGraw-Hill – did well. Likewise, Miller (cited in Trice and Beyer, 1993, p. 380) suggests that overly strong cultures create 'paths of deadly momentum . . . [so] productive attention to detail . . . turns into an obsession with minutia; rewarding innovation turns into gratuitous invention; and measured growth becomes unbridled expansion'.

Thinkpoint 5.6

Thinking back to Bob Ayling's comments about BA showing a rather 'macho' face to its public, and the 'dirty tricks' campaign waged by BA against Virgin, how might these episodes suggest that BA's new culture had by the early 1990s begun to demonstrate some of the problems relating to strong cultures discussed above?

Then there is the question of whether there is any real evidence that cultural change programmes guarantee *long-term* organizational success. Some commentators suggest that all we have available are 'brief, anecdotal stories of the dramatic impact of founders, leaders, heroes, in establishing or rescuing their enterprises' (Anthony, 1994, p. 15) – and we could also reflect on 'what happened next' at BA in the light of this argument.

Moreover, the validity and reliability of the texts establishing the culture–excellence link have been heavily criticized. Peters and Waterman, for example, have been accused of failing to focus on key US economic sectors like car manufacturing and financial services, as well as carrying out most of their interviews with senior managers who would be expected to sing the praises of their organizations. The companies they researched were also all high growth and employed large numbers of professional staff – both conditions that could be argued to make management-by-values more feasible, at least in terms of the required investment of resources and the likely reaction of the workforce.

Perhaps most damningly, by 1985 nearly a quarter of the firms surveyed by Peters and Waterman were having real economic difficulties; a point which is taken up by Chapman (2003) in the wryly titled *In Search of Stupidity*. The platform for Chapman's discussion is that it was the high-tech firms in particular in the Peters and Waterman sample that subsequently began to struggle. Chapman claims that these firms (perhaps *because* of their cultures – bearing in mind the argument above about strong cultures and complacency) often fail to learn from past mistakes and therefore continue to repeat avoidable errors. One example is Lotus' misguided 18-month long project to enable Lotus 123 to run on 640kb computers, by the end of which such machines were virtually obsolete.

Relatedly, it has been suggested that the 'has' theorists over-privilege culture as *the* factor that leads to business success. For example, consider this claim, taken from a biography of IBM founder Tom Watson. Here a former colleague is responding cynically to Watson's claim that IBM's success was founded on its corporate philosophy and not its capital investments, its R&D and so on:

> Well, what the hell could he say? He couldn't very well [say] that IBM had the money, recruited the scientists, or was ready to spend half a billion dollars . . . to take over the computer market by making everything in it, including IBM's own machines, obsolete. He couldn't very well say that it didn't make any difference what the company, or the employees, believed if they got eighty percent of the market. *(cited in Parker, 2000, p. 25)*

As we can see, then, it is possible to level several empirical and conceptual critiques at 'has' camp claims about the connection between culture and business excellence. Nonetheless, as Parker (2000, p.p. 12, 20 – emphasis added) suggests, 'these gurus *were* attempting an interesting reformulation of organizations and organizing' in their reinterpretation of the manager as committed champion of the organizational cause, not boring, numbers-obsessed cipher. This is also worth remembering with regard to the BA case study, the airline's more recent problems aside. That is to say, the cultural change effected by Colin Marshall did to some extent at least transform a moribund organization with a very formal and 'people-unfriendly' style of management into an outfit where staff apparently felt more valued, and translated this into better customer service.

Because of its emphasis on the ways in which organizational life can be constructed and reconstructed, moreover, the 'has' narrative reminds us of the fact that it is *people* who make organizational processes happen, not machines or money or information technology. In other words, it is only through human creativity, vision, efforts and interactions that goods are produced, services delivered, profits made, government targets met, budgets adhered to, shareholders satisfied, and so on.

But there are other issues we need to consider when analysing the contribution of the organizational culture orthodoxy. These relate specifically to what we might call its ontology – the assumptions about workplace reality on which its key assertions are based, and the various anthropological, sociological, political and ethical implications of those assertions. It is to these issues that we now turn in considering an alternative reading of organizational culture. Instead of suggesting that 'has' theory perhaps exaggerates the claims that it makes – as we did earlier in this sub-section – this perspective takes critical issue with *the ideas that lie behind* these claims.

The critical perspective

Introduction to the critical perspective, AKA culture is something that an organization 'is'

The broad alternative to understanding culture as something that an organization 'has', again in Smircich's (1983) formulation, is the claim that culture is something that an organization 'is'. This perspective is closer to the original anthropological conceptualization of culture than its mainstream counterpart. Indeed some 'is' theorists argue that 'has' theories have gone too far in their analysis of culture, because 'Most anthropologists would find the idea that leaders create culture preposterous: leaders [according to anthropology] do not create culture, it emerges from the collective social interaction of groups and communities' (Meek, 1988, p. 459).

On a related point, and emphasizing how 'is' theory shies away from the functionalist, technical, managerialism of 'has' theory, Alvesson (2002, p. 25) suggests that 'Advocates of the [is] . . . view of culture are inclined to play down the pragmatic results that can help management increase effectiveness in favour of more general understanding and reflection as the major emphasis of cultural studies.' That is to say, 'is' thinkers are interested in interpreting organizations rather than generating a series of management 'how to's' regarding improvement of the bottom line, as 'has' theorists are inclined to do. The focus of the 'is' perspective, then, is primarily a **practical-hermeneutic** one. In particular, it directs our attention to how coordinated action (without which, as we saw in the introduction to the chapter, organizations would not exist) becomes possible among disparate aggregates of individuals with varying aspirations, views, experiences and so on.

'Is' theorists begin from the claim that culture is *not* a variable – i.e. it is not just one organizational element. Instead they see it as a metaphor for the organization. If culture is something that an organization is, then everything in the organization is in some way cultural, evoking prevailing values, beliefs and norms:

> Seemingly 'objective' things, such as numbers of employees, turnover, physical products, customers, etc. become of interest (almost) only in terms of their cultural meanings. The size of a company may be seen as 'small is beautiful' . . . [or l]imited size may . . . signal exclusiveness and elitism.
> *(Alvesson, 2002, p. 25)*

Alvesson here clarifies how numbers of employees, for example, may be interpreted by 'is' theorists as signifying particular values. In the same way, turnover figures, product range, target market segment/s and so on would all be seen to express something about the relevant organization's culture. 'Is' theorists, then, focus on the symbolic significance of organizational phenomena as a way of understanding them.

The 'is' perspective also sees organizational culture as a *jointly produced* system of **intersubjectivity**. In other words, it develops the aforementioned notion of organizational common sense to examine how shared assumptions emerge and are passed on in day-to-day organizational activity. Here culture is an ongoing product of 'learning the truce' (Mills and Murgatroyd, 1991, p. 62). The principal values in any one workplace come about as the result of a collective accommodation between organizational requirements and individual members' aspirations. Here we see a particular understanding of freedom and identity: the common sense of culture allows workers to come to terms with what is asked of them at work, to arrive at a compromise between their own personal desires and the demands of their employment.

Ashforth and Kreiner (1999), for example, discuss what are usually referred to in the OB literature as **dirty jobs** in an attempt to understand the occupational cultures that grow up around this type of employment. They categorize these jobs as 'physically' dirty – where individuals deal with literal dirt, do dangerous tasks or work in areas that bring them into contact with death (e.g. refuse collectors, deep sea divers or mortuary attendants); 'socially' dirty – necessitating association with stigmatized groups or having to be servile in the job itself (e.g. prison warders and personal maids); and 'morally' dirty – the job is regarded as morally problematic or requires some form of 'cheating' (e.g. prostitution or professional gambling). Those involved in occupations like these, argue Ashforth and Kreiner, therefore work to reconcile their sense of themselves as upright and functional human beings with what they do for a living.

Thinkpoint 5.7

Think of examples where you have engaged in the process of reconciliation – maybe during your studies at university – or have observed others striving to do the same.

One example of this process of reconciliation, to which we have already referred, is Ackroyd and Crowdy's (1990) abattoir workers. Their work is both physically and morally dirty – it involves contact with blood, organs and excreta and centres on killing 'innocent animals' (p. 4). In the face of these exigencies, these men celebrate their own toughness and resilience – stressing, for example, that 'Only one in a thousand has the stomach for this job' (p. 8) – and attributing highest status to those who actually kill the animals. Their pride in what they do is also visible in the fact that they bring their sons to the plant for visits. Moreover, the men rarely shower before leaving the abattoir – indeed some deliberately splash themselves with blood before departing – and only change their overalls and hats when they are absolutely filthy. This culture therefore turns external social values upside down and prizes exactly what it is about the work that others view as negative. As Ackroyd and Crowdy (1990, p. 5) put it, 'the occupational culture of the slaughtermen grows out of the barrel of polluted products they are seen to handle' – it therefore insulates those who participate from wider society's moral condemnation and disgust.

For 'is' theorists, then, *everyone* participates – although, as we shall see, not necessarily as equals – in the ongoing construction of an organization's culture. It is not a matter of values being transmitted by managers and passively accepted by the lower ranks. This is a much more organic, 'socially emergent' view of culture as a product of the ways in which groups of people come to accept the limitations on their freedom or the challenges to their identity that working for a living entails. In short, culture here is understood to be a *coping mechanism* rather than a handy management tool. It involves the collective negotiation of a particular form of organizational reality, which allows workers to accommodate what they do for a living, however demanding or restrictive it might be.

Exercise 5.5

Another example of learning the truce can be seen in the 'dirty job' of prostitution. For example, sex workers rarely allow their punters to kiss them, and will almost always insist on the use of condoms at work when they may not bother in their personal relationships (see, for example, Brewis and Linstead, 2000, Chapter 8). How might selling sex for a living threaten a woman's identity, and how might these coping mechanisms allow her to deal with this threat?

'Is' theory therefore focuses on:

> explor[ing] the phenomenon of organization as subjective experience and . . . investigat[ing] the patterns that make organized action possible . . . When culture is [seen as] a root metaphor, attention shifts from concerns about what do organizations accomplish and how may they accomplish it more efficiently, to how organization is accomplished and what does it mean to be organized? *(Smircich, 1983, p.p. 348, 353)*

As already stated, of course, at least a measure of cultural agreement is necessary in order for organizations not simply to descend into anarchy.

Here we see further evidence that this is a very different approach to the one adopted by the 'has' camp, where a case is made for managers' ability to change, build or maintain culture in order to enhance competitive advantage, improve quality, increase productivity and so on. The 'is' camp, in contrast, understands culture as a means of adjusting to organizational demands, which develops jointly and gradually. Culture here turns on the daily accomplishment of an organizational reality within which members can feel psychologically 'safe' – where their identities are protected and they have come to terms with restrictions on their freedom. Perhaps, then, we should use different terms when referring to 'has' and 'is' readings of culture; 'corporate culture' when we are discussing interpretations based on the possibility of management-led cultural engineering initiatives, and 'organizational culture' for the 'is' claim that culture develops more organically (Linstead and Grafton-Small, 1992).

We now discuss the implications of 'is' theory's claims in more detail, as well as exploring a key debate around power and inequality within this area of the cultural literature.

Key issues and controversies

Because it sees culture as a day-on-day social product, enacted by all the members of the organization, the 'is' concept of 'culture-from-everywhere' emphasizes both the fragility of organizational life and its dynamics. 'Is' theorists attend closely to the ways in which *rank-and-file* members of organizations produce and reproduce systems of values, beliefs and norms – and therefore also amend and adapt them.

In addition, they emphasize 'cultural traffic' – the ways in which cultures shift 'with the flow of meanings and values in and around organizations'. For example, as new recruits join a firm, they may bring different ways of seeing with them, especially given the increased probability in our globalized world that these newcomers originate in another country. So culture here is understood as fluctuating in accordance with changing organizational circumstances (Alvesson, 2002, p.p. 191–192).

Exercise 5.6

BA apparently attempted to accommodate 'cultural traffic' – its growing numbers of non-British staff and customers – through its World Images rebranding exercise. But the initiative lasted only two years. Bearing in mind 'is' theory's suggestion that culture is an organic, collective product, can you suggest why it was so short-lived?

Because of these central precepts, 'is' theory is also much more emphatic than 'has' theory on the multicultural nature of organizations. In other words, it suggests that:

> ideas within a social group are not homogenous but plural and often contested . . . An organization's culture could thus be viewed as a struggle for *hegemony* with competing factors attempting to define the primary purpose of the organization in a way that meets their perceived definitions. *(Parker, 2000, p. 75 – emphasis added)*

'Has' theory does, as we have seen, accept that different cultures may exist in different organizational departments or functions because of the different challenges that they face. However, it tends to confine its analysis to the argument that managers need to devise ways of overcoming the resultant differentiation, whereas for 'is' theory this does not go far enough. For 'is' commentators, the organization represents a site in which there is an ongoing contest between various groups to make their voices heard, to control or have power over the overall direction that is taken, to shape activities in ways that meet their particular desires and aspirations. We will now develop this idea in a little more depth.

First, because of the idea that culture comes from 'everywhere' in an organization, 'is' theory makes the related claim that different sets of values, beliefs and norms (i.e. subcultures) *inevitably* develop at different loci within the organization in response to different situations. In other words, it sees cultural heterogeneity as 'situation normal' – especially given power structures within organizations and the fact that ordinary employees' experience of work may therefore be rather different from managers'. This heterogeneity and the consequent 'struggle for hegemony' often become very visible when workers feel their interests are being ignored or marginalized by management. The two episodes of industrial action at BA in 1997 and 2003, the UK firefighters' strike during the winter of 2002–03, the Association of University Teachers' strike in early 2004 and 24-hour stoppages by London Underground drivers are all good examples. 'Has' theory only rather grudgingly accepts that such heterogeneity *may* exist *despite* managers' best efforts. As Willmott (1993, p. 525) argues, it is 'responsive to the presence of value conflicts within modern (capitalist) organizations' but sees them 'as a sign of cultural weakness that can be corrected'. 'Is' theory, by way of contrast, suggests that organizations are *always* highly internally differentiated in terms of values – that they are almost mosaic-like in this respect.

Secondly, 'is' theory asserts that cultural differences are not just a product of varying experiences *inside* the organization: it adds to these considerations the issue of 'extra-organizational' identity. In other words, for 'is' theory, subcultures do not just spring up among those who participate in specific activities within the organization, but also among those who share things 'outside the factory gates'. These might include membership of a profession (like medicine, accountancy or academia), being male or female, belonging to a particular racial, ethnic or religious group, socio-economic or educational similarities and so on. Such affiliations will further cut across, dilute or undermine any connection employees have with the values, beliefs and norms that management attempt to hegemonically impose.

Thinkpoint 5.8

Think about the students in your year at university. To what extent would you say that they tend to 'split off' into subcultural cliques based on gender, racial, ethnic, religious, class or educational differences? If such 'divisions' are noticeable, how do they manifest themselves?

Moreover, these shared 'external' experiences may well be *reinforced* by internal organizational processes, perhaps creating subcultures that span organizational boundaries. A good example of this are the professional women's networks that bring together women from various organizations to discuss and advise each other on the challenges they face within traditionally masculine workplace hierarchies.[5]

This analysis also suggests further complications in that one person may simultaneously be a member of several organizational subcultures, the values, beliefs and norms of which potentially contradict each other. For example, I am female, a UMIST graduate, a Reader in Management, a lecturer in OB and research methodology, someone who researches the intersections between the body, identity and processes of organizing, the course leader for a specific Master's degree and Caucasian as well as Geordie[6] – all at the same time. This complexity could, moreover, mean that individual employees 'switch' between or emphasize specific cultural allegiances at different times in their working lives – for instance, when they receive a promotion or decide to blow the whistle (see Chapter 14 on the latter issue). It certainly makes the lines of 'Them' and 'Us' much more difficult to draw. In this understanding of organizational multiculturalism, then, 'Individuals are nodes on the [workplace] web, temporarily connected by shared concerns to some but not all the surrounding nodes' (Meyerson and Martin, 1994, p. 124).

So the 'is' version of multiculturalism means that organizational values, beliefs and norms are just as much the source of organizational *dis*agreement as they are of harmony and consensus. As Figure 5.2 indicates, for instance, some groups may buy into the culture that management wishes to impose, fervently and without reservation ('enhancing' subcultures that bolster the management message), others ('orthogonal' subcultures) accept the basic corporate culture but have an independent set of values of their own and still others ('counter' cultures) may be resistant to what management is attempting to instil.

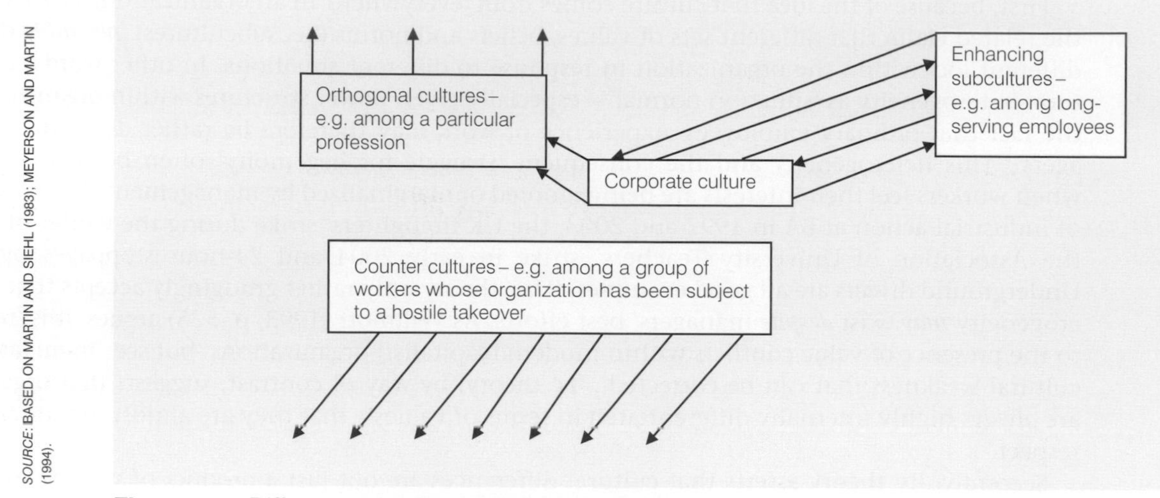

SOURCE: BASED ON MARTIN AND SIEHL (1983); MEYERSON AND MARTIN (1994).

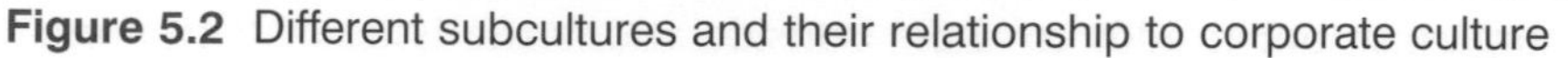

Figure 5.2 Different subcultures and their relationship to corporate culture

Thinkpoint 5.9

Thinking back to the early days of the BA cultural change initiative, how would you classify the former BOAC employees and the former BEA employees using the above framework – are these groups enhancing, orthogonal or counter cultures? Or are the lines not that easy to draw?

The argument here is that, instead of being passive recipients of management hegemony, employees will 'accept, deny, react, reshape, rethink, acquiesce, rebel, conform, and define and refine the[se] demands and their responses' (Kunda, 1992, p. 21) in various ways. This then raises the question of the extent to which it is actually possible for managers to change, maintain or build organizational culture – a capacity, which, as we know, is a central tenet of 'has' theory. 'Is' theory, however, is much more sceptical. Golden (cited in Brown 1998, p. 93) argues, for example, that there are at least four possible reactions to corporate culture as 'sold' by senior management:

- *Unequivocal adherence*. Unquestioning acceptance of management values, likely, as Brown asserts, 'to be the exception rather than the rule', and humorously depicted in the cartoon below.
- *Strained adherence*. Employees have concerns about the ethics or effectiveness of these values, but for the most part 'buy in'.
- *Secret non-adherence*. Workers outwardly comply with management values, usually because management have more power than they do and thus they fear for their jobs. But underneath this workplace 'act' they do not accept these values and will demonstrate this non-acceptance when it is safe to do so. Höpfl's (1993) BA research, for example, highlighted the potential flipside of the friendly greeting we receive when we board an aeroplane. One flight attendant told her that, while the staff are verbally wishing us 'Good morning', in their heads they are saying 'fuck you'. The 'fuck you' preserves some measure of personal identity and individual freedom in the face of corporate demands.

"This is wonderful—pathological loyalty is *exactly* what we're looking for!"

SOURCE: © JIM SIZEMORE/CARTOONSTOCK.COM

Image 5.11

Thinkpoint 5.10

Drawing on your experience of situations (at university or elsewhere) in which you were expected to behave according to particular values – e.g. respect for your seniors or neatness and tidiness – can you think of times when you have demonstrated secret non-adherence? An instance might be to have private, derogatory nicknames for disliked tutors to whom you show deference in public. You could also reflect on the following question: if workers display adherence to corporate values in public, does it matter whether they have actually taken them on board as part of their 'identities' or not?

- *Open non-adherence*. Out-and-out resistance to management values, such as the profound resentment displayed by certain brewery workers in Aktouf's (1996) research. Their dislike of colleagues who conformed to the corporate culture was manifest in insults including 'traitor', 'brownnose', etc. These epithets seem to demonstrate that these workers felt so strongly about their individuality, identity and freedom that they were not prepared to put on a workplace front even for the sake of a quiet life. Here Parker's struggle for hegemony again becomes very visible, as it did in the various forms of industrial action discussed above.

In short, 'has' theory is seen by 'is' theory to take a rather naive view of the extent to which culture can be managed. 'Is' theory sees meanings as contested within organizational settings. It emphasizes the multicultural character of organizations and suggests that different groups within a workplace constantly work to make their voices heard, to persuade others of the legitimacy of their interpretations of the organization. Here culture is the ongoing, dynamic product of contests of power, in which the advantage rests with managers because of their position within the organizational structure and the inequalities which this creates, but whose hegemonic attempts to persuade workers to take particular values on board are likely to be resisted in various ways.

For example, Kunda's (1992) fascinating study of High Technologies Corporation (Tech) suggests that management in this organization remorselessly reinforce their corporate message via manifold CTMs. Tech employees are thereby encouraged to invest in the company in terms of time, effort and identity, indeed to cease to think of themselves and their employer as separate entities. And these very overt forms of cultural control do seem to be successful: most Tech workers put in long hours and enjoy what they do for a living. But they also routinely distance themselves from the organizational ideology, describing it as 'the bullshit that comes from above', for instance (p. 158).

Nonetheless, while this may seem to undermine the Tech ethos, it actually serves as a safety valve through which employees can express frustration with management attempts at manipulation, thus forestalling any more damaging forms of dissent (such as industrial action). Workers also know that to *really* get on at Tech they must 'buy in' – mere behavioural compliance is not enough for managers who want to possess their hearts and souls, not just their time. Resistance to management 'bullshit' is therefore routinely tempered by the greater power that managers possess to shape and control staff's working lives.

In developing the idea of inequality in particular, moreover, some 'is' theorists pose a rather different set of questions. Rather than critiquing 'has' theory's naiveté for ignoring or downplaying organizational multiculturalism, contested meanings and worker dissent, they focus on what they see as its problematic aspirations. Willmott (1993), for example, claims that cultural management is similar in its objectives to the activities of the totalitarian[7] Oceania government in George Orwell's famous novel *1984*, because they both operate on the basis of what Orwell calls 'doublethink'. Cultural management initiatives, Willmott suggests, effectively promise autonomy for the individual employee if they submit to the company ideology. Such interventions therefore celebrate an idea (autonomy) while simultaneously rejecting it (through requiring submission). In other words, says Willmott, the 'has' gurus are recommending doublethink as a management tool, advocating that managers create a situation in which employees *believe* that they determine their corporate existence yet have no real freedom to make choices for themselves. So the basic 'has' theory message to managers is reinterpreted by this strand of 'is' thinking as follows:

> A stupid despot may constrain his slaves with iron chains; but a true politician [/ manager] binds them even more strongly by the chain of their own ideas; it is at the stable point of reason that he secures the end of the chain; this link is all the stronger in that we do not know of what it is made and we believe it to be our own work. *(Servan, cited in Foucault, 1977, p. 35)*

What this quote means is that overt forms of management control or open displays of management power – use of rules, reward and punishment, direct supervision and so on – are much more obtrusive and likely to be resisted than the subtle manipulation of employee values, especially where workers really do buy into what is being 'sold' to them. Authors like Willmott see this as the central tenet of 'has' theory. In this version of 'is' thinking, then, the emphasis is less on organizations as pluralist arenas in which a cacophony of different cultural voices can be heard, and more on the ways in which managers attempt to exercise their superior power to silence these voices, and impose their own hegemony. Our attention is thus drawn to the ways in which management values – such as the idea that 'the customer is always right' – might conceivably assume an organizational normality that is difficult to question. Instead, they may simply become what the organization and its members 'are all about'; just 'the culture'. 'Is' theory here becomes more explicitly political, more 'emancipatory', more to do with identifying the organizational forces that 'prevent [workers] from acting in accordance with their free choices' (Alvesson, 2002, p. 8).

Exercise 5.7

'**A bad manager says**
I'm sorry. You'll have to work all the hours that God sends.

A good manager says
I'm proud. This is a 24/7 organisation.'
(Beaton, 2001, p. 17)

SOURCE: © JIM SIZEMORE/CARTOONSTOCK.COM

"You do as you're told, we pay as we please. You work like a slave, we punish at random. That, in a nutshell, is our corporate culture."

Image 5.12

Why might this extract from Beaton (2001) be considered an 'emancipatory' 'is' theory joke about organizational culture? Is the manager in the cartoon a 'good' manager or a 'bad' manager in this respect?

We can reconsider the apparent 'success' stories told by 'has' theory in this light – like the one about the Honda worker who adjusts all the windscreen wipers on the Hondas he passes on his way home because he wants them to look perfect, or the Procter and Gamble employee who bought an entire range of P&G products in his local supermarket because the labels were wrongly positioned.[8] Colin Marshall's comments about the need to 'design' BA staff so that they give good customer service just as the organization designs seats, lounges and inflight entertainment are also relevant here. Perhaps these examples now begin to seem just a little sinister, a touch more like organizational cloning. Perhaps Honda, P&G and BA are examples of what Coser (1974) calls the **greedy institution**, demanding unswerving loyalty and enormous amounts of employee effort, such that its members have little time or energy for anything outside work, given the strength of the bond with their employer. Perhaps strong cultures such as these are apt to produce Whyte's (1957) **organization man** (/woman); employees who put what the corporation demands before their own needs, maybe without realizing that this is what they are doing. And then there is Kanter's (1983, p. 203) claim that strong corporate cultures offer workers 'a high' akin to that derived from alcohol or drugs – perhaps they are just as addictive as these substances, with equally problematic results? Here in fact the management of culture begins to look very much like a perpetuation of organizational inequalities and an abuse of management power.

Relatedly, we can also consider what 'is' theory would tend to identify as a gulf between the values senior management claim to promote in their public relations literature, annual reports, recruitment brochures and so on, and what it is actually like to work in that organization – what kind of values really shape organizational behaviour. A real-life example is the fact that most large organizations – and many smaller ones – now claim to be equal opportunities employers. They say they recruit, reward and promote all employees on the basis of merit and not ascribed characteristics like gender or race. But there are still marked inequalities between, for example, men and women in terms of their organizational experiences. These include the fact that full-time women workers in Britain are paid only 81 per cent of what their male counterparts earn (Equal Opportunities Commission, 2003, p. 11), and findings of this kind are only really explicable if we accept that sexism is still at large in the vast majority of workplaces.

Exercise 5.8

Following the launch of BA's 'Putting People First Again' initiative in 1999, one commentator wrote: 'Admirable though this may be, it does rather beg the question of where BA has been putting people recently' (*The Times*, 1999, p. 23). We know that the impetus behind this training intervention and its 1980s predecessor was to make staff feel good about themselves so they would also feel good about their dealings with customers. But then there are the various cost-cutting and redundancy exercises that have been characteristic of BA management practice since 1981, and which *The Times* journalist is presumably alluding to above. What might all of this suggest about what BA management claim regarding the organization's culture versus what it is actually like to work there?

In sum, then, the 'is' perspective is not functionalist or technical, but rather critical in the sense of refusing to accept things at their face value and appreciating the role of power and inequality in establishing organizational cultures. These writers emphasize that organizational values, beliefs and norms are both multiple and contested, that workplaces represent environments where there is an ongoing struggle for hegemony. However, an equally strong motif within the 'is' camp is that the management of culture can represent a problematic attempt by the senior members of the organization to clamp down on this multiplicity, to impose ways of thinking and feeling – to, in effect, brainwash employees into accepting the official organizational 'line'. So, while 'is' analysts generally seek to adopt a practical-hermeneutic stance on organizational culture because their key interest is to create meaningful knowledge about our working lives, as opposed to generating prescriptions about how to enhance the corporate bottom line, some as we have seen are also avowedly emancipatory. This later emphasis is even more at odds with the managerialist focus of 'has' theory because it views management activities as potentially oppressive.

In order to illustrate some of the issues discussed above in more depth, the chapter now considers two key empirical studies within 'is' theory. In contrast to those quoted for the 'has' camp, and perhaps reflecting different intellectual traditions in the two countries, these are both by British authors. They are Collinson's (1988) 'Engineering humour' and Ackroyd and Crowdy's (1990) 'Can culture be managed?'. These studies have been chosen because of their impact on the field of OB, and in particular their alternative take on some of the claims made by 'has' theory. Both studies, then, stress the idea of culture emerging as a coping mechanism, as well as suggesting that the specific cultures discussed are effectively counter cultures, resistant as they are to management ideology and precepts. Interestingly, however, Collinson and Ackroyd and Crowdy also go on to suggest that, despite their counter cultural form, neither generated unproblematically emancipatory consequences.

Important empirical studies

Collinson's (1988) study was set in the components division of a lorry-making factory in north-west England, where 250 men were employed. It examined humour in this context, and suggests that the various ways in which the men joked with each other 'reflected and reinforced the central values and practices of these male manual workers and contained elements of resistance and control, creativity and destructiveness' (p. 184). Examples included:

- Nicknames like 'Electric Lips', who couldn't keep a secret.
- Initiation rites – e.g. being sent to another colleague for 'a long stand'. The initiate would then be asked, after standing waiting for some time, 'Is that long enough?' (p. 189).
- Jokes at each other's or the management's expense, such as one colleague sending a rate-fixer (who set the payment rates for the men's work) to examine another rate-fixer's job, the implication being that he was not working hard enough.

The men's humour was generally unforgiving, macho, highly sexual and peppered with curses. Collinson suggests that it was a product of what we referred to earlier as 'learning the truce'. These men did repetitive, mundane work and also worked the longest hours in the company, in insecure jobs with very poor terms and conditions. This employment situation sent a clear message that they were both disposable and of little value. In the face of this challenge to their masculine pride, they established a culture that preserved their identities. The men's humour emphasized that, while they could laugh at themselves, they were also different from the managers and the white-collar workers, the 'twats and nancy boys' who didn't have the freedom to joke around (p. 186).

'Having a laugh' also helped them to get through the dull working day, plus it was a means of achieving group acceptance. Being able to withstand humiliation by one's colleagues as well as meting it out (i.e. being a 'real man') was a passport to becoming 'one of the gang'. But jokes were also directed at those who were seen as skiving (e.g. the rate-fixer gag above), because part of the men's wages was calculated using a collective bonus system. As Collinson points out, then, working in what appeared to be a creative culture of resistant shop floor humour was actually an edgy, competitive experience, which allowed no real basis for a sense of belonging. This is illustrated by a vote in 1983 where workers accepted a lump-sum redundancy payout with no resistance following the announcement of the closure of the components plant.

Recap

Collinson's key argument is that culture in this environment had evolved to allow the male shop floor employees to deal with the demands of their working lives, but that the humour involved did not really produce a cohesive or supportive community of co-workers or any basis for collective resistance to an oppressive regime in which these workers effectively colluded.

Like Collinson, and as we already know, Ackroyd and Crowdy (1990) discuss the culture in an English abattoir as a product of the particular demands of the occupation of slaughterman. The work here, like that in the lorry-making factory, is monotonous and partly remunerated using team-based bonuses. It is also dirty in moral and physical terms. Equally, the prevailing values are similar in some ways to those in the components division. The men emphasized hard and fast work, often not taking scheduled breaks, and taking pride in completing tasks in the shortest time possible.

Moreover, the slaughtermen's culture was macho and aggressive: every man had to measure up in terms of output as well as being able to withstand and/or participate in certain production line rituals. These included:

- 'Harassments' and 'degradations', where the men might speed up their own efforts such that work piled up at the stations of slower colleagues, or throw entrails at 'inadequate' workers.

- 'Demonstrations', where individual workers expressed boredom in acts such as spraying excreta from an animal's intestine and yelling 'It's raining' – identified here as a manifestation of that worker's individual toughness (p. 7).
- 'Set pieces', which were 'targeted', but 'also statements of [personal] effectiveness' (p. 7). These necessitated groups of workers cooperating to, for example, fill the boots of another with blood, having judged its temperature so that the unfortunate victim would not notice until it was too late.

Ackroyd and Crowdy's study, like Collinson's, is very evocative of the uncompromising atmosphere in the slaughterhouse, of the desire to show others up which lies beneath what might look like jolly workplace japes. They also emphasize though that there was little resistance from the lower status workers (usually the targets) to such 'japes'. But perhaps their central point is to question 'the extent to which a culture is something a management can create or control' (p. 4). Indeed they argue that the slaughtermen's culture, despite its contravention of health and safety regulations and formal abattoir hierarchies, actually suits management very well because the work gets done and there is no need for direct supervision.

Recap

Ackroyd and Crowdy's key argument is that this organizational culture developed organically to allow the abattoir workers to accommodate the exigencies of their employment, and that what resulted was highly competitive and highly macho. However, they also suggest that management had no need to intervene because the prevailing values among these men also guaranteed that they worked extremely hard.

Recap

Contributors to the 'is' perspective agree that culture:

- Is a metaphor for the organization – every organizational phenomenon says something about the prevailing values, beliefs and norms in that workplace.
- Is jointly produced by everyone in the organization, representing a means of coping with the demands of members' working lives.
- Is multiple and fragmented in complex and conflicting ways – different subcultures inevitably emerge in different organizational loci because of varying external and internal influences.
- Can therefore be very difficult to manage.

They disagree, however, on the extent to which managers are able to impose a culture on their employees – some see cultural management as tantamount to brainwashing, others suggest that groups of employees will often resist management attempts to manipulate them.

Conclusion

In drawing the chapter to a close, it seems plausible to conclude that some organizational values will be shaped by management, and taken on board in different ways by different member sub-groups, and others will be a product of collective or subcultural accommodation to the slings and arrows of organizational life. Moreover, although managers tend to act as what Hines (1988, p. 255) calls 'Official Communicators of [Cultural] Reality' ('has' theory), this does not mean that other groups within the organization do not try to influence the ways in which the organization operates ('is' theory).

We should take on board what 'has' theory says because it offers us another explanation of organizational success and failure, which we can add to more obvious factors such as technological innovation, high-quality products and market dominance. However, 'is' theory asks us to acknowledge that workers are not simply embedded in a culture where they passively accept what management feeds them. Even senior managers do not have this much power, and those further down the organization have even less in terms of their overall visibility, control over resources, numbers of people they interact with and so on – however much it may appeal to their vanity to believe the contrary.

Indeed, the more reflective analysis offered by the 'is' perspective, which seeks to understand how it is that people in organizations actually come together to work in more or less coordinated ways, is probably a precondition of any effective cultural initiative by management, as would be recommended by 'has' theorists. That said, the difficulty for many managers is that 'is' views are more complex, less accessible and do not assume the legitimacy of managerial values. 'Is' thinking is thus more likely to threaten managerial identity than to enhance and inflate it.

Finally, Smircich's (1983, p. 355) claim that thinking about organizational culture may encourage us 'not to celebrate organization as a value, but to question the ends it serves' also reminds us that organizations and management as we know them today are in themselves cultural (and relatively recent) phenomena. In other words, they are not natural, historical human activities. With this in mind, we can also think about the outcomes of organizations and management – which include space travel, university education (hurrah!) and the cure for smallpox, but also nuclear arms, developing world sweatshops and environmental destruction – and consider possible alternatives. As Alvesson (2002, p. 2) suggests, then:

> Insights and reflections [into/on organizational culture] may be useful in [relation] . . . to getting people to do the 'right' things in terms of effectiveness, but also for promoting more autonomous standpoints in relationship to dominant ideologies, myths, fashions, etc. To encourage and facilitate the thinking through of various aspects of values, beliefs and assumptions in industry, occupations and organizations seem to me to be a worthwhile task.

Discussion questions

1. What does it mean to say that culture brings an organization 'to life'?
2. Can you identify the four key differences between the 'has' perspective and the 'is' perspective on organizational culture?
3. What are some of the contingencies that might help managers to identify the 'right' culture for their organization?
4. Is a strong organizational culture always a good thing in terms of achieving business excellence? What other problems might such a culture create?
5. To what extent do you think it is possible to manage organizational culture?

Further reading

Important empirical studies

Ackroyd, S. and Crowdy, P. (1990) 'Can culture be managed? Working with raw material: The case of the English slaughtermen', *Personnel Review* 19(5):3–13.

Collinson, D. L. (1988) ' "Engineering humour" : Masculinity, joking and conflict in shopfloor relations', *Organization Studies* 9(2):181–199.

Deal, T. E. and Kennedy, A. A. (1988) *Corporate Cultures: The Rites and Rituals of Corporate Life*, Harmondsworth: Penguin.

Peters, T. J. and Waterman, R. H., Jr. (1982) *In Search of Excellence: Lessons From America's Best-Run Companies*, New York: Harper and Row.

Reading highlights

All the texts below represent good overviews of the organizational culture literature. You may find some more challenging than others.

Alvesson, M. (2002) *Understanding Organizational Culture*, London: Sage.

Anthony, P. D. (1994) *Managing Culture*, Milton Keynes: Open University Press.

Brown, A. D. (1998) *Organizational Culture*, second edition, London: Financial Times Pitman Publishing.

Linstead, S. (2004) 'Managing culture', in S. Linstead, L. Fulop and S. Lilley (eds.) *Management and Organization: A Critical Text*, Basingstoke and New York: Macmillan, p.p. 93–122.

Parker, M. (2000) *Organizational Culture and Identity: Unity and Division at Work*, London: Sage.

Smircich, L. (1983) 'Concepts of culture and organizational analysis', *Administrative Science Quarterly* 28(3):339–358.

References

Ackroyd, S. and Crowdy, P. (1990) 'Can culture be managed? Working with raw material: The case of the English slaughtermen', *Personnel Review* 19(5):3–13.

Aktouf, O. (1996) 'Competence, symbolic activity and promotability', in S. Linstead, R. Grafton-Small and P. Jeffcutt (eds.) *Understanding Management*, London: Sage.

Alvesson, M. (2002) *Understanding Organizational Culture*, London: Sage.

Anthony, P. D. (1994) *Managing Culture*, Milton Keynes: Open University Press.

Ashforth, B. E. and Kreiner, G. E. (1999) ' "How can you do it?": Dirty work and the challenge of constructing a positive identity', *Academy of Management Review* 24(3):413–434.

Barsoux, J-L. and Manzoni, J-F. (2002) 'Flying into a storm: British Airways (1996–2000)', INSEAD, Fontainebleau, France (case number 02/2002–4906).

BBC News Online (1999a) 'Business: The company file – Turbulent times at British Airways', 9 February. Online. Available at http://news.bbc.co.uk (accessed 5 July 2004).

BBC News Online (1999b) 'Business: The company file – Airline passengers Go against BA', 9 March. Online. Available at http://news.bbc.co.uk (accessed 5 July 2004).

BBC News Online (1999c) 'Business: The company file – British Airways hits more turbulence', 25 May. Online. Available at http://news.bbc.co.uk (accessed 5 July 2004).

BBC News Online (1999d) 'Business: BA to fly the flag again', 6 June. Online. Available at http://news.bbc.co.uk (accessed 5 July 2004).

Beaton, A. (2001) *The Little Book of Management Bollocks*, London: Pocket Books/Simon and Schuster.

Bjerke, B. (1999) *Business Leadership and Culture: National Management Styles in the Global Economy*, Cheltenham: Edward Elgar.

Brewis, J. and Linstead, S. (2000) *Sex, Work and Sex Work: Eroticizing Organization*, London: Routledge.

Brown, A. D. (1998) *Organizational Culture*, second edition, London: Financial Times Pitman Publishing.

Business Life (1997) 'The way ahead', July/August, p.p. 44–47.

Chapman, M. R. (2003) *In Search of Stupidity: Over 20 Years of High-Tech Marketing Disasters*, Berkeley, CA: Apress.

Clark, A. (2004) 'Heathrow turned into makeshift camp site as troubled BA hits fresh turbulence', *The Guardian*, 25 August. Online. Available at: http://www.guardian.co.uk (accessed 15 November 2004).

Collinson, D. L. (1988) ' "Engineering humour" ': Masculinity, joking and conflict in shopfloor relations', *Organization Studies* 9(2):181–199.

Corbett, J. M. (1994) *Critical Cases in Organizational Behaviour*, London: Macmillan.

Coser, L. A. (1974) *Greedy Institutions: Patterns of Undivided Commitment*, New York: Free Press.

Dalton, A. (2003) 'Peace deal in BA row over swipe cards', *The Scotsman*, 31 July. Online. Available at: http://news.scotsman.com (accessed 5 July 2004).

Daymon, C. (2000) 'Leadership and emerging cultural patterns in a new television station', *Studies in Cultures, Organizations and Societies* 6(2):169–195.

Deal, T. E. and Kennedy, A. A. (1988) *Corporate Cultures: The Rites and Rituals of Corporate Life*, Harmondsworth: Penguin.

Equal Opportunities Commission (2003) *Facts about Women and Men in Great Britain 2003*, January. Online. Available at: http://www.eoc.org.uk/cseng/research/factsgreatbritain2003.pdf (accessed 18 December 2003).

Foucault, M. (1977) *Discipline and Punish: The Birth of the Prison*, A. Sheridan (trans.), London: Allen Lane.

Handy, C. (1993) *Understanding Organizations: Managing Differentiation and Integration*, New York: Oxford University Press.

Harrison, R. (1972) 'Understanding your organization's character', *Harvard Business Review*, 50 (May–June):119–128.

Haurant, S. (2004) 'Drug testing at work "to increase" ', *The Guardian*, 28 June. Online. Available at: http://www.guardian.co.uk (accessed 5 July 2004).

Hines, R. (1988) 'Financial accounting: In communicating reality, we construct reality', *Accounting, Organizations and Society* 13(3):251–261.

Hofstede, G. (2001) *Culture's Consequences: Comparing Values, Behaviors, Institutions, and Organizations Across Nations*, Thousand Oaks, CA: Sage.

Höpfl, H. J. (1993) 'British carriers', in D. Gowler, K. Legge and C. Clegg (eds.) *Cases in Organizational Behaviour*, London: Paul Chapman, p.p. 117–125.

Innes, J. (2004) 'BA to test all staff for drug and drink use on duty', *The Scotsman*, 25 June. Online. Available at: http://news.scotsman.com (accessed 5 July 2004).

Jackson, N. and Carter, P. (2000) *Rethinking Organisational Behaviour*, Harlow, Essex: Financial Times Prentice Hall.

Kanter, R. M. (1983) *The Change Masters*, New York: Simon and Schuster.

Kotter, J. P. and Heskett, J. L. (1992) *Corporate Culture and Performance*, New York: Free Press.

Kunda, G. (1992) *Engineering Culture: Control and Commitment in a High-Tech Corporation*, Philadelphia: Temple University Press.

Legge, K. (1994) 'Managing culture: Fact or fiction?', in K. Sisson (ed.) *Personnel Management*, Oxford: Blackwell, p.p. 397–433.

Linstead, S. (2004) 'Managing culture', in S. Linstead, L. Fulop and S. Lilley (eds.) *Management and Organization: A Critical Text*, Basingstoke and New York: Macmillan, p.p. 93–122.

Linstead, S. A. and Grafton-Small, R. (1992) 'On reading organizational culture', *Organization Studies* 13(3):331–355.

Martin, J. and Siehl, C. (1983) 'Organizational culture and counterculture: An uneasy symbiosis', *Organizational Dynamics* Autumn:52–63.

Meek, V. L. (1988) 'Organizational culture: Origins and weaknesses', *Organization Studies* 9(4):453–473.

Meyerson, D. and Martin, J. (1994) 'Cultural change: An integration of three different views', in H. Tsoukas (ed.) *New Thinking in Organizational Behaviour: From Social Engineering to Reflective Action*, Oxford: Butterworth-Heinemann, p.p. 108–132.

Mills, A. and Murgatroyd, S. (1991) *Organizational Rules: A Framework for Understanding Organizational Interaction*, Milton Keynes: Open University Press.

Morgan, G. (1997) *Images of Organization*, second edition, Thousand Oaks, CA: Sage.

Morgan, O. (2003) 'Besieged BA left with strike baggage', *The Observer*, 27 July. Online. Available at: http://guardian.co.uk/Observer (accessed 5 July 2004).

Ouchi, W. G. (1981) *Theory Z: How American Business Can Meet the Japanese Challenge*, Reading, MA: Addison Wesley.

Parker, M. (2000) *Organizational Culture and Identity: Unity and Division at Work*, London: Sage.

Pascale, R. T. and Athos, A. G. (1981) *The Art of Japanese Management: Applications for American Executives*, New York: Warner Books.

Peters, T. J. and Waterman, R. H., Jr. (1982) *In Search of Excellence: Lessons From America's Best-Run Companies*, New York: Harper and Row.

Schein, E. (1992) *Organizational Culture and Leadership*, second edition, San Francisco: Jossey Bass.

Smircich, L. (1983) 'Concepts of culture and organizational analysis', *Administrative Science Quarterly* 28(3):339–358.

Tayeb, M. H. (1988) *Organizations and National Culture: A Comparative Analysis*, London: Sage.

The Times (1999) 'Not such a bad air day for Ayling', 10 February, p. 23.

Thompson, P. and McHugh, D. (2002) *Work Organisations: A Critical Introduction*, third edition, Basingstoke: Macmillan.

Trice, H. M. and Beyer, J. M. (1993) *The Cultures of Work Organizations*, Upper Saddle River, NJ: Prentice Hall.

Vedpuriswar, A. V. with Kamachandran, U. (2003) 'British Airways: Leadership and change', ICFAI Knowledge Center, Hyderabad, India (European Case Clearing House Collection, case number 403-044-1).

Whyte, W. H. (1957) *The Organization Man*, London: Jonathan Cape.

Willmott, H. (1993) 'Strength is ignorance, slavery is freedom: Managing culture in modern organizations', *Journal of Management Studies* 30(2):515–552.

Wilson, F. M. (2004) *Organizational Behaviour and Work: A Critical Introduction*, second edition, Oxford: Oxford University Press.

Wray, R. (2004) 'BA begins chaos inquiry', *The Guardian*, 30 August. Online. Available at: http://www.guardian.co.uk (accessed 15 November 2004).

Notes

1 Exercise 9.1, when you identified ways in which the staff at your university attempt to convey their 'philosophy', teach newcomers the 'rules of the game' and so on, would have identified some of the CTMs in use in this organization.

2 The management consultancy that Peters and Waterman – and indeed Deal and Kennedy – worked for at one time.

3 Management apparently threatened anyone planning to strike with removal of their staff perks, a block on promotion, dismissal or even being sued for damages.

4 These planes were subsequently phased out completely.

5 See for example the Business and Professional Woman UK website at http://www.bpwuk.org.uk/.

6 In other words I hail from the north-east of England.

7 Controlling all aspects of its citizens' lives and quickly and mercilessly suppressing any resistance.

8 He was, the story runs, reimbursed at a later date.

PART III
Emergent Issues

Part III provides a review of wider, emergent issues that are of contemporary significance. The global economy is examined within the context of the strategic plans of corporate managers who increasingly have to take some, if rather a limited, responsibility for the consequences of their activities for sustained ecological and environmental stability. The characteristics of new forms of organization, the nature of regulation and the relevance of ethics are examined from mainstream and critical perspectives.

6 Ethics at Work

Edward Wray-Bliss

Key concepts and learning objectives

By the end of this chapter you should understand:

- The core assumptions of mainstream writers on business ethics, and be aware of how these assumptions limit the ethical questions that mainstream writers have been able to ask of business.
- The connections between mainstream academic writing on business ethics and contemporary organization's socially responsible image.
- That there is a wealth of other, more critical approaches to ethics that enable us to question the appropriateness of this socially responsible image.
- How some of these critical approaches enable us to undertake a deeper examination of the values underpinning modern organizations.

Aims of the chapter

This chapter will:

- Examine the relationship between ethical values and organizational behaviour.
- Explore some of the key ideas and developments that have introduced ethics into the heart of the modern organization.
- Examine some key mainstream studies of business ethics.
- Explore some of the key ideas that mark the critical challenge to mainstream views of business ethics.
- Examine some key critical studies of ethics in organizations.
- Explore the linkages between ethics and the core concept of freedom, in order to better understand the issue of ethical values at work.

Overview and key points

Behaviour perpetrated within and on behalf of organizations affects all of us, everyday. Thankfully, much of the time we experience positive effects. So for instance, we buy products made within organizations. We drink water and eat food processed by organizations. We are educated and employed in organizations. However, organizational behaviour is not always so benign. We are also ripped off by organizations. Our environment is polluted by organizations. Many people are exploited or abused, harmed or even killed as a result of organizational behaviour. Much of this 'bad' organizational behaviour is regulated by the law. However, the law is often a very blunt tool. It can be limited in its reach. It is not always effectively enforced. It may be circumvented by the unscrupulous and the clever. It can even be blind to some seriously damaging events. There is, in short, potentially a large gap between how we may want organizations to 'behave' and how the law ensures that they behave. As a result of this, society is increasingly asking management to make sure that their organizations not only refrain from breaking the law but also, and this is potentially much more radical and far reaching though also less clearly defined, to ensure that organizational members behave *ethically*.

This chapter will examine this important emerging way of thinking about organizational behaviour. In the first section we explore the work of theorists in the academic field of business ethics. We examine how such writers have attempted to integrate the apparently quite different arenas of 'ethics' and 'business'. We also explore how the managers of business organizations have come to appreciate how important it is for their organization to now be seen to behave ethically, or, in the new ethical language of business, to demonstrate corporate social responsibility.

In the second section we take a more critical look at these recent developments in both the study and practice of 'ethics' in business. We re-examine the core assumptions of the business ethics/corporate social responsibility fields and highlight how these are themselves ethically questionable. As part of this we scrutinize the mainstream assumptions that organizations are or can be 'responsible'; the desirability of employees' subordination to managerial control; and the reduction of 'ethics' to the greater goal of 'profits'. By exploring the theories of critical writers and a number of compelling critical case studies, we see how critical approaches to the subject can help to reclaim ethics as a language that enables us to examine the values underpinning contemporary organizational behaviour.

Mainstream approach to values at work: Corporate social responsibility and business ethics

Introduction

The modern engagement with 'ethics at work' is conventionally thought to have started in the United Kingdom and the United States in the 1980s. The 1980s were shaped by neo-conservative governments that pushed an aggressively pro-business, 'freemarket' agenda. The agenda centred upon **deregulation of markets**, reducing the legal obligations upon business, and an ideology of self-management and self-reliance for both individuals and corporations. Crucially, for our account of the emergence of the modern engagement with ethics at work, this decade strongly promoted the idea and practice that business leaders should voluntarily *self-regulate*. The idea was that business leaders should be left alone to control their businesses rather than be more tightly regulated by the state or federal/national government. This was an ideology that the business community warmly welcomed then, and still jealously guards today.

Public faith in the effectiveness of business self-regulation was shaken, however, by a series of very public business scandals, disasters and frauds. People began to question the negative effects of business practice. Some even began to question the effectiveness of business self-regulation more generally. Of course, such scandals had occurred in the past, but in the 1980s more people (as a result of such things as the growth in small-scale share ownership) were directly affected by them, and social movements critical of business were better supported and had gained a greater visibility.

To regain public trust and ward off calls for more state regulation of business, the business community needed to reassure the public and policy makers that it was capable of taking responsibility for the potentially negative effects of its practices. This reassurance took the form of 'ethics'. The business community began to publicly present itself as concerned with the ethics of its actions and its effects upon the wider society. By drawing upon a discourse of 'ethics', business leaders could seek to reassure that they would take responsibility for their own actions. Business would be its own conscience if you like, and did not therefore need further governmental regulation. This modern concern by business leaders with issues of 'ethics' is generally given the shorthand title **corporate social responsibility** (CSR).

CSR is the term that has come to stand for the practices and policies undertaken by the business community to promote the idea that they are concerned with more than just profit at any cost. CSR practices can include:

- Appointing managers or directors with responsibility for CSR.
- Developing and publicizing ethical statements, policies or codes of practice.
- Joining environmental or other public groups or forums.
- Publicizing a track record of good corporate governance.
- Making well-publicized donations of money, time or resources to charities and other 'good causes'.
- Linking the business brand, through sponsorship, marketing, etc., with 'good' images such as ending child poverty, protecting the environment or inner city regeneration.

So widespread has the CSR movement now become that it is rare to find a large company these days that does not promote itself as 'socially responsible' (see Table 6.1).

However, just because business leaders now promote their organizations as 'socially responsible' does not mean that such claims are legitimate. One way the corporate world finds legitimacy for its claim to be socially responsible is through an association with the rapidly growing academic field of study called **business ethics**.

Table 6I Examples of corporate social responsibility practices

Company	Practices
	• Shell sustainable development 'We remain convinced that engaging with stakeholders and integrating social and environmental considerations better throughout the lifetime of our projects makes us a more responsive, competitive and profitable company, in the long and short term.' (www.shell.com)
Ford Motor Company	• Ford of Britain Charitable Trust • Environmental policies 'As the number of motor vehicles around the world increases, so do environmental concerns. However, we have always aimed to be a model for the industry in this area. So we're working to reduce the environmental impact of our products, while providing the utility, performance and affordability customers demand. We want it to be easy for people to say, "I'm an environmentalist and a car enthusiast." '(www.ford.co.uk courtesy of Ford Motor Company)
Nike	• Charitable donations • Code of conduct for subcontracted labour 'Nike's Corporate Responsibility mission is to be an innovative and inspirational corporate citizen in a world where our company participates. We seek to protect and enhance the Nike brand through responsible business practices that contribute to profitable and sustainable growth.' (www.nike.com)

SOURCE: AL SHELL UK LOGO COURTESY OF SHELL BRANDS INTERNATIONAL, BL FORD LOGO COURTESY OF FORD

'Business ethics' may be understood as the academic study and promotion of corporate social responsibility. Business ethics explores the ethical legitimations for, and effects of, a wide range of business practices. These academic arguments are then widely disseminated to students and managers through, for example, business ethics modules on MBA and other university management courses, through the large market for business ethics textbooks, and through a sizeable and constantly growing volume of academic journals, conferences and symposia on business ethics and CSR.

The field of business ethics is, as a result, broad and diverse and can therefore seem difficult to get an overall sense of. Despite this variety and volume, however, it is possible to discern a common approach in most mainstream business ethics work, consisting of:

- *A pro-business agenda.* Business ethics critiques particular business practices, but does not question the ethics of business more generally.
- *A free market agenda.* Business ethics endorses voluntary self-regulation of businesses rather than for instance control from outside (e.g. state regulation) as the way to ensure ethical practices.
- *A belief in the compatibility of 'profits' and 'ethics'.* Business ethics sees 'good ethics' as synonymous with 'good business'.

Recap question

- Summarize what 'corporate social responsibility' and 'business ethics' are.

CASE STUDY 6.1 Telebank PLC: A famous ethical organization[1]

Telebank PLC is a successful medium-sized UK financial institution employing around 4000 staff. These facts hardly make Telebank interesting. What does make it interesting is that Telebank was publicly heralded throughout the 1990s as perhaps the best example of a successful 'ethical business', a business that seemed to clearly, demonstrate that 'good ethics' and 'good business' could be synonymous. This case study, adapted from Wray-Bliss (1998) and

(2001), charts Telebank's rise to this moral and economic high ground.

In the United Kingdom prior to the 1980s financial service organizations were prevented from engaging in cross-sector competition. The market for financial service products that the 'big four' banks (Barclays, Lloyds, National Westminster and Midland) along with smaller banks like Telebank were involved in was protected by law, with many other financial service providers such as building societies prevented from supplying the banks' core products. Enjoying the benefits of a stable, protected and growing market, the big four had entered into an unofficial agreement not to undercut each other's products and services, thereby keeping their profits inflated. As a result, relatively small institutions like Telebank could carve out a profitable niche by offering service innovations that the 'big four' were reluctant to follow, and other financial service institutions such as building societies were legally prevented from providing.

In the 1980s, however, the UK conservative government radically changed the financial services market. The government embarked upon a programme of deregulating markets and freeing-up business and capital from historical constraints. As part of this programme historical restrictions on both banks and other financial service providers were lifted (e.g. The Building Societies Act 1986). The 'big four' banks now faced stiffer competition as other financial institutions could enter into their markets and undercut their products. The big four responded by providing their own new products and services, thereby competing more keenly both against each other and against smaller companies like Telebank whose profitable 'innovative' niche was suddenly under threat. By 1990 Telebank was making a loss of around £15 million.

Telebank had to do something, and fast. Its strategy was two-fold. First, like many of the other banks, it cut costs. It rapidly shed over 1000 employees, closed branches, dramatically cut staff numbers in its branches (typically from 40 to eight), and rerouted most of its contact with customers from over-the-counter face-to-face to telephone banking via remote telephone **call-centres**. Secondly, the management of Telebank decided to reinvent the bank as an 'ethical' corporation. In particular they represented Telebank as the bank that gave its customers the choice to invest their money ethically. Telebank management researched its customers' opinions on ethical matters, and then formulated and widely publicized a 12-point ethical policy, detailing whom the bank will and will not do business with. The policy prohibited the bank from investing its customers' money in, or indeed having business customers who are involved in, for example, the tobacco trade, the testing of cosmetics on animals or operating in countries with oppressive regimes. As the Telebank ethical policy booklet expressed it: 'Do you know, do you approve of how your money is being used when you are not using it? Do you think you have a right to know at least in principle? . . . Can you put up the Second World War defence – I didn't know?'

By so positioning itself as an 'ethical' bank, Telebank implicitly and explicitly distanced itself from the big four banks and also from the bad press that these banks had experienced through such practices as their involvement in apartheid South Africa and aggressive selling practices in the United Kingdom. For some business commentators and media analysts however, Telebank's reinvention as an 'ethical' company was contentious. The *Financial Times* newspaper remarked at the time that: 'Sceptics have been quick to suggest that Telebank is cashing in on ethics. A number also indignantly suggest that banks have no rights to preach to their customers or discriminate against potential recipients of loans.'

However, from this early scepticism, most detractors in the business world have now been converted to the good business sense of Telebank's ethical policy. They have come to understand it as an example of clever market positioning, with little risk to Telebank PLC, that served to attract the custom of more affluent, 'middle class', customers whose social conscience was matched with a solid bank balance. 'There's no denying this is a marketing initiative . . . why else do it? But we are not part of the long-haired sandal brigade, we are socially concerned bankers.' (managing director, Telebank). Indeed the bank's own economic turnaround speaks for itself. Telebank has increased its market share year-on-year since 1990. Deposits rose approximately 10 per cent in 1993, 16 per cent in 1994 and 20 per cent in 1995, with 44 per cent of new account openings being attributed to its ethical positioning. By 1996 the bank made a profit of almost £37 million, compared to its £15 million loss in 1990.

Questions

The case of Telebank PLC illustrates several elements that were also common to the emergence of CSR and business ethics more generally. Some questions:

- How does the case demonstrate connections between the free market economic context of the time and the emergence of the bank's ethical stance?
- How does the case illustrate the self-regulatory/voluntary nature of the bank's ethics?
- What relationship does the case suggest between the issues of 'ethics' and 'profitability'?

Key problems in this field

Case study 6.2 presents a celebrated example of one companys contribution to the problem of integrating 'ethics' and 'business'. In the section after this one, some important academic contributions to business ethics are discussed, but first we look at some of the key problems facing the field. A field that focuses upon practical business issues as diverse as A(lcohol policies at work) to

Z(imbabwe business bribery), and utilizes the framework of something as long-debated as ethical philosophy to do so, will clearly generate a great number of debates and controversies. To illustrate the complexities of ethical issues in organization, Box 6.1 raises just some of the questions that we might need to consider when thinking about the ethics of one organizational issue that effects everyone of us: pollution (see also Chapter 11).

From just this one issue, it should start to become clear that any attempt to consider the ethics of almost any organizational practice is problematic. So business ethics is full of 'problems' – but perhaps it should be. Business ethics is after all concerned with questions of ethics – with what is right and what is wrong, with how to live a 'good' life and not just a 'comfortable' or 'profitable' life – and these are far from easy issues.

Underpinning all the problems associated with specific organizational practices and issues (like pollution for instance), however, are a number of more general 'macro' problems that the field of business ethics needed to find a way to resolve if it was to justify its existence to sceptical managers of business organisations. We focus upon three such problems here: relevance; conscience; and translation.

The problem of relevance As an academic who works within the broad field of business ethics, the response that I invariably get when I tell people about my work is a look of bemusement followed shortly by the quip 'that's an easy job then . . . there aren't any'. The field of business ethics as a whole faces this same problem, that of connecting 'ethics' with 'business' in a context where many people see them as separate. Beaton's (2001) tongue-in-cheek advice to managers relies upon this commonly perceived disconnection between ethics and business for its humour: 'You cannot gain professional respect if your personal integrity is damaged. Prevent damage to your personal integrity by leaving it at home in the mornings.'

It is not just cynics like Beaton however that reproduce such ideas. The (in)famous US free market economist, Milton Friedman (1970), has argued that *the only* social responsibility of business is to increase its profits. Friedman has argued that the corporate executive or manager may *personally* feel responsibilities to particular charities, or good causes, but should only act on these responsibilities in the private sphere when at home or in the community. If as an employee s/he practises these or other expressions of 'social responsibility' in the corporation's time or with the corporation's money, then far from being 'ethical' s/he is being dangerously 'subversive', misspending the shareholders' money, and failing to act as s/he has been contracted to. For Friedman therefore: (quoted in White, 2000, p. 238).

> there is one and only one social responsibility of business – to use its resources and engage in activities designed to increase its profits . . . so long as it engages in open and free competition without deception or fraud.

Apart from pursuing profit as if it were a 'moral crusade', ethics has little or no place in the business world for Friedman. Instead ethics is seen as private and personal and should stay that way, and should stay out of business. It clouds and compromises the open pursuit of money-making.

Box 6.1: The complexities of ethics: The example of pollution

How should we understand the question of pollution by business? As immoral or as inevitable? Should it be stopped or only limited? Who has rights in this case: the business, the community, the natural environment, the shareholders, or the workers whose jobs may rely on the company producing, and thereby polluting? Do these rights conflict or coincide? How do we decide between them? Is pollution an evil that we must accept for the 'greater good'? Or does the community's right to clean air and good health outweigh all other moral appeals? And what health has a community without employment? Is it ethical to shift pollution-generating activites to other, poorer countries? Is it right to limit the goods that consumers can buy so that pollution is minimized? Who is to decide on each of these questions? On what ethical basis will such decisions be made?

Image 6.1

The problem of conscience Assuming that business ethicists somehow solve the above problem of making ethics seem relevant for business, who is to decide what ethics are relevant and how to enforce them? To encourage us to behave ethically, individuals have concepts such as conscience, or fear of God or gods, we have ideas such as damnation, karma, rebirth, salvation or enlightenment, we have the desire to please, or the desire to live according to our principles or precepts, and more, that encourage us to abide by what we understand to be ethical and good. But a business organization would seem to have none of these. Where is its god? Who is its conscience? Where is its desire to be principled? Who is to be its ethical authority, its guru, its lord, its cleric, its rabbi, its enlightened being? And, even supposing that such a figure or figures can be found, how are they to enforce the ethical conscience of the organization? And should this enforcement override the ethical values of dissenting others in the organization, or those with whom the organization interacts?

Thinkpoint 6.1

Power/knowledge and ethics

- Who do you think should be the 'ethical conscience' of an organization, and why?
- Reflecting further upon your answer, what assumptions have you made regarding who you think has knowledge about ethical issues in organizations and how this relates to the power you think these people should have to define an organization's ethics?

The problem of translation The third underlying problem facing business ethics is one of translation. Even if some body or bodies are identified as the 'ethical conscience' of the organization, are the languages of 'ethics' and 'business' commensurable? Ethics can seem to be all 'philosophical' and 'abstract', concerned with 'goodness' and 'virtue' and 'justice'. Whereas business is 'practical' and 'rational', concerned with 'efficiency', 'outputs', 'products', and 'costs'. Business relies upon measurement and calculability – everything must have a cost, a value, a purpose. Business has profit and loss accounts, stock control systems, payroll systems, delivery schedules, contracts, human resource planning and a wealth of other management systems to plan and measure each tangible aspect of organizational behaviour. Surely a business cannot hope to plan or measure something as intangible or spiritual as 'ethics'. And anyway, isn't ethics essentially individualistic, a matter of conscience, one's personal relationship with the divine (however this is understood)? Whereas organization is, by definition, concerned with collective purpose and collective effort. How can business ethicists possibly hope to translate 'ethics' into something intelligible to, and manageable for, business?

Taken together, these three problems of relevance, conscience and translation present a significant challenge for business ethics. In the next section we explore some of the key ideas and contributions in the field that have sought to address these issues.

Key ideas and contributions

Overcoming the problem of relevance To address the widely held belief that 'business' and 'ethics' are, and possibly should be, disconnected realms, social and economic arguments to the contrary have been made.

The social argument attests that business, its employees and management should properly be understood as part of the social world, rather than abstracted from it. They should be subject to similar expectations of ethical conduct that we would expect from other members of our communities. **Stakeholder theory** has been used to argue that shareholders are only one of the many groups of people whom business interacts with, and is therefore responsible for.

While shareholders principally demand profit, stakeholder theory argues that other stakeholders have equally valid demands that it would be unethical for the business to breach. For example, employees have the right to demand payment for their work and a safe and suitable working environment; suppliers payment for their goods or services; the local community employment and a non-toxic environment; the nation state taxes; and consumers safe, trustworthy and reasonably priced goods. Such expectations can be seen to form an implied *ethical contract* between business and the community, such that it is only by abiding by this contract that society effectively gives business the right to consume resources and be rewarded with profit. Even in the early 1980s this hidden, ethical dimension of legal contracts was being emphasized in response to the spate of corporate scandals.

> What is shocking about some of the current corporate scandals – bribery, falsification of records, theft, and corporate espionage – is that these acts violate the conditions for making contracts and market exchanges, conditions which are at the very heart of the free enterprise system. Such violations cannot be excused by saying that they do not appear on the contract. Such excuses are almost as absurd as someone defending the murder of a creditor by saying: I only promised to pay him back; I didn't promise not to murder him. Hence we can conclude that a company has moral obligations in the contract it makes with society and it has obligations to those moral rules which make contracts possible. *(Bowie, 1983 in White, 2000, p. 245)*

Business leaders must therefore ensure that their business is seen to be ethical, lest too many breaches lead us to start to question the usefulness of organizing our society according to the private profit making, free market, business model. We can see here a self-interested argument for the business community to be ethical. This self-interested reason for being ethical is even more clearly seen in the second type of argument for connecting ethics and business, the economic argument.

The economic argument presents ethics, in one way or another, as a business opportunity waiting to be exploited. Thus the company that is seen to be 'ethical' can attract more loyal staff and customers, can benefit from good public relations, can use their ethics as a unique selling point, can use ethics to develop a strong 'brand', and can even charge a premium for its products because of its ethical image. To impress upon business, and students of business, further the link between 'ethics and the bottom line' (Edwards and Goodell, 1994; Johnson, 1994) business ethics textbooks are frequently peppered with stories of highly profitable companies that have successfully traded upon a strong ethical image (such as Telebank PLC, above). Overall, the implicit, and increasingly explicit, message of many business ethics texts is that good ethics 'translates into increased profits' (Axline, 1990, p. 87).

Thinkpoint 6.2

Power/knowledge and ethics II

- What commercial organizations can you think of that have linked an 'ethical' or 'socially responsible' image with a profitable business?
- Can you think of organizations that have suffered or struggled because of an unethical public image?
- Your answers to these questions might illustrate further the ways that power, knowledge and ethics are related. By constructing in the public consciousness an image (knowledge) of being ethical, certain corporations have managed to become more economically powerful.

Overcoming the problem of conscience From the discussion above we can see that business ethics makes a confident appeal to the business community's own commercial self-interest to justify the contemporary focus upon ethics. But who is to control the organization's new-found ethics? Who is to be, in effect, the conscience of the organization? Once we reflect upon the way that much of the field has now effectively rendered 'ethics' a business resource, something from which profit and good public relations can be gained, then the answer that the business ethics field has come to might be fairly obvious – management.

Thinkpoint 6.3

Power/knowledge versus ethics?

- Can you think of any others inside or outside the organization who might question management's right to control what is defined as a matter of ethics? (We will pick-up this point later in the chapter.)
- Your answer might illustrate further the ways that the right to define the knowledge of what is ethical/unethical in organizations is itself contested. This is because there are 'power effects' that can arise as a consequence of such definitions. For instance, if working long hours is constructed as a marker of an employee fulfilling their ethical commitments to give their energy to their employing organization, then it will likely continue. However, if long working hours are constructed as an unethical demand by employers on employees' right for leisure and family time outside of normal working hours, then there is likely to be a challenge to these expectations.

In choosing management as the ethical conscience of the organization, business ethicists are reproducing the dominant managerialist thinking of mainstream Western industrial thought. As industrialized societies, since at least the time of F. W. Taylor, we are long used to understanding management to 'naturally' bear the responsibility for all 'higher' reasoning, all strategy and all 'important' thinking in the organization (see Chapters 3 and 6; see also Parker, 2002). Business ethics reproduces this managerialism by assuming that management should necessarily have the right to define the organization's ethics and ensure other organizational members' compliance to these ethics.

Overcoming the problem of translation If managers are to be the ethical agents or 'conscience' of organizations, this still leaves the question of how the language and concerns of 'ethics' can be translated into the rational or bureaucratic task of organizing?

Business ethics has managed this through simplifying ethics down to a process whereby management formulate and disseminate organization-wide ethical codes and/or policies. Through this mechanism the issue of ethics is thus reduced to a single, organizational-wide, unitarist series of rules. Ethics can now, in principle, be quite easily managed, with the manager merely having to decide whether the employee has broken the ethical rule or not.

Thinkpoint 6.4

Freedom power and ethics

- What ethical rules does your university or college have? (Does it have rules on cheating in exams, sexual harassment, bullying, discrimination?)
- What mechanisms are in place to enforce these rules, who enforces them, and how effective do you think these are in regulating your behaviour?
- Some universities, in response to worries about the safety of students, have started to introduce rules regulating who students may have sexual relationships with. As part of this, some universities have started requiring students to obtain formal written consent from a prospective sexual partner before they have sex. If your university or college introduced this policy, would you consider this an unjustified exercise of power and interference into your private sexual freedoms, or a responsible policy to ensure your freedom from possible sexual attack?

Key issues and controversies

So far, we have seen several problems with the attempt to integrate 'ethics' and 'business' and we have introduced the broad solutions to these problems presented by the business ethics field. These broad solutions are relatively uncontroversial within the field. There are disagreements in this field, however, and mostly these centre around the question of which philosophical ethical framework should be applied to evaluate and make sense of behaviour in organizations. The main frameworks that business ethics texts draw upon are utilitarianism, stakeholder theory, deontology, justice and virtue (see also Beauchamp and Bowie, 1997 and Snell, 2004 for useful summaries).

Originating in the work of British philosophers David Hume (1711–1776), Jeremy Bentham (1748–1832) and John Stuart Mill (1806–1873), utilitarianism understands the ethical value of an act to be based on its *consequences*. Acts that lead to the greatest good for the greatest number of people are judged to be moral. This apparently straightforward proposition, however, hides much complexity. What exactly constitutes a 'good' outcome, for instance, is very debatable. How are we to measure the sum total amount of good that each of a range of potential acts that we may undertake might lead to? How can a manager know, with any real certainty, the full consequences of her actions for others in a complex business situation?

One popular variation of utilitarian ethical approaches to business ethics is that of stakeholder theory. Stakeholder theory, as we have seen, argues that the management of an organization have responsibilities not just to consider the happiness or demands of shareholders, but to recognize that organizational behaviour affects a range of other 'stakeholders' both inside and outside the corporation. Stakeholder theory can be understood to modify utilitarianism, reminding us that when we are considering the ethical consequences of particular organizational actions, we must consider the potentially quite different interests of different constituencies. These can include employees, shareholders, the environment, the local community, even an unborn generation that may be harmed by a company's products or the pollution it generates.

Clearly, trying to take into account all the possible consequences for all stakeholders of every organizational act could lead to a paralysis of indecision. Utilitarian thinking, including stakeholder variants, in the contemporary business world has recognized this and tends to focus upon the development of ethical rules to guide behaviour. Rules such as 'do not break contracts' and 'do not falsely advertise products' may be argued to be those that the business should always observe because the *consequences* of not doing so would be a loss of faith in business in general. However, even this rule-based utilitarianism, popular in business ethics, is not without its problems. For any rule formulated for organizational members to follow, we can always ask such questions as: Who decided on the rule? How can we be sure that this rule doesn't just reflect their self-interest?

Why should we be certain that following this rule would indeed lead to the greatest sum of ethical outcomes?

Deontology, like rule-based utilitarianism above, is also based upon rules or laws. However, unlike utilitarianism, deontological ethics does not build its rules on the basis of anticipated consequences of actions. For deontology this would diminish ethics, reducing it to a means–ends calculation. To judge the ethics of an action on the basis of its contribution to, say, 'happiness' would be to elevate happiness *over* ethics – to, in effect, see ethics as a subset of happiness. According to deontology, ethics does not serve any such other ends, it is an end in itself. To act ethically an individual should not be attempting to second-guess the consequences of their actions, but rather should reason what universal *ethical duty* or law applies, and they should follow this without hesitation or regard to personal friendships, personal risks or any other contextual features. For deontology, these duties are worked out through pure reason on the basis of what German philosopher Immanuel Kant (1724–1804) argued was a 'categorical imperative' of 'universalizability'. Kant's categorical imperative can be understood as 'only act in ways that could be made a general law for all human behaviour'. On the basis of this universalizable imperative, all other ethical duties can be worked out through a process of logic and reason. Thus, for instance, murder cannot be moral because if murder was universalized as a moral duty logically not everyone could follow it (you can't follow a 'duty' to murder someone if you've been murdered yourself!). Therefore, refraining from murder is a logical universalizable moral duty.

This universalizable imperative translates into far more subtle moral duties as well. Perhaps most difficult to resolve in the context of today's organizations is the universal duty on all of us to respect the dignity and autonomy of others – a precondition if each person is to have the freedom to reason about what is ethical and act accordingly. This universal duty is often translated as the duty not to treat other people as only a *means* (i.e. as a resource to achieve what *you* want), but always to treat people as an *end* in and of themselves. Some business ethics writers (e.g. Arnold and Bowie, 2003) have suggested that this last duty presents a difficult challenge for contemporary businesses organizations in that they tend to use people instrumentally as disposable 'human resources'.

Another approach to ethics used in many business ethics articles is that of justice. Justice based approaches to ethics, formulated by among others British philosopher John Locke (1632–1704), focus upon rights and fairness (Snell, 2004). The *Universal Declaration of Human Rights 1948*, passed by the General Assembly of the United Nations, is perhaps the most famous attempt to formalize such a justice-based ethics and Amnesty International[1] the best known example of an organization attempting to turn these espoused rights into a reality. Justice-based approaches to ethics have some similarities with deontology (for instance the attempt to formulate universal rights, above); however, they can also be seen to depart in a crucial way. Whereas deontology focuses exclusively upon the observance of rational ethical duties, ethics of justice also focus upon the more emotional, and often emotive, issue of *fairness*. Thus under an ethics of justice, punishment of infringements and compensation for victims, for instance, might be justified if members of an organization have acted in ways that deny others' rights.

If the talk of ethical consequences, ethical duties and ethical justice so far seems a little impersonal, the next ethical theory used in business ethics texts turns our attention right back to the individual. Virtue-based approaches to ethics are often traced back – in Western thought at least – to the work of Greek philosopher Aristotle (384–322 BC). These approaches focus upon the *character* of the person who acts. After all, we could have all the information about the likely ethical consequences of our actions (as per utilitarianism) and we could know there to be clear duties that ethically we should not breach (as per deontology), but if we have failings in our character (if we lack 'virtue') we could still simply not choose to behave ethically. Within the business ethics field, this virtue-based approach to ethics can be seen in a range of material that focuses upon the moral education and character of managers (e.g. MacLagan 1998). Occasionally, when being least critical, virtue approaches can slip into a trap of individualism, where ethics depends upon heroic individuals possessing the special qualities required to resist temptations or engage in selfless 'good deeds'. This sometimes finds expression in business ethics texts celebrating charismatic senior managers as paragons of unimpeachable virtue, single-handedly spreading purity throughout their organizations.

Thinkpoint 6.5

Knowledge, identity and ethics

- Think about some examples at your university or college where you believe that you have acted ethically.
- Which of the approaches to ethics outlined above seems to best explain the reason why you acted this way. (For instance was it because you thought about the consequences of your actions (utilitarianism); because you were obeying an ethical rule that you would never consider breaching (deontology); because you were owed something that you took back (justice); because you are simply an ethical person (virtue); etc.).
- Could your evaluation of your behaviour as ethical be different if you applied one of the other understandings of ethics?
- The issue of ethics is central to our identity. We tend to justify our behaviour and selves using ethical arguments ('I did what I thought was right in the circumstances'; 'I followed the rules'; 'I followed my conscience'; 'I am a good person'; etc.). However, as the preceding section shows, there are different forms of knowledge about ethics. Not all of these would agree on what is the ethical course of action for any one situation. Given these disagreements, how secure is our valued 'ethical' identity?

A selection of important studies

Two studies are reviewed here – Denis Arnold and Norman Bowie's (2003) 'Sweatshops and Respect for Persons' and Bill Richardson and Peter Curwen's (1995) 'Do Free Market Governments Create Crisis-Ridden Societies?' – that, in their different ways, both reproduce several familiar aspects of the mainstream business ethics discourse and also push the business ethics debate forward.

Arnold and Bowie's (2003) article, published in *Business Ethics Quarterly*, uses a Kantian (deontological) ethical theory of respect for persons to critique the ethics of exploitative 'sweatshop' employment practices of **multinational corporations** (MNCs). For Arnold and Bowie (2003, p. 222): 'Persons ought to be respected because persons have dignity. For Kant, an object that has dignity is beyond price. Employees have a dignity that machines and capital do not. They have dignity because they are capable of moral activity.' The authors draw upon evidence from trade unionists, labour activists and non-governmental organizations to argue that **subcontractors** working for MNCs routinely breach such respect for persons in the conditions of labour that they impose upon their employees.

SOURCE: © ALISON WRIGHT/CORBIS

Image 6.2 An example of the overcrowded conditions common to sweatshops

Such conditions include widespread and well-documented breaches of labour law relating to wages and benefits, forced overtime, health and safety violations, sexual harassment, discrimination and environmental protection. Psychological and physical coercion to work also abounds. Such coercion can take the form of forced overtime through threat of job loss, and compulsion to work through verbal and physical assault. Working conditions are frequently appalling and include locking workers into the overcrowded and unventilated factories to prevent them leaving, resulting in fatalities when fires break out.

For instance, in 1993 200 employees were killed and 469 injured in the Kader Industrial Toy Company in Thailand because they were locked in. The Kader company produced toys for US MNCs such as Hasbro, Toys 'R' Us, J. C. Penney and Fisher Price (Arnold and Bowie, 2003, p. 231). In the 10 000-person Tae Kwang Vina factory in Vietnam, producing Nike products, employees were exposed to toxic chemicals at amounts up to 177 times those allowed under Vietnamese law (ibid.). Further, in addition to such unsafe, abusive and frequently illegal practices, these subcontractors producing goods for some of the worlds largest MNCs fail to provide workers with wages high enough even to meet basic needs for food, clothing and shelter, and this despite the fact that a living wage may only be as much as US$30.00 per week (see also Klein, 2001).

Drawing upon such evidence in conjunction with Kantian ethical philosophy and a variant of stakeholder theory, Arnold and Bowie (2003, p. 239) argue that MNCs are failing to meet their ethical responsibilities to these employees: 'We have argued that MNE managers who encourage or tolerate violations of the rule of law; use coercion; allow unsafe working conditions; and provide below subsistence wages, disavow their own dignity and that of their workers.'

Having criticised MNC treatment of their employees, the authors (ibid., p. 239) highlight MNCs as in a prime position to improve their ethics, thus reproducing the managerial focus of the mainstream business ethics field: 'MNE managers who recognize a duty to respect their employees, and those of their subcontractors, are well positioned to play a constructive role in ensuring that the dignity of humanity is respected.'

Thinkpoint 6.6

Inequality, power and ethics

- Critics of MNC's use of 'sweatshop labour' argue that these companies are unethical in exploiting stark inequalities in employment costs and conditions in developing countries compared to those in the West. Further, critics argue that MNCs are so large and powerful that they could, if they so wished, change these employment conditions and pay a sustainable wage.
- Imagine you are employed by one of the above companies and are given responsibility for improving your subcontractor's employment practices. What procedures would you recommend that the company undertakes?
- You may find it interesting to compare what Nike says about its own practices (www.nike.com/nikebiz/nikebiz.jhtml?page =25&cat=code) with what critics (such as those at www.corpwatch.org) say about the company's ethics.

Overall, Arnold and Bowie's argument is a powerful and important one. It blends traditional features of mainstream business ethics discourse with a powerful critique of the widespread exploitative practices from which the world's largest MNCs profit. It does, however, stop short of questioning the free market economic system that arguably encourages business to put profit before such ethical considerations. In the paper reviewed next we see an example of a mainstream business ethics article that does begin to question the prevailing freemarket economics.

Richardson and Curwen's (1995) article published in the *Journal of Business Ethics* is concerned with examining the causes of two fatal disasters, the *Herald of Free Enterprise* ferry disaster, and the Kings Cross underground fire, both of which occurred in the late 1980s. The 1987 *Herald of Free Enterprise* roll-on/roll-off passenger and freight ferry disaster occurred in good weather when the ferry capsized at sea after she sailed with both her inner and outer bow (loading) doors open. As a result, 150 passengers and 38 members of the crew lost their lives and many others were injured. The Kings Cross underground (below-ground passenger train) fire occurred in 1987, when grease and rubbish caught fire beneath the treads of the passenger escalators at the underground station level. The fire rapidly spread up the escalators and erupted into the ticket hall causing horrendous injuries and 31 deaths.

Analysing the causes of these disasters, Richardson and Curwen criticize management's inappropriate beliefs as contributing to, if not causing, the disasters by creating inappropriate organizational cultures, structures, systems and behaviour. They give an example (ibid., p. 556) of such inappropriate beliefs:

> Despite the existence of theoretical and real world warnings about the dangers inherent in organizations, a dominant premise of the free-market philosophy is one of organizations as economic (and only indirectly as social) wealth creators/bestowers. A society which concentrates excessively on the assumption that organizations are only – or even predominantly – beneficial wealth-creators, tends to be disaster prone.

The authors suggest that these fatal disasters are not 'one-off' examples of bad practice in an otherwise well-managed and safe economy. Rather, they highlight the free market economic system itself as strongly contributing to such inappropriate management beliefs: 'Free-market principles help sustain inappropriate beliefs about the nature of organizations and the kinds of cultures and systems which contribute to disasters' (ibid., p. 552).

So, we have in Richardson and Curwen what, for a mainstream business ethics article, is an unusually explicit criticism of top management's problematic influence upon the organization *and* of the freemarket philosophy that has so increased top manager's control. Though unusual in voicing these criticisms, however, the article also reproduces the managerialism and voluntarism of the business ethics field. Though critical of management for contributing to these fatalities, the authors see the solution merely as *management voluntarily changing the way they manage*. Managers, the authors conclude, must learn to 'think-upside-down' and develop a 'wider belief base for the creation of contexts by management strategies' (ibid., p. 558).

Ultimately, then, we have in Richardson and Curwen (1995) a compelling and persuasive critique of the most serious instances of organizational fatality and disaster. And while the authors reproduce the key assumptions of the business ethics field, they also push the field forward in examining more seriously the risks with management control and the free market economic system.

Although these studies are examples of some of the best work in the mainstream field of business ethics, critical approaches might suggest that they continue to display a number of serious limitations. We begin exploring these arguments by focusing upon the contribution and limitations of mainstream writing on business ethics in relation to the core concept of 'freedom'.

Limitations and contribution in relation to core concepts

Ethics is intimately connected to the idea of freedom. Ethics is concerned with choosing between different paths. At its simplest, ethics is choosing 'right' over 'wrong', 'good' over 'bad'. To choose, one must have the freedom to take different courses of actions, to make different choices. This core concept of freedom is illuminated in several different ways in the story of business ethics. First of all, the context of free market economics from which business ethics was born gave business more freedom from governmental control. Business self-regulation was to take the place of state regulation. With this freedom from state control came public examples of businesses abusing this freedom – leading to crisis, frauds, abuses, and disasters (much like those discussed above by Arnold and Bowie, 2003 and Richardson and Curwen, 1995).

Business ethics then emerged as a response to the problematic underside of this freedom, a response that promised to encourage business managers to think about the effects and ethics of their actions. Importantly, business ethics does not seek to limit the freedom that managers have under the free market/self-regulating economic system, it does not seek more state control, or stronger pressure groups, or unions, etc. Rather, business ethics endorses and reinforces the freedom and power of management to self-regulate, to be free from outside regulation, and to use this freedom to voluntarily behave more ethically.

The links between business ethics and freedom do not end here however. This is just the starting point of a whole series of questions regarding the nature of the 'freedom' that business ethics promotes. For instance, has the rise of business ethics and, 'corporate social responsibility' actually made the world freer from business exploitation, industrial accidents, environmental destruction, etc? Compelling evidence on this centrally important question is very elusive, but anecdotally it does not take much effort to find example after example of disastrous business behaviour in the local and national media – despite some of these companies having glossy ethical policies and codes. Indeed, if the industrial crises, abuses and disasters of the 1980s arose, as business ethics states, from a context of management having new found freedom to self-regulate, why does it make sense to see giving managers *more freedom*, freedom to define and police organizational ethics, as a likely solution to this problem?

Finally, under business ethics' managerial focus it is managers (and academics) only who have the freedom to define ethics – other employees and stakeholders seem to be cast in the subordinate position of merely submitting to these rules. Is their *unfreedom* the price that must be paid for more ethical organizations? Just how 'ethical' is it for a minority of organizational members (management) to impose their definition of ethics upon the majority?

Such questions and issues are among some of the concerns that critical approaches to the question of ethics at work address, which we turn to next.

Recap questions

- Why is 'ethics' considered important for today's organizations?
- Who in the organization is given responsibility for developing and enforcing ethical policy?
- Do you think organizations today are always ethical? If not, how would you like to see them improved?

Critical approaches to ethics at work

Introduction

One place to start an introduction to critical approaches to ethics at work would be to highlight the narrow range of ethical frameworks (utilitarian, deontological, justice and virtue) that mainstream business ethicists tends to draw upon. By so doing, business ethics tends to exclude a wealth of contemporary, and more critical, ethical systems including those of **feminism** (Brewis, 1998; though see Derry, 2002), **Marxism** (Wray-Bliss and Parker, 1998), and **post-modernism** (Phillips, 1991; Willmott, 1998).

Drawing upon such alternative ethical systems can provide us with fascinating and compelling different readings of ethics at work, readings that can make us radically question whether behaviour in today's organizations is indeed ethical. We start the introduction to critical approaches to ethics at work by questioning the ethics of organization; questioning the ethics of obedience; and questioning the corporate takeover of ethics.

Questioning the ethics of organization As we have seen, business ethics seeks to make organizations socially responsible by giving the managers of these organizations more power to define and control other organizational members' ethics. On the surface this seems like an effective way to bring ethics into the organization. However, by drawing upon the work of post-modern sociologist Zygmunt Bauman (1989, 1993) this can be seen as potentially disastrous for ethics at work. It may provide the conditions to actually increase unethical organizational practices.

Organizations, like crowds, are comprised of a mass of people. Organizations differ from crowds however in that the behaviour of people in organizations is regulated and controlled so that it meets the collective purpose of the organization. By and large, employees do what they are expected to do and this harnessing of their collective effort is what makes organizations so powerful (Knights and Roberts, 1982). To achieve this, organizations must eradicate unpredictable behaviour. Thus we have rules, procedures, uniforms, targets, quotas and all manner of other bureaucratic and cultural mechanisms to control employees' behaviour in organizations (see Chapters 8 and 12). Bauman argues that one effect of these organizational pressures towards conformity and uniformity is that individual ethical responsibility is squeezed out of the organization. Ethics means doing what one feels to be right, not what may be profitable, what everyone else is doing, or what your boss or shareholders may want you to do. Organization and its leaders thus work, consciously or otherwise, to eradicate this unpredictable and disruptive ethics from the organization – to stop organizational members from feeling and acting upon individual moral judgements about their and others' organizational behaviour.

An example of such eradication of individual moral responsibility at work could be seen in the fact that we tend to apply different standards to behaviour at work versus behaviour outside of work. For instance, while none of us would probably consider attempting to take from a stranger on the street their wages, their car and their job, we might well, as managers, follow an instruction to make some employees redundant resulting in the same effects. And while taking these things from a stranger would be outlawed as immoral, taking them from an 'employee', as actually happens in an organizational context and in an organized way, is typically not viewed in the same way. So we see here precisely what Bauman is alluding to, the same act is removed from ethical accountability because it happens to take place in an organization. The ultimate message to be drawn from examples like this is, argues Bauman, 'that the organization as a whole is an instrument to obliterate responsibility' (Bauman, 1989, p. 163).

The implications of this argument for how we should understand business ethics are profound. By promoting the idea that management should take responsibility for deciding and enforcing 'ethics', business ethics can be argued to be further *removing* ethical responsibility from individual organizational members. This explanation of Bauman's might help explain how modern organizations, populated with thoughtful and educated people who may well act perfectly morally outside of work have, and continue to, perpetrate unethical behaviour at work.

From the above, rather than promoting the idea of 'obedient' organizational members following rules laid down by management, as mainstream business ethics does, perhaps we need to question such obedience and search for ethics instead in acts of *disobedience* and *dissent*. We turn to critical contributions on this issue next.

Thinkpoint 6.7

Power versus freedom and ethics?

- Explain Bauman's argument that making more rules for organizational members to follow can encourage less personally responsible behaviour.
- What is the relationship between power, freedom, and ethics suggested in Bauman's writing?

Questioning the ethics of obedience A variety of ethical frameworks can be used to argue that one person's (e.g. an employee's) subordination to another (e.g. a manager) is unethical. For instance, it could be argued that employees' subordination is a breach of Kant's categorical imperative that states that a person cannot be used merely as a means by any other person. Alternatively, MacIntyre (1981) has argued that management can never be considered ethically virtuous because the concept and practice of management is manipulative. Management is about manipulating employees to do what they otherwise may not want to do (see Chapters 2 and 6; Roberts, 1984, also makes this argument very well). However, perhaps the most powerful critiques of the ethics of employees' subordination can be seen in Marxist critiques of capitalist working relations.

For Karl Marx what makes human beings unique is our potentiality and creativity. Through our collective effort (our labour) we transform ourselves, each other and the world around us. We fashion it according to our own designs and conscious intentions. However, under conditions of work in **capitalist societies**, many of us do not experience this human potentiality – even though our societies pride themselves on their 'freedom' and 'opportunity' and 'justice'. Our labour is bought by owners of corporations to service their need for profit. People are **dehumanized**, reduced to the status of things (e.g. 'human resources'), merely another factor of production to be used and exploited. Because of historical inequalities most people have to sell their labour for wages. Employees' labour then comes to seem like an alien thing to them, something owned by another. Work becomes resented – it turns into 'alienated labour' (Marx, 1844).

To help understand the concept of alienation, imagine some task either at home, work or at university that you really resented having to do – say a hated assignment for a course that you could not see the point of. Now imagine having to do such personally meaningless and hated tasks for the rest of your working life: this would start to give you an idea of Marx's concept of alienation at work.

As the group with a vested interest in ending their own alienation and exploitation, Marxism identifies employees as those most likely to act to challenge these dehumanizing workplaces. However, this group is routinely excluded from the decision-making processes in organizations, with such processes reserved for management. Therefore, Marxists focus upon employee resistance to management control as a potentially ethical and desirable act. Employee resistance is seen as employees' more or less conscious and strategic attempts to end their **alienation** and **exploitation**. This understanding of employee resistance as ethical is in direct contrast to the mainstream business ethics field that promotes increased managerial control as the only route to ethical renewal in organizations.

To illustrate the usefulness of this critical understanding of the ethical nature of workplace resistance, let's return to Richardson and Curwen's (1995) article 'Do Free Market Governments Create Crisis-Ridden Societies?' presented above. You will remember that this article was concerned with exploring the reasons behind two UK fatal disasters, the Kings Cross underground fire and the *Herald of Free Enterprise* ferry disaster. Throughout their paper the authors criticized top management as contributing to both disasters. Despite this the authors only identify *management* within the organization as providing any solution to such problems.

Drawing upon a critical understanding of the ethics of employee resistance, we can arrive at a less illogical solution. Taking the ferry disaster as an example, the investigation into this disaster discovered that it was caused because of the practice of ferries leaving port with bow doors open to save time on ferry turnaround and thereby maximize revenue. In this disaster 38 crew-members lost their lives, and many more were injured. All of these employees on board the ferry clearly had an acute vested interest in the safety and security of the ship their lives depended upon. An obvious conclusion from these facts would seem to be that if we are looking for a solution to improving workplace conditions and health and safety, we should be promoting employee resistance to such unethical and unsafe managerial demands. For example, by encouraging strong unions capable of voicing employee concerns, protecting them from victimization and generally exposing practices that put profit before people. This would seem to make more sense than, as the authors do, merely asking distant senior managers to develop a 'wider belief base', or indeed to write an ethical policy.

Thinkpoint 6.8

Inequality, power and ethics

- What is 'alienation' and why might employee resistance be seen as an ethical response to this?
- Your answer might illustrate the way that power even in a Marxist analysis does not just operate in one direction – i.e. *from* the powerful, *on* the powerless. Employee resistance demonstrates that employers are reliant upon employees behaving in productive ways. Once employees start resisting and not behaving in these expected ways, the workplace can be quickly transformed into a very difficult place to manage.

Questioning the corporate takeover of ethics From the above, we have an image of ethics as something that could and should be radical. We have an ethics that can be drawn upon to fundamentally question, for instance, the basis of management authority; the modern organizational form; and the basis of the capitalist economic system's promotion of local and global inequality. Understanding ethics as informing such wide-ranging critiques, how would critical approaches read the emergence of mainstream business ethics and corporate social responsibility? Perhaps the description that would fit best would be the 'corporate takeover of ethics'. Business ethics would be regarded as ethics made safe for business, where ethics is reduced to a corporate image exercise in support of the business drive for profits (see e.g. Parker, 2002).

By engaging in a few high-profile charity causes, producing some glossy ethical statements, or marketing themselves alongside images of smiling children, happy communities or green fields, business can apparently become wholesome and safe. For instance, giant fast food organizations according to their critics (e.g. Ritzer, 1993; www.mcspotlight.org) are complicit in reproducing health damaging obesity, environmental destruction and the rise in poorly paid, temporary 'McJobs'. However these organizations publicly project a very different image by linking themselves with children's charities and images of happy communities and families. We find, in short, ethics reduced to being just another resource that business can exploit to ward of criticism and/or attract the hapless consumer. This last point is illustrated well with a recent example from one of the world's largest defence (arms and weapons) contractors, Boeing (see Box 6.2).

Box 6.2: 'Boeing sacks finance chief in ethics row'

'Boeing, America's second largest defence contractor, yesterday dismissed Mike Sears, its chief financial officer, for unethical conduct in the hiring of a senior Pentagon official to run a $20bn (£11.8bn) refueling contract for the United States air force.

The aerospace group admitted that Mr Sears had violated company policy by communicating with Darleen Druyun about her future employment when she was still acting in her official government capacity on matters involving Boeing.

Ms Druyun – in effect head of air force procurement before joining Boeing as deputy head of its missile defence division – and Mr Sears covered this up, an internal investigation found. Ms Druyun was also dismissed . . . .

Mr Sears, who joined McDonnel Douglas in 1969, becoming head of its aerospace business in advance of Boeing's takeover in 1997, was widely tipped to succeed Phil Condit as chief executive when he steps down in 2006 . . . .

Mr Condit said "compelling evidence" of misconduct by Mr Sears and Ms Druyun had come to light "over the last two weeks", leading the board to order their dismissal . . . .

In July Boeing called in a former senator, Warren Rudman, from a prominent law firm to review its ethics programme and set up an office of internal governance. His work has now been extended to cover the hiring of government employees.

"Boeing must and will live by the highest standards of ethical conduct in every aspect of our business," Mr Condit said. "When we determine there have been violations of our standards we will act swiftly to address them."'

Source: David Gow, *The Guardian*, 25 November 25 2003, p. 17. © Guardian Newspaper Limited 1992.

In this example we might have expected a business that deals in the means to cause others' deaths to have some qualms about using a discourse of 'ethics' to describe its business. Not so. For critics of business ethics one possible reason why chief executive, Mr. Condit, finds the language of ethics so safe to use would be precisely because the field has functioned to bleach ethics of much of its critical potential. Instead of questioning business in general, business ethics has shied away from a serious analysis of the 'big picture', in favour of a blanket acceptance of capitalist society and the single-minded search for profit. The discourse of business ethics does not require Boeing to question the deadly business it is profiting from. Instead, ethics has been reduced to the much safer and much narrower question of whether its self-defined 'ethical' codes on recruitment have been followed. Instead of a serious, radical ethical critique of the nature of business in general, business ethics instead too often focuses upon local, specific and comparatively minor issues. This means, as Parker (2002, p. 98) argues, that: ' . . . business ethics is rarely utopian, or even moderately ambitious in its aims . . . if so little is expected, then perhaps little is likely to be achieved.'

This last point of Parker's is illustrated well by rereading Arnold and Bowie's (2003) business ethics paper critiquing the ethics of multinational corporations' use of sweatshop labour. This article (explored earlier) made a powerful ethical critique of the dangerous and exploitative conditions under which employees subcontracting for MNCs work. A radical critique of the ethics of such practices would likely lead one to question more generally the ethics of capitalism that promoted such disregard for the value of human life in the search for profits. However, Arnold and Bowie's paper, limited by its uncritical acceptance of the profit motive, does not argue for the above. Instead they merely ask that: 'MNEs and their contractors adhere to *local* labour laws, refrain from coercion, meet *minimum* safety standards, and provide a living wage for employees' (Arnold and Bowie, 2003, p. 222, emphasis added).

Critics of business ethics might suggest that we could be justified in feeling more than a little disappointed that an 'ethical' critique of such exploitative contemporary business practices ends by asking for so little. This last point is picked up in the following section, where we revisit the case study of the 'ethical' organization, Telebank PLC, showing what, for those critical of business ethics, would be the shallowness of the bank's ethical claims.

Key issues and controversies

Questioning Telebank PLC as an ethical organization The first of the critical approaches introduced above drew upon the work of Bauman. Bauman argued that organization exists by eradicating unproductive and unpredictable behaviour by its members, and especially such behaviour arising from employees' ethical sentiments. But how can we reconcile this argument with an organization such as Telebank PLC, which is celebrated for having explicit ethical commitments?

A critical reading of Telebank PLC might highlight how the bank's ethical policy functions as a controlling device. By taking the monopoly right to construct the bank's ethical policy, Telebank management can be understood to be taking this right *from* other organizational members. If others' concerns do not figure in what the bank's management has already defined as the ethical policy they are implicitly not a matter of ethics. The implications of these points can be seen in the history of Telebank's successful reinvention in the 1990s. Telebank PLC is celebrated for only *one* of its strategies in the 1990s: the publication of its ethical policy. However, if we return to Case study 6.1 we can see that its other major strategy at the time was a dramatic cost-cutting exercise:

> First, like many of the other banks, it cut costs. It rapidly shed over 1000 employees, closed branches, dramatically cut staff numbers in its branches (typically from 40 to eight), and rerouted most of its contact with customers from over-the-counter face-to-face to telephone banking via remote call-centres.

By taking control of what constitutes 'ethics', Telebank management effectively cast these redundancies as *not* an ethical issue. These redundancies, with their potentially devastating personal and social implications, are represented simply as a *financial* business decision. Returning to Bauman's arguments, we can see how this 'ethical organization' has effectively rendered redundancy outside of ethical discourse. As we will see below, this process of eradicating or removing issues from the status of ethics has occurred not only with the issue of redundancy at Telebank PLC. Other issues relating to conditions of employment are similarly absent from the organization's ethical policy.

Thinkpoint 6.9

Inequality, insecurity and ethics

- Do you think that redundancy should be regarded as an ethical, rather than a merely financial or legal issue? Why/Why not?
- Try to vividly imagine yourself in each of the following situations, and think whether your answer to the above question might have changed as a result:
  - (a) Imagine that a member of your family was being made redundant.
  - (b) Imagine that your job is to present before the board of directors the figures explaining the need for redundancies.
- Reflecting upon your answer to (a) and (b) above, can you see how our *closeness* to the effects of an action can change how we think about it ethically. It is very likely, for instance, that those who are made redundant and will experience the inequality of not having a job immediately and personally will understand redundancy as an acutely (un)ethical issue and not merely a financial decision. Whereas it is likely that those who get no closer to redundancy than providing some figures on corporate profitability may not experience the subsequent redundancies of people they may never meet as an ethical issue at all.

Questioning the ethics of obedience The second of the critical approaches to ethics and organization (introduced above) drew upon the writings of Marx. We saw how Marx's writings could be used to argue that one person's subordination to, and exploitation by, another is itself an ethical problem – it dehumanizes and alienates. Applying this critical ethical approach to the Telebank PLC case provides an unsettling and important reinterpretation.

The initial redundancies of 1000 employees can of course be critiqued as 'alienating' these employees from their productive human potential. Indeed there is perhaps little that can be regarded as more alienating in this respect than removing from people their ability to labour. However, oppressive and alienating relationships extend to those employees who remained in employment at the bank. We know from the case study that, in addition to the redundancies, many of the remaining employees were relocated in the bank's remote telephone banking call-centres. These types of organization have been criticized as oppressive places to work.

Call-centres are typically organized as large open-plan offices, where employees are permanently linked into a telephone and computer system that automatically distributes customers' calls to waiting staff. Staff have performance targets based upon number of calls answered per shift but little control over the automatic computerized allocation of their work. The work is high pressured and highly paced but routine, boring and repetitive. There is little chance for conversations and interaction among staff, so the social relationships that historically have been so important to quality of working life are damaged. There is little chance to interact with customers. The nature of the targets, the impersonal telephone service, and the lack of face-to-face interactions means that 'conversations' with individual customers typically last no more than a minute.

The chances for career progression are very limited, and salaries are not high. Timing on all of an employee's work (the number of calls they take, length of calls, actions between calls, time on breaks, time in the toilet, etc.) is recorded in the minutest detail by a central computer. Management can, at any time, examine each employee's statistics and make judgements about their performance, judgements that are linked to pay and/or discipline. Telebank staff have been seen to be crying at their desk after returning to work following holidays because of their intense dislike for the nature of the work. So notorious has the quality of working life at call-centres become that they have been described by some journalists and academics as the modern day equivalent of 'dark satanic mills' (Wylie, 1997).

For employees to experience their work so negatively, as so alien to their desires, and as so deadening of their potential, raises many ethical concerns about the nature of the work in Telebank's call-centres. For Telebank management, however, the working conditions were seen to be cost-effective – and matters of ethics just did not seem to figure. In fact, not one of the bank's celebrated 12 ethical commitments relates to the conditions their staff are required to work under. This indication of where management's priorities lie also lends weight to the suggestion of the critical writers that it is to employee resistance, rather than management largesse, that we should look if we wish to see such ethically questionable employment practices challenged. Indeed, an example of just this was when part-time Telebank employee, 'Sharon', refused to meet the target number of calls set by her manager, arguing that: 'If you pick up the phone 100 times a day and cut them off that's ok with the department manager. I'm at odds with him over targets, it's not good customer service. I've got a target of 40 calls but I don't care – I do the job as I think it should be done, we are here to help people' (Telebank employee 'Sharon', quoted in Wray-Bliss, 2001, p. 44).

Questioning the corporate takeover of ethics In Case study 6.1 I showed how Telebank PLC was rebranded as an ethical business. Through developing and publicizing a 12-point ethical policy and combining this with a profitable business, Telebank has become one of the hottest ethical business brands. The above critiques demonstrate how a business such as Telebank can gain this 'ethical' brand status despite serious questions that could be asked about shortcomings in its 'ethical' business practice. In particular, it has been argued here that it is often in the area of employment conditions that the contemporary business ethics discourse is most short-sighted. That so many redundancies and poor working conditions apparently do not affect a corporation's ability to brand itself as ethical can be seen to indicate just how successfully business has been able to take over the issue of ethics at work. What must be remembered from the Telebank case, and from similar celebrated ethical organizations, is that such organizations have not only deflected widespread public critical ethical scrutiny of such employment practices. More than this, they have been so successful in controlling what gets seen as an 'ethical' issue at work that they actually profit from the image of having the highest

Image 6.3 A call-centre

SOURCE: © SHERWIN CRASTO/REUTERS/CORBIS

ethical standards. For some critics, not only has business ethics removed its radical teeth, it is in danger of turning ethics into a lap dog of business (Neimark, 1995; Parker, 2002).

Important studies within the critical approach

In contrast to the often toothless nature of mainstream business ethics texts, the selection of articles in this section illustrate and emphasize the power and significance of critical approaches to ethics at work.

In her (1995) article 'The Selling of Ethics: The Ethics of Business Meets the Business of Ethics', Marilyn Neimark critiques mainstream business ethics, both in theory and in practice. Neimark draws upon the example of the multinational shoe-ware manufacturer 'Stride Rite' that sells its products under the registered trademark brands of Keds, Grasshoppers and Tommy Hilfiger Footwear. Like Telebank PLC, Stride Rite is celebrated for its ethical and socially responsible business practices, winning 14 social responsibility awards in the early 1990s. An example of the company's socially responsible policies published on its corporate website is paraphrased in Box 6.3.

However, also like Telebank PLC, Neimark argues that behind the public eye Stride Rite engages in practices that have a far less convincing 'ethical' justification. Alongside its ethical sentiments

Box 6.3: The Community Service and Volunteerism projects of Stride Rite Corp.

Stride Rite has made a strong commitment to 'do right' in the communities where the company works, and amongst the communities of its employees and associates.

- Stride Rite encourages its associates to take part in volunteer work during and after working hours. Projects, which this community service has contributed to include: Annual Service Day, Groundhog Job Shadow Day, Helping Hands, Netpals, and The United Way.
- Stride Rite has also made grants in terms of time and of and money to not-for-profit organisations which are dedicated to helping children, including the B.E.L.L. Foundation, Citizens' Schools, Peace At Home, and the Waltham Y.

Source: Paraphrased from http://www.strideritecorp.com/corporate.asp

and numerous awards, Stride Rite has closed down production plants in deprived areas in the United States and shifted production to low-wage overseas plants, mostly in Asia. In addition to the financial exploitation of impoverished Asian employees, we already know from studies such as Arnold and Bowie (2003) and Klein (2001) how appalling the conditions of work in low-cost overseas production facilities can be. The result of this cost cutting is that Stride Rite has made very healthy profits indeed. As a result, Neimark argues, it can afford to channel a small percentage of this profit into high-profile 'socially responsible' deeds, thereby creating an 'ethical' brand image.

The conclusion that Neimark draws from such examples is very interesting. She does not just argue that companies like Stride Rite are cynically manipulating an otherwise 'good' business ethics discourse. Rather, she concludes that Stride Rite's behaviour is *acceptable* within the business ethics discourse because Business Ethics endorses the profit maximizing, pro-business, free market agenda:

> Within that discourse there are no penalties for corporations like Stride Rite which, on the one hand, benefit from the positive public relations associated with doing good deeds and, on the other hand, act in ways that contribute to the increasing degradation and deformation of life in the USA and the exploitation of workers abroad.

For Neimark, business ethics does not represent the emergence of new ethical organizations or increased ethical scrutiny of business. Rather, as examples such as Stride Rite demonstrate, Business Ethics actually *deflects* such ethical scrutiny. Ultimately, business ethics risks turning ethics into just another resource to be cynically exploited in the construction of the corporate brand.

Neimark's article can be summarized as highlighting the danger of buying into corporations' claims to be 'ethical' and thereby failing to question their less well publicised profit-seeking behaviour. The next study highlights the dangers with business ethics' promotion of organizational members' obedience to managerial authority.

The (in)famous psychological experiments conducted by Stanley Milgram in the 1960s illustrate the importance of questioning authority (Milgram, 1974). Milgram and his colleagues explored the ethical limits of obedience to authority in the following way. They put up posters in a university asking for volunteers to take part in a study of 'memory and learning', for which the volunteers would receive a small payment for their time. People that responded to the advert were each given a time to turn up at a laboratory in the university. Here they were met by a scientist and another 'volunteer'. The scientist gave both volunteers their payment, and then proceeded to give them a brief background to the study, explaining that it was concerned with the effects of punishment upon learning. Both volunteers then drew lots, to see who would be the 'teacher' and who the 'learner'. The learner is then taken into another room, strapped into a chair, and electrodes places on both wrists. The teacher sees all this, before being taken to a separate room, from which s/he can hear but not see the learner. S/he is seated in front of an electric shock generating machine with switches ranging from 15 volts to 450 volts in 15-volt increments.

The teacher is told to read a list of word pairs into a microphone to the learner. Having read through the list, the teacher then starts with the first word and reads four possible pairs. If the learner gets the correct pair the teacher moves on to the next pair. If the learner gets it wrong they receive a shock and are told the correct answer. With every wrong answer the shock level increases. The scientist remains in the room with the teacher throughout the experiment and encourages them to continue where necessary.

There is, however, a catch. The teacher is a genuine naive subject – a volunteer such as you or I might be. However, the learner is not actually a volunteer, but a trained actor. They are not actually being shocked. The volunteer teacher does not know this, however, and hears an escalating series of protests from the learner as the 'shock' level rises. These protests range from a grunt of pain at a fairly low shock level, through to a demand to be released, an agonized scream, complaints of heart problems, through to absolute silence (presumed death). The point of the experiment is not, actually, to test memory and learning at all, but rather, to see how far ordinary people will proceed to administer pain to a protesting victim.

Thinkpoint 6.10

Before reading on!

- Imagine yourself in the position of being the 'teacher' and that experiment was being conducted at your own university or college. At what level do you think that you would have stopped giving what you believed to be electric shocks to the 'learner'?
- Would you have stopped at the first exclamation of pain? Or the first demand from the learner to stop? Perhaps the first agonized scream would have been enough for you? Or do you think that you would have continued past the point that you thought the learner was seriously hurt?
- Remember your answer, and you can compare it to the results of the experiment, next.

The result of these experiments was extremely disturbing. For far from disobeying the command at a very early stage, as *all* psychiatrists Milgram surveyed prior to the experiment predicted (and you probably indicated as your likely behaviour) most people continued administering shocks to the victim right to the end of the scale. As Milgram recorded:

> Many subjects will obey the experimenter no matter how vehement the pleading of the person being shocked, no matter how painful the shocks seem to be, and no matter how much the victim pleads to be let out. This was seen time and again in our studies and has been observed in several universities where the experiment was repeated. (*Milgram, 1974, p. 5*)

In short, the adult subjects of this experiment continued to 'shock' the victim, even though they thought they were seriously hurting, even killing, another person who was pleading to be released. Why might this have been the case? A possible explanation might be that perhaps the subjects were, for some reason, unaware or uncaring of the suffering and harm that the other person was apparently feeling. The extract in Box 6.4 from the transcript of just one of these experiments (picked up at the 315-volt stage) shows this not to be the case.

As we can tell from the extract, Fred was neither unaware nor uncaring about the pain he believed he was inflicting. He clearly wanted to stop the experiment, indeed on numerous occasions he said that he would not continue the experiment any further. And yet he did continue right to the end of the scale. He continued even to the point that he thought he had killed the man next door, as did many others. Why? For Milgram, the explanation lies in Fred's and the other subjects' acceptance *of the decisions of those in authority*: 'it is the extreme willingness of adults to go to almost any lengths on the command of authority that constitutes the chief finding of the study and the fact most urgently demanding explanation' (ibid., 1974, p. 5).

The Milgram experiments are a dramatic experimental illustration of the consequences of giving up control to a perceived legitimate authority. In the experiments the authority was a 'scientist' but it might have so easily been a 'manager' demanding unethical behaviour from a subordinate. From these experiments, Milgram draws a very powerful conclusion. He argues that far from endorsing obedience to authority as an unquestionable good (as the *managerialist assumptions* of mainstream organizational behaviour and business ethics texts leads them to do) we should question any organizational members' subordination to another's authority. In such obedience there is always the potential for a loss or abdication of ethical responsibility, and ultimately, the possibility for inhumanity.

Thinkpoint 6.11

Power, identity and ethics

- To reflect further on the implications of the Milgram experiments, imagine that you are employed in a job that you really like and have worked hard to get. Now imagine that your manager insists that you carry out a task you believe to be morally wrong, and won't listen to your protestations that you don't want to do it. Imagine that your family, your house mortgage payments, your children, perhaps your health premiums, not to mention your relationship with your boss, all rely upon you following this direct order.
- Just how bad would the task have to be before you disobeyed and risked everything? Would you really throw your job away over the first, small immoral act? Or would you wait until the act you were told to do was very wrong? Just when would you draw the line?
- Thinking about these questions, we can perhaps begin to see how, when illegal and immoral acts are perpetrated in organizational contexts the perpetrators so often proclaim that 'I am not responsible, I was just following orders'. In such protestations, individuals are separating off their sense of self, their ethical identity, from their actions. They put responsibility for their actions onto those in positions of power. This is a dangerous process. Zygmunt Bauman (1989) pursues these points in Chapter 6 of *Modernity and The Holocaust* when he uses the results of the Milgram experiments to help explain the very worst example of organized immorality ever perpetrated.

Box 6.4: Fred Prozi, Unemployed (transcript excerpt from Experiment 5) – from Milgram (1974, p.p. 73–76)

The subject is about 50 years old, dressed in a jacket but no tie; he has a good natured, if slightly dissolute appearance. He employs working-class grammar and strikes one as a rather ordinary fellow. He begins the experiment calmly but becomes increasingly tense as the experiment proceeds . . .

SUBJECT: I think something's happened to that fellow in there. I don't get no answer. He was hollering at less voltage. Can't you check in and see if he's all right, please?
EXPERIMENTER (*with same detached calm*): Not once we've started. Please continue, Teacher.
SUBJECT (*sits down, sighs deeply*): 'Cool – day, shade, water, paint.' Answer, please. Are you all right in there? Are you all right?
EXPERIMENTER: Please continue, Teacher. Continue please. (*Subject pushes lever*)
SUBJECT: (*swivelling around in his chair*): Something's happened to that man in there. (*Swivelling back*) Next one. 'Low – dollar, necklace, moon, paint.' (*Turning around again*) Something's happened to that man in there. You better check in on him sir. He won't answer or nothing.
EXPERIMENTER: Continue. Go on, please.
SUBJECT: You accept all responsibility?
EXPERIMENTER: The responsibility is mine. Correct. Please go on. (*Subject returns to list, starts running through words as rapidly as he can read them, works through to 450 volts*)
SUBJECT: That's that.
EXPERIMENTER: Continue using the 450 volt switch for each wrong answer. Continue please.
SUBJECT: But I don't get no anything!
EXPERIMENTER: Please continue. The next word is 'white'.
SUBJECT: Don't you think you should look in on him, please?
EXPERIMENTER: Not once we've started the experiment.
SUBJECT: But what if something has happened to the man?
EXPERIMENTER: The experiment requires that you continue. Go on, please.
SUBJECT: Don't the man's health mean anything?
EXPERIMENTER: Whether the learner likes it or not . . .
SUBJECT: What if he's dead in there? (*Gestures towards the room with the electric chair)* I mean, he told me he can't stand the shock, sir. I don't mean to be rude, but I think you should look in on him. All you have to do is look in on him. All you have to do is look in the door. I don't get no answer, no noise. Something might have happened to the gentleman in there, sir.
EXPERIMENTER: We must continue, go on please.
SUBJECT: You mean keep giving him what? 450 volts, what he's got now?
EXPERIMENTER: That's correct. Continue. The next word is 'white'.
SUBJECT *(now at a furious pace)* 'White – cloud, horse, rock, house'. Answer please. The answer is 'horse'. 450 volts *(Administers shock)* Next word, 'Bag – paint, music, clown, girl'. The answer is 'paint'. 450 volts *(Administers shock)* Next word is 'Short – sentence, movie . . .'
EXPERIMENTER: excuse me, Teacher. We'll have to discontinue the experiment.

Contrary, therefore, to the business ethics field's practice of giving management sole moral authority to define ethical policies to which other organizational members should obey, we should look towards organizational members' *disobedience* as an ethical imperative. If only Fred Prozi, and all those others in the experiment like him, had simply *refused* to shock the protesting victim we could be far more confident that unethical acts are not being perpetrated as a result of organizational chains of command. The final critical article introduced here draws these points out strongly.

In their (1994) article, 'Whistle-blowing as Resistance in Modern Work Organizations', Joyce Rothschild and Terance Miethe demonstrate the importance of employee **whistle-blowing** in challenging unethical organizational practices. They define whistle-blowing as an organizational member's 'disclosure of illegal, unethical or harmful practices in the workplace to parties who might take action' (ibid., p. 254).

Whistle-blowers tend to be well-respected and conscientious employees. They tend to believe that once they have informed the appropriate managerial authority of these illegal or unethical acts the organization will take the appropriate measures to change its behaviour. In reality, what whistle-blowers often experience is that the organization's management do not see whistle-blowing as an act of good organizational citizenship. Instead, management tend to see the whistle-blower as a trouble-maker, as a potentially dangerous and unpredictable organizational maverick, or just plain crazy. The result too often is that rather than investigating the unethical practices brought to their attention, management investigates the whistle-blowing employee. The whistle-blower is disciplined, victimized or even dismissed. Undoubtedly, some who experience this unexpected victimization may be bullied or frightened into silence. However, for others, the experience of being victimized reinforces a belief that management is morally corrupt. Some of these individuals go on to pursue the issue they raised with a stronger sense of moral purpose.

Rothschild and Miethe (1994) illustrate their study of whistle-blowers with empirical examples, such as that of 'Anne'. Anne, 37 years old, was grateful to be hired in the late 1990s as a casting operator for a company making rubber belts. Within just a few days of starting the job, Anne began to experience some strange physical reactions. However, she continued to work hard and got a special commendation from her supervisor as well as an expansion of her role to include training other employees. Only a few weeks later, however, Anne was experiencing worse physical symptoms, including burning in the nose and mouth, headaches and bone pain. She told her boss and said that she planned to send for the papers that should be displayed on the chemical drums they were using, which would give details of the nature of the chemicals in the drums. Her supervisor told her this was a good idea, but the next day she was dismissed. Anne refused to accept this treatment. She contacted other employees of the organization and found out they too had suffered similar health problems. She then contacted a local university. With their help Anne discovered that the company was exposing its workers, with no protective equipment or warning, to over 100 times the legal exposure to certain toxic chemicals, and further that it was dumping toxic waste illegally. As a result of her own short exposure, Anne now had tumours growing in her mouth, liver damage, her skull began to soften and she had irreversible lung damage. Despite these serious health effects, she continued to campaign to end the organization's unethical and illegal practices. She prepared a civil law suit against the company, provided witness testimony at a national level, and was interviewed by the national hard-hitting TV journalism program *60 minutes*. Rothschild and Miethe quote Anne:

> I felt so completely victimized by the company. I had been such a trusting person. When they hired me, I thought they had picked me because they could see that I was an intelligent and responsible person. Now I know that when they picked me they were picking out a person to murder.
> (*ibid. p. 263*)

Rothschild and Miethe (1994) argue that for whistle-blowers such as Anne, a clear sense of ethics emerges that is in stark contrast to that of the managers of the organization. To quote the authors:

> To a person (whistle-blowers) come to see themselves as strong and moral. They have developed an understanding of how greed and self-aggrandizement can result in deceptive practices, harmful products and fraudulent services being built into the fabric of many organizations. They feel free of the abuse and above it. (*ibid., p. 268*)

Whistle-blowers' 'disobedient' personal ethical integrity does not always mean that they are successful in changing organizational practices. Often the power and resources of the organization are just too vast for an individual, no matter how committed, to change. The conclusion that Rothschild and Miethe arrive at reflects this, and they call for more widespread and collective organizational resistance to unethical organizational practices. Rothschild and Miethe's work is thus in stark contrast to the endorsement of stronger managerial authority in mainstream business ethics texts. Rothschild and Miethe's research argues that if we wish to have organizations that perpetrate less illegal and more ethical practices, we must look to and support those who *challenge* and *resist* managerial authority.

Thinkpoint 6.12

Ethics and power

- Have you or someone close to you ever refused to do something you were instructed to do because you thought it was morally wrong?
- How difficult was it to refuse, and how did the person who told you to do it react to your refusal?
- What does your experience tell you about the relationship between ethics and power?

Rothschild and Miethe's research, alongside that of Milgram's experiments and Neimark's case study, demonstrate the significance of critical approaches to ethics and organizations. Such studies show that, despite some business ethicists' attempts to make ethics palatable and profitable for business, 'ethics' can still be drawn upon to call organizations to account for their exploitative, dangerous or oppressive practices. Critically informed ethical studies of organizational behaviour present a troubling and potentially radical challenge to unethical organizational practices.

Box 6.5: UK whistle-blowing legislation – 'The Public Interest Disclosure Act (PIDA) 1998

Following a number of high-profile organizational disasters including instances of the abuse of vulnerable people in some care homes and children's homes, the collapse of the Bank of Credit and Commerce International and the Clapham rail disaster, legislation was introduced in the United Kingdom to protect whistle-blowers from being victimized by their organization in the kind of ways described by Rothschild and Miethe (1994).

The legislation (PIDA 1998) makes it illegal to victimize or dismiss whistle-blowers where they raise genuine concerns about misconduct and malpractice, as long as certain conditions and procedures are followed. If a whistle-blower is victimized or dismissed as a result of his/her whistle-blowing they can take their case to an employment tribunal to seek compensation.

While clearly welcome, the actual usefulness and extent of this legislative protection must still be looked at critically. For instance, Dr David Kelly, the weapons expert and senior government adviser who whistle-blew on his concerns about the UK government's 'sexing-up' or misrepresentation of evidence for engaging in the 2003 war in Iraq, seemed to be very poorly protected by this legislation. Dr Kelly's name was given to journalists by government representatives, and a number of attempts were made by ministers to discredit him in the public perception by presenting him as paranoid and a fantasist. Dr Kelly committed suicide after these events, forcing a governmental inquiry. In addition to Dr Kelly's tragic case there have also been a number of other high-profile cases in the United Kingdom in recent years where senior professionals who have blown the whistle on practices ranging from child abuse, to medical malpractice (including the retention of dead children's organs without the parents' permission). Several of these people also seem to have been victimized and/or dismissed by their employing organizations despite the 'protection' of this legislation.

Such cases perhaps serve to illustrate again the argument that formal ethical 'rules' (including laws and/or company policies on whistle-blowing) do not take away the need for our continual ethical scrutiny of organizational behaviour.

For a comprehensive international review of whistle-blowing, see Drew (2003) at www.psiru.org.

Contribution and limitations of the critical approach to thinking about the field

Critical approaches to business ethics enable us to look again, and more deeply, at the ethics of business. Unlike mainstream business ethics, critical approaches are not tied to justifying their critiques in terms of what is profitable, comfortable or even necessarily sympathetic to business interests and managerial authority. Critical approaches enable us to understand that the consequences of and conditions of work are far from wholly positive or benign. They remind us that exploitation, oppression, abuse and rampant inequality abound in the contemporary business world. Critical approaches help us realize that management and other organizational participants can often have different, even contradictory, agendas and interests. They remind us that management practices are not necessarily those that lead to the most ethical outcome.

Critical approaches help us to reclaim 'ethics' as a language that can legitimize organizational members' right to radically question organizational behaviour. Overall, critical approaches help us to realize that ethical issues at work are far deeper, and more immediately pressing, than those contained within an organization's glossy 'mission statement' or 'code of ethics'. But, perhaps most importantly of all, critical approaches can help us reflect more deeply upon our *own* behaviour within, and assumptions about, organizations.

A limitation of some critical approaches is that, perhaps because they do not merely reproduce more widely accepted mainstream knowledge about organizations, they can sometimes seem abstract and distant from the lived-experience of working in organizations. Indeed, critical writers do not always help themselves in this regard, with academic critics of organization sometimes seeming to prefer the company of dusty old books and long-dead philosophers than the problems facing working people in today's organizations. As a result, you might find that some critical writing on organization needs to be persevered with – it may take some time to understand the densely packed arguments and concepts used. Persevere though, and your thinking about ethics and organization may be deepened, and changed, forever.

Thinkpoint 6.13

Power versus ethics?

- Why would critical writers see management control as ethically problematic?
- Why might 'corporate social responsibility' be viewed suspiciously from a critical perspective?

Conclusion

In this chapter we have explored the topic of ethics at work in a number of ways. In the first part of the chapter we examined the rise of business ethics as an academic subject area alongside the modern corporation's claim to be 'socially responsible'. We have unpicked these concepts and highlighted key assumptions upon which they have been built. These included assumptions that business and organization are generally ethical; that managerial authority is good; and that ethics and profits are compatible rather than contradictory.

In the second part of the chapter we saw how critical approaches to ethics at work enabled us to re-examine each of these assumptions. Through this critical lens we saw how, because it promotes and relies upon organizational members' conformity, organization is dangerous for ethics; how employee resistance can reintroduce alternative ethical values into organization; and how critical approaches are trying to wrestle 'ethics' back from the brink of becoming just another part of the corporate brand.

So this is what the chapter has done, but why do I think it has been important to do this? As an introductory chapter to ethics at work, indeed as an introductory book on organizational behaviour, this text is unusual in dedicating much of its space to critical approaches. These critical approaches have been introduced not just to give you more 'theories' to think about and learn (even though we have done so!). Nor are they included simply because academics love to argue with each other (although we do!). Nor even are they included principally because critical writers think that mainstream authors have been guilty of presenting a selective picture of organizations (although this would certainly be argued by many!).

Rather, as I understand it, critical approaches exist and have been presented to you principally because they signify an *ethical questioning* of, and unease with, the values and effects of organization. As I said at the start of this chapter organizational behaviour affects all of us, every day. Organizations are powerful, and this power can be beautiful and it can be terrible. For critical writers especially, organization must accordingly always be judged on ethical and not just on financial criteria such as profitability or share dividends. Critical approaches attend to the ethics of organizational behaviour, and do so whether the specific topic is motivation, bureaucracy, corporate culture, technology or any of the other chapters in this book. Critical approaches are always underpinned by ethical questions. Questions such as:

- Whether, and how, organizations contribute to happiness or suffering?
- How should we judge this?
- Who is harmed and who is helped by organizational behaviour?
- Whose lives and values have we neglected in the way we study and run our organizations?

Finally, and most importantly, such ethical questions and doubts should be regarded as never once-and-for-all resolved. Organizations do not stop being powerful, and the ethical questions about work and organization do not therefore come to an end either.

Discussion questions

1. Outline how mainstream business ethics overcomes the three problems of 'relevance', 'conscience', and 'translation' faced when trying to argue for a greater role for ethics in business.
2. Does the rise of interest in business ethics and corporate social responsibility mean that business is becoming more ethical? Answer this question first from a mainstream and then from a critical perspective.
3. From a mainstream perspective, can ethics be managed? And if so, how?
4. From a critical perspective, what is dangerous with the idea of trying to manage ethics?

Further reading

- Beauchamp, T. and Bowie, N. (eds.) (2001) *Ethical Theory and Business*, sixth edition, London: Prentice Hall. (Edited book. Includes a wealth of classic and contemporary writings on most mainstream aspects of business ethics.)
- Crane, A. and Matten, D. (2004) *Business Ethics: A European Perspective*, Oxford: Oxford University Press. (A thorough and sympathetic review of current thinking in business ethics.)
- Frederick, R. (ed.) (2002) *A Companion to Business Ethics*, Oxford: Blackwell. (Edited book of original articles. Mainly dealing with mainstream approaches, but with some critical work.)
- Jones, C., Parker, M. and Ten Bos, R. (2005) *For Business Ethics*, Oxford: Routledge. (An excellent critical discussion of business ethics.)
- Parker, M. (ed.) (1998) *Ethics and Organizations*, London: Sage. (Edited collection of critical writings on ethics and organizations. The first half reviews the main critical ethical approaches, while the second half critically explores a number of organizational practices. Not really written at an introductory level, but well worth persevering with.)
- Solomon, R. and Martin, C. (2004) *Above the Bottom Line*, third edition, London: Wadsworth Publishing. (Thoughtful textbook introduction to mainstream business ethics.)

Useful websites

- www.corpwatch.org (A website that pulls together critiques of contemporary business practice. A great resource for finding a wealth of unethical organizational behaviour.)
- www.McSpotlight.org (Similar to the above, with a strong focus on critiquing McDonald's restaurants in particular.)

References

Arnold, D. and Bowie, N. (2003) 'Sweatshops and respect for persons', *Business Ethics Quarterly* 13(2):221–242.

Axline, L. (1990) 'The bottom line on ethics', *Journal of Accounting* 170(6):87–91.

Bauman, Z. (1989) *Modernity and the Holocaust*, Oxford: Polity Press.

Bauman, Z. (1993) *Post-modern ethics*, Oxford: Blackwell.

Beaton, A. (2001) *The Little Book of Management Bollocks*, London: Pocket Books.

Beauchamp, T. and Bowie, N. (1997) 'Ethical theory and business practice', in T. Beauchamp and N. Bowie (eds.) *Ethical Theory and Business*, fifth edition, London: Prentice Hall.

Bowie, N. (1983) 'Changing the rules', in J. White (ed.) *Contemporary Moral Problems*, London: Wadsworth, p.p. 243–246.

Brewis, J. (1998) 'Who do you think you are? Feminism, work, ethics and Foucault', in M. Parker (ed.) *Ethics and Organizations*, London: Sage, p.p. 53–75.

Derry, R. (2002) 'Feminist theory and business ethics', in R. Frederick (ed.) *A Companion to Business Ethics*, Oxford: Blackwell.

Drew, K. (2003) *Whistle-blowing and Corruption: An Initial and Comparative Review*, Public Services International Research Unit (www.psiru.org).

Edwards, G. and Goodell, R. (1994) 'Business ethics', *Executive Excellence* 11(2):17–18.

Friedman, M. (1970) 'The social responsibility of business is to increase its profits', in J. White (ed.) (2000) *Contemporary Moral Problems*, London: Wadsworth, p.p. 233–238.

Gow, D. (2003) 'Boeing sacks finance chief in ethics row', *Guardian*, 25 November 2003:17.

Johnson, C. (1994) 'A free market view of business ethics', *Supervision*, 55(5):14–17.

Klein, N. (2001) *No Logo*, London: Flamingo.

Knights, D. and, Roberts, J. (1982) 'The power of organization or the organization of power?', *Organization Studies* 3(1):47–64.

MacIntyre, A. (1981) *After Virtue*, London: Duckworth.

MacLagan, P. (1998) *Management and Morality*, London: Sage.

Marx, K. (1844) *Alienated Labour* (ed. L. Simon, 1994) Cambridge: Hacket Publishing Company, Inc.

Milgram, S. (1974) *Obedience to Authority: An Experimental View*, London: Tavistock.

Neimark, M. (1995) 'The selling of ethics: The ethics of business meets the business of ethics', *Accounting, Auditing, and Accountability* 8(3):81–97.

Parker, M. (2002) *Against Management*, Cambridge: Polity.

Phillips, N. (1991) 'The sociology of knowledge: Towards an existential view of business ethics', *Journal of Business Ethics* 10:787–795.

Richardson, B. and Curwen, P. (1995) 'Do free-market governments create crisis-ridden societies?', *Journal of Business Ethics* 14:551–560.

Ritzer, G. (1993) *The McDonaldisation of Society*, Thousand Oaks, CA: Pine Forge.

Roberts, J. (1984) 'The moral character of management practice', *Journal of Management Studies* 21(3):287–302.

Rothschild, J. and Miethe, T. (1994) 'Whistle-blowing as resistance in modern work organizations', in M. Jermier, D. Knights and W. Nord (eds.) *Resistance and Power in Organizations*, London: Routledge, p.p. 252–273.

Snell, R. (2004) 'Managing ethically', in S. Linstead, L. Fulop and S. Lilley (eds.) *Management and Organisation: A Critical Text*, Basingstoke: Palgrave, p.p. 240–277.

White, J. (ed.) (2000) *Contemporary Moral Problems*, sixth edition, London: Wadsworth.

Willmott, H. (1998) 'Towards a new ethics? The contributions of poststructuralism and posthumanism', in M. Parker (ed.) *Ethics and Organizations*, London: Sage, p.p. 76–121.

Wray-Bliss, E. (1998) 'The politics and ethics of representing workers: An ethnography of telephone banking clerks' PhD Thesis, *Manchester School of Management*, UMIST, UK.

Wray-Bliss, E. (2001) 'Representing customer service: Telephones and texts', in A. Sturdy, I. Grugulis and H. Willmott (eds.) *Customer Service: Empowerment and Entrapment*, Basingstoke: Palgrave, p.p. 38–59.

Wray-Bliss, E. and Parker, M. (1998) 'Marxism, capitalism, and ethics', in M. Parker (ed.) *Ethics and Organizations*, London: Sage, p.p. 30–52.

Wylie, I. (1997) 'The human answering machine', *Guardian*, 26 July: 2–3.

Note

1 www.amnesty.org

7 Bureaucracy and Post-bureaucracy

Christopher Grey

Key concepts and learning objectives

By the end of this chapter you should understand:

- The two models of organizations – bureaucracy and post-bureaucracy – and what is claimed about the reasons for their existence and the benefits and limitations of each.
- The disputes about their value from the point of view of efficiency, but you should also understand that efficiency itself is a disputed concept.
- The different concepts of **rationality** in organizations and how these relate to the two models.
- The political and ethical issues that inform debates about the two models.

Aims of the chapter

This chapter will:

- Explain bureaucracy and post-bureaucracy as models of organization.
- Explain the deficiencies of each model from mainstream perspectives.
- Examine some major mainstream studies.
- Identify critical approaches to each model.
- Examine some major critical studies.
- Explain the strengths and weaknesses of the critical approaches.

Overview and key points

Bureaucracy is a model of organization based upon rules, hierarchy, impersonality and a division of labour and has been the dominant form of organization for over a century. However, it suffers from problems such as poor employee motivation, producer-focus and inertia. In view of this, post-bureaucracy has been proposed as a new organizational model more suited to today's business environment. Post-bureaucracy is based on trust, empowerment, personal treatment and shared responsibility. But this brings its own problems in terms of loss of control, risk and unfairness.

These models and problems derive from mainstream thinking. Such thinking is concerned with narrow views of efficiency and is guided by a search for control and performance. Critical approaches provide a more radical analysis of bureaucracy and post-bureaucracy. From a critical perspective bureaucracy is seen as dehumanizing and post-bureaucracy is interpreted as an extension of control. Moreover, both are criticized for seeking efficiency from the point of view of those with power, to the neglect of other people and of the ethical purposes and consequences of organization. However, among other limitations, critical approaches can be seen as utopian.

Mainstream approach

Introduction

Imagine that you have been asked to manage student admissions to your course, and imagine that for some reason you have to do the job from scratch. What kinds of things would you do? The chances are you would set up some kind of system. As a minimum, you might set up a system that established a closing date for applications; which sent out a standard letter acknowledging receipt of applications; which set a rule that once the closing date has passed you will accept the 100 best-qualified applicants; and which sent a standard letter of acceptance or rejection to each applicant, asking those you had accepted to confirm by a set date that they will take up your offer. You might well also employ other people to do some aspects of the job. For example, you might employ a secretary to send out the letters, but make the decisions about the wording of the letters and about whom to accept yourself. And on what basis would you have the right to make those decisions? Obviously, the fact that you are the Admissions Manager.

Thinkpoint 7.1

What other kinds of procedures might you put in place?

No doubt there would be quite a lot of other aspects of the system you devised. What is sure is that you would devise a system, and that if you did not then you would be unlikely to do a very good job. Think for a minute about what would happen if you did not adopt a system similar to that just outlined. You might accept or reject applicants when later on you got better or worse qualified applicants; you would write a different letter each time you dealt with an application; you would accept applicants on the basis of something other than qualification (at random? first come, first served? the sound of their name? where they were born?), and you would have no way of knowing who had accepted their places because you had not asked them to confirm acceptance of your offer.

In order to perform this relatively straightforward task efficiently, you would have designed a system characterized by:

- rules (e.g. closing date)
- standardized procedures (e.g. letters)
- rationality (e.g. accepting applicants for a logical reason)
- division of labour (e.g. between you and your secretary)
- hierarchy (e.g. you are in charge of your secretary)
- authority (e.g. you have the right to make decisions).

Take any other task of any size and you will find that these kinds of systems will enable you to do the job better than any alternative. What does 'better' mean here? It means more efficiently (with less waste of time and resources) and more effectively (in terms of getting the result you require).

Exercise 7.1

Imagine another task you might be asked to organize. What system would you put in place and how does it illustrate the characteristics discussed? Can you design a system that would be effective that does *not* have these characteristics?

This example illustrates themes that have been at the heart of the theory and practice or organization for at least 100 years. One of the founding figures of organizational behaviour was Max Weber (1864–1920), a German social scientist who was interested in a wide range of social and political questions in his time. One of these was the question of what held societies together, and this, he thought, was to do with authority.

Authority comes in different forms in different societies at different times. It may be based on 'charisma' (the personal authority of particular individuals) or on 'tradition' (the established authority of institutions, such as the monarchy). But according to Weber, modern societies were increasingly based on rational-legal authority – that is, systems of rules (e.g. legal rules) devised for rational reasons. Hence the term rational-legal. People in society accepted that they had to follow the dictates of these systems. Hence they were a form of authority.

Rational-legal authority was the basis not just of the legal system, but the state, the civil service, industry and most other kinds of organization. We can already see how it relates to the example of setting up an admissions system, where terms such as 'rule', 'reason' and 'authority' appeared. Applied to organizations, rational-legal authority means bureaucracy. Nowadays we often use this word to imply something inefficient – 'red tape' (and we will come back to that later). But in its pure form (which Weber called an 'ideal-type') it refers to a highly efficient form of organization. Indeed, this was the reason why, according to Weber, it was becoming more and more dominant from the late 19th century onwards. Bureaucracy, he said, was the most technically efficient and rational form of organization. It simply got the job done better than any other system, and this was why it was adopted.

Let's take a closer look at what these bureaucracies consist of:

- *Functional specialization*. There is a formal division of labour so that some people are paid to do one kind of function as their official duty and they do not do anything other than their official duty. They are employed full-time within the context of a lifetime career structure and are appointed and promoted on the basis of qualifications and experience.
- *Hierarchy of authority*. There is a structure such that those holding a superior position have the authority, solely by virtue of holding that position, to give orders to those in subordinate positions. Subordinates, in turn, report upwards to their superiors.
- *System of rules*. Everything that goes on in the organization is based upon following a formal, written set of rules about procedures and practices that must be adhered to.
- *Impersonality*. Rules are followed and authority is held with regard for emotions, personality or personal preferences. Employees and customers are treated in accordance with these rules.

Some of these ingredients look pretty obvious to us. Does it really need to be said that people get paid in money? But Weber was trying to pin down all the features that separated bureaucracy from

SOURCE: COPYRIGHT © CANAL +

Image 7.1 Cogs in the machine?

all other kinds of organization. Other features are familiar from the admissions system example – which isn't surprising because Weber's 'model' was based on his observation of what efficiently organized systems actually did. Some features look a little dated – full-time, permanent jobs for life, for example, are not necessarily a feature of modern bureaucracies. But overall, the reason why the list seems obvious is that Weber was right to think that these kinds of organizations were becoming dominant. Now,they seem so familiar that we hardly recognize them as anything other than 'the way things are'.

However, a bureaucratic way of organizing is one bound up with tasks of a particular kind. Specifically, it is effective in situations where very large numbers of identical, standard operations are needed – processing social security claims or mass producing cars, for example. It also suits situations where a rigid chain of command is favoured, where little training or initiative is required, since all that people need to do is to follow rules and orders.

Many commentators believe that these kinds of conditions no longer obtain or, at any rate, are increasingly rare. Since at least the 1970s, but with a growing insistence, it has been claimed that such 'industrial' conditions are giving way to a 'post-industrial' era. This argument takes many forms, but in essence it says that the economy has moved from the mass production of standard products towards short product runs for niche markets. At the same time, it is suggested that people in organizations need – and perhaps want – to be more flexible and innovative, rather than simply following orders.

Thinkpoint 7.2

What do you regard as the benefits and costs of a working in a bureaucracy from the point of view of the employee?

Against that background, there has arguably been the development of a range of new organizational forms. These are given many different names, but as an umbrella term we can call them 'post-bureaucracies'. Charles Heckscher (1994), one of the leading writers on post-bureaucracy, has devised a list of characteristics he calls the post-bureaucratic ideal-type, in contrast to Weber's ideal-type of bureaucracy:

- Rules are replaced with consensus and dialogue based upon personal influence rather than status. People are trusted to act on the basis of shared values rather than rules.
- Responsibilities are assigned on the basis of competence for tasks rather than hierarchy, and are treated as individuals rather than impersonally.
- The organization has an open boundary, so that rather than full-time permanent employment, people come into and out of the organization in a flexible way, including part-time, temporary and consultancy arrangements. Work is no longer done in fixed hours or at a designated place.

CASE STUDY 7.1 Universal

Robertson and Swan (1998) explain the development since 1986 of a consultancy firm that specializes in advising high-tech companies and start-ups on innovation and the exploitation of intellectual property rights. The firm – which they call 'Universal' – is also involved in incubating (providing resource and assistance for new ventures) and taking equity shares in some client companies. The Universal case is an interesting one for illustrating aspects of the basic models of bureaucracy and post-bureaucracy and also some of the complexities of these models, which we will come to later in this chapter.

To give a very brief summary, Universal grew from a charismatic founder and handful of consultants in 1986 until it employed around 120 consultants plus almost the same number again as associates in other countries. In the early years, Universal was explicitly egalitarian, non-hierarchical and non-bureaucratic. Many of the early members were recruited from more traditional consultancies and were attracted by the freer atmosphere. Project teams were self-organizing and trusted to do their work well and efficiently. Projects were initiated on the basis of their scientific value. People joined projects that interested them and rewards were fairly equally shared. Knowledge about projects was shared on a word of mouth basis. In short, bureaucracy was not much in evidence. From the early 1990s onwards, the combination of growth and also tougher market conditions led to the creation of divisions and divisional managers. Under a new performance management system, each division and each individual was given a revenue target, and this was linked to financial rewards. Projects were undertaken on the basis of their financial viability. Although there was still relatively little formal hierarchy, there was an informal pecking order among staff. There was an internal labour market for project staff, which used e-mail systems to advertise opportunities.

Exercise 7.2

Imagine that you had joined Universal in 1986. How might you feel about the changes now?

Case commentary

How we read this case depends on where we look from. Entering Universal now, we might see it as a good example of a post-bureaucratic organization. It is relatively flatly structured and project based, and it makes heavy use of 'virtual' organization. Looked at by someone who had worked at Universal since 1986 we might see it as a good example of an organization which has become more bureaucratically structured in order to compete in tougher market conditions by increasing efficiency. Although we will return to the case as we go through the chapter, the point to note for now is that bureaucracy and post-bureaucracy are to some extent relative terms. In other words, reality is usually less clear-cut than the models or 'ideal-types'. Robertson and Swan (1998, p. 561) make almost exactly this point when they show how cultural and systemic forms of control are interlinked at Universal.

Key problems

Bureaucracy Although bureaucracy has been adopted in probably every large organization in every country in the world, organization theorists and analysts have always recognized that it poses problems. Some of these problems are to do with the social impact of bureaucracy, and these will be picked up in the 'Critical approach' section later in this chapter. But there are also problems from the more narrow perspective of organizational design and efficiency. Many of these are the kinds of problems that give rise to the everyday sense that bureaucracy equals 'red tape' – needless waste and pedantic obsession with rules. Later, we will cover some of the technical reasons for these problems, but for now we will just give a brief outline of them.

Bureaucracy can be thought of as a form of organization which is like a 'machine'. In principle, each part is perfectly designed to perform its task, and the whole thing operates 'like clockwork' in an entirely predictable, standard way. It is this that makes a bureaucracy efficient. But it also means that the people within the organization have to function as if they were mere 'cogs' within the machine. This leads to at least three key problems for bureaucracy.

One is the problem of motivation (see Chapter 2). Because people in bureaucracies have to follow rules, and have no choice or discretion about doing so, they may well have little personal commitment to the organization, and gain little interest or stimulation from their work. Theorists of motivation have long recognized that very often motivation is linked to factors such as job satisfaction and to a sense of achievement and responsibility at work. Bureaucracies rarely deliver this and, *if* high motivation leads to better work performance then it follows that employees will perform sub-optimally in bureaucracies. In this sense, they may not be so efficient as they seem at first sight.

Linked to this is the problem that bureaucracies, as rule-based systems, may not be very good at customer service. If the workforce are poorly motivated they are unlikely to care much about customer service but simply follow rules grudgingly or blindly. These rules are there for the good of the organization rather than customers, and will not be changed to suit the particular demands an individual customer may have. For this reason, bureaucracies are sometimes described as producer-focused. There is an expression – 'a jobsworth' – which describes the typical mindset of an employee of a bureaucracy. When asked by a customer to bend the rules in some particular case, such an employee replies 'that would be more than my job's worth'. They know that failing to follow rules will lead to their being punished, or even sacked. This can also lead to a situation where no decision is taken until it is passed up to the competent 'authority'. This 'buck-passing' leads to people 'hiding behind the rules' and is sometimes called bureaupathy.

This kind of inflexibility is a microcosm of a third key problem for bureaucracy: it seems to be resistant to innovation and to change (see Chapter 10). Rules, once made, are enshrined for all time and will only change very slowly. This may not matter in contexts of, say, producing large quantities of standard products the specifications of which do not vary for long periods of time, perhaps several years. However, in more volatile and uncertain conditions bureaucratic inertia will mean that these organizations fail to adapt and therefore will either disappear when faced with competition; or survive only because of being protected by government from competition, but deliver goods and services in an inefficient way.

Thinkpoint 7.3

How does the system for student admissions, described at the beginning of this chapter, illustrate the problems of bureaucracy?

Post-bureaucracy Post-bureaucracy is very much a response to the kinds of problems believed to characterize bureaucracies and it proceeds, as we have seen, from the analysis that many or most sectors are in fact unstable and rapidly changing. This means that bureaucratic inertia will indeed be a problem. However, as an alternative model of organizations, post-bureaucracy generates its own set of problems, many of them, of course, being precisely those which bureaucracy seems to solve.

If bureaucracy is like a machine, then post-bureaucracy is more like an organism – a living, growing, changing entity with a mind of its own. But this means that it is far less predictable than a machine, and prey to illnesses and malfunctions. Again, we can see at least three linked problems.

The first of them is that of control. Bureaucracies use detailed rules to control what goes on in organizations. Without such rules, how can control be exercised, especially in large organizations that may spread over many countries? In essence, post-bureaucracy proposes a different, normative, form of control based upon some version of culture management (see Chapter 9) and trust. But that is a rather fragile form of control, resting as it does on self-control rather than external monitoring. Trust may be difficult to sustain, especially over long distances where relationships are mediated 'virtually' rather than face-to-face, and trust, of course, may be betrayed. Since post-bureaucracies are also characterized by a 'porous' organizational boundary, this means that employees will be coming in and out of the organization on short-term and consulting contracts. These seem like particularly unpromising conditions to build shared values and trust. In short, there is a danger that post-bureaucracies will descend into anarchy.

Related to this problem of control, there is the problem of risk. It is all very well to give people more freedom to innovate and to do away with rules, but what happens if this freedom leads to decisions that go wrong? The consequence will be failures of service delivery and lost money. Fixed

Image 7.2

rules may deter good ideas and improvements to products and services, but they also prevent bad ideas and damage. We can see that, in the case of Universal, these issues informed the development of more bureaucratic systems. Whereas, in the early days, projects were developed with little concern for their financial consequences, the later systems tried to ensure that these consequences were considered.

The third main problem is also linked to the issue of control. As well as the business risks of innovation there are also questions of fairness. Bureaucratic systems are impersonal; they do not discriminate between people except on the basis of experience and qualifications. Post-bureaucracy stresses individual treatment – again, a move away from rigid rules. But this opens up the possibility of all kinds of irrationalities and prejudices. For example, while you might want to be treated 'as an individual', would you want your promotion prospects to depend upon whim? Suppose a male project leader only chooses attractive young women to work on prestigious contracts. Wouldn't those of us who are not attractive young women (and, indeed, those who are) prefer to be chosen on the basis of a rational system? And the issues here are not only moral but also pragmatic, since businesses that allow discrimination may face legal penalties and also suffer sub-optimal decisions about staffing. This also applies to the flexible treatment of customers. We might be delighted if an organization, say, rushed our order through and so responded flexibly to our needs. But what about the other customer whose order is therefore pushed down the queue? Would that customer be so pleased?

Thinkpoint 7.4

How does the development of Universal illustrate an attempt to deal with the problems of post-bureaucracy?

Key ideas and contributions to thinking

Because bureaucracy has had such a long history, there is a very wide range of studies that have tried to understand and refine it. Post-bureaucracy has a shorter history, but this has coincided with an upsurge in writing and thinking about organizations, so there is plenty of material to cover there as well. However, it would not be unfair to say that the earlier generation (say, 1945–1970) of organizational theorists, who were concerned with bureaucracy and its problems, contributed more to the key ideas in this area. This is partly because ideas about post-bureaucracy have actually been around for a long time (as we will see later) and so the earlier theorists had already developed several ideas about them. And it is partly because the later generation (say 1970 to the present) seem less to generate new ideas as to reformulate what has become something like an orthodoxy about the deficiencies of bureaucracy.

Does size matter? In much of the earlier material, and explicitly in the case study of Universal, it has been implied that there is something significant in the impact of organizational size upon bureaucracy. And this is surely true. If we go back to the opening example of an admissions system for a university course, then it is fairly obvious that if, for the sake of argument, there were only three applications for the course, it would hardly be necessary to devise the systems described. There would be no need for standardization of letters, no need for a division of labour and no need for an authority structure. There might still need to be a rule on whom to accept (if, for example, there was only one place available) but this would hardly call for a bureaucratic system.

There can be no doubt that part of the reason Weber observed a growth in rational-legal, or bureaucratic, organization was because he also lived at a time that was witnessing a phenomenal growth in organizational size – whether that meant the army, the state or factories. Later studies confirmed this. Some of the classic work was done by Peter Blau (1955, 1970). In studies in the United States of over 50 government employment agencies involving over 1200 branches and 350 head offices, Blau found a consistent relationship between bureaucratization (which he measured in some technical ways that do not matter here) and organizational size, measured in numbers of employees. As employee numbers increased, so to did bureaucratization. An organization with, say, 10 000 employees was much more bureaucratized than one of 10, or even 100.

But, more than that, although bureaucratization increased with size, it did so at a declining rate. In other words, adding employee numbers to small organizations had a bigger impact on bureaucratization than adding the same numbers to large organizations. It is not difficult to see why. Imagine a firm employing 10 people, which then expands to employ 510. That is likely to call for all kinds of new systems and rules. But imagine a firm of 20 000 people that expands to 20 500. That will have much less impact. So numbers of employees increase bureaucratization, but at a declining rate, and this observation gives rise to the 'Blau curve'.

That size was linked to bureaucracy was also supported by the Aston Studies, conducted at Aston University in the United Kingdom in the 1960s and 1970s (Pugh, Hickson and Hinings, 1968; Pugh and Hickson, 1976). These studies asserted a causal relationship between size and bureaucratic structure. However, their explanation was different, and more complicated, to that of Blau. The Aston researchers proposed that in larger organizations there was a greater **statistical probability** of recurrent and repetitive events. This being so, such organizations were more likely to develop standardized rules since they were faced with standardized situations. And standardized rules are, of course, at the heart of bureaucracy. One way of understanding the developments at Universal consultancy is to see a growth in size as leading to the development of more standardized systems.

Although there is an obvious common-sense appeal in the idea that size is what drives bureaucracy, it is important to realize that the situation is less straightforward than common sense might suggest. First, there have been studies which argue that if there is a relationship between size and bureaucracy, then its causality may run against that proposed by the Aston Studies. In other words, it may be that sometimes size is a consequence, not a cause, of bureaucracy. Aldrich (1972) reanalysed the Aston data and argued that this was so. Why? Imagine an organization setting up a new division (e.g. a personnel division or an overseas office). This is an increase in the division of labour, one of the measures of bureaucracy. This new division has to be staffed, so more people are employed. So an increase in bureaucratization has led to an increase in size, not vice versa.

Another classic study questions the size–bureaucracy link in a different way. Joan Woodward, who was not just one of the pioneers of organization studies but one of the few women among those pioneers, looked at the relationship between technology and bureaucracy. She studied around 100 manufacturing firms, of varying sizes, in the United Kingdom and argued that what affected the extent of their bureaucratization was not their size but the type of technology they employed (Woodward, 1965). Thus firms engaged in mass production of standard goods did indeed have bureaucratic structures, but those – even large firms – that were developing one-off products (e.g. hydroelectric turbines), or that had continuous high-tech production technologies (e.g. chemical refining), were far less bureaucratized.

How do these questions relate to post-bureaucracy? Is the implication that large organizations must be bureaucratic? This can be answered in two ways. First, the case for post-bureaucracy rests heavily on the proposition that new information and communication technologies have had a decisive impact upon ways of organizing. So the Woodward findings are relevant to this, because they suggest that there is not an iron law linking size and bureaucracy. Technology also comes in to the

SOURCE: © RONNIE KAUFMAN / CORBIS

Image 7.3 Pre-industrial or post-Fordist?

Image 7.4

equation. Secondly, at least since Peters and Waterman's influential thinking on organizational culture it has been claimed that organizations can 'be big' and 'act small' at the same time. They can use cultural norms, instead of bureaucratic rules, to combine personalized service and organizational control. Whether that is true remains, of course, an open question.

The dysfunctions of bureaucracy Whatever it is that leads to bureaucracy, what are its effects? Classic studies here have focused on whether bureaucracy is really as rational as it appears. We have prefigured this question when, in discussing the problems of bureaucracies, we considered how efficient they were. A group of writers, sometimes called the 'bureaucratic dysfunctionalists', posed these issues with considerable sharpness, by probing some of the realities of bureaucratic life.

The American sociologist Robert Merton (1940) addressed a core theoretical and practical issue with his concept of goal displacement. He argued that, over time, people in bureaucracies came to see 'following the rule' as the goal or purpose, rather than the effect that the rule was supposed to produce. This is the theoretical way of talking about the 'jobsworth' mentality referred to earlier. What matters in goal displacement is, so to speak, 'doing the thing right' rather than 'doing the right thing'. A slavish adherence to the rules as an end in itself is central to the 'red tape' associated with bureaucratic life.

To see how it might work, let's return to the hypothetical admissions system discussed at the start of this chapter. Imagine that having set up the system described you receive an application from a student who has not filled in the application forms, but has provided evidence of already having achieved six 'A' grade A-levels at the age of 16. She also has an impressive record of non-academic achievement and a clutch of references attesting to her academic and personal qualities. But, for some plausible reason, she needs a decision on whether she will be accepted to the course before the closing date for applications has passed.

A reasonable response might be to offer her a place. You know that she fills the criteria and is almost certainly better qualified than any other applicant you will get. Yet the rules say that application forms must be completed and that no decisions will be made before the closing date. So, quite legitimately, you refuse to give a decision and she goes elsewhere. This is goal displacement. Goal displacement does not just mean that you have been inflexible. The point (or 'goal') of the rule is to ensure that the organization maximizes the quality of its student intake. Yet the effect of applying the rule has been to sub-optimize the intake: the person who takes the place you might otherwise have offered the unorthodox applicant will not be as well qualified. You have acted as if the goal of the rule is to *follow* the rule.

Exercise 7.3

How would a post-bureaucratic organization deal with this applicant? What problems might this lead to?

A particular version of the goal-displacement thesis is found in the work of Philip Selznick (1949). His studies suggested that the divisionalized structures of a bureaucratic organization led inevitably to people identifying with the aims of their divisions, not the aims of the organization as a whole.

Thus they would pursue divisional interests at the expense of the organization. In this way, a bureaucracy not only could, but, because of the divisionalization most likely would, deliver organizationally sub-optimal outcomes. This line of thinking has opened up significant wider issues in organizational analysis, including the relationship between sub-cultures and organizational cultures (see Chapter 9) and the nature of organizational politics (see Chapter 8).

All this might seem to deal a fatal blow to the whole theory of bureaucracy. The key idea of this theory is that a system of rules enshrines the most efficient way of doing things. Yet goal displacement suggests that following the rules does not always lead to the best outcome. Someone might respond by offering this (sophisticated) defence of bureaucracy. The defence would be that bureaucracy offers not an optimum solution to each case it deals with but an optimum *average* solution. In other words, overall a bureaucratic system is more efficient even if, in particular cases, it is less than optimal.

Yet, against this, we would have to set the argument presented by Peter Blau. Apart from the Blau curve, this researcher also advanced a very elegant argument suggesting that bureaucracy *always* delivers sub-optimal solutions to problems. Blau observed the trade union tactic called 'work to rule'. A work to rule falls short of a strike and consists of workers refusing to do anything other than follow the formal, established rules of their workplace. Anything that they do which is not in their contracts and not in the organizational rulebook, they refuse to do. If the rules say that they stop at 5.00pm, they stop at 5.00pm on the dot, for example. Similarly, if the rules fail to specify how a particular job should be done then they repeatedly ask for assistance or guidance before doing it. Blau explains that the reason why a union adopts 'work to rule' is in order to disrupt the organization (typically, in pursuit of a pay claim). Yet, if bureaucratic rules enshrine the most efficient way of organizing, then how could it be that following those rules to the letter made the organization less efficient? Blau's answer is that, in fact, following the rules exactly is *not* the most efficient way of organizing, just as goal displacement tells us that following the rules, rather than trying to meet the underlying purpose of those rules, is inefficient. But this means that bureaucracy is not the most efficient kind of organization. Therefore, the whole model of bureaucracy must be wrong.

These insights are very much in line with the case for post-bureaucratic organizations. This case invites us to 'tear up' the rulebook and allow individual discretion. Yet, although this is plausible in the light of Blau's analysis, it has its own problems. Workers may, in following the set rules, be less efficient than if they had used their own discretion. But it does not follow that, left to themselves, they would have adopted the most efficient way of working. They might have adopted an even less efficient approach than that enshrined in the rules. If so, a post-bureaucratic way of working would not only be less efficient during times of industrial action, it would be less efficient at all times!

Thinkpoint 7.5

Do you think that Universal is more or less efficient because it has adopted a more bureaucratic system? Do you think that the admissions system would be more or less efficient if it adopted a post-bureaucratic system?

The studies of Merton, Selznick and Blau show us that the close following of bureaucratic rules may not lead to efficiency. But there is also a second stream of work within the bureaucratic dysfunctionalist literature that advances a diametrically opposed set of problems. Here the issue is not one of an over-attachment to the rules but the observation that, very often, organizational rules are completely ignored. This was Crozier's (1964) finding – that employees in bureaucracies did, as a matter of fact, indulge all manner of prejudices whether or not the formal rules allowed it. These prejudices may be presumed to be sup-optimal from the point of view of organizational efficiency, but this is not necessarily so (as they might be cases of the Blau finding that ignoring organizational rules offers better outcomes than those delivered by the rules). But whether or not they are sub-optimal, they certainly deal a blow to the idea that bureaucracies are impersonal.

The work of Alvin Gouldner elaborates Crozier's insights by introducing the concept of mock bureaucracy. Gouldner (1954) found cases of organizations that have elaborate rulebooks but, in practice, the rules are ignored. Examples include safety regulations. In many dangerous industries, from mining (discussed by Gouldner) to building sites, it is commonplace for the formal rules to exist but not to be followed – as the phrase has it, 'more honoured in the breach than the observance' – because people see them as inconvenient or getting in the way of the job. Other examples might include equal opportunities regulations.

Mock bureaucracy and goal displacement are opposites – one is about following rules blindly, the other about ignoring rules – but both undermine the rational, machine-like picture of organizations found in the bureaucratic model. But their implications for post-bureaucracy are different. An over-attachment to rules vindicates the case for post-bureaucracy as a solution to this myopic inertia. But if bureaucracies ignore rules and find their own way of working then it might be argued that, in practice if not in theory, they end up being little different to organizations that dispense with rules, so why not stick with bureaucracy?

Key issues and controversies

Many key issues and controversies have already been indicated in the chapter, such as why do bureaucracies exist, whether they are efficient and what is the alternative? However, the major overriding controversy is whether bureaucracy is being, or should be, consigned to history to be supplanted by post-bureaucracy (see also Chapter 4).

The idea that bureaucracy is on the way out is one which has been touted for many decades – certainly since the mid-1960s when Warren Bennis (1966) proclaimed the imminent death of bureaucracy. His case for this was very similar to that heard today – namely that there was no longer the stable business environment within which bureaucracy made sense, and that more collaborative organizational relations rendered the rigid rules of bureaucracy obsolete. This analysis was disputed at the time, for example by Miewald (1970), and later by Perrow (1979), on the basis that bureaucracy, at least for large organizations, retained an efficiency advantage, and that the extent to which environmental turbulence had increased was exaggerated.

Despite this, there have been continual claims along the same lines as those of Bennis, although the vocabulary shifts over time. For example, Piore and Sabel (1984) advanced the idea that the world was moving from mass production and stable markets towards niche production in volatile markets. This in turn had the implication of a move from bureaucracy to '**flexible specialization**'. More recent outings of the argument have probably been more widely, or at any rate more vocally, made than ever before. In particular, management gurus such as Tom Peters and Charles Handy have been highly influential in proclaiming versions of the same basic claim. This analysis has also been popularized by more public policy oriented writers such as Charles Leadbetter (1999) and in this way it has informed political debate in many countries, especially the United Kingdom and the United States. At the political level, the end of bureaucracy thesis links to attempts to reform public sector organizations and to devise education and training policies that are consistent with the emerging 'knowledge-economy' (see Chapters 5 and 12).

SOURCE: © ISTOCKPHOTO.COM / SEAN LOCKE

Image 7.5 Brave new world?

But it would be wrong to see all these arguments as deriving from the self-publicizing efforts of some influential popular writers. On the contrary, their claims are only accessible versions of some very sophisticated studies. For example, Manuel Castells has written several very detailed analyses (e.g. Castells, 1996) pointing to the rise of the **network society** and **network organizations**, which he links strongly to the information technology revolution of the last quarter of a century. More directly in the organization studies community, Heckscher and Donnellon (1994) have provided both a theoretical framework and several empirical illustrations of post-bureaucracy.

As with earlier predictions of the demise of bureaucracy, the more recent obituaries have also been met with a great deal of scepticism (see Chapter 4). Warhurst and Thompson (1998) have been particularly acute critics arguing that mass production and, for that matter, manufacturing are by no means in decline globally, and that new working practices based on trust and empowerment are more rhetorical than

SOURCE: © DREDGE & RIGG / PRIVATE EYE

Image 7.6

real. About the only attribute of the post-bureaucratic model that is unequivocally proven is an increase in the use of part-time and short-contract workers. But, even if increasing, this is not new, and it does not in and of itself demonstrate post-bureaucratization.

Later in this chapter we will return to some of these issues from a different perspective, but in terms of mainstream views, what is the answer to this controversy? In a sense, precisely because it is a controversy, there is no definite answer. It may be that it is just too early to tell. It may be that, as with Universal, there is no absolute answer because it depends on where, and when, you look at things. Thus it is possible to interpret Universal as being bureaucratic or as being post-bureaucratic. This perhaps reflects another important issue: both bureaucracy and post-bureaucracy as 'ideal-types' may not actually exist in practice. Instead, organizations may exhibit a range of characteristics, some of which are bureaucratic and others post-bureaucratic.

Finally, though, precisely because of the long history of this controversy, it is interesting to consider the now classic work of Burns and Stalker (1961). Their study suggested that organizations might be mechanical or organic (meaning roughly bureaucratic or post-bureaucratic) depending on 'contingencies' such as the nature of their business environment, the technologies they used and the skill levels of their workforces (a similar finding to the Woodward studies discussed earlier). This **contingency approach** might suggest to us that the idea that all organizations are, or will become, post-bureaucratic is simplistic. It is notable that most of the empirical examples given of such organizations are in high-tech business sectors such as computing and biotechnology, which are yet to 'mature'. In the end, then, the mainstream answer to the current version of its main controversy may be a restatement of contingency theory.

Important empirical studies

In the chapter so far, we have identified many of the main empirical studies in this area, all of which would repay closer attention. Because the theme of bureaucracy, in particular, has been present since the start of organization studies (indeed, in some ways, it is the bedrock of the subject) there are an almost literally endless number of studies we could examine. But the three discussed here are especially interesting.

The first study is Melville Dalton's (1959) classic *Men Who Manage*. This was in many ways a pathbreaking piece of research because it represents one of the first applications of **ethnographic** methods to the study of organizations. Although ethnography had been used from at least the 1920s to study social groups within Western societies, they had tended to focus on 'marginal' or relatively powerless groups, such as street gangs or prostitutes. Dalton's study was innovative because it was one of the first ethnographies of powerful elites.

Men Who Manage was a study of four bureaucratic organizations, codenamed Milo, Fruhling, Attica and Rambeau, but the centrepiece of the book was the study of Milo, which was the most extensive of the four cases. Strictly speaking, we should in fact say that, as its title implies, this was a study of bureaucratic managers rather than of entire organizations. Apart from being methodologically innovative, this study was highly revealing about the realities of managerial work and did much to debunk the rational image of such work and, indeed, bureaucracy itself. Among other things, it illustrates some of the issues that Crozier discussed concerning how individual prejudices (e.g. about religious beliefs) were not left outside the office but played a central part in decision making about, for example, who to employ and promote. The study also illustrates Selznick's point about how different divisions within bureaucracies pursue their own goals through political in-fighting, rather than there being a single, shared, organizational goal (see Chapter 8).

A second study in a recognizably similar tradition to Dalton's is Rosabeth Moss Kanter's (1993) book, *Men and Women of the Corporation*. The title itself seems to stand in some kind of relation to Dalton's work, published almost 20 years earlier. For not only had organizations become somewhat less male dominated in the intervening period but, more to the point, Kanter was one of the pioneers of applying feminist ideas to the study of organizations. Thus, while much of the detail of her study of the firm code named Indsco reveals some similar issues to that of Dalton, Kanter draws particular attention to how they relate to gender. For example, Kanter suggests that the relationship between (largely) male managers and (exclusively) female secretaries takes a form that is recognizably pre-bureaucratic and is quite resistant to the rational-legal ideal-type of bureaucracy. She suggests that the relationship is highly personalized and therefore unstandardized, and is in part bound up with displays of status on the part of both manager and secretary.

Good studies of this detailed type post-bureaucracy are, as yet, more difficult to find. The 'after-word' to the second edition of Kanter's book is worth reading in this regard as it updates some of the Indsco story into the 1990s. A less academic study of post-bureaucracy is Ricardo Semler's (1993) account of his company Semco, a Brazilian engineering firm. Semler regards himself as a 'counsellor' rather than a chief executive, and this illustrates the idea that post-bureaucracy discounts hierarchy. Overall, Semco is characterized by an approach that rejects formal rules, employees set their own working hours and pay rates, and is relaxed about unionization and strike activity.

It is important to recognize that this study is the work of someone describing and justifying his own experience and activities: it does not purport to be detached or analytical, and it would be interesting to hear the voices of others within the firm to see how far they endorse Semler's account. Nevertheless, there is no doubt that Semco represents a departure from traditional bureaucratic models of organiz-ing and, moreover, that it has been able to perform profitably and successfully and that it is no small high-tech start-up. From that point of view it offers a documented example of the existence and viability of something like the organizations that Heckscher and others argue are the future of work.

Limitations of the mainstream approach

Like most of the mainstream approach to organizations and management, a major limitation of its treatment of bureaucracy and post-bureaucracy is its one-sided and restricted focus on efficiency. Weber's ideal-type of bureaucracy has – wrongly, as we will see – been treated as if it were a design template for how organizations should be. In the process, this has elevated one particular kind of rationality – **instrumental rationality** – at the expense of others.

Why is this a limitation? There are two related reasons. One is that by its focus on *means*, instru-mental rationality is only concerned with the 'how' of organizing and not with the 'why'. In the next section we will explore why this is such an important omission. Secondly, by seeing efficiency in terms of minimum inputs and maximum outputs, the mainstream only considers efficiency from the partial viewpoint of someone who has an interest in this kind of efficiency. Normally this means the powerful – the people who own and run businesses being the obvious example. As soon as we shift position, efficiency can look quite different.

Think of the now common way that all kinds of organizations use automated telephone systems. When we phone up, we are told to press different keys for different options and eventually, probably after waiting in a queue, we are connected to an operator. This is efficient for the organization as it is a low-cost way of managing enquiries, partly because some of the work of transferring calls formerly done by a paid employee is now done, for nothing, by the caller. Sometimes, as with computer support lines, for example, the caller actually pays while they do this unpaid work for the organization. So from the caller's point of view it is not efficient because it involves a waste of time, sometimes a cost and, often, frustration. It also usually leads to a less personalized service (compare, for example, the traditional contact between a customer and a bank manager with that offered by national call-centres).

Thinkpoint 7.6

What other examples can you think of where things that are efficient for an organization are inefficient for you as a customer?

SOURCE: © JAGADEESH / REUTERS / CORBIS

Image 7.7 Back to the future?

This one-sided view of rationality and efficiency can be seen to run through almost all of the debates about bureaucracy and post-bureaucracy discussed so far. For example, concerns about 'motivation' in bureaucracy are animated by the idea that demotivation will lead to employees working less hard – it is not a concern about happiness or well-being (see Chapter 2). Much of the bureaucratic dysfunctionalist literature is concerned with the alignment (or otherwise) between the formal rules of the bureaucracy and what actually happens. Something similar could be said of Dalton's preoccupation with politics 'getting in the way' of rationality.

As for post-bureaucracy, the whole basis of the shift towards these new organizational forms – if, indeed, the shift is occurring – is the fear that failure to do so will lead to declining competitiveness and shrinking profitability. The more trust-based ways of working, like traditional concerns with motivation, are animated by a belief that these will render employees more productive, which again reveals the underlying view of efficiency in the mainstream approach. It is surely no coincidence that moves away from bureaucracy are typically associated with harder work and more stress. So, again, we must ask the question: efficient for whom?

Exercise 7.4

Thinking of the admissions system and the changes in the Universal case, for whom are they efficient and for whom are they inefficient?

In this sense, the limitations of the mainstream approach are, partly, to do with the partial picture it offers. But more fundamentally, it is to do with power. On the one hand, most mainstream approaches are concerned with deriving organizational methods – whether bureaucratic or post-bureaucratic – that best exert power and control over employees. On the other hand, by having this focus, mainstream approaches conform to and support the view that what 'matters' are the interests and perspectives of the privileged, the powerful and the elite.

Critical approach

Introduction

In many respects, the central dividing line between mainstream and critical approaches to bureaucracy and post-bureaucracy runs back to Max weber. Perhaps we could even say that it runs 'through' him.

For Weber on the one hand was persuaded that bureaucracy was becoming the dominant organizational form while, on the other hand, he bemoaned and even despaired of this fact. Weber did not use his term 'ideal-type' to mean that bureaucracy was a desirable ideal, or the ideal form of organization, but this is how mainstream approaches to organization studies have often interpreted it.

'There is quite an interesting story that helps to explain why the mainstream did this (although there are many other reasons). Weber's work (which was written in German) was for a long time not widely read in the United States, where the bulk of organization studies has been conducted. It became popular through the translation of eminent Harvard sociologist Talcott Parsons. Parsons' translation and interpretation of Weber put a 'spin' on it that emphasized bureaucracy as an 'ideal'. This had an impact on the development of the organization studies field in a general way, but more particularly on Merton, who was a student of Parsons. Merton in turn supervised Blau, Gouldner and Selznick. As we have seen, these authors provided the bedrock of the literature on bureaucracy.

A different (and it is fair to say that most scholars would agree a more defensible) interpretation of Weber is to see his work as being concerned with two different kinds of rationality. One is the technical or instrumental rationality which, as we have seen, bureaucracy embodies. The second is value or **substantive rationality**.

It is worth dwelling a little on the rather complicated issue of why substantive rationality is sometimes called value rationality. This is because deciding whether an outcome is rational involves a value judgement – is something good or not? Some people believe that this is not just a matter of opinion but can be decided on rational principles. Others would say that what is good or bad is a matter of what we generally agree is good or bad. So, for example, most people would accept that child pornography is bad (and those who think that these judgements have a rational basis might say that it is also irrational because it treats children as objects rather than people with rights). From this point of view, no matter how efficient an organization was in producing child pornography (that is, no matter how instrumentally rational it was), that organization would not have value or substantive rationality. If this seems complicated, there is an easier version of the definitions. We could say that instrumental rationality means 'doing the thing right' and substantive rationality means 'doing the right thing'. Of course, someone might object that instrumental rationality *does* embody a value – the value that efficiency is the sole criterion in deciding what to do. This is true, but it is present as a hidden value and one which, when made explicit, would then provoke debates about its ethical adequacy which are suppressed when it is simply assumed that instrumental rationality is 'a good thing'.

Actually, even when the theory seems obscure and abstract, in practice we are all familiar with the kinds of issues that are at stake. Is it right (or rational) for organizations to produce guns, cigarettes or instruments of torture? And outcomes of organizational actions are not just to do with their products but with their by-products. So, for example, is it right (or rational) for organizations to pollute the environment? This latter case is especially interesting because it does help to explain why there might be a link between what is right and what is rational. If it is the case that organizations need to live in a sustainable environment (e.g. because they need clean water to operate), then is it rational (let alone right) if they despoil that environment (e.g. by polluting water supplies)?

Exercise 7.5

What other examples of substantive irrationality can you think of?

A concern with substantive rationality is central to critical approaches to bureaucracy and post-bureaucracy, and later on we will return to it in several different ways. In one respect, it is another version of the question: efficient for whom? Is the efficient producer of landmines efficient for the Angolan child whose limbs are blown off? Is the efficient producer of cigarettes efficient for a Chinese peasant (who may never have heard about the risks) dying from lung cancer?

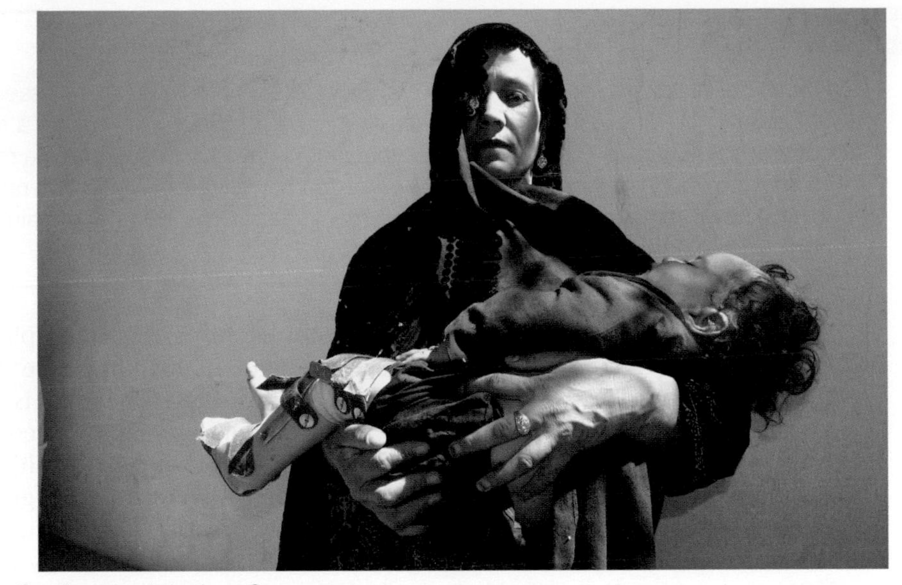

SOURCE: © ADOPT-A-MINEFIELD-WWW.LANDMINES.ORG.UK

Image 7.8 Getting the job done?

Thinkpoint 7.7

One of the big management problems facing the British National Health Service is 'bed blocking' – which normally happens when an elderly person is using a hospital bed because no suitable nursing home place is available. In 2004, Barbara Salisbury, a nurse, was convicted of attempting to murder such elderly patients. According to the prosecution, her motive was that she was trying to improve the efficiency of her ward. Was she a good bureaucratic manager?

Specific products aside, Weber's case for thinking that bureaucracy was substantively irrational was based upon his reading of the overall societal effects of its rise. These he described as creating an 'iron cage of rationality'. Here the idea is that, because bureaucracy is becoming dominant, so more and more of people's lives are lived within the constraints of a rationalized (i.e. instrumentally rationalized) system. Living in a world in which every experience was organized, literally from the hospital in which we are born to the undertakers who take us to the grave, is there a sense in which bureaucracy undermines our very humanity? In particular, the experience of work within bureaucracies is, from a critical perspective, not just demotivating but actually dehumanizing. That is, by treating people as parts of a machine, bureaucracy denies everything that makes people human rather than inanimate objects – perhaps this was what made possible the hospital murders referred to in Thinkpoint 7.7? Again it can be said that this is both wrong and also irrational. Fundamentally, the functional reason for having organizations is to meet needs that no one could satisfy as an individual. But if the effect of organization (in its bureaucratic form) is to negate our human needs then there is a logical contradiction. Dehumanization, then, is not just wrong, it is irrational, and it is a profound negation of identity and freedom.

We will return to these issues shortly, but the final introductory point to the critical approach is to consider post-bureaucracy. In many respects it might be thought that, as an alternative to bureaucracy, this addresses some of the points made by the critics. Overtly, there is a stress on organizational values and a much less dehumanizing approach to work. However, as has been discussed in other chapters (e.g. Chapters 4 and 9), critical approaches are by no means reassured by such developments. At the heart of the problem is again the issue of power and control. Critical commentators believe that there is not an either/or opposition between the control of employees under top-down formal rule systems like bureaucracy and the freedom of employees under top-down value-based systems. Rather, both are seen as forms of control, the former operating at the level of behaviour and bodily actions; the latter at the level of belief and the mind. Indeed, many critical theorists regard the latter as the more insidious, because it seeks to exert control over the 'whole person'.

Thinkpoint 7.8

In a corner of the Dog and Duck, John and Richard are comparing their bosses. John is saying that his manager is inspirational: 'She just has a way of making you feel as if you want to do a really good job, for her and for the company'. Richard is impressed. 'Wow, you should have my boss – she's a real slave driver', he complains.

Who do you think works the longer hours, John or Richard? Would you rather be coerced into doing something, knowing that it was coercion, or be manipulated into doing something, without knowing that you were being manipulated?

One way of thinking about these issues is in terms of employee skill levels. Bureaucratic organizations rely upon, and to some extent create, a situation where skill levels are low. They require that employees follow set rules and work in standardized ways. Skill is in many ways a form of power. If skill levels are low, then employees are easily replaceable and so reducing skill levels is an effective way of increasing organizational control. If the employees do not like the organization, well, there are plenty of people who can replace them. When skill levels are higher, then this gives more power to employees possessing these skills. In Joan Woodward's work, discussed earlier, it was assumed that the bureaucracy was linked contingently to the type of technology being employed. But perhaps a better way of rendering that link would be to say that technologies that required a skilled workforce gave more power to that workforce and, hence, they could not be managed bureaucratically.

By extension, post-bureaucratic organizations are obliged to create (or at least pay lip service to) employee responsibility because such organizations are predominantly in business sectors that need high levels of skill. These employees, who Reich (1993) calls 'symbolic analysts' and who have also been called (Kelley, 1990) 'gold-collar workers' (to distinguish them from blue-collar, or manual, workers and white-collar, or clerical, workers) have the power to command better treatment. Such employees are the consultants and professionals who possess a knowledge that resides in their heads. Craft workers had such knowledge, until it was broken down by Taylorism (see Chapter 6). And, wherever it can be achieved, symbolic analysts are similarly de-skilled, one example being attempts to replace accountants with IT-enabled audit factories. More generally, expert systems are used to replace professional employees. Even academics, traditionally a very difficult occupation to rationalize, are increasingly required to produce work in standard formats, such as this book, and perhaps eventually could be replaced with computer software.

So, on this reading, post-bureaucracy reflects an accommodation with those occupations whose skill level cannot be bureaucratized and it will only persist until such time as it can. In the meantime, post-bureaucracy uses the discipline of value-based or **normative control** to get the maximum amount of work out of its employees.

These kinds of ideas can sound, at first hearing, like pure nonsense. After all, control is about stopping people from doing what they want. So if people choose to do what they want to do then they are free,

Image 7.9

Image 7.10 Girl power?

not controlled. But consider the haunting, and slightly scary, title of Nikolas Rose's (1999) influential book, *Governing the Soul*. Who we are, and what our choices signify, may not be as simple as we think.

Thinkpoint 7.9

John has now left the Dog and Duck and is in the supermarket. There is an endless array of things to choose from. He buys some toothpaste because it gives him double reward points (he hasn't noticed that it is twice the price of the value brand). Then he considers whether to buy some traditional English sausages or the own-brand version – he chooses the traditional option because the packet is cardboard with a picture of a farmyard. The own brand are wrapped in cellophane. They are cheap and, frankly, look it (he doesn't know that both sausages are identical and come from the same factory) and after all he has been economical with his choice of toothpaste. He chooses some beer and, because everyone knows that German lager is passé, he gets a Hungarian brand (he doesn't remember that he saw an advert for it last night – it's just what he fancies). At the checkout there is a display of hand-cooked potato crisps with a Malaysian curry flavour and he puts one in the trolley – he wouldn't have thought of buying them if the supermarket hadn't helpfully put them there. Then he sees a sign that says he can have a second bag free, so he chooses to take two (he doesn't know it yet, but next time he goes to the supermarket he will seek out these crisps, even though they won't be on special offer).

John has made several choices. Is he free? Are you any different to John?

Key issues and controversies

One of the most remarkable books ever written about organizations is almost never mentioned, much less discussed, within mainstream literature on bureaucracy. The book in question is Zygmunt Bauman's *Modernity and the Holocaust* (1989). Bauman explores how the Nazi Holocaust, which murdered at least six million Jewish people as well as those from many other groups, was related to a highly developed European civilization. He analyses this is many ways, but in particular he explains how the genocide instigated by the Nazis represents the extreme application of a bureaucratic logic. What makes the Holocaust peculiarly horrifying is the way in which the mass extermination was conducted industrially – with a system of rules, impersonally applied, which made it as technically efficient as a genocide could be. The capacity to register and monitor populations so that Jews, communists, gypsies, homosexuals and the other categories to which the Nazis objected was itself a considerable administrative achievement. The shipping of these people to the camps was another, and their systematic extermination a third.

SOURCE: © AUSCHWITZ MAIN GATE, DECEMBER 1994, PHOTO BY SKIP SCHIEL, COPYRIGHT 2005

Image 7.11 Where it all ends?

The British novelist, C. P. Snow, has one of his characters, a wartime civil servant in London, reflect that, just as he was handling the memoranda relating to the development of atomic weapons, so his counterpart in Berlin would be reviewing figures on the death rate of Jewish people under different dietary regimes in the labour camps (this was written before the extermination programme was known about). That bureaucratic practice, the impersonal, scientific, ethically neutral pursuit of means made the Holocaust instrumentally rational while, clearly, not being substantively rational. This is perhaps the clearest illustration of how these two definitions of rationality differ. Bauman says that we should not, therefore, see the Holocaust as an aberration or anomaly when compared with mainstream Western culture: rather, it was a manifestation of the habitual ways of organizing within that culture.

The Holocaust example is very important, and not for emotive reasons. Almost everyone can agree that the extermination of a race of people is irrational on any meaning that might be given to that term. Yet the fact that (instrumentally) rational methods could be applied to it, as easily as to the production of toy cars or, for that matter, the distribution of food aid, serves to underscore the moral blindness of bureaucracy. It is not that bureaucratic techniques are necessarily 'immoral' but that they simply do not consider morality. So, if we want to live in a civilized society, we cannot simply be concerned with efficiency as envisaged by bureaucracy: we have to think about the purposes to which bureaucracy is put. Bureaucracy does not consider values: people do.

Thinkpoint 7.10

You are (probably) on a management course. Would you be willing to devise the most efficient way to exterminate people? If not, how is your course helping you to make moral judgements about how to use your skills?

Although the moral deficiencies of bureaucracy are a key issue within the critical approach, are they a key controversy? The British sociologist Paul du Gay (2000) has offered a sophisticated and important defence of bureaucracy although not, of course, one that would condone its genocidal use. It is worth pausing to reflect upon the context within which du Gay has made his arguments. It is a context in which the public sector within the United Kingdom (and elsewhere) has been accused of being far too bureaucratic, not in the sense of being amoral but in the traditional sense of being mired in 'red tape'. It stands accused of being characterized by goal displacement, producer focus and all the other mainstream complaints about bureaucracy. These complaints have their counterpart in other critical analyses which see bureaucracy as dehumanizing and morally blind (see also Chapter 14). Fighting on both flanks, du Gay argues, in the title of his book, *In Praise of Bureaucracy*.

Bureaucracy, du Gay explains, is actually imbued with morality, not because of Weber's concerns about substantive rationality but because of the demands of instrumental rationality for maximum efficiency. To satisfy these demands, argues du Gay, requires an ethic of impersonality and fairness so that employees and customers or clients are treated without prejudice. So, for example, bureaucracy does not care about employee's gender or ethnic background – it only cares about qualification since this is what will be most efficient. Clients, too, are treated the same, whoever they may be. Bureaucracy is a safeguard against discrimination. In this way it embodies, rather than ignores, a morality of fairness and due process. Post-bureaucracy or, as du Gay says, enterprise, has no such formal code.

Exercise 7.6

How does the admissions system example illustrate du Gay's point that bureaucracy is fair? In the last few years there have been many criticisms of the elitism of university admissions procedures, especially at Oxford and Cambridge. What would be better; a system based on A level results, an interview system or, as some have suggested, a standardized aptitude test? In what ways might each approach relate to bureaucracy and post-bureaucracy? Would there be a conflict between efficiency and fairness in each of these approaches? Would it be greater in some rather than others? Assuming you are at a university, do you feel that your application was dealt with efficiently or fairly or both?

In one way, there is no doubt that du Gay is correct. And his work has been important in answering the charge that bureaucracy is morally blind. Yet in another way it assumes far too much. It assumes that bureaucracies do, in fact, conform to Weber's ideal-type. Yet studies from the mainstream show how, in practice, bureaucracies allow all kinds of prejudice and discrimination – Crozier, Dalton and Kanter are all examples. Du Gay is right to say that the formal model of bureaucracy embodies an ethic. But it would be wrong to conclude that bureaucracy does invariably, in practice, exhibit this ethic.

Exercise 7.7

Jackie decides to rent a house with five other students. When they move in they draw up a rota to share the cooking, cleaning, shopping and so on. This is a (simple) kind of rule-based system with a division of labour. One of its features is that it divides the work up fairly. In your experience, is this likely to work in practice? What difference might it make if all Jackie's house-mates are male?

Du Gay's arguments are important because they question whether bureaucracy is discredited. Although he flies against mainstream thinking, he has a strong case. For all of the arguments against the death of bureaucracy advanced in the 1960s continue to hold true, and the basic advantages of bureaucracy, as illustrated by the admissions system example, are undeniable – both in terms of efficiency and those of fairness. But whether fairness is enough to offset the moral deficiencies of bureaucracy that Bauman illustrates is less clear – and remains a controversial issue.

A selection of important studies

There are many ways in which bureaucracy and post-bureaucracy can be criticized. Studies have focused on the problems of the former, of the latter, or of the distinction between them. From the many possibilities, we have chosen some that represent a range of these positions and are the most articulate in advancing their analyses.

One of the more readable studies of bureaucracy is George Ritzer's widely praised book *The McDonaldization of Society* (2000). Ritzer's is in effect a re-working of Weber's concerns about the iron cage of rationality – the idea that there is no escape from the growing presence of bureaucracy. But Ritzer updates this analysis by focusing on McDonald's, the fast food chain, which he says is the template for contemporary forms of bureaucratization, with its standardized menus, architecture and, even, the words used by employees. At the heart of Ritzer's critique is the familiar complaint that bureaucracy dehumanizes both employees and customers. The impersonality that is central to the bureaucratic ethos may, as du Gay says, guarantee fairness, but it also means that the 'person' is irrelevant and subservient to the organizational machine. McDonaldization exemplifies the logic of standardization, which is what bureaucracy is all about, and Ritzer sees standardization as spreading into all kinds of areas of life: the national curriculum and modularization in education; package holidays and mass-build housing estates, for example.

Thinkpoint 7.11

When you eat at McDonald's, sit in a lecture theatre or go on a package holiday, do you feel dehumanized? And if you do not, does that mean that Ritzer is wrong or that you have become so tamed that you do not even notice the iron cage around you?

Ritzer, like Weber, is critical of the instrumental rationality of bureaucracy. Kathy Ferguson puts a particular spin on such a critique in elaborating *The Feminist Case Against Bureaucracy* (1984). Within the mainstream approaches we saw how Kanter's work indicated the male biases within bureaucratic organization, but Ferguson's arguments are much more radical. She sees the instrumental rationality of bureaucracy as being one that is in principle 'masculinist'. Whereas, for critics in the Weberian tradition, instrumentality is an expression of specifically modern and industrial ways of viewing the world and organizations, for Ferguson they embody something more – a masculine search for control and mastery. The structures of hierarchy are an expression of this both in the simple sense of being an example of such masculinism and, in a more complex way, by positioning employees and customers as passive and dependent in a way that Ferguson, borrowing the expression first coined by Simone de Beauvoir, sees as analogous to the traditional position of 'the second sex' or women.

In a wider ranging way, Ferguson sees the development of bureaucracy as being part and parcel of the way in which the modern world has been divided into a public and private sphere. The public sphere, where bureaucracy is located, is characterized by masculinity, competition, aggression and rationality, while the private sphere of families and households is characterized by femininity, cooperation, tolerance and emotionality. In this way, a range of archetypically feminine experiences and values are seen to have been excluded from the public sphere of bureaucracy and not just excluded but also disparaged and discounted.

Thinkpoint 7.12

Think about the ways you behave with your friends and family and compare them with how you behave at work or in classes. How are they different? Why? What would happen to you if you behaved in the same way in both settings?

The next study is one less concerned with theory and more focused on the lived-experience of, in particular, post-bureaucracy. Richard Sennett's *Work and the Corrosion of Character* (1998) looks at a series of lives affected by the changing nature of work. In many cases, Sennett returns to people and workplaces he had visited 25 years before as part of the research for an earlier book, giving a useful insight into these changes. For example, he revisits what was formerly a Greek bakery run along bureaucratic rules by a stable unionized workforce with intimate knowledge of baking techniques. It is now part of a huge multinational firm, and uses a shifting workforce of non-unionized migrant workers operating computer-controlled ovens. These latter allow production to shift flexibly from one type of bread to another, yet the operators know nothing at all of baking techniques: they simply click on icons on a computer screen.

This example is interesting because it shows how new post-bureaucratic working conditions of flexibility (in employment and production) do not imply an idyllic, empowered kind of organizational life. Rather, the new ways of working are as 'alienating' and dehumanizing as before, if not more so, because the bonds of community among the employees (and with customers) and the involvement of the workers with their work and product has been fractured. But it is also interesting because the loss of the traditional bureaucracy serves to point to the ways in which such organizations are not necessarily as dehumanizing as the work of someone like Ritzer claims, nor as devoid of emotionality as Ferguson's analysis might imply.

Finally, a more conventional kind of empirical study, but one of the very best of its kind is Rick Delbridge's *Life on the Line in Contemporary Manufacturing* (1998). Like Dalton's classic book on managers, this is an ethnography reporting on the author's time in two British factories. One is a Japanese-owned electronics plant (Nippon CTV), the other a European-owned producer of automotive components (ValleyCo). Although strictly speaking this is not a study of bureaucracy and post-bureaucracy, it does contrast the more traditional approach at ValleyCo with the 'Japanized' approach at Nippon CTV where there is a focus on lean production, just-in-time management, innovation, customer focus and HRM. This is, at least, an adjacent theme to that of the present chapter.

While Delbridge found a number of contrasts between the plants, it is fair to say that his overall conclusion is that there is a considerable similarity between 'traditional' and 'new' forms of working in terms of things like hierarchy, participation or trust. His findings are very much in line with those in the various contributions to Thompson and Warhurst (1998) in relation to scepticism about post-bureaucracy: 'There is little to suggest that contemporary manufacturing is best characterized as "postfordist" and that the shop-floor is a hotbed of worker autonomy and knowledge creation' (Delbridge, 1998, p. 192).

One feature of this study which makes it 'critical' rather than mainstream is that it captures the experience and perspective of the front-line – or shop floor – workers rather than being an idealized and self-interested account written from a managerial perspective. In this regard it represents an antidote to some of the more hyperbolic claims made about the 'new economy' such as those found in the mainstream literature on post-bureaucracy.

Contributions and limitations of the critical approach

Contributions Perhaps the most important contribution of the critical approach is to move away from a narrow focus on efficiency and the techniques of bureaucracy and post-bureaucracy towards a recognition of the political and ethical values that come into play when organizations are designed (see also Chapter 14). The idea that managing and organizing are not 'neutral', technical issues is one that runs throughout critical approaches, as is clear from most other chapters in this book.

Post-bureaucracy, of course, is claimed by its advocates to be precisely an organizational form concerned with values. They argue that it liberates employees and consumers alike from the stifling 'red tape' and inflexibility of bureaucracy. Critical approaches are unpersuaded by such arguments. Crucially, as with culture management (see Chapter 9), the problem is that values are defined hierarchically and within an overall purpose of gaining control. Another way of saying this would be that post-bureaucracy, as much as bureaucracy, is defined by an instrumental – and, feminists would argue, masculinist – rationality. It may use a different set of techniques to get the job done, but it is still, essentially, an exercise of power, using people as instruments in pursuit of some other goal. The examples of Sennett's bakers or of customers' experience of automated phone systems both illustrate this.

In any case, the other main contribution of critical approaches is to point out that the lived experience of post-bureaucracy is by no means the utopia that its advocates suggest. Bureaucracy dehumanized its employees, but at least offered the security of set routines. Post-bureaucracy marks an increase in insecurity and anxiety because it promotes job insecurity, an intensification of time pressures (the '24/7' society) and places the accent on the responsibility of individuals to manage their careers and lives without the collective protection that bureaucracies can offer.

Thinkpoint 7.13

Thinking about the people you know, particularly older people like your parents and their friends, do you think that they are anxious and insecure about work? Or do you think that people your age face more of a problem?

Thus critical approaches question a **binary** logic: either bureaucracy is 'right' or it is 'wrong'. A simple version of the mainstream–critical divide would be based on binary logic. Bureaucracy is good, post-bureaucracy is bad. Or post-bureaucracy is good, bureaucracy is bad. We have seen that many of the protagonists in the debate follow just this logic. Almost all of today's management gurus, and most policy makers, say that bureaucracy is bad. Paul du Gay is one of the few examples of writers who say the opposite. However, in our discussions of the mainstream approach we found that evidence was split and we also found that the division between bureaucracy and post-bureaucracy was much less clear-cut. Critical approaches go further, though. It is not just a matter of trying to find evidence on one side of the argument or the other. Rather, it is to see that there are continuities, based on instrumental rationality, between both.

Limitations Despite what was just said about a refusal of binary logic within critical approaches, it is also true that some individual studies within these approaches do have a tendency to oversimplify. Ritzer, in particular, seems to imply that because bureaucracy is 'bad' then anything that is not bureaucracy is 'good'. Thus some of the forms of resistance to McDonaldization that he proposes end up endorsing some of the niche marketing practices associated with post-bureaucracy. Defences of bureaucracy, too, can carry a danger of romanticizing such organizations as places of fairness and, even, communities. Studies like Delbridge's can be a useful antidote to this kind of danger.

A second difficulty with critical approaches, which seems to be present in Weber's discussion of the iron cage and, again, in Ritzer is the problem of **determinism**. Many mainstream positions show this problem – for example, most cases for the rise of post-bureaucracy rest on the determinism of computer technologies – but so too do some critical approaches. The idea that bureaucratization is a 'juggernaut' that will inevitably sweep aside other forms of organization because of its technical efficiency is a common one in critical theory. The limitation of this view is that it pays no attention to the choices that people and societies make about how to organize themselves. In this respect determinism is a double problem. First, because it ignores choices, it is analytically problematic. Secondly, because it promotes the view that whatever choices are made they will have no effect, it encourages fatalism and quietism and is therefore a political problem as well.

Exercise 7.8

Politicians often use phrases like 'there is no alternative' or 'the fact of the matter is . . . '. Parents often respond to small children's favourite question ('why?') by saying 'that's just the way it is' or 'because I say so'. Many economists tell us that 'you can't buck the market' and some biologists say that 'it's all in the genes'. All these are, in different ways, deterministic arguments. How valid are they? Can you think of other examples?

Somewhat related to this is a third difficulty for critical approaches, especially the argument that post-bureaucracy is no more than the spread of even more intense forms of power and control. This then makes it very difficult to know what kinds of reform can be envisaged that would be acceptable to critics. If dehumanization and humanization at work are both versions of control, then what proposal for change does that leave? The answers typically seem highly utopian: for example, the suspension of masculinist and instrumental rationality. Given that this seems unlikely in the immediate future, does this mean that there is nothing to be done but bemoan the existing state of affairs until a complete social transformation has occurred?

Conclusion

In this chapter we have seen how a complex series of issues are involved in thinking about bureaucracy and post-bureaucracy. It is undoubtedly true that bureaucratic organizations have been one of the defining features of modern life. Weber was right to observe that they were becoming so in his time and right to predict that they would become more so in the future. Yet almost no one who has studied them seriously, whether from a mainstream or a critical perspective, has concluded that they are without problems. Mainstream and critical writers differ in the radicalism with which they explain these problems, however. As a broad generalization, mainstream approaches stress the ways in which reality diverges from the rationality of the bureaucratic model, while critics draw attention to the defects of the very rationality that underpins that model. Mainstream writers may be more likely to see possible reforms to bureaucracy but are perhaps over-optimistic about the likely efficacy of such prescriptions. Critics are likely to highlight the oppressive and dehumanizing consequences of bureaucracy and therefore will tend to want to reject it root and branch.

But of course things are never quite so simple. In recent years, there have been very pronounced rejections of the bureaucratic model from within mainstream thinking on organizations and, also, some defences of bureaucracy from critics. The mainstream proponents of post-bureaucracy, who repeat many earlier claims in their case, are in some senses 'critics' of bureaucracy, but not in the way normally implied by the term 'critical approaches'. This is because they make their case from within mainstream assumptions about efficiency and organizational purpose. They are saying, in effect, bureaucracy was fine for its time, but times have changed and now they favour post-bureaucracy. They do not question the underlying idea that organizations exist to deliver efficient outcomes for their owners, nor the need to maintain control. They just want to do it in a new way.

For that reason, critical approaches are critical of both bureaucracy and post-bureaucracy. They question the narrowness of the mainstream understanding of efficiency and the acceptability of pursuing control over others in pursuit of that efficiency. Although to polarize mainstream and critical approaches too much would be to fall into the trap of binary logic, there are some real and substantive differences between them. These differences reflect very serious and profound divergences of thinking, not just about organizations but about society as a whole. Critical approaches tend to be explicit that it is these political issues that are at stake, whereas mainstream approaches typically prefer to leave them implicit, and to treat organizational design as if it were simply a matter of developing and applying the most efficient technique. However, as we have seen, embedded within the very notion of efficiency there are some political assumptions, principally about the question of for whom organizations are efficient.

The mainstream approach is, in this regard at least, untenable, and its more reflective practitioners know it. Within the myriad of debates about bureaucracy and post-bureaucracy, what is ultimately at stake is how people choose to organize their collective activities and this goes to the heart of what we think those collective activities should be, and how we go about them. These are inescapably moral and political questions.

Discussion questions

1. Why did bureaucratic organizations come into existence?
2. Does the literature on 'bureaucratic dysfunctionalism' prove that bureaucracy is inefficient?
3. What kinds of contingencies could explain whether an organization will tend to be bureaucratic or post-bureaucratic?
4. Charles Heckscher says that the world is becoming more post-bureaucratic. George Ritzer says it is becoming more bureaucratic. Who is right? Could they both be right?
5. Is it substantively rational to make a profit? If so, then aren't private sector bureaucracies necessarily rational in all meanings of the word?
6. What kind of organizations would satisfy the critics of bureaucracy and post-bureaucracy? Do any exist?

Further reading

du Gay, P. (2000) *In Praise of Bureaucracy: Weber, Organization and Ethics*, London: Sage.

This is not an easy read, but it must stand as one of the most important books written in this area for many years. It offers what some might think is an audacious case for the virtues of bureaucracy, and challenges much conventional thinking in this regard. At its heart is a claim that bureaucracy embodies a specific ethic of impartiality that is of enduring value.

Ferguson, K. (1984) *The Feminist Case Against Bureaucracy*, Philadelphia, PA: Temple University Press.

Again not an easy book, but it should feature in any list of readings because it provides a fundamental challenge not just to bureaucracy but to the logic that informs many claims about post-bureaucracy. For Ferguson, bureaucracy exhibits a masculinist logic of control and this opens up the very fundamental terrain of the values underpinning any form of organization.

Head, S. (2003) *The New Ruthless Economy: Work and Power in the Digital Age*, Oxford: Oxford University Press.

Written from the perspective of an economist, this book provides an accessible exposé of how working conditions in the 'knowledge economy' are subject to intensified pressure and control. The writing is lively and fluent, and although the analysis is not always deep it provides a compelling account of post-bureaucracy.

Ritzer, G. (2000) *The McDonaldization of Society: An Investigation Into the Changing Character of Contemporary Social Life*, second edition, Thousand Oaks, CA: Sage.

This is a provocative, well-written book that makes the case that modern society is becoming increasingly bureaucratized and standardized, with McDonald's as the defining example. It offers an interesting reworking of Weber's concerns about bureaucracy in a way that is much more accessible than the original writings.

Sennett, R. (1998) *Work and the Corrosion of Character: The Personal Consequences of Work in the New Capitalism*, London: WW Norton.

This book can be commended for its readability. It offers very personalized accounts of how shifts from traditional bureaucratic organizations to those of post-bureaucracy impact upon the lives of real people. Sceptics might say that Sennett offers us stories not analysis, but, carefully read, this book provides a convincing critique of contemporary life.

Whyte, W. H. (1956) *The Organization Man*, New York: Simon & Schuster.

This classic work, which is available in many editions, was an early and perceptive critique of life in bureaucracy. Although 50 years old, it still reads freshly, not least because many of the features described seem to apply to post-bureaucracy as well, which in itself should caution us against an overly polarized view of the two 'models'. Whyte's concern that individuals are subsumed within the organizational order has a disturbingly modern feel.

References

Aldrich, H. (1972) 'Technology and organization structure: A re-examination of the findings of the Aston group', *Administrative Science Quarterly* 15:26–43.

Bauman, Z. (1989) *Modernity and the Holocaust*, Cambridge: Polity.

Bennis, W. (1966) 'The coming death of bureaucracy', *Think*, November: 30–35.

Blau, P. (1955) *The Dynamics of Bureaucracy*, Chicago: Chicago University Press.

Blau, P. (1970) 'A formal theory of differentiation in organizations', *American Sociological Review* 35:210–218.

Burns, T. and Stalker, G. (1961) *The Management of Innovation*, Oxford: Oxford University Press.

Castells, M. (1996) *The Rise of the Network Society*, Oxford: Oxford University Press.

Crozier, M. (1964) *The Bureaucratic Phenomenon*, Chicago: University of Chicago Press.

Dalton, M. (1959) *Men Who Manage*, New York: John Wiley & Sons.

Delbridge, R. (1998) *Life On the Line in Contemporary Manufacturing*, Oxford: Oxford University Press.

du Gay, P. (2000) *In Praise of Bureaucracy: Weber, Organization and Ethics*, London: Sage.

Ferguson, K. (1984) *The Feminist Case Against Bureaucracy*, Philadelphia, PA: Temple University Press.

Gouldner, A. (1954) *Patterns of Industrial Bureaucracy*, New York: Free Press.

Heckscher, C. (1994) 'Defining the post-bureaucratic type', in C. Heckscher, and A. Donnellon (eds.) *The Post-bureaucratic Organization: New Perspectives on Organizational Change*, Thousand Oaks, CA: Sage, p.p. 14–62.

Heckscher, C. and Donnellon, A. (eds.) (1994) *The Post-bureaucratic Organization: New Perspectives on Organizational Change*, Thousand Oaks, CA: Sage.

Kanter, R. M. (1993) *Men and Women of the Corporation*, second edition, New York: Basic Books.

Kelley, R. (1990) *The Gold-collar Worker: Harnessing the Brainpower of the New Work Force*. Reading MA: Addison-Wesley.

Leadbetter, C. (1999) *Living On Thin Air: The New Economy*, London: Viking.

Merton, R. (1940) 'Bureaucratic structure and personality', *Social Forces*, May: 560–568.

Miewald, R. D. (1970) 'The greatly exaggerated death of bureaucracy', *California Management Review*, Winter: 65–69.

Perrow, C. (1979) *Complex Organizations*, Englewood Cliffs, NJ: Prentice Hall.

Piore, M. and Sabel, C. (1984) *The Second Industrial Divide*, New York: Basic Books.

Pugh, D. and Hickson, D. (1976) *Organisation Structure in its Context: The Aston Programme*, London: Saxon House.

Pugh, D., Hickson, D. and Hinings, C. R. (1968) 'Dimensions of organisation structure', *Administrative Science Quarterly* 13:65–103.

Reich, R. (1993) *The Work of Nations*, London: Simon & Schuster.

Ritzer, G. (2000) *The McDonaldization of Society: An Investigation Into the Changing Character of Contemporary Social Life*, second edition, Thousand Oaks, CA: Sage.

Robertson, M. and Swan, J. (1998) 'Modes of organizing in an expert consultancy: A case study of knowledge, power and egos', *Organization* 5(4):543–564.

Rose, N. (1999) *Governing the Soul*, London: Routledge.

Selznick, P. (1949) *TVA and the Grass Roots: A Study in the Sociology of Formal Organizations*, Berkeley CA: University of California Press.

Semler, R. (1993) *Maverick*, London: Century.
Sennett, R. (1998) *Work and the Corrosion of Character. The Personal Consequences of Work in the New Capitalism*, London: WW Norton.
Thompson, P. and Warhurst, C. (eds.) (1998) *Workplaces of the Future*, Basingstoke: Macmillan.
Warhurst, C. and Thompson, P. (1998) 'Hands, hearts and minds: Changing work and workers at the end of the century', in P. Thompson and C. Warhurst, (eds.) *Workplaces of the Future*, Basingstoke: Macmillan, p.p. 1–24.
Woodward, J. (1965) *Industrial Organization: Theory and Practice*, Oxford: Oxford University Press.

Glossary

Action Behaviour that is socially meaningful or purposeful; it is influenced or interpreted by oneself or others. Thus moving one's leg might be seen as behaviour (unless agreed as a pre-arranged signal), whereas kicking a ball in a football match might be seen as action (unless as a deflection).

Action-based A concept used to describe the dynamics of organization. It assumes that political rule is dependent on the practices of organizational members and limited by the norms, values and foresight of informed actors.

Actor-network theory or analysis (ANT or ANA) A theory that does not restrict action to that performed by humans but also involves non-human action as performed by material artefacts such as cars, phones or social institutions insofar as they and humans affect one another. Every technological device is dependent on a heterogeneous network, which supports the specific ways in which this device has been designed and used.

Agency The sense of acting from an individual's own volition.

Alienation Marx famously employed this concept to describe the experience of **labour** under capitalism; a condition in which individuals feel separated or estranged from some part of their existence (e.g. the product or process of their labour) because they are subjected to external controls.

Ambiguous figure system The situation where the development of informal relations may clash with the formal hierarchy leading to considerable ambiguity as to who is responsible for what and/or to whom.

Anticipatory socialization A process of learning to behave in ways appropriate to particular future roles, relationships or occupations. An example would be anticipating what is the expected behaviour of a student prior to leaving college.

Anxiety Unlike fear, which has an identifiable source, anxiety has no specific object to which it responds. It is a *general* feeling of malaise or dis-ease for no particular reason, and indeed cannot be understood. In extreme form, it may be associated with **neurosis** or **psychosis**.

Apolitical Absence of any acknowledgement of politics and power.

Appropriating Taking possession of another's goods. Marx described it as legal theft since the law protected the capitalist when 'stealing' the surplus derived from labour, rather than returning it in the form of wages.

Ascribed Behaviour that is imposed upon people by virtue of their position or role. In earlier societies roles were often ascribed at birth rather than achieved through demonstrating competence.

Asset specificity Where an asset such as a skill, knowledge or machinery cannot easily be transferred to another organization and/or for which there are no ready substitutes.

Atomistic methodology Approach to knowledge where complex 'reality' is broken down into simple 'components' that are then studied in abstraction from their natural habitat – in laboratories or other artificially constructed conditions. These components – or atoms – are then recombined to build ideal-typical models, which are then used to test, measure and intervene in the world.

Authority Legitimate *right* to control, prohibit and judge the actions of others. It is when someone has the right to exercise power over you (e.g. tell you what to do) It is often distinguished from power, where there can be physical coercion or force, for that is based on 'might' not 'right'. Authority establishes rights recognized by subordinates as well as exercised by superiors.

Autocracy A political regime or person that rules by tradition or coercion rather than consent, as might be expected in a democratic regime.

Barriers to entry Corporate practices that develop or are deployed to deny or deter potential competitors entering the market.

Basic assumptions A term used by Schein to refer to the origins of **values** and **cultural artefacts** in organizations. Basic assumptions are shared and deeply embedded presuppositions about issues such as whether human beings do or should live for the moment (immediate gratification) or see their activities as a means to a future end or goal (deferred gratification).

Binary Division into two and only two opposites as in body/mind, female/male, black/white, positive/negative, true/false or the code of 0 and 1 in computing. Criticisms of this way of thinking, sometimes described as dualistic, argue that there are other alternatives that lie in between or beyond the two extremes.

Black box Metaphorical term for describing something that need not be or never is investigated. It is as if to uncover what is inside the black box would destroy its benefits, much like discovering the sleight of hand of magicians undermines their mystique. The black box is often at the basis of **technological determinism**.

Boundary management Strategies and actions intent on controlling the interface between different elements (or departments) within an organization.

Bounded rationality Stipulates the existence of limitations in the human capacity to process information without resort to some arbitrary or non-rational selection. It suggests that these limitations restrict individuals to constructing simplified models that extract only the basic elements of a problem and thereby neglect its complexity.

Bourgeois Critics of capitalism use this term to denote the privileged complacency of the relatively affluent middle classes.

Brainstorming Involves people in a group exercising their creative skills to generate new ideas or innovations. The key aspect of it is that, in the early stages, all ideas put forward are considered valid and no criticism or selection is allowed until later on when ideas are evaluated.

Bureaucracy Describes a form of business administration based on formal rational rules and procedures designed to govern work practices and organization activities through a hierarchical system of authority. Bureaucratic organization is often thought to be rigid, inflexible and overburdened by hierarchical rules sometimes pejoratively referred to as 'red tape'.

Business ethics The academic study, and promotion, or the existence of, ethical practice in business.

Business process re-engineering (BPR) An approach to organizational redesign that proposes that information technology should be the catalyst for revolutionary organizational change, leading to improved measures of performance in terms of costs, speed, quality and service.

Call-centres Offices where staff are employed principally to process telephone calls with customers. Such centres involve heavily routinized and disciplined work processes where staff often work at very high levels of intensity and under conditions of technological surveillance and close monitoring.

Capital In Marxist critical theory, capital is defined as assets (e.g. property, machines, money) used to finance the production of commodities for the private gain of the capitalist classes. Capitalists invest their capital in the production of commodities and accumlate profits by selling goods at a value exceeding the costs of their production.

Capitalist society The dominant economic system around the world today. An economic system that concentrates the majority of wealth in private hands (capitalists) and requires the majority of people to sell their labour to secure a wage from this group.

Chain of command Links within a hierarchy between the most senior and least senior of managers or supervisors.

Classical school Writers who have focused on the formal organization of work. Classical theorists assume that an organization's structure formally unites organizational members into a well-integrated team dedicated to the pursuit of common goals.

Classify Places ideas, phenomena, practices or events into categories that are then named. Most sciences begin by classifying the types of objects they study (e.g. types of plants in botany).

Cliques Small exclusive group of friends and associates who constitute part of the **informal** structure of an organization.

Coalitions **Informal** liaison between two or more interest groups intent on increasing their joint power and control with respect to another group or groups.

Co-determination Form of influence predicated on the cooperation of parties with possibly opposing or competing interests in the pursuit of a mutual or common outcome.

Codified knowledge A type of knowledge that has been written down or stored in a book or computer system, for example. It is therefore explicit, but might be better seen as information rather than knowledge.

Coercive power Where compliance is achieved through the threat of withholding valued rewards.

Cognitive Associated with thinking or mental processes such as perception; or traditional views of understanding such as those that are gained by reading or classroom learning.

Cognitivism Psychological perspective on human behaviour that emphasizes the mental processes of thinking and perception rather than other influences such as the subconscious or social factors.

Colonized Process where usually a larger, richer or more powerful unit (organization, country) takes control of a weaker one – as when, for example, in the 18th and 19th centuries, European states appropriated the wealth and labour of Africa, Far East Asia, the Indian subcontinent, Latin America and the New World.

Committee system Where decisions are taken by committees rather than individuals – a situation that can lead to a proliferation of committees dominating the decision-making process of an organization.

Commodity Something that can be exchanged for a price. While normally seen in terms of physical goods or services, the term is sometimes extended to human beings where they are treated, in a **dehumanized** manner, purely in terms of their economic value (price) as labour.

Common sense What is assumed to be self-evident, obvious and fundamentally correct. It is often used to silence all alternative understandings on the basis that common sense is clearly and universally authoritative and dependable.

Communities of practice (COPs) Refers to groups of people who interact (through meeting personally or electronically) and in so doing share knowledge and learn from each other through the interaction. Precise definitions vary, but emphasis is typically placed on the **informality** of such groups and interactions.

Competitive advantage What is deemed to make an organization or nation more competitive or economically successful than another, such as access to important resources.

Conception What characterizes human creativity is that it begins with a mental process of imagination or conception.

Consent Wide-scale agreement relating to **authorities** and their decisions. For example, where production workers assent to, and approve of managerial strategies and mechanisms of work organization.

Content theories of motivation These theories tried to identify the specific factors – individual needs, task factors, management styles – that shape individual motivation.

Contestability Extent to which something can be disputed and debated.

Contextual embeddedness Way in which any action on the part of, for example, managers or employees is ascribed different meaning and significance depending on the context in which it occurs. Highlights the historical and cultural conditioning (and relativity) of what may appear to be normal and natural.

Contingency approach Way of analysing organizations so that rather than there being a single way of doing things, there are different ways depending (or 'contingent') upon different situations. For example, **technological determinists** believe that organizations have to adopt different structures depending upon the technology that they use.

Corporate social responsibility (CSR) The practices and policies undertaken by organizations to promote the idea that they have concerns that extend beyond efficiency, performance, productivity and profit to embrace the public, customers, the environment and other stakeholders.

Critical structuralist Critical theory that identifies the political activity of organizations to be directly linked to the capitalist productive economy.

Cultural artefacts Phenomena accessible to the senses, including architecture, myths, rituals, logos, type of personnel employed and so on, which signify the **values** in an organization's culture.

Cultural barriers Are seen to prevent the transfer of ideas and practices because of differences in what is viewed as acceptable in different contexts.

Cultural differentiation Refers to differing sets of values, beliefs and norms, which co-exist in one organization. Also see **multiculturalism** and **subculture**.

Cultural engineering Attempt to change an organization's culture to accord with the interests or **values** of managers. It depends on a view that a 'culture is something that an organization has' rather than 'is'. If organizational relations are defined by culture, it is more difficult to impose a unified set of values, beliefs and norms that are designed to provide to impose a unified set of values, beliefs and norms that are designed to provide the basis for all organizational actions and decisions.

Cultural transmission mechanism (CTM) Techniques used by managers to build, maintain or change a particular organizational culture, to encourage employees to adopt specific values, beliefs and norms. Examples include **management by example** (MBE) and deliberately recruiting new staff who embody the desired culture.

Culture An anthropological term that refers to the shared values, beliefs and norms about key priorities and ways of undertaking particular tasks, or relating to colleagues among members of a particular organization.

Custom and practice Workplace behaviour that has been repeated over a lengthy period and is therefore routinely taken for granted.

Customer relationship management (CRM) A broad management approach that emphasizes the financial value of developing long-term relationships with and detailed knowledge of customers. For example, through the use of information systems databases, it is assumed that customers can be 'captured' so that customized goods and services may be targeted appropriately to them.

Death of distance View popularized by Cairncross, that, for the purposes of organizing, the importance of physical location and geographical distance is no longer a constraint because of the developments in information and communication technologies.

Decision objectives Aim/goal of a decision and the criteria through which outcomes can be evaluated.

Decision premises Structures and processes that constitute the apparatus of decision making. An example of a decision premise is the agenda for meetings. Control of this agenda can enable one to manipulate how a decision is approached.

Decision process Sequential processes and structures involved in the deliberation of a decision.

Decision theory School of thought that emphasizes the importance of constructing systematic procedures for approaching and solving problems.

Dehumanized A process by which human beings are treated like objects or things and thus their humanity is denied.

De-layering Reducing the number of levels in the hierarchy so as to have fewer managers.

Delegated The process of passing the responsibility to make management decisions down the **hierarchy** to those in less senior positions.

Dependency Indicates some degree of reliance upon others.

Deregulation of markets Process whereby greater competition is encouraged between commercial organizations through reducing regulations that previously restricted their behaviour or entry into certain markets.

Determinism View that there is an inevitable direction in which events move, as a result of some cause that is independent of the event. In organization studies and in everyday life, the idea that 'human nature' determines social arrangements is possibly the most common. See also **technological determinism**.

Dialectic of control Contested process whereby work and other activities are socially accomplished. Every activity is seen to involve an interdependence between diverse individuals and groups, such as managers and workers. While exercising differential power associated with their access to scarce and valued resources such as income, status and qualifications, none of these enjoy a monopoly of control. This is because each individual or group has a degree of dependence on the other.

Digital divide The term refers to the disparities between those who have access to the new information and communication technologies and those who do not – and who are therefore excluded from the 'brave' new digital economy. Research and debate on the subject typically focus on whether the social impact of computers reinforces or reduces existing social and economic inequalities.

Direct democracy System of collective decision making in which there is an opportunity for everyone to participate and influence how 'things' get done or are organized.

Direct management control Describes conditions where workers have little or no scope to decide how work is organized and conducted.

Dirty job A job that carries with it some form of social stigma and so may require its incumbents to reconcile this with their sense of themselves as 'decent' human beings. Examples include jobs that deal with literal dirt (e.g. refuse collection, lavatory cleaning) or involve what is regarded as morally problematic behaviour (e.g. prostitution, crime).

Discourse Often taken to mean the same as language or the spoken word and written text, but may also refer to a broad category of talk or text such as *managerial* discourse. Some approaches extend the meaning of the term to what is possible in a given context or era and to meaningful behaviour as well (discursive practices). Here, the term can be summarized as what can be said (and done).

Disembodied Analysis that relies purely on the cognitive aspects of human conduct, completely ignoring how bodily and emotional life is central to human existence.

Disintermediation Abandonment of intermediaries (e.g. wholesalers, retailers) that facilitate the distribution of goods and services so that producers trade directly with consumers. Mail order and internet trading represent common examples of disintermediation.

Dispositional factors Internal personality aspects, traits and beliefs that are specific to each individual and may be seen to motivate a person to behave in a certain way. They are opposed to situational factors where the behaviour is due to factors or circumstances external to the individual.

Division of labour The way that people divide up different tasks or jobs between one another to achieve greater levels of efficiency and productive output. Emile Durkheim (1947) argued that the division of labour was not only economically efficient but also socially effective in that it made clear how we are all dependent upon one another and this knowledge would help to generate social solidarity – a necessary condition of social survival.

Double-loop learning (DLL) Involves highly reflective and creative actions that, through continuous feedback processes of self-learning, testing and exploration, facilitate organizational change. DLL is contrasted with single-loop learning (SLL), which is more incremental and mechanical and often likened to the role of a thermostat that regulates a domestic heating system in accordance with external temperatures.

Dysfunctions Action, procedures and processes that impede or disrupt the ability of an entity to achieve its aims.

Economic deregulation Part of the 'New Right' politics where there is an attempt to remove various restrictive practices on trade so as to open up companies to greater competition.

Elite Selected group of presumably gifted or otherwise distinguished individuals.

Emancipatory Political term associated with emancipation or freedom from control. An example is freedom from slavery, but freedom remains an important issue in other contexts, even where control may be less visible.

Empowerment The distribution of power to people lower down the hierarchy so that they can feel a degree of autonomy and sense of personal identification in the decisions they make.

Entity Something that exists as a solid or concrete thing. May refer to human institutions, such as organizations, as well as to objects.

Environment What exists external to the organization, such as available technologies, markets and government.

Epistemology Logic (*logos*) of knowledge (*episteme*). It is associated with the founding assumptions that make it possible to develop any kind of knowledge; and thereby it defines the methods and limits by which knowledge is constructed and advanced.

Equity theory These ideas focus on the importance people attach to perceptions of fairness in how managers deal with them relative to others.

Esprit de corps Positive morale – strong sense of belonging and purpose shared by a work group or organization.

Essence That which is fundamental and unchanging in an 'object', situation or person and most commonly recognized in the phrase 'human nature' (see **determinism**). There is an assumption of some deep, inner essence that can be discovered and which defines the individual. Once an essence is attributed to an object, no further examination is seemingly required. That is why a phrase like human nature or commonsense gives the impression of providing the final and ultimate explanation of anything.

Ethnography A form of study where the researcher lives and works as a member of the group being studied. It aims to provide an 'insider' account but, because it is conducted by a researcher, it has a degree of 'outsider' detachment. Ethnography developed from the techniques used by anthropologists to study what were often seen as exotic cultures or societies outside their own.

Experiential Pertaining to direct experience rather than thought or imagination.

Exploitation A process where people are used merely to further someone else's goals. In an economic context, 'exploitation' refers to using others for the purpose of creating a surplus that enables the exploiter to live without working or to supplement their income in this way.

Externalization The process of creation through which what has been conceived in the mind comes to be embodied through work in an object.

Feminism The theory and politics associated with critiques of society that make gender and the oppression of women as their central focus.

Flexibility Systems of production and working arrangements that allow material and human resources to be utilized speedily to meet the fickle and fluctuating demands of the market and customer taste.

Flexible specialization Approach to production and the organization of work that emphasizes the need for adaptation rather than repetition. Companies following this strategy simply transform their production regularly as there is a demand for more distinctive, customized products and services. **Flexibility** can come in the form of producing non-standard products for niche markets; varying the number of employees according to fluctuations in demand; and/or requiring employees to undertake multiple tasks.

Fordism System of mass production based on hierarchical management control pioneered by Henry Ford during the early 20th century, adopted throughout most Western economies up until its decline in advanced capitalist economies in the 1970s when product differentiation and changing markets demanded more flexibility.

Functionalism Theoretical model or framework that presumes organizational consensus and posits that activities continue to exist only because they perform the indispensable function of maintaining a coherent integration of the organization. Consensus is presumed to be the natural state of affairs and conflict pathological.

Globalization Notion that countries are becoming economically, politically, technologically and culturally closer to each other. Examples of this process include the European Union, the internet and the worldwide popularity of branded products like Coca-Cola, Nike shoes and Mercedes cars.

Goal displacement Occurs when the pursuit of a secondary or marginal objective assumes greater importance than the primary objective and/or when the means (e.g. complying with a procedure) becomes more important than the ends (e.g. attaining the objective).

Greedy institution Coser's term for organizations that require unstinting effort and immense dedication from their employees.

Groupthink Term used by Janis to refer to situations in which group make problematic decisions because individuals over-conform to the group ethos and fail to express personal doubts. There is comfort in groupthink in that the group as a whole feels protected given that the decision is collective, but silence is presumed to imply consent whereas it may signify a fear of resistance.

Headcount Staff or employee numbers in an organization.

Hegemonic Form of control that includes, if not focuses on, the control of people's values, their 'hearts and minds'. An example would be the instilling of a sense of respect for authority or for property rights or, more contemporaneously, a commitment to the organization. All these may help ensure that we do what we are supposed to do and want what we are supposed to want by those in authority such as employers and governments. This renders control through more overt reward or punishment (e.g. job loss) less necessary.

Hierarchy/Hierarchical levels Positions in an organization associated with different levels of status, power and economic reward.

Hierarchy of needs Maslow suggested that individual needs were organized in a hierarchy from physiological needs, to safety needs, to needs for love, affection and belonging, to esteem needs and finally at the top of the hierarchy the need for self-actualization.

Human capital People or employees, as distinguished from other forms of (physical) capital, such as technology and buildings. It also suggests a particular, and restricted, view of people as economic assets.

Hybrid Combination of two or more elements or characteristics that are normally separate.

Idealized picture Description of a situation in a way that portrays only positive elements and it is cleansed of any negative aspects.

Idea-type An ideal-type is the purest, most fully developed version of a particular thing (usually a concept). It does not mean that the thing itself is ideal. The ideal-type of a sadistic serial killer would be someone with all the characteristics of the cruelest mass murderer imaginable – but that does not mean that there is anything desirable about serial killers! It does not mean that the 'ideal' is good or bad. Instead it simply refers to an abstract, exaggerated image or a benchmark by which actual behaviour (e.g. the acts of an actual serial killer) can be assessed.

Ideology A related set of ideas and beliefs held together by a set of values and sometimes used to justify particular political or sectional interests. A patriarchal ideology, for example, justifies male domination. However, definitions differ in the extent to which ideology is seen as reflecting or distorting the truth.

Idiographic approach to personality An approach that is suspicious of the value of generalized 'scientific' categories of classification and thereby understands personality in the terms used by individuals to described themselves. It perceives individuals in terms of personal experience; their personality is learned through social and cultural interaction as opposed to biological or genetic determination.

Impersonal and disembodied Relates to the way that our relations with one another can lack any sense of personal intimacy and be so instrumental and calculative or cerebral and cognitive (i.e. linked to powers of the intellect and logic) as to deny any bodily and emotional content.

Individualizing The process through which people come to see themselves as separate from others and personally responsible for their actions and life chances rather than interdependent.

Informal or Informality Behaviour that is not officially recognized or approved.

Inhibition Inability to do or say something that one desires to say or do. There are numerous sources of inhibition from the fear of embarrassment of being wrong to the consequences of speaking your mind when in a position of subordination.

Innovation The process of imaging something new in a given context (e.g. invention) combined with developing that idea into an applied form.

Institutional approach A perspective that highlights the social shaping of activities at a broad level whereby institutions such as the state, education, professions and the church are seen to condition how things are done in a similar way within these contexts. Emphasis is placed on the importance of practices (such as managing employees) being seen as socially legitimate rather than necessarily technically efficient. When such practices and their legitimacy become taken for granted and established, they are said to be institutionalized.

Institutionalization Process whereby people are fully integrated into an institution (repeated and routine practices) so as to rarely think to challenge them.

Instrumental rationality Behaviour that is exclusively concerned with a self-interested end-result such that the end always justifies the means. It seeks the most efficient (i.e. high output/effort ratio) means to achieve a given end. The two terms often but need not go together to emphasize how the behaviour is single-minded in its 'technical' and non-emotional pursuit of specific goals.

Intangibles Difficult or impossible to measure accurately yet remain important. For example, a new procedure or system might be seen to increase productivity or employee satisfaction, but the benefit is difficult to isolate and measure.

Integral A necessary or inherent part of something.

Intellectual property rights (IPR) A legal term referring to ownership of knowledge or ideas. For example, the copyright assigned to authors, editors or publishers means that others have to ask permission and, often, pay to reproduce material. Likewise, inventions might be patented.

Internalized When an idea, norm or value is completely embedded in individual consciousness such that there is often an unawareness of its existence and influence on behaviour.

Interstices That which exists in between two 'objects'.

Intersubjectivity The existence of consensually shared ideas, values, beliefs and norms. Organizational **cultures** are a form of intersubjectivity.

Invoked The drawing out, or encouraging, of some idea or action.

Isomorphic A term associated with the **institutional approach** that means 'takes the same or a parallel form'. In particular, it refers to the ways in which organizations adopt the same practices as their peers in a given social context, because they are required to do so by **standard-setting bodies**, see it as 'best practice' or are uncertain of what to do and so copy others.

Japanization Process of adopting practices associated with Japan. In particular, it refers to the adoption in the West of certain production practices such as team meetings based on quality improvements.

Job enrichment Work arrangements that are designed to expand the number of tasks and roles workers perform to provide opportunities for them to gain greater satisfaction, reward, recognition and achievement.

Kaizen This is the process of continuous improvement developed in the Japanese organization of work and then introduced as an important element in Western organizational designs, such as **total quality management**.

Knowledge diffusion The spread of knowledge across contexts such as between organizational or national boundaries, as if knowledge acts like a gas. Recent challenges have been made to this traditional view such that knowledge does not exist independently, like a gas, but is produced and adapted or **translated** in context. See **contextual embeddedness**.

Knowledge-economy One not based upon producing physical things but on using knowledge to deliver services. Consultancies like Universal, advertising agencies, software development houses, even universities are all examples of the knowledge economy. It is characterized by knowledge-intensive firms, knowledge-sectors and knowledge-workers.

Knowledge management Process of capturing and codifying knowledge for management (e.g. profitable) purposes. It is often associated with information systems that store 'knowledge' in databases, but has become associated with the broader activity where management seek to **appropriate** the tacit as well as the explicit knowledge of their employees (see also **tacit skills**).

Labour People or class people involved in the productive work, and can be distinguished from those who manage the processes of productive work.

Labourist That which is seen to reflect, represent or celebrate the views of manual labour especially, but the working classes more generally.

Leakage Used to refer to the **knowledge diffusion** where it was not intended, such as the loss of commercially sensitive information.

Lean production/manufacturing System of production, first used in Japan, to maintain the smooth flow of production by using minimum resources to reduce cost, work in progress and other overheads. It is associated with just-in-time services and stock inventories where companies do not retain excess labour or stocks of goods but use information technology to ensure recruitment or reordering of stocks when actually needed.

Learning organization Recent and managerially fashionable term to describe organizations that value collective and not just individual learning. May be reflected in more participative structures and a managerial emphasis on continuous learning (i.e. organizational improvement).

Learning styles Variations in approaches to learning and the extent to which it is attributed to individual, cultural or other background differences, and subject to change.

Legacy systems Old technology practices that have been superseded but still have to be serviced or managed since the cost and effort involved in merging all the data files and procedures to the new system is greater than the benefits of just allowing it to be 'run down' until extinct.

Legitimacy Condition in which decisions or practices are widely acceptable to those whom they affect because there is broad level of consensus about the form or process of their adoption.

Liberal enlightenment Belief in reason and rationality and generally supporting the freedom and autonomy of the individual.

Luddites Name originally given to late 18th and early 19th century textile workers who, in defence of their livelihoods, set out to resist the mechanization of their trades. 'Luddite' is often employed as a term of abuse to describe those who attempt to stand in the way of 'progress'.

Management by example (MBE) A symbolic leadership device, or **cultural transmission mechanism**, which involves managers embodying the values, beliefs and norms they wish employees to adopt in everything they say and do.

Management knowledge Often associated with apparently discrete management ideas such as human resource management, but more generally linked to different types of knowledge used or possessed by management.

Managerialism or managerialist Term applied by critical academics to describe the type of social science output that serves the objectives of managers, as these critics see them, rather than offering an independent or alternative perspective. Managerialism usually entails the idea that effective management is the solution to an array of socio-economic problems.

Marxism Theory and politics associated with the writings of Karl Marx. The principal focus is a critique of the oppressive effects of social class in a capitalist economy.

Masculine discourses Communication consciously or unconsciously reflects and reproduces a sense of being analytical and technical, and masterly and in control generated largely but not exclusively by men.

Mass production The large-batch/mass assembly line/conveyor belt systems of production, often referred to as Fordism because of its association with Henry Ford's production line.

Matrix A form of organization where there are parallel lines of authority criss-crossing one another so that staff are accountable simultaneously to managers in a hierarchy and other specialists horizontally.

Mean production Describes how critical theorists interpret lean production. They see it as having subtle controls and forms of surveillance over workers that result in work intensification.

Mechanistic organization Similar to Weber's model of rational-legal bureaucracy. Includes a specialized division of labour within which each individual carries out an assigned and precisely defined task comparable to the discrete parts that comprise a machine. It is the opposite of **organic organization**.

Mentors Those assigned the task of supporting others by providing advice and assistance to help in their personal and career development.

Mobilization of bias Manipulation of decision-making premises, processes and objectives so as to ensure that a specific point of view or intention is supported.

Modernist Label attached to a range of phenomena, including art and architecture. Here, it is a set of beliefs associated with the historical period of modernity. These beliefs value progress and include a faith in the rationality of science to discover truth and control nature. Things like ambiguity, chance, play, fun, unmanageability and multiple truths or rationalities (e.g. based on custom, religion, lifestyle) are denied or subjected to the scientific gaze in modernism. For example, emotion might be seen in terms of a quantitative measure of emotional intelligence. By contrast, such things are celebrated or brought to the foreground in what has come to be known as post-modernist views.

Monopoly A market where only one supplier of a product or service exists. There is no competition and thus no other sources of the commodity, so the supplier is able to completely dominate the consumer. Also see **oligopolistic** and **oligopoly**.

Multiculturalism In the organization studies context, another term for **cultural differentiation** or the existence of **subcultures** in an organization.

Multinational corporations Very large corporations that have operations crossing multiple nations. Such corporations have been the focus of sustained criticism for the enormous economic and political power they wield.

Multi-skilling Working arrangements in which workers acquire the full range of necessary skills required to perform a number of jobs, tasks and duties efficiently under minimum supervision.

Multi-tasking Working arrangements where it is claimed that workers acquire the various skills needed to perform a number of jobs, tasks and duties.

Narcissism Preoccupation with self-image, and with making the world enhance this image. In the ancient Greek myth, Narcissus became fixated with his mirror image as he saw it reflected in a pool of water.

Negotiated order The idea that social reality is open to a degree of interpretation and mutual adjustment between actors (e.g. between members of a team or between a boss and a subordinate). This element of negotiability make possible a process of manoeuvring to influence other actors.

Neo-classical economics A form of economics that emphasizes free markets and non-intervention by the state. It contrasts with the post-war consensus around Keynes's ideas of state intervention and public spending to maintain economic growth.

Neo-imperialism Colonization other than by military force, typically associated with the spread of a particular dominant set of ideas such as religious beliefs or consumerism.

Network organization Organizations which are not structured hierarchically but which make lateral connections, and connections across functions. Usually associated with claims of increased flexibility and often claimed to be modelled on 'Toyotaism' rather than Fordism.

Network society A society composed of network organizations. More generally, a society in which there is a great deal of fluidity in social relations, multiple sources of information and multiple sources of authority, rather than fixed hierarchies and roles.

Neurosis Unhealthy compulsion and attachment to routines or behaviour patterns that if taken away stimulate feelings of nervousness and anxiety.

Neutering Rendering impotent or ineffective.

New Right Political development or strategy popular in the final quarter of the 20th century where the 'free market' is advocated and state intervention stigmatized. New Right policies favoured the privatization of public sector corporations such as gas, electricity, the railways, etc.

Nomothetic approach (to personality) Distinguished by the beliefs that there are underlying universals (e.g. of personality) against which everything and everyone can be measured and classified. Personality, for example, tends to be understood as an inherited phenomenon and one that is the product of biology, genetics and heredity. The nomothetic approach is based on large-scale quantitative and scientific study with the aim of discovering the mechanisms and 'laws' that explain human behaviour.

Non-participant observation Method of research that observes the detailed activities of research subjects without participating directly in the experiences and tasks they perform.

Non-rigorous Usually a pejorative term meaning the absence of in-depth analysis or systematic research procedures.

Normalize A term to describe how discourses and practices are defined or perceived as proper and normal such that they become unquestioned; it serves to control or discipline individuals by transforming them into subjects that obey certain cultural or political norms or rules.

Normative What is commonly accepted as normal and/or appropriate to an organization. Critical political analysis draws attention to the evaluation of behaviour using normative criteria, often the criteria favoured by supporters of the status quo (e.g. managers), as an exercise in classification and control. See **normative control**.

Normative control Another term for the control of the 'hearts and minds' of employees. So when a manager or professional 'chooses', apparently from free will, to work through the night to complete a task because of values of being responsible, then s/he is being controlled, by being self-controlled.

Objectification The end point of the creative process at which point what has been produced comes to have an independent existence in the world.

Objective Free from bias, prejudice, judgement and emotion.

Oligopolistic Market where a small number of very large suppliers of a product or service have removed the competition and are thereby able to dominate the consumer since there are few alternative sources of supply.

Oligopoly The noun that describes the type of market discussed above.

One best way Refers to anything that is regarded as the one solution for all organizational ills.

Ontology Theories of reality; claims about the nature and contents of the natural and social worlds. It includes a concern with the nature of human existence or what it is to be human, so it is about our relationship to the world as a whole person, not just in terms of some aspect such as personality, motivation or attitudes.

Opportunism Acting in one's own best interests regardless of others or any sense of wider social obligation or commitment.

Organic organization An emphasis is placed on knowledge as a contributing resource rather than restricted to a specific job specification. There exists a continual adjustment to tasks as they become shaped by the nature of the problem rather than predefined. Opposite of **mechanistic organization**.

Organizational chart Stylized but clear representation of the organization that may provide a basis for the analysis of decision-making processes.

Organizational politics Label given to activities surrounding the competition between individuals, groups, units, departments or divisions for scarce rewards and resources within organizations. See also **negotiated order**.

Organization man The term used to refer to a worker who is so committed to the organization that s/he automatically and perhaps even unconsciously prioritizes their job demands above what they themselves require or want.

Outsourcing Business practice involving greater levels of intermediation (see **disintermediation**). Producers of goods and services establish contracts with other companies or specialists (e.g. payroll, web management, call-centres, or even distribution) to supply essential parts of their business. It has a long tradition stretching back to the early 19th century when producers bought their labour from contractors, but became less common in the 20th century, as companies directly employed their labour forces.

Panacea This refers to a remedy that cures all complaints. Teamwork, for example, might be commended as a technology of work organization that solves all production problems from control, to productivity, to retention and commitment.

Paradox Something that appears to be absurd, impossible or self-contradictory, but might be true.

Participant observation Method of research originating in social anthropology where the researcher engages with the subjects of their study by attempting to live like them for some time.

Pathological Derives from psychology or psychiatry to refer to mentally disturbed individuals. Emile Durkheim used the term 'social pathology' to describe a situation where individuals failed to see society as an objective reality, as discovered by the science of sociology, and thereby failed to see how their egoistic actions were destroying the very social fabric that is a necessary condition of civilized life. Managers tend to regard workers as pathological ('awkward', 'bloody-minded', 'uncooperative', etc.) when they fail to comply with the logic and reason of management.

Pathologized See **pathological**.

Piece-work Payment on the basis of what is produced rather than the time taken to produce it.

Pluralist A recognition of diverse legitimate viewpoints, interests or approaches. A pluralist vision of organizational politics emphasizes the free interplay of interest groups as operating to check and balance the potentially authoritarian tendencies of governing bodies.

Political questions These are characterized by an inquiry into how social relations are created, reproduced and charged.

Political structure Balance of competing pressures from interest groups seeking to realize, or gain recognition of, their own particular concerns.

Political system Boundaries, goals, values, administrative mechanisms and hierarchy of power, which constitutes a particular organization.

Politics of truth Refers to the process of giving voice to ideas and voices that compete over what is taken to be accepted knowledge or **ideology**.

Positivism Term used especially by critical analysts to identify a method of social science research in which the differences between the 'natural' phenomena of the physical sciences and human phenomena are downplayed. Positivists are those who presume, and or seek to emulate, the causal methods of the natural sciences. In doing so, they neglect the problems of meaning and interpretation, or how researchers are active agents (not merely passive recorders) in constructing the events and behaviour they may claim merely to report.

Post-Fordism Describes flexible systems of production that are designed to produce differentiated goods and services for niche markets.

Post-modern Has two broad meanings – an historical era following modernity and a philosophical/theoretical perspective. Both are seen to celebrate what modernism devalues and/or represses – surface appearances, emotion, play, chance and indeterminacy in life – the value of different rationalities (e.g. based on experience) rather than a single authoritative science or **truth**. See also **modernist**.

Post-modernism The theory and politics principally associated with contemporary French thinkers. Post-modernism may be understood as a reaction to and critique of **modernism**.

Power Often conceived as ability of A to influence B to do something that B would not ordinarily have done without A's influence. The attribution of power to individuals or groups as their 'possession' has been challenged by a view of power that is 'relational' – such as the disciplines and ideologies that operate to constrain as well as enable those to whom power is attributed by the 'possessive' view.

Power as plural Pluralists perceive organizational relations as defined by bargaining, competition and the use of power to resolve conflicts and represent conflicts of interest. See **pluralism**.

Practical-hermeneutic Describes theories that seek to understand and reflect on organizations as opposed to reporting them or issuing prescriptions as to how to manage them more effectively. Can be contrasted to **managerialist** theories and in some instances also to **emancipatory** theories.

Precepts Refers to general instructions on a course of action and a set of principles that provide guidance. Taylorism, for example, has some explicit precepts such as a distinction between conception and execution, standardization, etc.

Privatization Selling off public corporations, in part or in full, to individuals or corporations that anticipate increasing their wealth or value from this acquisition. See **New right**.

Procedural justice Like equity theory, procedural justice is interested in the effects, either positive or negative, that arise from how fairly and transparently managers implement decisions affecting their staff.

Process theories of motivation These theories look at motivation as the outcome of a dynamic interaction between the person and their experiences of an organization and its management. Such processes depend critically on the sense individuals make of their experiences at work.

Processual Theoretical approach that focuses more attention on the political but also cultural and strategic process within organizations rather than the structure of the organization.

Procrustes An ancient Greek mythological character who either stretched his guests to fit the bed or chopped off their legs, if they were too tall. Eventually, the same fate befell Procrustes himself!

Product differentiation Refers to one way in which firms can maintain their competitive advantage; they differentiate their product, in ways that appeals to the customer, from all others on the market.

Product life cycle Refers to how products move from being new to being mature to being obsolete. This impacts on the pricing and marketing of goods as well as the degree of competition.

Progressive Favouring and believing in progress or moving forward by improving on the past.

Project teams Group of people working together on a particular task with a discrete objective and time frame. Often such groups include different specialists, perhaps drawn from different departments, for the purpose of achieving the project task.

Psychodynamic approaches Defined by a concern with internal processes and forces within the psyche that clash and conflict with varying degrees of intensity in each individual and in ways that take time to resolve. In this approach, individual behavioural routines, oddities or little peculiarities and idiosyncrasies are seen as surface acts of behaviour that are really 'symptoms' of more underlying, deep-seated and unconscious forces and desires. In the Freudian approach to analysis, psychodynamic forces are understood to reach eventual compromise or 'settlement' through the negotiation of a series of relatively well-defined stages – the anal, the oral and the oedipal, for example – the resolution of which help stabilize personality.

Psychological contract The invisible or implicit set of expectations that employees have of their organizations (e.g. challenging, stimulating work that allows for career progression) and that their organizations have of them (e.g. loyalty and flexibility), but are not laid down in the formal contract of employment.

Psychosis Breakdown of our normal ways of thinking and perceiving in which objects in the world lose definition and precision, merging and collapsing into one another in a surreal and agitated, highly charged riot of images. Objects in the world and even the sound of words can come to take on a seemingly malevolent force. In Freudian terms, psychosis is associated with the collapse of the distinction between the conscious and the unconscious so that our waking world takes on dream-like qualities.

Purposeful actors Belief that individuals retain rational control (e.g. in their pursuit of self-interest and sectional loyalties) throughout the processes of organizational decision making.

Quality circles These are meetings of group of workers committed to continuous improvement in the quality and productivity of a given line of production.

Quality of working life movements Denotes programmes of organizational design and development dedicated to improving productivity and workers' retention and commitment by bettering the relationship between employers and employees and the work environment.

Quotas Limits placed on something; in trade usually refers to limits placed on the number of goods, for example cars, which can be exported from one country to another.

Rationality A commitment to reason, rather than faith, intuition or instinct. In the study of organizations, rationality is often claimed to consist of the adoption of optimally efficient means. However, critical approaches suggest that this is a one-sided view of rationality since it usually considers efficiency in terms of narrow goals such as profitability, without considering whether organizations are efficient for realizing the well-being of members of the organization, or for society more widely.

Rationalizing Measures intended to increase the efficiency and/or improve the effectiveness of work practices. See **rationality**.

Rational process Process that incorporates goals and a mechanism calculated to achieve agreed aims largely irrespective of its consequences for other dimensions of social existence (e.g. community well-being).

Receivership Term used to describe a company that has gone bankrupt and has its assets taken over by an independent auditor who then allocates a distribution to the various creditors.

Red tape A term of abuse applied to bureaucracies that enforce rules more elaborate and inflexible than is considered necessary. See **bureaucracy**.

Regression Compulsion to repeat or return to earlier patterns of behaviour and interaction as a way of avoiding the challenges associated with more adult or demanding situations and relations. In everyday language we often hear people say 'stop being so childish!' This is often associated with behaviour that is deemed inappropriate for adults.

Reification Describes the tendency to treat a human creation (say organization or technology) as if it had an independent existence of its own rather than being the product of human thought and work.

Relations of production The basic set of social relations that allow production to take place. Typically they are the relations between those who own property and their agents (managers) and those who are dependent on them for their wage labour.

Relative power Assumption that power exists in relation to the will and objectives of both superordinates and subordinates.

Representative democracy A form of political reality in which democratic influence is predicated on legitimate forms of electoral selection, accountability and representation.

Rhetoric Art of persuasion and may encompass a range of rhetorical techniques aimed at changing an audience's views or behaviour. It is also sometimes seen as meaning false or exaggerated, and is contrasted with reality or truth – 'that's just rhetoric or someone trying to convince you of their beliefs. For those who hold that knowledge is ambiguous, perhaps especially in management, and that what we say comes to shape what we do and think, the distinction is itself viewed as rhetorical, not least because it implies some direct or privileged access to reality.

Routinization of charisma Charismatic leaders have been seen to inspire an organization by the force of their energy and passion but create a situation of over-dependence on one person. In order to remove the uncertainty and unpredictability associated with this dependence, an organization establishes routines, rules and procedures that institutionalize and thereby routinize the practices that have evolved.

Rule system System of governance based on rules.

Sabotage Conscious intention to disrupt 'normal service' or production. It is often considered a deviant activity. See **pathological**.

Satisficing Describes (and sometimes prescribes) a situation where a satisfactory resolution to a problem is adopted, rather than an optimum resolution.

Scientism A view where ideas and techniques that comply with [. . .] protocols are believed to be **objective** and politically neutral.

Self-esteem A psychological term referring to how one thinks or feels about oneself in an evaluative (i.e. positive or negative) way.

Shareholder value Associated with the idea that the first responsibility of firms is to deliver value to shareholders. Therefore, the interests of employees, consumers and communities are secondary. Most associated with US and UK firms.

Shop floor Location in factories where industrial or manufacturing workers are employed.

Silos Discrete functions, departments or divisions within an organization that through the routines of repetition have become ossified and self-absorbed.

Social capital Economic value to organizations of the social contacts and networks people have, especially those where there is a sense of obligation (e.g. to return a favour). This concept has been given increasing attention in recent years as the learning value of networks has been recognized. For example, contacts, especially those outside of normal organizational relations, are useful as sources of new knowledge or innovation. Close relationships, by contrast, are seen as more suited for the transfer of elusive or tacit knowledge.

Social construction of technology (or SCOT) A more radical variant of the approach known as the **social shaping of technology**. According to constructivists, in order to understand technological developments we need to study the social interpretations that have produced the definitions of what problems can or should be solved by a given technology. These interpretations, SCOT argues, guide the choices made by the designers, manufacturers and users. Technical choices in other words are not merely the application of an abstract techno-logic but are also vehicles for the expression of perspectives and ideologies of those social groups (including designers, opinion formers, users, non-users, etc.) that have a stake in the development of a particular technology. Technologies are therefore the offspring of alternative constructions and compromise.

Social constructivists or constructivists, those who adopt the **constructivist** approach.

Socialization A term used in psychology and sociology that refers to the process by which an individual internalizes values, norms, beliefs and behaviours present within the socio-cultural environment in which s/he lives.

Social shaping of technology A sociological approach that rejects the **technologically determinist** view of **technology** as being distinct from the rest of society. It focuses on social and economic interests as key influences on the eventual shape of the technology. For those who follow this approach, technology is just one aspect of the way we live socially (and is not inherently different to organizations, art or politics).

Social system Refers to a specific pattern of relationship, maintained by a certain flow of interactions and a common goal.

Span of control The number of people for whom a manager has responsibility.

Sponsor–protégé relationship Informal relationships between senior and junior personnel, often motivated by mutual advantage.

Stakeholder theory The idea that business owes responsibility to more groups than merely its shareholders. Stakeholders may include customers, the environment, suppliers, the local community, future generations. etc.

Standard-setting bodies Regulatory organizations that set and monitor standards of practice for organization, such as those in health and safety or financial accounting.

Start-ups New small businesses that have just begun to trade.

Static structural A way of understanding that does not allow for processes of change over time and which presumes that the phenomenon can be divided into layers or structures. So, for example, knowledge can be classified as of different types that do not change over time.

Statistical probability The chance of a given event happening across a population of events. For the probability to be robust, the population must be sufficiently large to be statistically significant.

Statistical process control A statistical technique used by quality managers to ensure that product quality standards are maintained.

Stickiness Sometimes used to denote how difficult it can be to **transfer knowledge** from one context to another – e.g. the **tacit skill** of a craft worker, developed over years of practice.

Strategic contingency Theory suggesting that uncertainty for an organization stems from its systems of operation, which include technology and work operations from its environment.

Structuralist approach Concentrates on the complexity of the design or structure of an organization independently of the human dimension. It tends to see organizational structures as determined by external conditions characterized as the environment.

Subcontractors Those working to provide goods or services for one company but who are employed by another company. See also **outsourcing**.

Subculture A set of values, beliefs and norms that is specific to one group in the organization, and may be at odds with the 'official' culture as promoted by senior management. See also **cultural differentiation** and **multiculturalism**.

Subjectivity The sense of being-in-the-world that includes but is not reducible to the sense of identity and meaning that is associated with it.

Substantive rationality Substantive rationality means whether the outcomes of an action are rational from the point of view of the actor regardless of the efficiency of the action itself. **Instrumental rationality** is concerned with means. Substantive rationality is concerned with ends.

Sub-system One part (e.g. the heart) of numerous interdependent elements that comprise the wider system (e.g. the body).

Suggestion box Box in which employees can write down their ideas for improvements.

Supply chain Stages through which materials and other resources are passed in the process of their being combined, assembled and delivered to their ultimate customer.

Sustainable development A term generally used to refer to a concern with balancing economic demands with a concern for future generations. For example, the use of timber is now controlled in many but by no means all of world, so that for every tree cut down another is planted in its place.

Sweatshop labour This term generally describes any form of labour in factories or smaller workshops that is done in conditions where labour is poorly treated, lacks adequate rights, health and safely conditions are poor, and wages low.

Tacit skill A form of knowledge that cannot be made fully explicit, such as in a training manual or through verbal instruction. Examples include riding a bike or changing gear in a manual car.

Teamworking Working arrangements in which workers themselves are given responsibility for the planning and coordination of some aspects of their work and the roles and tasks they are required to perform.

Technical In an organization studies context, this term refers to theories or ideas intended for application by managers so that they can improve the organizational 'bottom line'.

Technocratic Form of governance, which is exercised through the technical knowledge of experts.

Technological determinism Determinism is the view that there is an inevitable direction in which events move. For technological determinists, the cause is technology. According to technological determinists, certain key technologies are the primary movers in developments in organization, the economy or even society itself.

Technological determinists Those who adopt the approach defined above.

Technology At the most basic level the term 'technology' is used to refer to the 'entire set of devices' that facilitate the adaptation of human collectivities to their environments. A fuller definition of technology includes the human activities, knowledge and skills that are necessary in order to create, understand and operate such devices.

Theory X McGregor used this term to characterize a set of negative assumptions by managers about the attitudes and capabilities of employees; people are passive and need to be persuaded, rewarded, punished and controlled if they are to align their efforts with the needs of the organization.

Theory Y McGregor used this term to characterize a set of positive assumptions by managers about employees; that people are cooperative, able to take responsibility and set their own goals if managers provide the conditions under which they can do this.

Third way Compromise political strategy that seeks to restrict state intervention to the minimum necessary to avoid the 'free market', having consequences that result in the less well off being excluded from certain aspects of society.

Tolerance of ambiguity Used in Hofstede to differentiate between cultures that seek rules for everything and will not take action outside of a rule, and those cultures where rules are lacking and who use their own initiative and creativity.

Total quality management A system of quality control that is designed to build in quality at every stage of production to minimize waste and defective parts that would otherwise be detected at the end of the production process.

Transaction cost economics Theory that explains the existence of an organization in terms of its superiority, relative to markets, in controlling the cost of matching the supply of goods and services with their demand.

Transferability of knowledge The capacity to move knowledge from one context or form to another. This may vary according to the people involved. For example, it might be easier to help another engineer learn a new theory of mechanics than it would be to teach an engineering novice (see also the **knowledge diffusion** and **cultural barriers**).

Transferable skills Employee skills or knowledge that can be readily applied to a wide range of tasks.

Translated Changed from one form to another. This might be in the sense of a complete transformation, as an idea is adapted to a particular context, or a more modest change such as a (good) linguistic translation (see also the **knowledge diffusion** and **cultural barriers**).

Transnational This term emphasizes the importance of flows across the world but retaining contacts and lines across national boundaries. The term 'transnational corporation' is sometimes used to convey the same meaning as the term multinational.

Transnationality Indicates that some or many of the assets, sales and employees of a firm are based outside its home base.

Truth A common-sense term relating to that which is accepted as factual or verified beyond doubt, but also a philosophical issue, or claim, of some complexity. A core theme here would be the contrasting views on whether there can only be one truth or many truths.

Typologies Form of classification that involves grouping together entities or subjects with like themes and ensuring that these groups are mutually inclusive and mutually exclusive from all other groups. For example, cars and aeroplanes might be different groups of entities within a typology of transportation.

Uncertainty Branch of political analysis which argues that leadership and influence within organizations tends to be enjoyed by those perceived as dealing with the sources of greatest ambiguity.

Unitary Form of management in which the views of top management are assumed to be shared by everyone. Conflict is treated as is **pathological** rather than a reflection of different interpretations and interests.

Universalist Theories that claim applicability across all locations and all times.

Unobtrusive Intangible forms of control, which appear not to intervene overtly in a worker's daily activity and yet have the ability to influence their conditions of work (e.g. a racist canteen culture).

Utilitarian Useful, especially in a practical way, but also refers to utilitarianism, which is a doctrine that judges actions on their outcomes in terms of overall increases in 'good' or happiness, for example.

Value free That which is seen to be **objective** – i.e. detached from particular personal values. Critical theory questions its existence.

Value maximizing Pursuit of rational decision-making strategies that require the individual to select options based on their ability to best achieve the ultimate goal (e.g. if the goal is to seek promotion, value-maximizing would involve steering one's career away from activities that would undermine this objective). Often the 'value' is translated into material terms, such as salary improvements or value-for-money.

Values Has a variety of meanings in organization studies, but in the specific sense intended by Schein it encompasses his 'middle level' of organizational culture, located between **basic assumptions** and **cultural artefacts**. Values derive from basic assumptions and inform cultural artefacts. They involve shared organizational responses to questions such as 'What are we doing?' and 'Why are we doing it?', and might include a commitment to profit maximization or a focus on equal opportunities.

Vignettes Brief excerpts from a larger story that may help us to understand 'what happens' to people in everyday life.

Whistle-blowing When an organizational member tells the wider world of unethical or illegal practices being conducted inside their organization.

Work intensification Working conditions in which workers are subject to constant pressures to increase output and productivity levels.

Working to rule Way employees, when in dispute with employers, may revert to formally prescribed ways of working that disrupt efficiency and effectiveness by replacing informal practices with rigid and often time-consuming procedural requirements.

Work–life balance General term to refer to how far work dominates people's lives over and above any other considerations.

Index